Teen Genreflecting 3

Recent Titles in Genreflecting Advisory Series

Diana Tixier Herald, Series Editor

Fluent in Fantasy: The Next Generation
Diana Tixier Herald and Bonnie Kunzel

Gay, Lesbian, Bisexual, and Transgendered Literature: A Genre Guide
Ellen Bosman and John Bradford; Edited by Robert B. Ridinger

Reality Rules!: A Guide to Teen Nonfiction Reading Interests
Elizabeth Fraser

Historical Fiction II: A Guide to the Genre
Sarah L. Johnson

Hooked on Horror III
Anthony J. Fonseca and June Michele Pulliam

Caught Up in Crime: A Reader's Guide to Crime Fiction and Nonfiction
Gary Warren Niebuhr

Latino Literature: A Guide to Reading Interests
Edited by Sara E. Martinez

Teen Chick Lit: A Guide to Reading Interests
Christine Meloni

Now Read This III: A Guide to Mainstream Fiction
Nancy Pearl and Sarah Statz Cords

Gay, Lesbian, Bisexual, Transgender and Questioning Teen Literature: A Guide to Reading Interests
Carlisle K. Webber

This Is My Life: A Guide to Realistic Fiction for Teens
Rachel L. Wadham

Primary Genreflecting: A Guide to Picture Books and Easy Readers
Susan Fichtelberg and Bridget Dealy Volz

Teen Genreflecting 3

A Guide to Reading Interests

Diana Tixier Herald

Genreflecting Advisory Series

 LIBRARIES UNLIMITED

AN IMPRINT OF ABC-CLIO, LLC
Santa Barbara, California • Denver, Colorado • Oxford, England

Copyright 2011 by Diana Tixier Herald

Library of Congress Cataloging-in-Publication Data

Herald, Diana Tixier, 1954-
  Teen genreflecting 3 : a guide to reading interests / Diana Tixier Herald.
    p. cm. — (Genreflecting advisory series)
  Includes bibliographical references and index.
  ISBN 978-1-59158-729-3 (acid-free paper) 1. Young adult fiction, American—Bibliography.
2. Young adult fiction, American—Stories, plots, etc. 3. Fiction genres—Bibliography.
4. Teenagers—Books and reading—United States. 5. Young adults' libraries—Collection development—United States. I. Title.
Z1232.H472 2011
[PS374.Y57]
016.813008'09283—dc22   2010040791

ISBN: 978-1-59158-729-3

15 14 13 12 11   1 2 3 4 5

This book is also available on the World Wide Web as an eBook.
Visit www.abc-clio.com for details.

Libraries Unlimited
An Imprint of ABC-CLIO, LLC

ABC-CLIO, LLC
130 Cremona Drive, P.O. Box 1911
Santa Barbara, California 93116-1911

This book is printed on acid-free paper ∞
Manufactured in the United States of America

For Jack, Mark, Patrick, and Hazel

Contents

Acknowledgments

Thanks to all the authors of teen novels who have kept me enthralled for hours on end and the publishers who provide access to those stories.

My deepest appreciation goes to Barbara Ittner, the editor who makes it all make sense.

Several book clubs have provided me access to discussing books with teens. Thanks to members of the Bistro Book Club, the Fruita Middle School Bistro, Grand Junction High School Book Club, and Central High School Book Club. This book could not have been done without the helpful contribution of opinions on books from dozens of teens, including Ursula, Logan, Harrison, Anthony, Morgan, Rebecca, Hope, Michael, Anika, Mary, Noah, Shelby, Trina, Sierra, Delainey, Tyler, John, David, Andrea, Ryanne, Spencer, Linsey, Tori, Ash, Courtney, Kissondra, Katherine, Katie, Elizabeth, Chavilah, Schuyler, Amanda, Amber, Briana, Flor, Nicholas, and Jasmine. Thanks also to the wonderful librarians working with those groups: Cappi Castro, Sarah Shelp, Barb Kidder, Ronda Scroggins, and Shanna Smith.

A special thank-you to the teens who shared their opinions on their favorite genres: Jordan, Lindsay, Brooke, Shelby, Alice, Andrea, Elle, and Lizzie.

Robbie Johnston, former teen book club member, current book blogger, and future librarian, provided many words of wisdom and helpful suggestions. His assistance has been invaluable in writing this book.

As always, thanks to Rick Herald for putting up with all the drama that went into writing this book.

Introduction

The most dedicated readers in the country are teenagers.—Sherman Alexie, "In His Own Literary World: A Native Son Without Borders," *New York Times,* October 20, 2009 (http://bit.ly/bzsn7)

The genre of young adult or teen fiction is at a new peak at the time of this writing. Teen books are best sellers, they are being made into movies, and adults, and the targeted audience of readers twelve to eighteen years old are reading them voraciously.

"No one disputes the fact that the young adult population is growing" is how the second edition of *Teen Genreflecting* started. At that time I also said libraries cannot afford to disregard these demographics, nor they can they afford to cling to the assumption that teens don't read or use libraries. In the time that has elapsed since the last edition was released, this has become startlingly clear, as the phenomenal success of the <u>Harry Potter</u> series demonstrated that books for teens could become mainstream best sellers. And of course, the Harry Potter phenomenon was followed by the more recent Stephenie Meyer phenomenon, which has now been followed by *The Hunger Games.*

Today's Teen Readers

The current population of young adults includes the last of the Millennials, the generation born between 1980 and 1995 and the very beginning of what Wikipedia is calling Generation Z, or what Don Tapscott (2009) identifies in *Grown Up Digital: How the Net Generation Is Changing Your World* as the "Net Generation." The Net Generation is defined as those born between the beginning of 1977 and the end of 1997, which places all teens in the year 2010 firmly in this demographic, numbering approximately 81.1 million people, or 27% of the U.S. population.

In 2006 there were more ten- to nineteen-year-olds in the United States (42 million) than adults over age 65 (37 million) (Goldberg 2006).

Teens and Reading

This is a generation that reads, as evidenced by sales of teen books, even though many adults have also become hooked on the genre. Sherman Alexie, the National Book Award–winning author of *Diary of a Part-Time Indian,* has said: "A lot of people have no idea that right now Y.A. is the Garden of Eden of literature" (Raab 2008.).

The teen books that get read are often those that are considered genre fiction. While writing *500 Great Books for Teens,* author Anita Silvey (2006) asked hundreds of teens to name their ten favorite books. Reading their responses and studying sales figures of recently published teen books, she determined that genre fiction—fantasy, mystery, suspense, adventure, romance—was surging.

Teen literature has become big business. This is documented by *Publishers Weekly*'s sales figures for 2008 (McEvoy and Coffey 2009). Nine young adult titles sold over a million copies in 2008, while only six adult titles topped the million mark (Roback 2009). And the teen titles outdid the adult titles by a huge margin. The number one teen best seller was *Breaking Dawn* by Stephenie Meyer, which sold 6,051,981 copies; the number one adult best seller, *The Appeal* by John Grisham, sold only a little more than 1,320,000. If the best-seller lists for books published for adults and the children's and teen markets were combined, *The Appeal* would have come in fourth. The story was much the same in 2009. Five or six adult hardcovers sold in excess of a million copies (Facts & Figures 2009 Revised 2010), whereas eleven titles labeled as children's surpassed that mark (Roback 2010).

Publishers have definitely noticed this trend. Harlequin established its reputation on publishing romance novels for women, but has now entered the teen genre with both its Kimani Tru, imprint featuring young African American protagonists, and a new imprint, Harlequin Teen, which debuted in 2009.

Stephenie Meyer, the author of the Twilight series, was even named one of the 100 most influential people in *Time* magazine after being nominated and profiled by Orson Scott Card (2008). In 2010 Suzanne Collins, another author for teens, was named to the *Time* 100 list (Skurnick 2010).

Membership in the Young Adult Library Services Association (YALSA), a division of the American Library Association, has boomed in recent years, and it was the fastest-growing division in the library world in 2009. More than 3,380 (Kuenn 2010) libraries celebrated teen read week, registering at the teen read week Web site. More than 11,000 teens voted for the Teens Top Ten (ala.org/ala/mgrps/divs/yalsa/teenreading/teenstopten/teenstopten.cfm).

The Michael L. Printz award, which recognizes literary excellence in young adult literature, and the Alex award, which is given to adult books that young adult readers will enjoy, were new awards when the last edition of this guide was published; now they are well established. Some titles, usually those with abundant "literary merit," that are published as adult books in other countries, such as Great Britain and Australia, are being published in the United States as young adult books. There has been conjecture that this is due to the importance of the Michael L. Printz award (Going 2004).

There is no doubt that adults are reading teen fiction in great numbers. A novel being published as YA or teen is not a judgment on its quality or level of literary merit. This is merely the category in which the publisher believes it will sell the most copies. And as Michael Cart said, "The line between Y.A. and adult has become almost transparent" (Raab 2008).

Teens are reading more than ever. According to a 2008 NEA survey, "Best of All," the most significant growth has been among young adults, the group that had shown the largest declines in earlier surveys. The youngest group (ages eighteen to twenty-four) has undergone a particularly inspiring transformation, from a 20 percent decline in 2002 to a 21 percent increase in 2008—a startling level of change.

Serving Teen Readers

The key to motivating teens to read is to provide them with the reading materials in which they are most interested. Even reluctant readers can become avid readers if they find the right material.

As individuals, teenagers have unique needs—physically, intellectually, and emotionally—and their reading tastes and habits differ from those of children and adults. Teens are struggling to define themselves as individuals, to redefine their relationships with family members, and to find out how they fit into the larger world. Because they are involved in this identity search, teens enjoy exploring different roles and personae that help them come to terms with who they are. Coming-of-age stories are particularly pertinent to teens, as are stories that address issues of family, friends, and society.

Teens are curious—they are interested in the latest trends and hottest issues, so books with current, topical focuses intrigue them. As teens stretch their intellectual abilities, they enjoy practicing their problem-solving skills through suspense stories and stretching their imaginations to fantasy and science fiction tales.

Today's teens are also under tremendous stress, and reading can provide a soothing retreat from youthful angst. A gentle romance with a happy ending or an enthralling historical novel provides relief to some readers, whereas the successful resolution of an action-packed survival story, with a strong definition between good and evil, reassures others.

Genre fiction fits various needs of young adult readers. Like other readers, teens like to know what they are getting. They want an identifiable product from which they will receive a certain something that they desire. Genres organize the world of literature into understandable segments. Teens often identify themselves by what they read, and they can be very definite about that: " I only read romances," " I never read science fiction," or " I love fantasy the most." Developing and marketing your collection by genre is one way to provide teens access to the books they want and most enjoy. By grouping similar books together—whether through spine labeling, shelving, and display or by creating and distributing lists—you can make it easier for teen readers to find what they want.

With all the 2.0 technology, it is easier than ever to connect teens with the books they want to read. Grouping books according to their appeals and utilizing genre categories acts as an indirect readers' advisory technique to make your job easier and works well with social networking sites such as GoodReads and Shelfari as well as in blogs.

Many individuals enter adolescence as readers and regular library users but quit sometime before entering adulthood. Teen years are busy, with many distractions and new experiences, and whatever it was that got them hooked on books is too often not strong enough to keep them reading.

However, teens needn't lose interest in reading. Often all they need is support and encouragement—and help in finding the right reading material. Librarians and book-sellers are in the perfect position to make the difference. By supplying teens with the books they like to read in friendly surroundings, we can make that difference. When librarians and booksellers encourage reading in the teen years, they make friends for life. Identifying those books is what this guide is all about.

With the abundance of new titles, the evolution of genres and their popularity, and the changing interests of teens, this guide will help readers and librarians find starting places that lead to enjoyable reading experiences.

Library Services for Teens

Library services for teens have had many ups and down throughout history. We are currently in an era that is focusing on teen services in libraries. Even though the United States is just coming out of a recession and unemployment is high, libraries are hiring young adult librarians and creating dedicated spaces in new buildings and in library remodels for teens. For a more detailed overview of the history of serving teens in libraries, check "200 Years of Young Adult Library Services History," compiled by Anthony Bernier, Mary K. Chelton, Christine A. Jenkins, Cathi Dunn MacRae, and Jennifer Burek Pierce (http://pdfs.voya.com/VO/YA2/VOYA200708chronology_long.pdf). A new edition of Michael Cart's *Young Adult Literature: From Romance to Realism*, which was first published in 1996 and chronicled the first fifty years of young adult literature, is due out in the second half of 2010.

Since the last edition of this book was published, library services for teens have grown by leaps and bounds. At the time that the first edition of *Teen Genreflecting* was written, there was only one half-time librarian in a Colorado public library with the title of young adult librarian; now many libraries have a designated staff member for services to teens, even libraries on Colorado's rural western slope, from the Mesa County Library District, serving a population of over 120,000, to Telluride, with a population of approximately 2,200 in a county that only numbers 6,594.

Services and programming for teens have blossomed in both public and school libraries. The Ann Arbor library district publishes a quarterly newsletter of their programs that recently featured sixty-eight programs for teens. School libraries have become meeting places for book clubs, chess clubs, and groups of teens who like to work on puzzles. Both public and school libraries often offer programs related to gaming, with Guitar Hero competitions being popular, and manga and anime programs reaching an audience that frequently eats sushi and is learning how to speak Japanese. Other popular programs include "how-to" workshops for various crafts, including how to make snow globes and how to do Indian Mehndi designs with henna. A popular new trend in programming is workshops on creating media productions using blogs, podcasts, and video. The creation of book trailers—book previews that feature images, film clips, and music to promote specific books—seems to be on the rise. Teens who are active with social networking love making content for their pages and find the library a natural place to get started.

Book clubs remain a popular activity for teens in the library, and even seem to be growing. Teens generally prefer a book club model different from their English lit classes. In the Bistro Book Club, each participant selects from the newest books in the collection, then reports back on what was read via a booktalk at the next meeting. The Bistro Book Club is held every week at the same time and same place, so that when teens have to miss several sessions due to school, sports, or extracurricular activities, they know that when those activities are over, they can still attend book club. Teens who have submitted written or audio reviews that are published on a Web site get first dibs on any new books or books that are booktalked by other members.

Some libraries, particularly public libraries, have had great success with homework help programs. Programs that train and assign teens to volunteer activities within the library have also seen success.

Food is often deemed essential for successful teen programs. It has been said that "if you want teens to stay away, don't serve snacks." Of course, the whole reason for providing programs is to have teens attend, so food is highly recommended.

Teen advisory boards draw on teen preferences to give the librarians insights into what teens want in programs and materials, and participating in them gives the teens a meaningful activity to include on their resumes.

Teen summer reading games keep teens reading over the summer and can be a way to interact with teens who are too busy to read much for pleasure during the school year. It is also a great way for kids who move during the summer to meet other teens in their new communities. Again, like book clubs, it is important that the program not look or feel like school. Any way a summer reading game can be structured to make the reading and use of the library and its resources intrinsically enjoyable, rather than requiring so many pages or minutes for rewards, pays off in the long run.

One of my favorite ways to do a summer reading game is to introduce a large measure of chance. Prizes are awarded weekly, but everyone gets one chance to win in a drawing for every book read or listened to and every activity completed, so the more a teen participates, the more chances he or she has to win. This removes much of the competition of someone trying to outread everyone else for the big prize. For the younger end of the teen spectrum, particularly if there is a big party or social event at the culmination of the summer game, it works well to let them team up and participate as a group, so they have someone to attend with.

Readers' Advisory for Teens

The most important tenet of providing readers' advisory services to teens is to treat the teen reader with respect, in the same way one would work with an adult. Readers' advisory seldom starts at the desk. The best RA involves creating a book-centered relationship between librarian and reader, and the best place to start that is in the stacks. Once a sense of trust is built up, the reader will approach the librarian at the desk. Occasionally a parent will bring a teen to the desk and request readers' advisory assistance for the teen. In these situations, it is important to direct questions to and focus on the teen.

Readers' advisory is about readers, not about the advisor. It is also important to acknowledge that no two people ever read the same book, so your experience reading a particular title may be quite different than that of a teen reader, who has lived through a different set of experiences and thus has a different set of filters and understandings in place while reading.

Give teen readers permission to not like suggested books, as well as permission to stop reading a book that is not being enjoyed. Surprisingly enough, many people feel they have to finish any book they start, which can make reading on onerous task. Emphasize to the reader that he or she should be having fun and enjoying the reading experience.

It helps to suggest the reader take several books, so if one doesn't captivate the attention, the reader can switch to one of the other titles. Let teens know that you do not require them to like the books you have suggested.

Genre fiction is often timeless, but teens are far more conscious of the age of a book than adults are. However, even though many teens are adamant about only wanting to read new books, often they have not noticed the original publication date—instead they base their judgment on the look of the cover art. In response to this phenomenon, publishers of teen fiction commonly reissue titles with updated covers, and sometimes even give the books new titles! Genre fiction with high author recognition allows some books to remain popular long after the time that most of their age mates have been retired from the collection. This is something librarians should keep in mind as they create book displays or make purchases for their collections.

Readers' advisory is an art, not a science. As a readers' advisor you will likely have some beautiful pairings between reader and book, as well as some that don't work as well. Be honest with readers and communicate with them the fact that readers' advisory is a process that grows and sharpens over time spent working together.

Purpose of This Book, and Its Audience

This guide is intended to help readers' advisors connect readers who like teen or young adult literature to the books they will most enjoy. It organizes and describes more than 1,500 fiction titles by genre, subgenre, and theme, grouping them according to specific appeals and reading tastes. In addition to the annotations, you will find notes on the genres—their distinctive features, characteristics, and tips for inviting readers.

This guide is not intended to be an all-inclusive compendium of authors who write genre fiction for teens. It is not a scholarly or historical treatise on the subject of young adult genre fiction. Nor is it meant to provide a comprehensive list of titles by specific authors. It is not intended to identify "safe" or "clean" books for inclusion in censored collections, or even those identified the "best" teen fiction according to literary standards. It is merely a guide to help readers' advisers and others understand the genres as they currently appear in young adult or teen fiction and assist readers to find the books they want to read. It is hoped that public and school librarians, educators, booksellers, and other adults who work with teen readers will find it a valuable professional tool and readers' advisory resource.

Scope, Selection Criteria, and Methodology

Major fiction genres popular with readers of teen fiction are represented in this book, including contemporary fiction, issues fiction, historical fiction, fantasy, science fiction, paranormal, and multicultural fiction. It covers titles published specifically for the teen audience, as well as books published for children and adult readers that are also popular with teens. Most of the titles in this book were published in the last seven years, but some classics and older but highly popular titles are included, as they are commonly available in library collections. (Those interested in learning more about older titles are encouraged to consult previous editions of this guide.) Selections of older titles here are based on popularity with teen readers and, in some cases, because the titles help to define the genre. Award recommendation lists from library and educational associations, genre writers organizations, and public libraries with active services to teens were consulted in making the final selections. Personal reading and consultation with teen readers were also sources of information.

Many of the authors represented in this guide are prolific and well-established, but readers will also find new authors who are expected to grow in popularity. There are some authors of great stature whose output is limited.

Organization and Features

As noted previously, the titles for this book are arranged according to genres, subgenres, and themes. The chapters, sections, and subsections are meant to group books with similar appeals together, so users can readily identify read-alikes. Chapters include broad sections for specific types, common themes, or both. Types represent distinct genres and subgenres in which books share genre conventions such as mystery or epic fantasy. Other titles may share a single, appealing theme, for example, vampires or humor. Although types represent a stronger and more multifaceted unity among titles, many readers are interested in specific themes.

In many cases, an argument can be made to place a specific title in more than one category. Obviously, the final decision of where to place a book in a guide like this involves some subjectivity. The judgments made here are based on publisher information and personal experience as a readers' advisor. An appendix of special lists and a detailed subject index provided additional access points for users.

Books in series are listed under the author's name and series title. In cases in which multiple authors have contributed to a series, the series is placed alphabetically by series title rather than author. Individual titles within a series are placed in series (chronological) order, rather than alphabetical order, because as readers we wish to read the titles in series order.

Author, title, and publication date are provided for all titles, along with an indication of interest level. Designations used are as follows:

- **M** middle school, grades 6 through 8
- **J** junior high school, grades 7 through 9
- **S** senior high school, in grades 9 through 12
- **O** mature teens, senior high school students, grades 11 and 12

These designations are based on reviews, library catalogs, and, again, personal experience and judgment. The overlap reflects developmental pace of readers and rapidity of change at the younger end of adolescents. Users should also keep in mind that these designations are subjective. Often one resource recommends a title for grades five through eight, whereas another recommends the same title for ages fourteen and up. It cannot be over emphasized that teens should read what they are comfortable with and what they find interesting and exciting, regardless of the assigned grade range. Books with a low or easy reading level that have high appeal and may interest struggling teen readers are indicated by the designation "High-Low."

Major awards and honors are one way to find the best of the best each year for different audiences, and this is something educators, in particular, need to do. The following awards and honors are noted in the annotations:

Alex — The Alex Award, for books published for adults but of interest to teens. Ten titles are given the award each year.

BBYA — Best Books for Young Adults, a list created by a committee of the Young Adult Library Services Association, a division of ALA; YALSA retired the list after 2010.

IRA — The International Reading Association Award for promising new authors of young adult books

IRA YAC — The Young Adult Choices list of books selected by teen readers for the International Reading Association

Morris — The Bill Morris Award for best first novel

PP — Popular paperbacks, selected by a YALSA committee

Printz Award — The best book published for the teen market, based on literary quality and selected by a YALSA committee

Printz Honor — Books selected by a YALSA committee as having outstanding literary merit

Quick Picks — A list created annually by a YALSA committee recommending books that have high appeal for young adults who do not ordinarily like to read

TTT — Teens Top Ten list, nominated and voted on by teens

VOYA — Outstanding books for middle school readers, selected by the reviewers and editors of *Voice of Youth Advocates*

Other awards, not specifically for teen books or that have a narrower focus, mentioned in the annotations, include the following:

NBA	National Book Award, awarded by the National Book Foundation and selected by a five-member panel of respected authors for each of four categories, one of which is Young People's Literature
Newbery Award	Awarded by the Association for Library Service to Children, for contribution to American literature for children. The committee considers books with an intended audience through age fourteen. One book is the award winner and up to four are honor books.
Edgar Award	Awarded annually by the Mystery Writers Association. There is a young adult category.
Norton Nebula Andre Norton Award	Awarded by the Science Fiction and Fantasy Writers of America for a young adult novel as part of the Nebula Awards; first awarded in 2005
Hugo Award	Voted on by members of the World Science Fiction Convention vote. Although there is no teen or young adult award, the award for best novel has occasionally gone to novels published for teens.
Mythopoeic Award	Awarded annually by the Mythopoeic Society. The award for children's literature considers books from picture books to young adult novels. It is occasionally awarded to an entire series rather than to individual books.
Pura Belpré	Administered by the Association for Library Service to Children, "presented to a Latino/Latina writer and illustrator whose work best portrays, affirms, and celebrates the Latino cultural experience in an outstanding work of literature for children and youth"
Schneider Family Book Award	Administered by the American Library Association. "The Schneider Family Book Awards honor an author or illustrator for a book that embodies an artistic expression of the disability experience for child and adolescent audiences." Award divisions include middle school and teen.

Coretta Scott King Award   Administered by EMIERT, a division of ALA. Awarded to "annually recognize outstanding books for young adults and children by African American authors and illustrators that reflect the African American experience."

Changes and Revisions

This edition differs a great deal from its predecessor. Most titles included are new to this edition, having been published since 2003. Issues novels and fantasy are still very popular, but paranormal novels have experienced a huge surge in popularity.

Of course, new subgenres, authors, and titles show up constantly, and it is impossible for a book such as this to remain completely up-to-date. Scanning reviews, talking to teens, and reading new genre titles are good ways to keep current. In addition, Readers' Advisor Online www.readersadvisoronline.com) incorporates books from the Genreflecting series and is regularly updated, adding new titles on a constant basis.

Readers may be interested in the author's Web site, Genrefluent (http://www.genrefluent.com/), where new titles are added between editions of *Teen Genreflecting*.

How to Use This Guide

This guide may be used in a number of ways. Perhaps the most common way to use this book is in identifying read-alike books. Books with similar characteristics and themes are grouped together. When the reader is looking for another book just like the last one he or she read, look for the title in the title index, and you'll find similar titles in the same section. Once the user finds a genre or subgenre of interest, a quick scan of the annotation indicates whether a specific title will be of interest to the reader. Grade levels, awards, the age of the protagonist, setting—all provide clues to finding the best choice for the reader. Some teens may wish to consult the book directly, so share the guide, rather than hiding it behind the reference or user services desk.

Of course, the book may also be used to simply familiarize readers' advisers with genre fiction for young adults. Book lists and narrative material help clarify what the genres are and which books and authors they contain.

Librarians wishing to expand their genre fiction collections for teens may find some of the newest and more popular titles in this guide. It may also be used as a source for book lists, displays, and other passive readers' advisory techniques. Whatever the specific application, this book should be used to share the joy of reading and books.

Other Resources for Finding Books Popular with Teen Readers

With the popularity of young adult fiction and the proclivity of teens and those who work with them to participate in 2.0 activities, the problem in finding books for teens isn't finding out what books teens are reading; it's more a matter of filtering the enormous quantity of information to come up with something usable. There are a multitude of bloggers focusing on teen books, and several groups on social networking sites that focus on them. For clickable links check out the Teen Genreflecting links at the Genrefluent site (www.genrefluent.com).

As of the writing of this guide, popular sites included the following:

- Teens Read—www.teensread.org. Formerly the Center for Adolescent Reading, the Bistro Book Club has a variety of reviews by teen readers, accomplished and emerging.

- Ed Spicer's Teen Book Reviews—www.spicyreads.org/Welcome.html

- Teens Read Too—www.teensreadtoo.com/BookReviews.html

- Flaming Net Book Reviews—http://flamingnet.com/bookreviews/index.cfm

- Reading Rants—www.readingrants.org/

- Cynthia Leitich Smith—www.cynthialeitichsmith.com. An author who writes for teens and children maintains this wonderful Web site.

Closing

Use this guide to put teens together with the books that they will enjoy, that will entertain them, make them laugh or cry or shiver, that will help them shape their own lives. Use this guide to find books you will enjoy and remember that not all readers of teen lit are teens. More and more adults are finding the pleasures of tightly plotted novels published as teen novels. In an August 2009 article, "Good Books Don't Have to Be Hard," Lev Grossman wrote:

> [M]illions of adults are cheating on the literary novel with the young-adult novel, where the unblushing embrace of storytelling is allowed, even encouraged. . . . Let's be honest: Why do so many adults read Suzanne Collins's young-adult novel *The Hunger Games* instead of contemporary literary fiction? Because *The Hunger Games* doesn't bore them.

Eliminate boredom. Share a teen book.

References

Card, Orson Scott. 2008. "Stephenie Meyer." *Time*, May 12, 110.

"Facts & Figures 2009 Revised." 2010. *Publishers Weekly*, April 5, 32-40.

Going, K. L. 2004. "Michael L. Printz Honor Speech." *Young Adult Library Services* [online] 3, no. 1 (Fall): 28-41. Available from Academic Search Elite, Ipswich, MA (accessed February 25, 2010).

Goldberg, Steven. 2006. "Demographics: Think About Teens." *Kiplinger*, May 5. Available at www.kiplinger.com/columns/picks/archive/2006/pick0605.htm (accessed May 23, 2010).

Grossman, Lev.2009. "Good Books Don't Have to Be Hard." *Wall Street Journal*, August 29.

Kuenn, Stephanie, YALSA Communications Specialist. 2010. E-mail message to author, February 25.

Kruse, Ginny Moore. 2008. Interview.I Spring. CCBC Cooperative Children's Book Center, School of Education, University of Wisconsin. Available at www.education.wisc.edu/ccbc/friends/kruse.asp (accessed May 23, 2010).

McEvoy, Dermot, and Michael Coffey.2009. "Bestselling Books 2008: Hardcover Old and New." *Publishers Weekly*, March 23, 17–22.

Raab, Margo. 2008. "I'm YA and I'm OK." *New York Times Book Review*, July 5. Available at www.nytimes.com/2008/07/20/books/review/Rabb-t.html (accessed May 23, 2010).

Roback, Diane. 2009. "Bestselling Children's Books 2008: Meyer's Deep Run." *Publishers Weekly*, March 6, 30–37.

Roback, Diane. 2010. "The Reign Continues." *Publishers Weekly*, March 22, 33–42.

Silvey, Anita. 2006. "The Unreal Deal." *School Library Journal*. (October 1). Available at www.schoollibraryjournal.com/article/CA6376083.html (accessed August 20, 2010).

Skurnick, Lizzie. 2010. "Suzanne Collins." *Time*, April 29. Available at www.time.com/time/specials/packages/article/0,28804,1984685_1984940_1985512,00.htm (accessed August 20, 2010).

Tapscott, Don. 2009. *Grown Up Digital: How the Net Generation Is Changing Your World*. McGraw-Hill, 16.

Chapter 1

Contemporary

Realistic fiction is fun for me to read because it is easy to relate to. I like that I am able to picture myself in the character's position, and am able to compare similar situations from my life and what occurs in the book.
—Jordan, age 14

The books in this chapter, if published for adults, would be called mainstream or general fiction. Because teens see life somewhat differently than adults and distinguish between preferred genres more often, calling this type of novel contemporary helps them find what they often consider to be real-life or reality fiction more easily.

The genre is characterized by a recognizable contemporary setting with situations the reader could see actually happening. Sometimes, as in the Meg Cabot <u>Airhead</u> books, the premise falls outside contemporary reality, but readers identify with the realistic setting despite the science fiction–like premise. This genre features teen protagonists trying to live their lives and focuses on how they do. Even though they face some challenges (there would be no story without them), the focus of these books in on the protagonist's life, not on the issues he or she faces.

Readers who like contemporary fiction often enjoy the reality of "issues" and "romance" fiction that does not feature exotic locations or other time periods—in other words, anything in other genres that is set in an identifiable here and now.

Identity

Finding one's identity is one of the primary needs in teens. Adolescence is a time of trying on new personas, trying out new ideas, and forming new relationships. Some teens have a hard time figuring out who they are, while others just sail through. Sometimes one's identity is tied closely to one's ethnic or racial background, gender or sexuality, or faith.

Cabot, Meg.

Airhead. 2008. 9780545040525. **J**

Sixteen-year-old Emerson wakes up after a terrible accident to discover that she now has the body of a supermodel. Her life-in-another body adventures continue in *Being Nikki* (2009, 9780545040563) and *Runaway* (2010, 9780545040600). (PP)

Read-alikes: Readers may also enjoy *Switch* by Carol Snow, another story involving a teen girl finding herself wearing a glamorous body.

Subjects: Body Switching; Models

Franklin, Emily.

The Other Half of Me. 2007. 9780385734462. **S**

As the offspring of an anonymous sperm donor, sixteen-year-old Jenny Fitzgerald feels different than her younger half siblings in more ways than just being an artist in a family of athletes. Signing up on the Donor Sibling Registry, she discovers that she has a half-sister.

Subjects: Siblings

Korman, Gordon.

Jake, Reinvented. 2003. 9780786856978. **S**

Paralleling the story line of *The Great Gatsby*, this novel tells the story of the new kid at a high school, Jake Garrett, former nerd who reinvents himself in an attempt to win the heart of Didi; it features hard-partying high school students. (BBYA, PP)

Subjects: Humorous

Lockhart, E.

The Disreputable History of Frankie Landau-Banks. 2008. 9780786838189. **J** **S**

Turning gorgeous and curvy during the summer between her freshman and sophomore years, Frankie attracts the attention of popular senior, Matthew. When she discovers he is a member of an all-male secret society at their elite boarding school, she figures out a way to infiltrate it. (BBYA, Printz Honor, NBA Finalist, TTT, IRA YAC)

Subjects: Boarding Schools; Pranks; Secret Societies

Perkins, Mitali.

First Daughter: White House Rules. 2008. 9780525479512. **J**

In this sequel to *First Daughter: Extreme American Makeover* (annotated in chapter 2), sixteen-year-old Sameera attempts to escape the scrutiny and restriction being placed on her as the Secret Service tries to keep the Pakistani American adopted daughter of the president of the United States safe.

Rosoff, Meg.

Just in Case. 2006. 9780385746786. **S**

Fearing that Fate has it in for him after he barely saves his baby brother from certain death, fifteen-year-old David Case changes his name to Justin and acquires a whole new look. (BBYA)

Subjects: Brothers

Wollman, Jessica.

Switched. 2007. 9780440240525. **J**

Identical sixteen-year-olds, one the daughter of a wealthy family, the other the daughter of the cleaning woman, switch places (à la *The Prince and the Pauper*) and find themselves.

Subjects: Darien, Connecticut; Wealth

Zevin, Gabrielle.

Memoirs of a Teenage Amnesiac. 2007. 9780374349462. **M J S**

A lot can happen in four years. When sixteen-year-old Naomi Porter falls on the school steps, she discovers that she has lost four years' worth of memories—including the fact that her parents got divorced, her mother remarried, and the people who claim to be her best friend and boyfriend are almost strangers to her. (BBYA, IRA YAC)

Read-alikes: Readers intrigued with the amnesia angle may also enjoy *The Adoration of Jenna Fox* by Mary E. Pearson and *Kat Got Your Tongue* by Lee Weatherly.

Subjects: Amnesia; Step-families

Ethnic and Racial

Dealing with ethnic and racial identity can be a major issue in life. Conflict in these titles often involves discovering one's background and facts surrounding racial or ethnic identity, and figuring out what they mean.

Alegria, Malin.

Sofi Mendoza's Guide to Getting Lost in Mexico. 2007. 9780689878114. **S**

When high school senior Sofi defies her parents and goes to a pregraduation party in Mexico, she finds out she is not a legal resident of the United States and can't go home. She ends up moving in with relatives she never met who live in Tijuana. As Sofi waits for resolution and a way home, she learns to live with no Internet access, no telephone, and an outdoor bathroom. In trying to figure out if she is Mexican, American, or just what, she discovers her own ties to her family roots and finds love.

Subjects: Illegal Immigrants; Latinos; Mexico; Romance

Alexie, Sherman.

Absolutely True Diary of a Part-Time Indian. 2007. 9780316013697. **J S**

Accidentally breaking his geometry teacher's nose takes fourteen-year-old Arnold off the rez and makes him the only Indian in his new school. Now he isn't the funny looking, smart kid anymore, but a basketball star with a hot girlfriend. (BBYA, NBA, BBYA Top 10)

Subjects: Basketball; Native Americans

de la Peña, Matt.

Mexican White Boy. 2008. 9780385733106. **S**

Because of being half-Mexican, Danny Lopez had always felt like an outsider in his preppie private school, but when he goes to National City, just south of San Diego, he feels like an outsider because he looks so white and speaks no Spanish. In the course of the summer he teams up with Uno, a kid who is half African American and half Hispanic, in a scheme using his phenomenal pitching skills to make money. With their winnings, he can go to Mexico to visit his dad, and Uno can move to Oxnard to live with his dad. Danny also falls for a gorgeous half-Mexican girl who doesn't speak any English, which makes their relationship kind of tough. This great coming-of-age story has interesting baseball action and compelling characters set in a warm but also menacing environment, where danger lurks alongside the ubiquitous graffiti and gangs.

Subjects: Baseball; Fathers and Sons; Latinos; Mixed Race

Headley, Justina Chen.

Girl Overboard. 2008. 9780316011297. **J** **S**

Chinese American Syrah Cheng, the fifteen-year-old daughter of a billionaire, loves to snowboard, but when an accident takes her away from the slopes, she has the time to figure out who she really wants to be.

Subjects: Asian Americans; Snowboarding; Wealth

Nothing But the Truth (and a Few White Lies). 2006. 9780316011310. **J** **S**

At Stanford math camp, Patty Ho begins to come to terms with her mixed heritage, but then her long-winded, lecturing Taiwanese mother shows up. (PP)

Subjects: Asian Americans; Camp; Mathematics; Mixed Race

Lisle, Janet Taylor.

The Crying Rocks. 2005. 9780689853203. **J** **S**

Joelle's adoptive mother keeps telling her strange stories about how she came to be part of her family, while the little girl across the street worships her and thinks she is a long-lost princess. Meanwhile Carlos has problems of his own, believing that he heard his brother's cries at a Naragansett historical site called the Crying Rocks and ran away in fear, leaving him to die.

Subjects: Adoption; Native Americans

McDonald, Janet.

Off-Color. 2007. 9780374371968. **J** **S**

When her mother loses a job and they have to move from their mostly white Brooklyn neighborhood to the projects, fifteen-year-old Cameron is worried about being a white girl in a minority neighborhood. When she finds a photo of the father she never knew, all her ideas about racial identity are turned upside down.

Subjects: Housing Projects; Mixed Race

Myers, Walter Dean.

The Dream Bearer. 2003. 9780064472890. **M**

Twelve-year-old David lives in Harlem with his hard-working mom, mentally ill dad, and older brother who seems to be getting into drugs. He and his best friend meet an old man named Moses (who looks homeless) while they are playing basketball. Moses tells them he is 300 years old and is a dream bearer. Whenever they meet, he tells them some of the dreams he's been carrying—dreams of slavery.

Subjects: African Americans; Basketball; Drugs; History; Mental Illness; Slavery

Sonnenblick, Jordan.

Zen and the Art of Faking It. 2007. 9780439837095. **M**

Starting at a new school in a new town, eighth grader San Lee sounds pretty knowledgeable when the subject of Zen comes up in his world history class, but that's only because he studied it at his last of many schools. With his con man dad absent, he and his mom struggle to get by, so his Chinese face, lack of a winter coat or boots, and Zen expertise convince some of the other kids he is a Zen master, which just may get him the girl.

Subjects: Asian Americans; Con Games; Zen

Valdes-Rodriguez, Alisa.

Haters. 2006. 9780316013086. **S**

Sixteen-year-old Paski moves from Taos, New Mexico, to Orange County, California, after her cartoonist father is hired to turn his comic book, *Squegeeman*, into a movie. Suddenly they have money, but Paski must leave her friends behind to start attending a snobby school where everyone is beautiful and the popular kids, called "Haters," try to make life miserable for others.

Subjects: Cartoonists; Latinos; Motocross; Mountain Biking; Psychics

Gender and Sexual Identity

What does it mean to be a girl? A boy? A boy who likes girls, a boy who likes boys, a boy who is really a girl, a girl who is really a boy, a girl who likes girls, a girl who likes boys? Who one is and to whom one is attracted are a huge part of teen identity. The books in this section deal with teens who explore those issues. Some are proactively exploring because of its importance in their lives. Others have the exploration thrust upon them, like Sam in the comedic *Boy2Girl*, who finds out a lot about himself when he agrees to masquerade as a girl.

The teens in these stories are dealing with who they are, finding their own identity, in the context of gender and sex. Books in which gender and sexual identity provide the focus around which the conflict in the book lies are annotated in the "GLBTQ Parents, GLBTQ Teens" section of chapter 2.

Blacker, Terence.

Boy2Girl. 2005. 9780374309268. **M** **J**

When Sam's mom dies he is sent to England to live with his aunt, uncle, and cousin Matthew Burton, who is thirteen, the same as Sam. Matt and his pals have a gang called the Sheds, not like the Crips and Bloods, but like the kids playing in a vacant lot type of gang. Their adversaries are members of the Bitches, a girl gang. When the obnoxious Sam Lopez gets the Sheds banned from their favorite hamburger joint, he offers to do whatever they dare him as atonement. They decide that the diminutive, long-haired Sam should spend the first week of school masquerading as a girl to find out what the Bitches are up to. He ends up really shaking up the school, perceptions, and the entire thirteen-year-old male–female culture. Gender roles, a great fortune, and a money-hunting criminal enter into the mix.

Hartinger, Brent.

Russel Middlebrook. **J** **S**

Russel Middlebrook is an ordinary high school student with a couple of great friends. Russel is gay, his friend Min is bi, and Gunnar is straight. All of them are looking for the right person to fall in love with.

Subjects: Gay–Straight Alliances

Geography Club. 2003. 9780060012236.

When high school sophomore Russel meets another gay teen online and discovers that he goes to the same school, they decide to form a club for the gay, lesbian, and bi teens to meet and talk, with such a boring name that nobody else will join.

The Order of the Poison Oak. 2005. 9780060567323.

When Russel, Min, and Gunnar take jobs as counselors at a summer camp, Russ ends up dealing with a tough group of ten-year-old burn survivors, who run roughshod over him until he finds grounds for mutual respect. Along the way he finds romance. (PP)

Subjects: Camp

Split Screen: Attack of the Soul-Sucking Brain Zombies / Bride of the Soul-Sucking Brain Zombies. 2007. 9780060824082.

Parallel stories told in two different novellas set while Russ and Min, now sixteen, work as extras on a teen zombie movie.

Subjects: Movies

Juby, Susan.

Another Kind of Cowboy. 2007. 9780060765170. **J** **S**

After his drunken dad wins Turnip, a horse, in a poker game, Alex and Turnip become a winning Western riding team. However, Alex, who is secretly gay, really wants to ride dressage. Wealthy Cleo O'Shea is forced to ride dressage whether she wants to or not. Together Cleo and Alex form an unlikely but real friendship. (BBYA)

Subjects: British Columbia; Canada; Gay Boys; Horses; Humorous

LaRochelle, David.

Absolutely Positively Not. 2005. 9780439591102. **J** **S**

Sixteen-year-old Steven is absolutely positively sure he is not gay. So why is it that he finds his new health teacher so extremely handsome and fascinating? (BBYA, IRA YAC)

Subjects: Gay–Straight Alliances; Humorous

Levithan, David.

Boy Meets Boy. 2003. 9780375832994. **J** **S**

In a whimsical utopian version of our world, high school sophomore Paul has always known and been accepted as gay. The 6-foot-5-inch-tall homecoming drag queen, Infinite Darlene, is also captain of the football team; the quiz bowl team rules; and the gay–straight alliance exists to turn the straight kids into better dancers. But even in a nearly perfect world, first love can be hard. Paul discovers that when he falls for Noah, loses him, and tries to win him back. (BBYA, PP)

Subjects: Drag Queens; Gay Boys; Humorous; Quiz Bowl

How They Met, and Other Stories. 2008. 9780375848865. **S**

This collection of stories featuring eighteen different relationships displays Levithan's wit and his observations of the human condition.

Subjects: Gay Boys; Lesbians; Romance; Short Stories

Myracle, Lauren.

Kissing Kate. 2003. 9780142408698. **J** **S**

Sixteen-year-old Kate and Lissa are best friends until they share a passionate kiss. Then, as Lissa tries to figure out her sexuality, Kate avoids her. (BBYA)

Subjects: Lucid Dreaming

Sanchez, Alex.

Getting It. 2006. 9781416908982. **S**

Fifteen-year-old Carlos has his gay friend Sal make him over as he tries to get his crush, Roxie, to become his girlfriend. His payment to Sal is to help him start a gay–straight alliance at their high school.

Subjects: Gay–Straight Alliances

Rainbow Series. **S**

Three boys attending the same school represent a few facets of the gay spectrum—from closeted to out—as they find friendship and romance.

Subjects: Gay Boys

Rainbow Boys. 2001. 9780689841002.

Jason, Kyle, and Nelson are all gay, but all different in other ways. They all go to the same high school, but Nelson is very much "out," whereas Jason, a jock, has a girlfriend. Though all the issues are covered, this is also a welcome romance tale. (BBYA, IRA YAC)

Rainbow High. 2003. 9780689854774.

As high school seniors, the three boys face big changes. After Jason comes out, he loses his college scholarship. Kyle knows that going away to Princeton will change things between him and Jason. And Nelson's boyfriend is found to be HIV positive.

Rainbow Road. 2005. 9780689865657.

When a new GLBT high school in California invites Jason to be the keynote speaker at their opening ceremony, he, Kyle, and Nelson head across America on a road trip. (PP)

Wittlinger, Ellen.

Love and Lies: Marisol's Story. 2008. 9781416962311. **M**

Marisol from *Hard Love* is the star of this story as she decides to defer college for a year to concentrate on writing a novel. Taking a novel writing class, she falls for her teacher, Olivia.

Subjects: Lesbians; Writers

Faith

Faith plays a major role in the lives of many teens. Sometimes a religion with which they have been raised becomes constricting; at other times teens without faith find it. Until recently this area had been largely neglected in teen literature. The following books all feature teens in a contemporary setting dealing in some way with how faith or religion impacts their lives.

Like novels in which the characters find their identity through, or despite, their ethnicity, race, or sexual identity, the characters in the following novels are trying to figure out what makes them who they are, only in these cases in terms of their faith.

Abdel-Fattah, Randa.

Does My Head Look Big in This? 2007. 978-0439919470. **J** **S**

Amal, a typical eleventh grader, attends a private school in Melbourne. She decides to start wearing the hijab full time, which makes it pretty obvious that she is the only Muslim in her school. She has a couple of Islamic girl friends, but they attend a different high school. Her two best friends at school also see themselves as outsiders: Eileen is Japanese Australian, and Simone thinks she is fat. Two very attractive boys start hanging around with the girls. Like Hassan in John Green's *An Abundance of Katherines*, Amal finds she can stay true to her faith and still be a real contemporary teen.

Subjects: Australians; Muslims

Bradley, Kimberly Brubaker.

Leap of Faith. 2006. 9780803731271. **M**

When Abby starts attending a Catholic school because she's been expelled from the public school, she tells her parents she is going to convert to Catholicism in an attempt to make them pay attention to her, but along the way she finds real faith.

Subjects: Catholics; Conversion

Brande, Robin.

Evolution, Me & Other Freaks of Nature. 2007. 9780440240303. **M** **J** **S**

After being kicked out of her fundamentalist Christian church, Mena starts her freshman year of high school with no friends and many enemies. In her science class, run by the amazingly cool Ms. Shepherd, she is teamed up with lab partner Casey, a brilliant student who is also kind of cute. She is totally restricted by her parents, but with some duplicity and the help of Casey's older sister Kayla, Mena spends a couple of hours every day with Casey's family as they build their science project around the litter of lab puppies at his home. When the church kids start protesting Ms. Shepherd's teaching of evolution, Kayla enlists Mena to write an anonymous column for the student paper. Lovingly drawn characters; a fast-moving plot; and a thoughtful exploration of identity, religion, and science make this a winner. (BBYA, IRA YAC)

Subjects: Dogs; Fundamentalist Christians; Science

Cooney, Caroline B.

A Friend at Midnight. 2006. 9780385733267. **M** **J**

Horribly angry at her deadbeat dad who abandoned her little brother at the airport, fifteen-year-old Lily finds her faith in God challenged.

Subjects: Dysfunctional Families; Abandonment; Brothers and Sisters

Levitin, Sonia.

Strange Relations. 2007. 9780440239635. **J** **S**

When seventeen-year-old Marne goes to Hawaii to stay with her aunt's family, the secular Jewish Los Angeleno finds culture shock as well as a sense of family with her Hasidic relatives.

Subjects: Extended Families; Jews

Reinhardt, Dana.

A Brief Chapter in My Impossible Life. 2006. 9780375846915. **J**

Sixteen-year-old Simone has never really cared to know anything about her birth mother, but her parents bring her together with Rivka so she can know her before Rivka dies from cancer. Along the way, she also discovers her ethnic and religious roots. (BBYA, PP)

Subjects: Adoption; Cancer; Jews

Roth, Matthue.

Never Mind the Goldbergs. 2005. 9780439691895. **S**

Hava may be an Orthodox Jew, but she has figured out how to keep her faith while still exhibiting her own punk-flavored style. However, keeping her faith poses challenges when she goes to LA to perform in a sitcom about an Orthodox Jewish family. (PP)

Subjects: Actors; Jews

Sanchez, Alex.

The God Box. 2007. 9781416908999. **S**

How can Paul reconcile his deeply felt Christianity with his attraction to other boys?

Subjects: Christians; Gay Boys; Latinos

Coming-of-Age

Coming-of-age is a universal theme, and it's rife with possibilities. Coming-of-age doesn't happen all at once. It can take years. It can involve tragedy or comedy. The titles in this section deal with teens figuring out who they are as individuals and how they want to live. Although the stories have much in common with those in the "Identity" section, the teens in this section are not discovering themselves through faith, race, or sexual identity.

Anderson, Laurie Halse.

Prom. 2005. 9780142405703. **S**

High school senior Ashley has no interest in anything school related, but when the new math teacher absconds with the prom funds, she is roped into helping her best friend Natalia put on the best prom ever. (IRA YAC, PP)

Subjects: Proms

Twisted. 2007. 9780670061013. **S**

After a graffiti stunt lands seventeen-year-old Tyler Miller in trouble with the law, his life changes. Formerly he was pretty much unnoticeable, but after a summer of physical labor to pay restitution and fines, he's looking buff. In fact, he attracts the notice of Bethany Milbury, queen of his high school and daughter of his father's boss. Even though his dysfunctional family hasn't changed, Tyler finds he has grown through the experience. (BBYA, Quick Picks, TTT, IRA YAC)

Subjects: Community Service; Dysfunctional Families; Graffiti

Birdsall, Olivia.

Notes on a Near-Life Experience. 2007. 9700440421610. **M** **J**

Just when she is ready to get serious about her crush, Mia, a middle child, watches her upper-middle-class family fall apart after her dad moves out.

Subjects: Divorce; Proms; Psychotherapy

Brugman, Alyssa.

Finding Grace. 2004. 9780440238331. **J** **S**

Eighteen-year-old Rachel takes a job taking care of Grace, a brain injured woman, because the job is near the university. As she comes to know and care about Grace, she learns much about herself, and she also meets an interesting guy.

Subjects: Australians; Brain Injuries; Caregivers; College Students

Caletti, Deb.

The Fortunes of Indigo Skye. 2008. 9781146910077. **S**

High school senior Indigo's life is changed, and not necessarily for the better, after one of the diners she serves in her waitressing job leaves her a $2.5 million tip. (BBYA)

Subjects: Waitresses; Wealth

Honey, Baby, Sweetheart. 2004. 9781416957836. **S**

Sixteen-year-old Ruby McQueen becomes the girlfriend of wealthy and glamorous Travis Becker and starts doing things that are completely out of character. When her librarian mom and her boss stage an intervention, she finds herself on a road trip with a group of senior citizens. (NBA Finalist)

Subjects: Librarians; Motorcycles; Senior Citizens

Cameron, Peter.

Someday This Pain Will Be Useful to You. 2007. 9780374309893. **S**

Even though he is supposed to be going to Brown University in the fall, recent high school graduate James Sveck, working in his mother's New York art gallery, fantasizes about throwing it all over and moving to the Midwest. (BBYA)

Subjects: Art Galleries; Gay Men

Castellucci, Cecil.

Beige. 2007. 9780763630669. **J** **S**

Katy is not happy about having to go to LA to spend the summer with Rat, her punk rocker dad, whom she hasn't seen in years. Her dad was actually banned from entering Canada because of his heroin habit. Conservative in apparel and lifestyle, Katy finds the punk scene very alien. The chapter titles make a terrific punk playlist. (BBYA, Quick Picks)

Subjects: Celebrities; Playlists; Punk Rock; Skateboarders

Boy Proof. 2005. 9780763627966. **J** **S**

Egg, on track to be valedictorian, is a science fiction geek who dresses like her favorite character and tries to keep others out of her life, until Max, a newcomer at her school, refuses to keep his distance. (BBYA. Quick Picks)

Subjects: Actresses; Film Industry; Science Fiction; Special Effects

Cohn, Rachel.

Cyd Charisse. J S

Named after the famous dancer, Cyd Charisse, this California girl loves working as a barista and loves her boyfriend, Shrimp. Her mom, who never married her dad, and her stepfather are named Nancy and Sid, names familiar to teens who love old punk rock. Cyd Charisse only met her bio-dad once, when she was little and he gave her a doll. The doll, Gingerbread, to whom she talks, adds a touch of whimsical magical realism to the story.

Other titles in the series are annotated in chapter 9.

Subjects: Baristas; Step-Families

Gingerbread. 2002. 9780689860201.

When sixteen-year-old Cyd Charisse stays out all night with her boyfriend Shrimp, her mom Nancy and stepdad Sid send her off to her bio-dad in New York, where she meets her older half-sister, who calls her "Daddy's little indiscretion" and her gay half-brother, who becomes her friend. (BBYA, Quick Picks, IRA YAC)

Cohn, Rachel, and David Levithan.

Naomi and Ely's No Kiss List. 2007. 9780375844409. S

Growing up in the same New York apartment building, Naomi and Ely, age eighteen, have always been best friends. Even though Ely is gay, Naomi has always figured she would someday marry him, but when he kisses her current boyfriend their relationship crashes.

Subjects: College Students; Gay Boys

Cross, Shauna.

Derby Girl. 2007. 9780805080230. S

She was small town Texas girl Bliss Cavender; and she meant to follow in her mother's and grandmother's footsteps to become the next Miss Bluebonnet, but now she is Babe Ruthless, skating for the Hurl Scouts in the roller derby. (BBYA, Quick Picks, Film—*Whip It*)

Subjects: Beauty Pageants; Roller Derby

Denman, K. L.

Mirror Image. 2007. 9781551436654. J M

Ninth grader Sable, who only wears black, is dismayed when she is forced to work with Lacy, who always wears pink, on a joint art project for school. The two girls, who seem to be absolute opposites, discover things they have in common as they spend time at each other's homes and meet each other's mothers.

Subjects: Art; Goth; High-Low

Dessen, Sarah.

Just Listen. 2008. 9780142410974. **S**

The devastating experience that changed Annabel Greene's life is slowly revealed after she spends a summer in virtual exile and then finds a friend in loner, Owen, when she starts her junior year of high school. (BBYA, TTT)

Subjects: Eating Disorders; Models; Outsiders

DuPrau, Jeanne.

Car Trouble. 2005. 9780060736750. **J S**

Seventeen-year-old Duff Pringle has a job designing computer games waiting for him in California and only six days to drive there. Unfortunately things start going wrong shortly after leaving his Virginia home, when his car breaks down, but then he finds a car that needs to be driven across country, links up with a drifter, and eventually the daughter of the car owner's con artist mother joins them on the journey.

Subjects: Con Games; Gaming; Road Trips

Ferraro, Tina.

Top Ten Uses for an Unworn Prom Dress. 2007. 9780385733687. **J S**

Being dumped by her boyfriend two days before the prom is just one of the problems littering Nicolette Antonovich's life.

Subjects: Breaking Up; Proms

Gonzalez, Julie.

Imaginary Enemy. 2008. 9780385735520. **M J**

Many kids have imaginary friends, but Jane White has Bubba, an imaginary enemy upon whom she blames all the mishaps in her life.

Green, John.

An Abundance of Katherines. 2006. 9780142410707. **S**

Colin Singleton, a one-time child math prodigy, has had nineteen girl-friends, all named Katherine, and nineteen breakups. His pal Hassan, a bright slacker, drags him off on a road trip, and they end up in Gutshot, Tennessee, lured by a highway sign offering tours of the grave site of Archduke Franz Ferdinand, whose assassination was the trigger for World War I. They soon start working with Lindsey Lee, the daughter of the factory owner who is the main employer in the area, on an oral history project. All three of them are smart, talented, and kind people. Colin gets all hung up in making a mathematical model of how relationships work and fail; Hassan, an observant Muslim, discovers new things about himself; and Lindsey finds out a lot about her town, her mom, and who she really is. (BBYA, Printz Honor, PP)

Subjects: Anagrams; Muslims; Road Trips

Looking for Alaska. 2005. 9780525475064. **S**

Geeky sixteen-year-old Miles Halter, known as Pudge, leaves Florida for boarding school in Alabama, where he finds other brilliant teens with whom he smokes, drinks, and plays pranks. When he falls "in lust" with Alaska, a troubled, beautiful, intelligent girl who lives down the hall, his life is bound to change. (BBYA, Quick Picks, TTT, Printz Award, IRA YAC, PP)

Subjects: Boarding Schools; Obituaries

Ha, Thu-Huong.

Hail Caesar. 2007. 9780439890267. **S**

Written by a fifteen-year-old, this portrait of a seventeen-year-old boy, called Caesar for his power over others, tells the story of his growth after a new girl comes to town and he begins to realize that he isn't all he thinks he is.

Subjects: Teen Authors

Halpern, Julie.

Into the Wild Nerd Yonder. 2009. 9780312382520. **S**

Jessie, a high school sophomore, had two best friends, but over the summer they went poseur punk, while Jessie has pretty much stayed the same. She is a good student and loves to sew A-line skirts using themed fabrics. Looking for friends who will act like friends, she discovers some different groups in her school, meets a cute nerd, and finds like-minded souls. (BBYA)

Subjects: Positive Families; Sewing; Gaming

Han, Jenny.

Shug. 2006. 9781416909439. **M**

As seventh grader Annemarie Wilcox, called Shug, enters adolescence, she develops a crush on her best friend, Mark, who rejects her. She also sees her parents' relationship falling apart and tries to figure out who she is and where she fits in.

Subjects: Crushes; Divorce

Hartnett, Sonya.

Stripes of the Sidestep Wolf. 2005. 9780763634162. **S**

High school drop out Satchel O'Rye is trying to support his family in a dying town after his father has totally given up. When he spots an unusual looking dog and mentions it to local outcast Chelsea Piper, he begins to think he may have spotted a Tasmanian tiger, thought to be extinct. (BBYA)

Subjects: Animals; Australians; Drop-Outs; Literary

Johnson, Maureen.

13 Little Blue Envelopes. 2005. 9780060541439. **J** **S**

A packet of letters found posthumously sends seventeen-year-old Ginny on a tour of Europe, fulfilling various tasks set by her artist aunt. (BBYA, TTT, IRA YAC, PP)

Subjects: *Art; Travel*

Jones, Patrick.

Nailed. 2006. 9780802796486. **S**

Sixteen-year-old Bret faces first love and betrayal while at odds with his father, who tells him that the nail that sticks out the farthest gets hit the hardest. Jones delves into Bret's feelings, depicting him as a very real, complex person who grows throughout the course of the story. The relationship between Bret and his father is well drawn as well, and even the villain of the story is sympathetically portrayed.

Subjects: Bands; Fathers and Sons

Koja, Kathe.

Kissing the Bee. 2007. 9780374399382. **S**

High school senior Dana, sidekick to her best friend Avra, begins to see their relationship in a new light while researching bees. Avra plans to flee their town after graduation with her boyfriend Emil, who has kissed Dana.

Subjects: Bees; Proms

Korman, Gordon.

Born to Rock. 2006. 9780786809219. **J** **S**

Leo Carraway, president of the Young Republican Club and recipient of a full-ride scholarship to Harvard, sees his plans go up in flames when he is unjustly accused of cheating about the same time that he discovers his biological father is King Maggot, an eighties punk rock star. Since he has lost the scholarship and is going to need money for college, Leo joins the Purge tour. (PP, Quick Picks)

Subjects: Celebrities; Punk Rock; Road Trips

Lockhart, E.

Ruby Oliver. **J** **S**

Ruby "Roo" Oliver, in therapy for her panic attacks, faces problems at school and home.

Subjects: Breakups; Houseboats; Humorous; Panic Attacks; Private Schools; Psychotherapists; Scholarship Students

The Boyfriend List: 15 Guys, 11 Shrink Appointments, 4 Ceramic Frogs, and Me, Ruby Oliver. 2005. 9780786809219.

> Fifteen-year-old Ruby Oliver prepares a list for her shrink of boys she has had a crush on, been friends, with, or even just known. When it gets out to the school at large, she becomes a pariah. (Quick Picks)

The Boy Book: A Study of Habits and Behaviors, Plus Techniques for Taming Them. 2006. 9780385732093.

> Roo Oliver now has a driver's license, new friends, and three possible love interests, but she still sees Dr. Z. (IRA YAC)

The Treasure Map of Boys: Noel, Jackson, Finn, Hutch, Gideon. 2009. 9780385904377.

> Roo's junior year of high school continues much the same, with boy dilemmas, panic attacks, and now a bake sale. A sequel, *Real Live Boyfriends: Yes, Boyfriends, Plural. If My Life Weren't Complicated, I Wouldn't Be Ruby Oliver*, is due out in December 2010. (BBYA)

Mackler, Carolyn

The Earth, My Butt, and Other Big Round Things. 2003. 9780763620912. **J S**

Fifteen-year-old Virginia is growing up fat in an otherwise perfect family. She has created rigid rules and an agenda for her relationship with Froggy Welsh the Fourth. With her best friend moving away, Virginia is on her own as she comes to the realization of who she really is, and that everyone else in her family is not as perfect as they look. (BBYA, IRA YAC, Printz Honor, PP)

Subjects: Body Image; First Love; Plus Size; Self-Esteem

Guyaholic. 2007. 9780763628017. **S**

V, eighteen, finds love when she is hit in the head with a hockey puck, but she doesn't really believe she deserves it, so she blows it big time by cheating on Sam. Leaving her grandparents' home, she heads to Texas, and along the way she figures out what's important in her life. (Quick Picks)

Subjects: Road Trips; Self-Esteem

Vegan Virgin Valentine. 2004. 9780763626136. **J S**

Mara's practically perfect life as a high school senior on her way to being valedictorian goes off track when her sixteen-year-old niece, V, a reputed slut, moves in. (Quick Picks, IRA YAC)

Marchetta, Melina.

Saving Francesca. 2004. 9780375829833. **J S**

Eleventh grade is going to be hard enough for Italian Australian Francesca Spinelli. She is one of only thirty girls who will attend the formerly all-male St. Sebastian's, but then her college professor mother falls ill with depression, leaving her with a father and younger brother who all are trying to figure out what to do. (BBYA, PP)

Subjects: Australians; Depression; Private Schools

Naylor, Phyllis Reynolds.

Alice Series. J S

As Alice has gotten older in this series that follows her life from sixth grade, when she loses her mother, through adolescence, so has the grade level for appeal. Readers do not have to read the entire series, and in fact the early titles in the series are intended for a middle grade readership, while the most recent titles are decidedly for teens.

Patiently Alice. 2003. 9780689826368

Alice discovers lots of changes when she returns home after working as a camp counselor for three weeks following her freshman year of high school. (IRA YAC)

Including Alice. 2004. 9780689826375.

With the big wedding finally happening, Alice, who always wanted her dad to marry Sylvia Summers, feels left out.

Read-alikes: High school readers who like the conflicting emotions Alice feels about her father's marriage may also enjoy C. Leigh Purtill's *All About Vee.*

Alice on Her Way. 2005. 9780689870903.

A sophomore class trip to New York and a stay in a hotel are on the agenda for Alice and her friends Pam, Liz, and Gwen.

Alice in the Know. 2006. 9780689870927

Working at a department store during the summer between tenth and eleventh grades, Alice McKinley discovers a world of problems.

Read-alikes: In *The Sisterhood of the Traveling Pants* by Ann Brashares, Tibby learns a lot about life and problems while she is working in a discount department store.

Dangerously Alice. 2007. 9780689870941.

In Alice's nineteenth adventure (twenty-second if you count the prequels) the high school junior sheds her good girl image by attending a party she isn't supposed to and discovers that every decision has consequences.

Read-alikes: Facing the consequences of being in the wrong place is also a theme in *Harmless* by Dana Reinhardt.

Purtill, C. Leigh.

All About Vee. 2008. 97811595141804. S

Eighteen-year-old Veronica May, a plus size actress, full of confidence from years as a success in community theater, heads for Hollywood when her widowed father decides to remarry, her job evaporates, and the director of the community theater decides to stage a production that has no place for her. A talented, larger-than-life performer, Vee discovers that not being a size 0 makes her stand out in a bad way in Hollywood, after a few horrible auditions where people aren't interested in her talent, just her size. She has moved in with a friend from high school, one of the Vs, who is now going by the name Reed, which is actually her last name. Between movement classes, yoga class, and acting class, Vee takes a job as a barista. Her hunky boss is a former actor who does not date employees, and she becomes pals with a gay coworker and a paranoid conspiracy theorist. Entertaining, heartfelt story.

Subjects: Actresses; Hollywood, California; Plus Size

Qualey, Marsha.

Just Like That. 2005. 9780142408308. **J** **S**

Failing to warn a couple on a snowmobile about thin ice, eighteen-year-old Hanna is devastated when she later discovers they have died. As she tries to get over the tragedy, she meets Will, the jogger who found the accident. Hanna falls for him, even though he is younger than she is. (BBYA)

Read-alikes: Readers who like the romance between an older girl and slightly younger boy may also enjoy *Lombardo's Law* by Ellen Wittlinger.

Reinhardt, Dana.

How to Build a House. 2008. 9780375844539. **S**

Sixteen-year-old Harper decides to leave the disaster that is home, now that her stepmother and siblings have moved out to spend part of the summer helping re-build a family home in small town Tennessee that had been destroyed by a tor-nado. (BBYA)

Subjects: Bailey, Tennessee; Construction; Divorce

Scott, Elizabeth.

Bloom. 2007. 9781416926832. **S**

Lauren stays closed off by choice. Even though she has been dating Dave, the most popular boy in school, she and her one friend are not popular, merely tolerated by the popular crowd. After her mother abandoned Lauren and her philandering fa-ther, a series of women moved in and out of the house, but now she has made her dad promise to not move another one in until she goes off to college. When she was eight, Evan and his mom moved in for a brief time, and he became her friend. Now he has turned up in her history class and incites feelings in her. She likes hav-ing a popular boyfriend, but doesn't really connect with him. Everyone thinks they have a sex life, but he has chosen celibacy. What he wants is a low key rela-tionship centered around church like his parents have. Lauren starts seeing Evan in secret when he gives her a ride home one day, but she doesn't break up with Dave. Meanwhile she becomes friends with another girl who is in her music class. As Lauren tries not to be the kind of person who cuts and runs like her mom, she never even thinks about cheating on her boyfriend as being like her father, who al-ways has a new girlfriend lined up before breaking up with the old one. (PP)

Shusterman, Neal.

The Schwa Was Here. 2004. 9780142405772. **J**

Calvin Schwa is functionally invisible; that is, people just don't notice him. He thinks it may be genetic. When he was little, his mother disappeared from a gro-cery store, leaving him in the shopping cart. Antsy Bonano notices him when he steps up to return the head of a plastic dummy that Antsy and his pals have been trying to destroy as a product test for Mr. Bonano. Antsy knows an opportunity when he sees one, and soon he and Calvin (aka the Schwa) are raking in the bucks based on bets and dares, utilizing the Schwa's functional invisibility. Things change when they break into Old Man Crawley's apartment to steal a dog bowl. (Crawley had fourteen Afghan hounds, named for the seven sins and seven virtues.) Their punishment is to walk the sins and virtues every day, but everything changes when Crawley's blind granddaughter turns up and both boys fall for her. Antsy's adventures are continued in *Antsy Does Time* (2008, 9780525478256). (BBYA, IRA YAC, PP)

Subjects: Dogs; Invisibility; Missing Persons

Spinelli, Jerry.

Smiles to Go. 2008. 9780060281335. **M** **J** **S**

Will Tuppence, a ninth grader who is interested in astronomy, skateboarding, and chess, has huge conflicts with his much younger sister, Tabby.

Subjects: Accidents; Brothers and Sisters; Friendship; Romance; Love Triangles

Stein, Tammar.

High Dive. 2008. 9780375830242. **J** **S**

When nineteen-year-old Arden travels to Sardinia to say good-bye to her family's beloved vacation home following the death of her father and her mother's deployment to Iraq, she meets a trio of college students and joins up with them on their tour of Europe.

Subjects: Grieving; Road Trips

Triana, Gaby.

Backstage Pass. 2004. 9780060560195. **S** **J**

Sixteen-year-old Desert McGraw has lived her life on the road with her father, "Flesh," lead singer of the rock band Crossfire, and her mom, the band's manager. Now she is in a comfortable Florida suburb, attending public school for the first time. She finds a boyfriend named Liam Blanco, who unfortunately has a stepmother who is a tabloid reporter, and a best friend named Becca, who is a gay girl being raised by her elderly grandmother in a tiny shacklike home. (IRA YAC)

Subjects: Lesbians; Rock Bands

Cubanita. 2005. 9780060560225. **S**

Teaching art at a camp in the Everglades the summer before heading off to college, Isabel Diaz finds herself at odds with her Cuban-born mother over her new boyfriend and eschewing of Cuban values. (PP)

Subjects: Camps; Everglades; Latinos

Van Draanen, Wendelin.

Confessions of a Serial Kisser. 2008. 9780375842481. **J** **S**

Looking for love after she and her mother move out of their luxurious home following her parents' breakup and after her father's girlfriend, the mother of one of her teammates, moves into her own home, sixteen-year-old Evangeline embarks on a quest for the perfect kiss.

Walters, Eric.

Splat. 2008. 9781551439860. **M**

After their fathers volunteer them to work on the annual tomato festival in their small town, Keegan and Alex work on making the tomato toss a success to provide funding for a new skate park, but when a tomato war breaks out, they find themselves in real hot water.

Subjects: High-Low; Skateboarding; Small Towns

Wittlinger, Ellen.

Zigzag. 2003. 9780689849985. **J** **S**

When her boyfriend abandons seventeen-year-old Robin for a summer in Rome, she ends up traveling across country with her aunt and two problematic cousins. (BBYA, PP)

Subjects: Cousins; Road Trips

Zeises, Lara M.

Contents Under Pressure. 2004. 9780385730471. **J** **S**

Feeling distanced from her friends, fourteen-year-old Lucy Doyle is excited when her brother returns home from music school, but she wasn't expecting to have to share her room with her brother's pregnant girlfriend, especially not just as she may be embarking on her own first romance. (IRA YAC)

Subjects: Brothers and Sisters; Pregnancy

Ziegler, Jennifer.

How Not to Be Popular. 2008. 9780385734653. **J** **S**

Sixteen-year-old Sugar Magnolia Dempsey, Maggie to her friends, is devastated when her Hippie parents decide to move to Austin, Texas, where she decides that to avoid being crushed when her family moves on again, she will not make any friends. She also thinks the best way to do that is to do everything that is the opposite of what one would do to be popular. She dresses herself in goofy clothes from the secondhand shop her parents run and unconsciously starts a trend at school for hokey lunch boxes, mechanic's coveralls, and rubber galoshes. In the school cafeteria, outcast Penny sits with her and Jack, who looks like a young republican and wants to date her. Using Penny as a roll model for dorkdom, Maggie joins the Helping Hands club and starts going to a water aerobics class made up mostly of senior citizens. As her plans blow up in her face, Maggie finds out who she is and where she belongs. (IRA YAC)

Subjects: Austin, Texas; Outsiders; Volunteering

Relationships

Teens are all about relationships—with those they are attracted to, those with whom they live, and those with whom they spend all their time. Friendship is at its most intense during adolescence, and many teen novels deal with friendships evolving and changing during this turbulent time. Adolescence is also when teens evaluate what family means to them; for many it is a time of drawing away, but for others it is a time of clinging to those lifelong relationships.

Family

Abbott, Hailey.

The Bridesmaid. 2005. 9780385732208. **M** **J**

After years working in their parents' wedding hall, Abby and Carol have seen the ugly side of weddings and vowed they will never act like the odious brides they've encountered. When Carol graduates from college and starts planning her own wedding, fifteen-year-old Abby is dismayed to find her sister is turning into a bridezilla.

Subjects: First Love; Sisters; Weddings

Auseon, Andrew.

Funny Little Monkey. 2005. 9780152054137. **S**

Fourteen-year-old twins Arty and Kurt Moore are not anything alike, but the one thing they have in common is their rabid dislike for each other. Arty, standing at 4 feet, 2 inches, uses his sarcasm and treachery in his battle against his 6-foot-1-inch twin, who physically tortures him.

Subjects: Brothers; Humorous

Bondoux, Anne-Laure.

Life as It Comes. 2007. 9780440239697. **J** **S**

When their parents die, responsible fifteen-year-old Mado becomes the ward of irresponsible twenty-year-old sister Patty. Because Mado can be sent to foster care if anything goes wrong, Patty hides her pregnancy.

Subjects: France; Orphans; Pregnancy; Romance; Sisters

Cohn, Rachel.

The Steps. 2003. 9780689874147. **M**

Her mom is off to Hawaii with her boyfriend, so Anabel goes to Sidney, Australia, to see her dad, Jack, over Christmas vacation. In Sydney she discovers she has a sister, Lucy, who is the same age; a younger stepbrother, Angus; and a baby half-sister, Beatrice.

Subjects: Blended Families; Siblings; Sidney, Australia; Step-Siblings

Friedman, Aimee.

The Year My Sister Got Lucky. 2008. 9780439922272. **J** **S**

Katie and Michaela, New York City ballet students, are uprooted when their parents decide to move upstate to Fir Lake, where eighteen-year-old Michaela slides into their new rural lifestyle with ease, but fourteen-year-old Katie feels like a fish out of water.

Subjects: Ballet Dancers; Rural Life; Sisters

Friesen, Gayle.

For Now. 2007. 9781554531332. **J** **S**

Jes's mother has married Cal, whose practically perfect daughter Angela, also a high school junior, has now moved in with them, but all is not as it appears on the surface. Jes finds herself at odds with Angela just as her best friend almost deserts her in the interest of first love, and Sam, her male best friend, starts looking more and more attractive. (BBYA)

Harmel, Kristin.

When You Wish. 2008. 9780385734752. **J** **S**

Star Beck, a teen pop star, runs away to Florida, where she works incognito in a pizza restaurant and tries to connect with the dad she had always been told had abandoned her.

Subjects: Celebrities; Runaways

Johnson, Maureen.

Suite Scarlett. 2008. 9780439899277. **J** **S**

Fifteen-year-old Scarlett Martin, along with her three siblings, works in their family's hotel—a hotel that has seen better times. Scarlett is in charge of maintaining the room of Mrs. Amberson, a larger-than-life actress who has moved into the hotel, and is soon swept into her plots to write a book, wreak revenge on another actress, and help Scarlett's brother and his underground theater company succeed, in surprising ways. Scarlett's adventures continue in *Scarlett Fever* (2010, 9780439899284). (BBYA)

Read-alikes: Readers who like the relationships between the siblings may also enjoy the <u>Casson Quartet</u> by Hilary McKay.

Subjects: Hotels; Humorous; Manhattan, New York; Siblings; Theater

Kadohata, Cynthia.

Outside Beauty. 2008. 9780689865756. **J**

Twelve-year-old Shelby is very close to her three sisters, who all have different fathers. When their beautiful mother, who collects men and jewelry, is injured in a disfiguring accident, they are dispersed to their fathers and fight to reunite.

Subjects: Beauty; Disfigurement; Sisters

Kephart, Beth.

House of Dance. 2008. 9780061429286. **J S**

Feeling abandoned by her mother's affair with a married man, fifteen-year-old Rosie spends the summer on a project to cheer up her grandfather, who is dying of cancer.

Subjects: Dance; Dying; Grandchildren; Grandparents

Lurie, April.

The Latent Powers of Dylan Fontaine. 2008. 9780385731256. **J S**

Fifteen-year-old Dylan Fontaine and his musical prodigy older brother, who smokes too much weed, are pretty much on their own, with a dad who works almost all the time and a mom who moved out to live with an artist.

Read-alikes: Anne-Laure Bondoux's *Life as It Comes* also deals with a younger sibling looking out for an older one.

Subjects: Brothers; Musicians

Shoup, Barbara

Everything You Want. 2008. 9780738712277. **S**

When college freshman Emma's family wins big in the lottery, life is bound to change.

Subjects: Wealth

Voorhees, Coert.

The Brothers Torres. 2008. 9781423103042. **S**

Frankie Towers navigates the perilous waters of high school in northern New Mexico while trying to get the girl of his dreams. Half Anglo, half Hispanic, he works in his parents' Mexican restaurant, Los Torres, and has a best friend who has the disgusting habit of frequently pulling out his glass eye. His crush is Rebecca Sanchez, daughter of the town's chief of police. Frankie's older brother Steve, a soccer star, doesn't have to work in the restaurant, has been given a car, and is popular at school but has recently started running with the *cholos*. (BBYA, IRA YAC)

Friends

At no time in life are friends more important to an individual than in adolescence. Many teens feel that their primary relationships are those with peers, so it is no wonder that books dealing with friendship are prevalent in novels for teens. Through them they see reflections of themselves and their friends.

Brian, Kate.

The V Club. (alternate title: *The Virginity Club*). 2004. 9780689860652. **S**

High school friends Kai, Mandy, Debbie, and Eva all want to win a big new scholarship, so they start the Virginity Club, a service club, so they can meet the scholarship requirement of "must exemplify purity of soul and body." (PP)

Subjects: Scholarships; Service Clubs; Virginity

Castellucci, Cecil.

The Queen of Cool. 2006. 9780763634131. **S**

Beautiful, affluent, and wildly popular, sixteen-year-old Libby Brin decides she wants to change her shallow life and starts volunteering at the zoo.

Subjects: Volunteering; Zoos

Friesen, Gayle.

The Isabel Factor. 2005. 9781553377382. **J** **S**

Anna and Zoe, fifteen, are inseparable, until Anna goes off to camp as a junior counselor while Zoe stays behind with a broken arm. At camp Anna befriends free spirit Isabel, but when Zoe shows up, so does confusion over identity and being a friend.

Subjects: Camps; Canadians; Identity

Johnson, Maureen.

The Bermudez Triangle. 2004. 9781595141552. **S**

When Nina Bermudez leaves her two lifelong best friends Avery and Mel behind to attend a summer leadership program at Stanford, the summer before their senior year in high school, she doesn't know that they will change as much as she does over the summer. (PP)

Subjects: Camp; First Love; Lesbians

Koertge, Ron.

Boy Girl Boy. 2005. 9780152058654. **S**

Best friends Larry, Teresa, and Elliot plan on all leaving together right after high school graduation to make new lives for themselves in California, but as graduation approaches they begin to realize that perhaps they won't always be together.

Subjects: Gay Boys

Margaux with an X. 2004. 9780763626792. **S**

Danny's wardrobe looks like a pile of rejects from a secondhand store. He lives with his aunt who has MS, and volunteers at an animal shelter. Margaux is the beautiful, intelligent, and accomplished daughter of a con man. Both of them have deep secrets; and as unlikely as it may seem, they become friends. (BBYA)

Subjects: Con Men; Multiple Sclerosis; Popularity; Volunteering

Lockhart, E. , Sarah Mlynowski, and Lauren Myracle.

How to Be Bad. 2008. 9780061284229. **S**

Two sixteen-year-old friends and a coworker leave Niceville, Florida, where they work in a waffle restaurant, to head for Miami for a weekend. Vicks is going to see a boyfriend who has just gone off to college; Jesse is running away from her mother's cancer diagnosis; and Mel, a rich new-comer, wants in on the friendship between Jesse and Vicks. The novel is written from the viewpoints of each of the three protagonists, each by a different author.

Subjects: Multiple Narratives; Road Trips

MacCullough, Carolyn.

Drawing the Ocean. 2006. 9781596430921. **J S**

Ever since sixteen-year-old Sadie's twin brother died four years ago, she has drawn or painted every day, haunted by his ghostly presence. Moving to a new school across the country, Sadie becomes part of the popular crowd, but she is really drawn to friendship with Fryin' Ryan, a poet and outcast.

Subjects: Bereavement; Outsiders; Poets; Twins

Nelson, Blake.

Prom Anonymous. 2006. 9780142407455. **S**

Growing up, Laura, Jace, and Cloe were best friends, but high school has moved them into different groups. As the prom approaches, Laura decides it would be perfect for all three of them to go.

Subjects: Proms

Ockler, Sarah.

Twenty Boy Summer. 2009. 9780316051590. **J S**

Anna and Frankie have been best friends forever, but the year Anna turns fifteen is full of grief for both of them: Frankie's brother Matt dies just weeks after becoming Anna's secret boyfriend. Anna and Matt had planned to tell Frankie about their relationship when Anna was to have accompanied the family on their annual beach vacation, but it didn't happen because of the tragedy. A year later, Frankie challenges Anna to meet twenty boys in the time they are at the beach.

Subjects: Beaches; Grief; Siblings; Vacations

Spinelli, Jerry.

Love, Stargirl. 2007. 9780375813757. **J S**

After moving from Arizona to Pennsylvania, fifteen-year-old Stargirl writes an ongoing letter to Leo, while befriending an assortment of various people, from five-year-old Dootsie to lonely, elderly Charlie. This is a sequel to *Stargirl*.

Subjects: Epistolary Novels; Outsiders

Passions

Young adults are full of passion in many different areas of their lives. Many contemporary teen novels deal with the protagonists in relation to the activities that often consume them. Many of these involve endeavors in the arts, but activism, sports, and even gambling provide strong themes that set these books apart.

Art

Many teens feel great passion for art, wanting to create representations, no matter how abstract, of their visions of life, love, and angst.

Bauer, Cat.

Harley's Ninth. 2007. 9780375837364. **S**

With a gallery exhibition looming and a possible pregnancy, Harley continues her passion for painting, introduced in *Harley, Like a Person* (2000).

Subjects: Adoption; Family Secrets; Pregnancy

Konigsburg, E. L.

The Mysterious Edge of the Heroic World. 2007. 9781416953531. **M**

While helping a neighbor, sixth grader Amedeo Kaplan discovers a drawing signed by Modigliani, which leads him into finding out about the Nazi repression of modern art.

Subjects: Degenerate Art; Florida; Nazis

The Outcasts of 19 Schuyler Place. 2004. 9780689866371. **M**

Margaret Rose Kane, age twelve, declines to participate in any camp activities, and as a result is picked up by one of her elderly uncles, who lives with his brother in a neighborhood that has been through many transformations. The towers they built over the previous forty-five years are slated for destruction by yuppie lawyers in the neighborhood. Margaret Rose, along with the handyman from the camp and her mother's old childhood playmate, create a protest and a plan to save the towers as fine examples of "outsider" art. (BBYA)

Subjects: Activism; Camp; Outsider Art; Uncles

Sones, Sonya.

What My Girlfriend Doesn't Know. 2007. 9780689876028. **J** **S**

Robin Murphy, age fourteen, is a talented artist but social outsider. He sees his life differently after he is invited to audit a Harvard art class, and Sophie, one of the popular girls at school, falls for him. (Quick Picks)

Subjects: Verse Novels

Music

Music plays an important role in the lives of teens. It often defines their generation, and they often use the music they are passionate about to define themselves whether they are making music, studying it, or listening to it. A popular recent trend in teen novels is the inclusion of playlists featuring music to listen to as one reads the book. Cecil Castellucci uses song titles as chapter titles in her novel *Beige* to set the tone for the story as it progresses.

Cohn, Rachel.

Pop Princess. 2004. 9780689852053. **S**

Fifteen-year-old Wonder Blake's life took a turn for the worse when her singer-songwriter sister was killed and the family moved to a small town where she is a definite outsider. Now with her own recording contract and a hit song, her life will change again.

Subjects: Bereavement; Fame; Outsiders

Cohn, Rachel, and David Levithan.

Nick and Norah's Infinite Playlist. 2006. 9780375846144. **S**

The story of a single night told in alternating chapters by Nick and Norah, who meet at a Manhattan club one night and fall in love as they go from club to club listening to different bands. (BBYA, Quick Picks, IRA YAC, PP, Film)

Subjects: Playlists; Punk Rock; Romance

Flinn, Alex.

Diva. 2006. 9780060568467. **S**

Sixteen-year-old opera student Caitlin, recovering from a relationship with an abusive boyfriend, is at odds with her mother, who wants people to believe they are sisters, and who is having an affair with a married man.

Subjects: Dysfunctional Families; Mothers and Daughters; Opera

Hughes, Mark Peter.

Lemonade Mouth. 2007. 9780385735117. **J S**

Five Rhode Island high school freshman meet in detention, and the band Lemonade Mouth is formed, in this story told in six alternating voices by members of the band and a fan.

Subjects: Bands; Parallel Narratives; Rhode Island

Krovatin, Christopher.

Heavy Metal and You. 2005. 9780439743990. **S**

Sam Markus loves heavy metal music and life on the edge at his expensive prep school, but things change when he starts going out with "straight-edge" Melissa. (BBYA, Quick Picks, IRA YAC)

Subjects: Prep Schools; Rock Music; Straightedge

Nelson, Blake.

Rock Star Superstar. 2004. 9780670059331. **S**

Bass guitar player Pete, age sixteen, discovers the real nature of the rock music business when he joins a rock band that is on its way to stardom. (BBYA, Quick Picks)

Subjects: Explicit Sexuality ; Musicians; Portland, Oregon; Rock Bands

Sports

Sports is a passion for many teens. Even in times of declining school budgets, sports are not cut because they are one of the incentives that keep many teens in school. Not all sports are traditional, and the novels that feature athletes show their true characters despite decades of "jock" stereotyping.

Beam, Matt.

Getting to First Base with Danalda Chase. 2007. 9780525475781. **M**

Loving baseball and getting to kiss Danalda Chase are on seventh grader Darcy Spillman's mind as he learns about girls from Kamna Singh and teaches her about baseball.

Subjects: Baseball

Green, Tim.

Football Genius. 2007. 9780061122736. **M**

Troy White, age twelve, has the uncanny ability to predict football plays, but that doesn't help with his own coach, who has him sitting on the bench, or with the Atlanta Falcons when his mother is fired from her PR job. (IRA YAC)

Subjects: Atlanta; Football

Football Hero. 2008. 9780061122743. **M**

Twelve-year-old orphan Ty Lewis loves football, but has to work in his uncle's cleaning business. (IRA YAC)

Subjects: Football

Krech, Bob.

Rebound. 2006. 9780761455431. **J** **S**

Seventeen-year-old Ray Wisniewski loves basketball, but he is white, and at his New Jersey high school it is the African American guys who play basketball. That means he has to wrestle if he wants to participate in a sport. (BBYA, IRA YAC)

Subjects: Basketball; New Jersey; Racism

Lupica, Mike.

The Big Field. 2008. 9780399246258. **M** **J**

Hutch, age fourteen, has always been a short stop, playing the position his dad played as a professional, but now there is a new kid in town, and Hutch has been moved over to second base. (IRA YAC, VOYA)

Subjects: Baseball; Fathers and Sons; Florida

Heat. 2005. 9780142407578. **M**

Cuban American pitching phenomenon Michael Arroyo is benched when the coach of a rival team accuses him of being older than twelve. With his birth certificate lost in Cuba, and he and his brother keeping their father's death a secret, Michael's dream of pitching in the Little League World Series is now in peril. (VOYA, PP)

Subjects: Baseball; Brothers; Cuban Americans; New York; Orphans

Danny Walker. **M**

Danny Walker loves basketball, but even though he is a great player, he is often overlooked by his coaches because of his small size.

Subjects: Basketball; Fathers and Sons

Travel Team. 2004. 9780142404621.

Twelve-year-old Danny Walker, who is a savvy, smart basketball player, is cut from the travel team because of his small stature; but his dad, a former professional basketball player, is trying to reconnect with him and starts up another travel team.

Summer Ball. 2007. 9780399244872.

Now thirteen, Danny finds new challenges at a tough basketball camp.

Subjects: Camp

Murdock, Catherine Gilbert.

Dairy Queen. **M** **J** **S**

If D. J. can run the family dairy farm and train a star quarterback, why shouldn't she go out for football herself?

Subjects: Farming; Female Athletes; Football; Wisconsin

Dairy Queen. 2006. 9780618863358.

D.J. Schwenk has always played football with her brothers so, in her fifteenth summer, the summer all the farm chores have fallen to her because her father was injured, she ends up training the rival school's quarterback and decides to go out for football herself. (BBYA, VOYA, PP)

The Off Season. 2007. 9780618934935.

D.J.'s junior year in high school starts off pretty well; she is playing football, and Brian is now her boyfriend, but things start going wrong. She injures her shoulder and can't play, she realizes Brian doesn't want to be seen with her, and then her older brother suffers a broken neck on the football field. (BBYA)

Front and Center. 2009. 9780618959822.

With football season behind her, D. J. turns to basketball and thoughts of college as scouts pour into her town.

Myers, Walter Dean.

Game. 2008. 9780060582951. **J** **S**

High school senior Drew Lawson is counting on basketball, which he loves, to get him into college and dreams of making it in the NBA.

Subjects: African Americans; Basketball; Harlem

Peet, Mal.

Keeper. 2005. 9780763632861. **S**

When a well-respected sports journalist interviews "El Gato," the goal keeper who led his soccer team to the World Cup victory, he is surprised to hear a tale of a boy growing up in the South American rainforest who was taught soccer by a ghostly presence. (BBYA)

Subjects: Journalists; Soccer; South America

Tharp, Tim.

Knights of the Hill Country. 2006. 9780553495133. **J** **S**

High school senior Hampton Green lives in a small Oklahoma town where football rules and he is a star, but off the field, his life is not all that great. (BBYA, IRA YAC)

Subjects: Football; Oklahoma

Wallace, Rich.

One Good Punch. 2007. 9780375813528. **S**

Michael Kerrigan, an all-around good kid, looks forward to his senior year as captain of the track team and editorial assistant at the newspaper, but when marijuana is found in his locker everything changes. Will he? (BBYA)

Subjects: Honor; Newspapers; Obituaries; Track

Weaver, Will.

Motor Novels. **J** **S**

This series, set in the Midwest, features several characters of different ages and walks of life involved in stock car racing.

Subjects: Car Racing; Midwest; Minnesota; Multiple Points of View

Saturday Night Dirt. 2008. 9780312561314.

Told from multiple viewpoints, this story of dirt track car racing on one Saturday in Minnesota illuminates the sport through the eyes of the daughter of the track owner, who is trying to keep it solvent; several teens who are racing; the older man who flags the race; and others. (Quick Picks)

Super Stock Rookie. 2009. 9780374350611.

Trace Bonham's racing career takes off when he picks up a sponsor, but he is not sure he wants to move on when he discovers what the world of Super Stock racing entails.

Theater

A passion for theater and performing is another avocation that keeps teens motivated and in school. Many dream of going on to Broadway, and the lure of the footlights is apparent in novels for teens.

Jones, Carrie.

Girl, Hero. 2008. 9780738710518. **M** **J**

High school freshman Lily, not yet recovered from the death of her stepfather, wins a lead role in the school play as she tries to figure out who she is.

Subjects: Abuse; Bereavement; Dysfunctional Families; Father Figures; Wayne, John

Lockhart, E.

Dramarama. 2007. 9780786838158. **J** **S**

Best friends Sayde and Demi go off to Drama camp, where he can shine as a gay African American and she discovers that being a major talent in her high school doesn't make her one in the bigger world. (BBYA, PP)

Read-alikes: Readers who enjoy the friendship between a straight girl and a gay boy may also enjoy *Naomi and Ely's No Kiss List* by Rachel Cohn and David Levithan.

Subjects: Camp; Friends; Gay Boys

Ruditis, Paul.

Drama! **J** **S**

Drama is always foremost at a posh Malibu school specializing in theater.

The Four Dorothys. 2007. 9781416933915.

Local politics determines that four different actresses are cast in the starring role in Orion Academy's latest production.

Everyone's a Critic. 2007. 9781416933922.

A famous Broadway producer, director, and choreographer visits Orion Academy to pick one boy and one girl to go to New York for his exclusive summer theater program.

Show Don't Tell. 2008. 9781416959052.

Sam is thrilled that it is time for the Renaissance Fair, and Bryan's secret just may be revealed.

Entrances and Exits. 2008. 9781416959069

> Romance, sexual orientation, hormones, and one-act plays are on the agenda for fall.

Wood, Maryrose.

My Life: The Musical. 2008. 9780385732789. **J** **S**

> Emily and Philip, both sixteen, are obsessed with the Broadway musical *Aurora*, so when rumors fly that it is going to close, they jump in to try to save it.

> **Subjects:** Broadway; Grandmothers; Long Island

Cards

Not all of the passions that teens embrace fall into accepted extracurricular areas. In Sachar's *The Cardturner*, Alton's passion for bridge puts him outside the mainstream. Most of the books dealing with cards involve gambling, which is one of those passions. Often the protagonists have extraordinary skills at figuring percentages and probabilities, but this is not an activity that keeps them on the straight and narrow.

Hautman, Pete.

All-In. 2007. 9781416913252. **J** **S**

> Seventeen-year-old Denn Doyle is making his living as a high stakes gambler in Las Vegas, until he meets the girl of his dreams and his luck changes. This is a stand alone sequel to *No Limit*, a book that was originally published with the title *Stone Cold*.

> **Subjects:** Con Games; Las Vegas; Poker Tournaments

Hautman, Peter, ed.

Full House: 10 Stories About Poker. 2007. 9780399245282. **S**

> Stories by K. L. Going, Francine Pascal, Adam Stemple, Alex Flinn, Gary Phillips, Mary, Bill Fitzhugh, Walter Sorrells, Pete Hautman, and Will Weaver about poker and teens who play the game.

Luper, Eric.

Big Slick. 2007. 9780374307998. **S**

> After "borrowing" $600 from his father's dry cleaning business to enter a poker tournament he is sure he will win, sixteen-year-old Andrew and his friends try to find a way to pay it back before he is found out.

> **Subjects:** Mathematics; Poker Tournaments

Sachar, Louis.

The Cardturner. 2010. 9780385736626. **J** **S**

> When sixteen-year-old Alton is recruited to drive Trapp, his wealthy blind great uncle, to his bridge club and assist him during play he is not thrilled. Tori, the granddaughter of Trapp's bridge partner from decades ago, had been the previ-

ous card turner but had committed a major faux pas and been fired as card turner, though retained as protégé. Alton is gradually seduced by the complexities of bridge and begins to secretly play bridge with Tori. A subtle paranormal element complicates life.

Volponi, Paul.

The Hand You're Dealt. 2008. 9781416939894. **J** **S**

Huck Porter's dad was the best poker player in their small Arizona town. He even won the watch blessed by the pope in the poker tournament that supports the local recreation center. When his dad has a stroke and has to miss the tournament, Huck's horrible math teacher wins and sneaks into the ICU to take the watch from Mr. Porter's wrist just before he dies. Now Huck wants to win the tournament and get the watch back, but what will it cost him to do that?

Humor

Contemporary stories that tickle the funny bone are a welcome diversion from teen angst. Even though the following books are humorous, and some downright laugh-out-loud funny, many deal with real events and feelings in the lives of teens. Unfortunately humor, which is often difficult to write, is seldom recognized with awards. Readers who enjoy humorous novels will also find some in other sections of this guide, including chapter 10, by looking for humor in the subject index.

Bradley, Alex.

Hot Lunch. 2007. 9780525478300. **J** **S**

When Molly and Cassie, high school sophomores, get into a food fight in the cafeteria at their alternative school, they are sentenced to be lunch ladies until they can get along. It doesn't help that they both like the same boy.

Subjects: Alternative Schools; Cafeterias; Recipes

Cheshire, Simon.

Kissing Vanessa. 2004. 9780385732123. **M** **J** **S**

When Kevin, a fifteen-year-old photographer, follows his friend's advice on how to win a girl, things go wildly wrong.

Subjects: Great Britain; Photography

The Prince and the Snowgirl. 2007. 9780385733427. **J** **S**

Tom, age fifteen, looks so much like Prince George that he has a job impersonating him, but things go awry when he does his impersonation to get the girl, and the real prince shows up.

Subjects: Great Britain; Impersonators; Scotland; Skiing

Collins, Yvonne.

The Black Sheep. 2007. 9781423101567. **J** **S**

Leaving her uptight, Manhattan parents to switch families for a reality TV show, fifteen-year-old Kendra Bishop ends up in the big California Mulligan family, headed up by hippie parents. Kendra does have an attractive new "brother," Mitch, who dreams of becoming a marine biologist, and a new interest in activism to save sea otters.

Read-alikes: Readers who like the reality TV situation may also enjoy *Never Mind the Goldbergs* by Matthue Roth.

Subjects: Fish Out of Water; Reality TV; Romance

Cooney, Caroline B.

Hit the Road. 2006. 9780385729444. **M** **J**

Sixteen-year-old Brit takes off on an epic road trip when her parents drop her off to stay with Nannie, her eighty-six year-old grandmother, who is determined to round up her old college buddies so they can all attend their sixty-fifth college reunion. (PP)

Read-alikes: Other humorous novels featuring teen girls on a road trips with elderly women are *Honey, Baby, Sweetheart,* by Deb Caletti and *Rules of the Road* by Joan Bauer.

Subjects: ; Kidnappings; Road Trips; Senior Citizens

Ehrenhaft, Daniel.

Tell It to Naomi. 2004. 9780385731294. **J** **S**

Trying to find a place to fit in, high school sophomore Dave Rosen starts writing an advice column for his high school paper, but the fatal flaw in his plan is that everybody believes it is his older sister, an unemployed journalist, who is writing it.

Subjects: Advice Columns; Crushes; Secret Identities

10 Things to Do Before I Die. 2004. 9780385734066. **S**

Believing he has been fatally poisoned, Ted Burger, age sixteen, decides to accomplish the ten things on his "to do" list before he dies during the first twenty-four hours of spring break, including partying with his favorite band and losing his virginity.

Juby, Susan.

Alice MacLeod series. **J** **S**

Alice MacLeod had been homeschooled by her nonconformist parents for ten years before venturing into traditional schooling.

Alice, I Think. 2003. 9780060515454.

When fifteen-year-old Alice, who has always been homeschooled, starts attending high school, she keeps a diary of the hilarious goings on with her hippy parents, the people she meets, and her counselors. (BBYA)

Miss Smithers. 2004. 9780060515461.

> Charmingly eccentric Alice enters the Miss Smithers pageant, writes a zine, and reflects on her small-town life.

Alice MacLeod, Realist at Last. 2005. 9780060515522.

> Seventeen-year-old Alice is finding summer trying, with a breakup, a new therapist, and dealing with her activist mother's incarceration.

Kizer, Amber.

Gert Garibaldi's Rants and Raves. **S**

Self-centered fifteen-year-old Gert rambles on about anything that catches her attention, including romance and sex.

One Butt Cheek at a Time. 2007. 9780385734301.

> Fifteen-year-old Gert categorizes everyone in her life, including her gay best friend, his boyfriend, and the boyfriend's twin, upon whom she has a crush. She also takes to heart her sex education teacher's suggestion that girls examine their own bodies.

From Butt to Booty. 2008. 9780385904407.

> Dumping a boyfriend who is an inept kisser, Gert continues in her sophomore year dealing with SATs, sex, soccer, and a job.

Korman, Gordon.

Son of the Mob.

Growing up as the son of a mobster is tough for Vince Luca, who wants to make his own honest way in life.

Subjects: Film; Mafia

Son of the Mob. 2002. 9780786815937. **J S**

> Seventeen-year-old Vince Luca, a mobster's son, and Kendra, an FBI agent's daughter, fall in love. (BBYA, Quick Picks, PP)

Son of the Mob: Hollywood Hustle. 2004. 9780786809196. **S**

> Vince and Kendra are off to different colleges in California, where Kendra winds up acting in Vince's roommate's movie. (BBYA, Quick Picks)

Lubar, David.

Sleeping Freshmen Never Lie. 2005. 9780142407806. **J S**

> As high school freshman Scott Hudson signs up for too many activities in an attempt to be close to his crush, he finds himself covering a losing sports team instead of writing book reviews, serving on the student council, and working on the stage crew for the school musical—all of which gives him a horrendous schedule that doesn't leave much time for sleep. Meanwhile he chronicles all his trials and tribulations in a guide for his yet-unborn sibling. (BBYA, IRA YAC)

Subjects: Brothers; Clubs

Moloney, James.

Black Taxi. 2005. 9780060559380. **J** **S**

When sixteen-year-old Rosie Sinclair's grandfather gives her the keys to his big black Mercedes when he goes to jail, the attached strings have her ferrying senior citizens around town at the ring of a cell phone.

Subjects: Senior Citizens

Paulsen, Gary.

Lawn Boy. 2007. 9780385746861. **M**

When a twelve-year-old unnamed narrator is given a riding lawnmower, he turns it into a lucrative financial empire with the help of a prizefighter and a stockbroker. His adventures continue in *Lawn Boy Returns* (2010).

Subjects: Entrepreneurs; Inheritances; Small Businesses

Selzer, Adam.

How to Get Suspended and Influence People. 2007. 9780440421603. **M**

Leon, an eighth grader, creates an uproar when he makes an avant-garde sex education movie.

Pirates of the Retail Wasteland. 2008. 9780385734820. **M**

Fourteen-year-old Leon stages a filmed protest against a chain coffee shop in an attempt to save a quirky downtown area.

Shaw, Tucker.

Flavor of the Week. 2003. 9780786818907. **J** **S**

Overweight Cyril loves to cook, and loves Rose, who loves his cooking. When his old best friend moves back, he takes on a Cyrano de Bergerac-like role by cooking for Rose and passing it off as being done by Nick. (PP)

Read-alikes: Readers who like the Cyrano type story may also enjoy *Undercover* by Beth Kephart, which also has a contemporary setting. *Fairest* by Gail Carson Levine and *Cyrano* by Geraldine McCaughrean may also be of interest.

Subjects: Cooking; Recipes

Soto, Gary.

Mercy on These Teenage Chimps. 2007. 9780152062156. **M**

Ronnie Gonzalez and Joey Rios find themselves feeling chimp-like when they turn thirteen, face lots of physical changes, and start noticing cute girls.

Tracy, Kristen.

Lost It. 2007. 9781416934752. **S**

Sixteen-tear-old Tess Whistler's junior year in Idaho is far different than she expected.Her parents go off to a wilderness survival camp, her grandmother moves in, and Tess finds a boyfriend and loses her virginity.

van de Ruit, John.

Spud. 2007. 9781595141705.

Though technically a historical novel, as it is set in 1990 in South Africa as apartheid is dying, this comedy with lots of descriptions of bodily functions deals with crazy life in a boy's boarding school.

Subjects: Boarding School; South Africa

Wizner, Jake.

Spanking Shakespeare. 2007. 9780375840852.

Shakespeare Shapiro, age seventeen, writes an unflinching and hilarious memoir detailing his senior year of high school, complete with religion, masturbation, and defecation. (BBYA)

Di's Picks

Alegria, Malin. *Sofi Mendoza's Guide to Getting Lost in Mexico.*

Alexie, Sherman. *Absolutely True Diary of a Part-Time Indian.*

Cross, Shauna. *Derby Girl.*

Lubar, David. *Sleeping Freshmen Never Lie.*

Lupica, Mike. *Heat.*

Ziegler, Jennifer. *How Not to Be Popular.*

Chapter 2

Issues

I like to read about other people's lives and what they've been through or are going through.—Lindsay, age 15

Books about issues, those often called "problem novels," are frequently what people think of as young adult literature. Issue-driven novels are a large genre in publishing for teens and have a big following, although they rarely hit the popularity levels that science fiction, fantasy, and paranormal books achieve. Perhaps because they are most like mainstream fiction, issue-driven novels are often on recommended lists and win awards.

Just as there are myriad issues, there are many different reasons these books appeal to teen readers. Some teens like to read about someone else who has the same problems in their lives, or perhaps has even worse problems than the ones they are facing. Some readers enjoy the tragic stories, often the ones about death and dying, because they enjoy the catharsis of crying over a book, rather than finding something in their own lives to cry about. Others love the style of particular authors who write in the genre.

Over time the issues change in teen literature, just as the issues teens face in real life change.

Multiple Issues

Teens facing tough issues often have multiple problems. Also, it seems to hold true that "birds of a feather flock together." Troubled kids find each other in fiction as well as in life. And with many book characters, just as in real life, problems seem to cascade and snowball, with one issue creating situations that cause additional issues to arise.

Bildner, Phil.

Busted. 2007. 9781416924241. ⊙

At Coldwater Creek High School, the principal claims to have a zero tolerance policy, but in reality there is a lot he is willing to overlook. Drinking, sneaking out of rooms, and sex can get the school's elite banned from prom and graduation, but a bully who sexually harasses other students, beats them up, and torments a teacher is tolerated. Just what is up at the Creek?

Subjects: Bullying; Promiscuity; Substance Abuse

Brooks, Kevin.

Candy. 2005. 9780439683272. **S**

Fifteen-year-old Joe goes into London for an appointment and meets Candy, who is a junkie and a prostitute. Obsessed with Candy, Joe takes her to his family's country cabin to get her off drugs, but then her pimp kidnaps Joe's sister. (IRA YAC)

Subjects: Addiction; Kidnapping; Prostitution

Charlton-Trujillo, E. E.

Feels Like Home. 2007. 9780385733328. **J** **S**

After their mom abandoned them and their drunken father, Mickey and Danny had only each other and S. E. Hinton's classic novel *The Outsiders*. But six years ago a tragedy changed Danny from town golden boy/football hero to pariah, and he abandoned Mickey, too. Now looking at graduating from high school and with her father, who had been sober for a year, being buried, Mickey is devastated when Danny comes home. She can't remember exactly what happened during his senior year that killed his best friend and ruined his life, but she is going to have to if she wants to get on with her life. Her confusion causes a rift with her best friend Christina and may be standing in the way of her first real relationship with a boy.

Subjects: Alcoholics; Death; Missing Persons; Siblings

Cohn, Rachel.

You Know Where to Find Me. 2008. 9780689878596. **J** **S**

Before her cousin killed herself, she and Miles would take prescription drugs in the tree house. Now Miles takes them by herself as she tries to deal with her senior year without Laura.

Subjects: Cousins; Drug Abuse; Suicide

Corrigan, Eireann.

Ordinary Ghosts. 2007. 9780439832441. **S**

What Emil has in life is a dead mom, missing brother, distant dad, and a key that gives him access to every room in his prep school.

de la Peña, Matt.

We Were Here. 2009. 9780385906227. **S**

Miguel did something awful, something so awful that he ended up in juvie before being sent to live in a group home. Although he's not friends with Mong or Rondell, one a psycho and the other mentally deficient, he goes on the run with them. But, as he spends time with them and they trek toward Mexico along the California coast, all three boys discover that nothing has to be exactly as it looks. (BBYA, Quick Picks)

Subjects: African Americans; Anger; Asian Americans; California; Developmental Disabilities; Group Homes; Hispanics; Mental Illness; Runaways

Draper, Sharon M.

The Battle of Jericho. 2003. 9780689842337. **J** **S**

Sixteen-year-old Jericho and his cousin Josh pledge in the Warriors of Distinction, an exclusive private club, only to find cruelty, humiliation, and the horrors of hazing. (IRA YAC, Coretta Scott King Honor)

Subjects: African Americans; Secret Societies

Flinn, Alex.

Fade to Black. 2005. 9780060568429. **S**

Alex Crusan has transferred to Pinedale High because of a family move and isn't any happier about it than the kids who go there, who don't want some AIDS-infected kid from Miami contaminating their school. Clinton Cole, football player, former fat kid, and downright mean and angry, may be the most outspoken opponent to Alex's presence. When Alex is sitting in his car at an intersection while making a doughnut run one morning, he is attacked with a baseball bat and ends up hospitalized. Daria Bickell, the only witness, knows what she saw, but the poem-like thoughts of this girl with Down syndrome are difficult for her to convey to others. (IRA YAC)

Subjects: AIDS; Assault; Down Syndrome; Violence

Nothing to Lose. 2004. 9780060517526. **J** **S**

Michael Daye, aka Robert Frost, tells his stories, the one of now and the one of a year ago, in alternating chapters. Now he is a carny, running a Whack-a-Mole game at a traveling carnival. Then he was a football player, and the stepson of a wealthy lawyer, living in a huge beachside home. Now his mother is on trial for murder. Then she was an abused wife who he was powerless to protect. Now he has a sharp and sympathetic lawyer. Then he had a beautiful girlfriend named Kirstie. (PP)

Subjects: Carnivals; Mothers and Sons

Giles, Gail.

Right Behind You. 2007. 9780316166362. **J** **S**

When Kip was nine he did something horrific that changed his life and those of several others forever. At fourteen, released from a secured mental facility in Alaska and using a new name, he moves with his father and stepmother to Indiana, where he finds friendship and success as a high school swimmer, but he still can't get over what he did. (IRA YAC)

Subjects: Criminals; Hidden Identities; Secrets

Going, K. L.

Fat Kid Rules the World. 2003. 9780142402085. **J** **S**

When a skinny homeless kid saves him from throwing himself in front of a train, seventeen-year-old Troy, obese and lonely, finds a new identity as drummer for Curt's band, Rage/Tectonic. (BBYA, Printz Honor)

Subjects: Music; Obesity; Suicide

Saint Iggy. 2006. 9780152062484. **J** **S**

Iggy Corso tries, he really does, to get along in school, but things just seem to always go wrong for him. His mother has disappeared, and his father is always stoned; so when he gets kicked out of school for what may be the last time, he realizes that he really has no one to go to. He looks up Mo, a former mentor who dropped out of law school and the mentoring program, and finds himself at the digs of the dealer who has made his life hell. When he is taken to Mo's parents' home, he sees what life is like outside the projects. Mo's mom sees the goodness in Iggy and tries to help him, but Iggy's life is on its own path. (BBYA)

Subjects: Drug Abuse; Homelessness

Hartnett, Sonya.

What the Birds See. 2003. 9780763636807. **J** **S**

In this darkly atmospheric literary tale, a lonely nine-year-old Australian schoolboy imagines that the three new neighbor children may really be the same three who recently went missing.

Subjects: Australia; Literary; Missing Children

Hautman, Pete.

Godless. 2004. 9781416908166. **J** **S**

Hulking Jason (J) Bock, agnostic and leaning toward atheism, comes up with the idea of starting his own religion that worships the ten-legged god, the town's water tower. The followers include Magda, a sexy girl from his TPO classes at the Catholic church; Henry, a remarkably intelligent and well-read bully who knows how to get to the top of the tower; Dan, the Lutheran minister's son, who is more or less a vanilla nonentity; and Shim, his spidery best friend, who seems to be descending into schizophrenia as he writes the holy book of the Chutengodians. (BBYA, NBA, PP)

Subjects: Mental Illness; Religion

Hegamin, Tonya.

M+O 4EVR. 2008. 9780618495702. **S**

Opal has always loved Marianne, but in high school M decided to be popular, and O had to wait for any scraps of time she could spare. When M dies, O, the only African American girl in their small town, must figure out how to cope.

Subjects: African American; Death; Mixed Race

Hopkins, Ellen.

Identical. 2008. 9781416950059. **O**

Kaeleigh and Raeanne are the sixteen-year-old identical twin daughters of prominent parents. Between them they deal with a plethora of issues: sexual abuse, promiscuity, bulimia, cutting, and substance abuse. (TTT, Quick Picks)

Subjects: Verse Novels

Hyde, Catherine Ryan.

The Day I Killed James. 2008. 9780375841583. **S**

After her boyfriend breaks up with her, seventeen-year-old Theresa invites James, a young veteran who has long had a crush on her, to take her to a party, where she ends up back with her boyfriend. When James is killed after leaving the party, Theresa, overcome with guilt, tries to run away from her problems.

Subjects: Abused Children; Death; Homelessness

Johnson, Angela.

Bird. 2004. 9780142405444. **M** **J** **S**

Told in three voices, this short tale of thirteen-year-old Bird, who runs away to Alabama to try to bring her stepfather back; Jay, who lost his brother; and Ethan, who gained a second chance at life through a heart transplant, are just the type of characters, genuine and real, that have brought Johnson such well-deserved acclaim. (BBYA)

Subjects: Bereavement; Runaways; Stepfamilies; Transplant Patients

Jones, Patrick.

Chasing Tail Lights. 2007. 9780802796288. **O**

Trying to be invisible, believing she is ugly white trash, Christy carries a world of problems on her shoulders. Living in a decaying part of Flint, Michigan, a dying city, she keeps house for her mom, who works two jobs and drinks too much. Other characters include her evil older drug-dealing brother Ryan; her brother Mitchell, who is only a year younger and shared the same father; and the light of her life, her niece Bree, the daughter of her stone-cold killer brother Robert, who is doing life in prison. As Christy flashes back to her past—the way she acquired her best friend Anne, a rich doctor's daughter, and the friendship of a teacher who turned her on to some very good reads—the reader can feel and understand exactly what Christy feels.

Subjects: Abuse; Flint, Michigan

Cheated. 2008. 9780802798473. **O**

After a night of drinking and poker, fifteen-year-old Mick and a couple of acquaintances encounter a homeless man, who ends up dead.

Subjects: Cheating; Drinking; Gambling; Violence

Levithan, David, ed.

This Is Push: New Stories from the Edge. 9780439890281. 2007. **S**

This anthology features stories by edgy writers including Eireann Corrigan, Markus Zusak, Brian James, Chris Wooding, Billy Merrell, Kristen Kemp, Christopher Krovatin, Coe Booth, Tanuja Desai Hidier, Kevin Brooks, Samantha Schutz, Patricia McCormick, Eddie de Oliveira, Matthue Roth, and Kevin Waltman.

Subjects: Issues; Short Stories

Lopez, Jack.

In the Break. 2006. 9780316008747. **O**

A fight with his stepfather drives fifteen-year-old Jamie to run away. Heading for Mexico with his sister Amber and best friend Juan, the three camp and surf along the way, with danger always on their heels.

Subjects: Abuse; Latinos; Runaways; Surfing

Lynch, Carol Williams.

Messed Up. 2009. 9780823421855. **J** **S**

Fifteen-year-old R. D. is struggling through his second year of eighth grade when his grandmother runs off with a trucker, leaving him with her Vietnam veteran ex, who is not long for this world. With his mom in prison, his dad unknown to him, and a suspension from school when he tries to do the right thing, it looks like life is all downhill for R. D., but he takes his life in hand amid all the complications. (BBYA, Quick Picks, VOYA)

Subjects: Death; Latino

McDaniel, Lurlene.

Briana's Gift. 2006. 9780440238690. **J**

Decembers are bad for thirteen-year-old Sissy. Her dad died in December, her mother got sick in December, and her sister ran away in December. Now Briana has returned home, pregnant. What will December bring this time?

Subjects: Comas; Death; Pregnancy

Neri, G.

Surf Mules. 2009. 9780399250866. **S**

The summer after senior year, Logan and his best friend Z-Boy have to deal with the loss of their friend, who died in a surfing accident. They embark on a cross-country road trip as marijuana mules.

Subjects: Death; Friendship; Marijuana; Surfing

Oates, Joyce Carol.

Small Avalanches and Other Stories. 2003. 9780060012175. **S**

A dozen stories about the choices girls make and the consequences that result.

Subjects: Short Stories

Pagliarulo, Antonio.

A Different Kind of Heat. 2006. 9780385732987 . **J** **S**

Seventeen-year-old Luz Cordero lives in a group home because her rage over a cop shooting and killing her brother got her involved in a police brutality protest that turned into a riot. A former gang member, she struggles with anger issues and also has problems with a mother who is in prison.

Subjects: Bereavement; Bronx, New York; Foster Care; Gangs; Group Homes; Shootings

Pearson, Mary E.

A Room on Lorelei Street. 2005. 9780312380199. **O**

Tired of taking care of her alcoholic mother, Zoe, age seventeen, moves out on her own, willing to do anything necessary to keep her new life. (BBYA)

Subjects: Alcoholism

Spinelli, Jerry.

Eggs. 2007. 9780316166478. **M**

Depressed by the death of his mother and his father's absence, nine-year-old David resists everything his grandmother wants him to do, but when he unhappily participates in an Easter egg hunt, he finds what he thinks is a dead girl in the woods. Actually she is thirteen-year-old Primrose, who lives in a van outside the tiny house where her mother tells fortunes. Their friendship grows, and the two help each other with their complicated lives.

Volponi, Paul.

Black and White. 2005. 9780142406922. **S**

Two talented basketball players from a bad neighborhood become robbers to get the money they want for new sneakers. When they accidentally kill one of their victims, one of them goes to jail. (BBYA, Quick Picks, IRA, IRA YAC, PP)

Subjects: African Americans; Basketball; Criminals; Race

Rucker Park Setup. 2007. 9780670061303. **S**

Two talented best friends have always wanted to play in the legendary street basketball tournament, but now one is of them is dead. (Quick Picks)

Subjects: Basketball; Death; Guilt

Woodrell, Daniel.

Winter's Bone. 2006. 9780316066419. **S**

If she is going to save the family home for her two little brothers, seventeen-year-old Ree Dolly must find her bail-jumping dad in time for his court date. (BBYA)

Subjects: Adult Books for Teens; Criminals; Mental Illness; Methamphetamines; Ozarks

Outsiders

The feeling of alienation, or being an outsider, seems to hit most teens at one time or another. In fact, one of the benchmark titles in the world of young adult literature is *The Outsiders* by S. E. Hinton. In some of the following books, the state of being an outsider is fatal; in others, the outsider is able to change and improve those who are members of cliques.

Brugman, Alyssa.

Walking Naked. 2004. 9780440238324. **J** **S**

When Megan, a popular member of the dominant clique at her Australian high school, has to spend time in detention, she meets Perdita, an outsider called "The Freak," who loves poetry.

Subjects: Australia; Poetry; Suicide

Choyce, Lesley.

Skate Freak. 2008. 9781554690428. **M** **J**

Dorf's mom has moved west to learn to operate big equipment, and he and his unemployed dad have moved from their small seaside community to the city. Dorf finds the kids who hang at the skate park hostile, and the local cops hate skateboarders. The bright spot in his life is a girl skater, who falls in love with his old town when he takes her there to skate the rocks.

Subjects: High-Low; Romance; Skateboarding

Howell, Simmone.

Notes from the Teenage Underground. 2007. 9780747585121. **O**

Gem, Lo, and Mira, a trio of outcasts, make an underground film that threatens to destroy their friendship.

Subjects: Australia; Film Making

Koja, Kathe.

The Blue Mirror. 2004. 9780374308490. **S**

Maggy, a talented sixteen-year-old artist, a nonentity at school, and at home the caretaker of her drunken mother, is drawn into the dangerous web of a homeless boy and his entourage. (BBYA)

Subjects: Artists; Homelessness

Buddha Boy. 2003. 9780142402092. **M** **J** **S**

Justin is unhappy to be assigned to work on a team project with Jinson, the new boy at school, who faces torment from the school's predators with unusual peacefulness. (BBYA, IRA, PP)

Subjects: Art; Buddhism; Bullying

Korman, Gordon.

Schooled. 2007. 9781423105169. **M** **J**

When thirteen-year-old Capricorn Anderson's grandmother falls from a tree and is hospitalized, Capricorn must leave the commune where he has never watched TV or held money to live in a foster home and attend a middle school full of bullies. (VOYA, IRA YAC, PP)

Subjects: Bullying; Communes; Foster Care

Portman, Frank.

King Dork. 2006. 9780385734509. **O**

1

Tom Henderson, aka King Dork, finds himself unchallenged by school, unappreciated by his peers, and unimpressed by *Catcher in the Rye.* However, he is very good at coming up with band names and inventing song titles and cover art with his friend Sam. (BBYA)

Robson, Claire, ed.

2

Outside Rules: Short Stories About Non-Conformist Youth. 2007. 978-0892553167. **S**

Fourteen stories about teens who are outsiders, who assert their own identities no matter the costs to themselves. The authors include Sandell Morse, Wally Lamb, Sandra Cisneros, Akhil Sharma, Jacqueline Sheehan, Rand Richards Cooper, Annette Sanford, K. Kvashay-Boyle, Claire Robson, Caitlin Lonning, Katharine Noel, Reginald McKnight, Chris Fisher, and Rebecca Rule.

3

Subjects: Outsiders; Short Stories

Death, Disability, and Disease

4

Death, disability, and disease are three of the most dramatic situations that can impact a teen's life. Lurlene McDaniel is the author most known for illuminating the lives of teen characters through stories dealing with these issues. Many books of this type deal with multiple issues, often precipitated by a death. Sometimes a death is the result of other issues. Currently, accidents that cause injuries and death are common in teen fiction; in the first edition of *Teen Genreflecting*, suicide and disease, particularly AIDS, were more frequent catalysts for the stories.

5

Acampora, Paul.

6

Defining Dulcie. 2006. 9780142411834. **J** **S**

When sixteen-year-old Dulcie's beloved father dies, her mother moves them from Connecticut to California. Dulcie is miserable, and when her mother plans to sell her father's old truck, she takes off in it. Her plan is to head back to her grandfather, but along the way she befriends an abused girl.

Subjects: Abuse; Bereavement; Grandfathers; Janitors; Pickup Trucks

7

Asher, Jay.

Thirteen Reasons Why. 2007. 9781595141712. **J** **S**

Two weeks after Hannah Baker commits suicide, high school senior Clay Jenson receives a package holding thirteen cassette tapes directing him to places she wants him to visit, and explaining why she did what she did. (BBYA, Quick Picks, IRA YAC)

8

Subjects: Edgy Fiction; Posthumous Messages; Rape; Suicide

Clinton, Cathryn.

The Eyes of van Gogh. 2007. 9780763622459. **J**

High school senior Jude, a talented teen artist who has moved from place to place, finds friendship, an unsatisfactory relationship, and a connection with her comatose grandmother, but attempts suicide, fearing she is becoming too much like her dysfunctional mother.

Subjects: Artists; Suicide

Crutcher, Chris.

Deadline. 2007. 9780060850890. **S**

After being diagnosed with a terminal illness, a high school senior, Ben Wolf, decides to do everything he wants to do in the one year of life he has left. (Quick Picks)

Subjects: Abuse; Brothers; Football; Humor; Romance

Downham, Jenny.

Before I Die. 2007. 9780385751834. **O**

Sixteen-year-old Tessa has been fighting leukemia for four years but now, knowing she only has a few months or weeks left, she decides to do tall the things she wants to before she dies. (TTT, BBYA)

Forman, Gayle.

If I Stay. 2009. 9780525421030. **J** **S**

Mia, an exceptionally talented seventeen-year-old cellist, is waiting to hear if she has been accepted to Julliard. She's madly in love with her punk rocker boyfriend, who shares her passion for music, and close to her wonderful parents and little brother. A family outing takes a strange turn when Mia finds herself outside the car, seeing her dead parents, and then realizes she is outside her own body. The novel follows her through the next twenty-four hours as she is taken to a Portland hospital, where she tries to decide whether to go on with her parents or stay in this world. (BBYA, Quick Picks)

Subjects: Accidents; Musicians; Oregon; Out of Body Experiences

Fullerton, Alma.

In the Garage. 2006. 9780889953710. **S**

B. J. has never been popular, but she has always been able to depend on her friend Alex, who is gorgeous, smart, kind, and talented. Everything changes when a couple of the popular girls start paying attention to B. J. Told in alternating sections of Alex's poetic journal and BJ's narrative, as the story unfolds the reader waits for the awful event to happen.

Subjects: Betrayal; Gay Boys; Homophobes; Journals; Musicians

Gonzalez, Julie.

Ricochet. 2007. 9780385732284. **M** **J**

When a bully intimidates three other boys into playing "Idiot's Roulette" in a deserted room, one of them dies and all their lives are changed forever, including fifteen-year-old Connor, who is charged as an accessory in the death of his best friend. (Quick Picks)

Subjects: Bullies; Crime

Harazin, S. A.

Blood Brothers. 2007. 9780385733649. **S**

When his best friend, in a drug induced rage, tries to kill Clay and he defends himself, this hard-working teen's life is changed forever. (Quick Picks)

Subjects: Bicycling; Comas; Drugs; Hospitals

Hernandez, David.

No More Us for You. 2009. 9780061173332. **S**

Told from the alternating viewpoints of Carlos, who has just started a job as a museum guard, and Isabel, who is close to the one-year anniversary of her boyfriend's death, this story relates how the two are brought together by Vanessa, a new girl at their school who works with Carlos at the museum. A double date changes their lives when Vanessa and her date are killed in a car accident. (BBYA)

Subjects: Art; California; Latinos; Museums; Romance

Jocelyn, Marthe.

Would You. 2008. 9780375837036. **J** **S**

Natalie, on the verge of her junior year in high school, and her older sister Claire get along well, and Natalie knows life will be different when Claire heads off to college in a couple of weeks, but when Claire is seriously injured in a late-night car accident, everything changes

Johnson, Maureen.

The Key to the Golden Firebird. 2004. 9780060541408. **J** **S**

When their father dies of a heart attack in his beloved Pontiac Firebird, the three "Tall, Blond, and Wonderful" teen Gold sisters must figure out how to go on.

Subjects: Cars; Sisters

McDaniel, Lurlene.

Letting Go of Lisa. 2006. 9780385731591. **J**

When his mother gives birth to twins, Nathan Malone, who was previously homeschooled, starts his senior year at a regular high school. There he meets Lisa Lindstrom, who suddenly disappears.

Subjects: Brain Tumors; Death; Home School

Mitchard, Jacquelyn.

All We Know of Heaven: A Novel. 2008. 9780061345784. **J** **S**

Two best friends who look quite a bit alike are in a horrific accident. One lives and the other dies, but there is confusion about their identities. Is the girl in the coma Bridget Flannery or Maureen O'Malley?

Subjects: Comas; Death; Mistaken Identity

Morgenroth, Kate.

Echo. 2007. 9781416914389. **S** **J**

Justin keeps reliving the worst day in his life, the day he killed his younger brother and destroyed his own life.

Subjects: Brothers; Do-Overs

Noël, Alyson.

Saving Zoë. 2007. 9780312355104. **S**

When fifteen-year-old Echo is given her late sister's diary, she discovers much that she did not know.

Subjects: Death; Diaries; Grieving; Secrets; Sisters

Oates, Joyce Carol.

After the Wreck, I Picked Myself Up, Spread My Wings, and Flew Away. 2006. 9780060735272. **J** **S**

After her mother is killed in a horrible accident on a bridge, fifteen-year-old Jenna tries to recover from her own injuries and goes to live with her aunt's family in New Hampshire. There she finds drugs that help block out some of the pain of her multiple losses, but then she meets Crow, a gorgeous biker, and her life takes a different turn.

Subjects: Bikers; Car Accidents; New Hampshire

Rabb, Margo.

Cures for Heartbreak. 2007. 9780385734035. **S**

With her mother dead from cancer, her father in the hospital with heart disease, and her boyfriend hopefully recovering from leukemia, high school freshman Mia questions why her family has had such a tragic history.

Subjects: Holocaust; Jews; Leukemia; New York

Schmidt, Gary.

Trouble. 2008. 9780618927661. **J** **S**

After his brother is killed in a car accident, fourteen-year-old Henry Smith sets out to climb a mountain in Maine—one that the two brothers had planned to climb together—along with a rescued dog and his best friend. Along the way they are picked up by a fellow student, a Cambodian immigrant who was driving the car in the accident. (VOYA, BBYA)

Subjects: Brothers; Cambodians; Dogs; Immigrants; New England; Racism

Stein, Tammar.

Light Years. 2005. 9780440239024. S

Astronomy major Maya gets through her first year in America at the University of Virginia while she tries to recover from the death of her boyfriend, killed in a Tel Aviv suicide bombing. (BBYA)

Taylor, Brooke.

Undone. 2008. 9780802797636. J S

Serena, who has been unable to worm the identity of her unknown father out of her mother, became best friends with Kori, a former cheerleader turned bad girl, when they were in eighth grade. Kori pushes Serena into doing all kinds of dangerous things, including smoking, drinking, and getting high, but when she dies, Serena takes on Kori's list of five ways to tempt fate and sets out to fulfill them all.

Subjects: Family Secrets; Gaming

Vande Velde, Vivian.

Remembering Raquel. 2007. 9780152059767. J S

When fourteen-year-old Raquel dies on her way home from the movies. she becomes the center of attention. This episodic story is told by Raquel's acquaintances. (Quick Picks)

Volponi, Paul.

Rooftop. 2006. 9780142408445. S

Clay and Addison, first cousins, hadn't seen each other in years. They come together again in a rehab/school day program. Clay has been sent by his parents because they discovered he was smoking weed. Addison was caught selling crack on a street corner. One evening on their way to a school function, Addison and Clay end up on a roof in the projects, where Addison is shot and killed by a police officer. A local politician comes into the mix, using what he considers a case of a white cop killing a black teen to further his own goals and putting words in Clay's mouth. (BBYA, Quick Picks)

Subjects: Drug Abuse; Shootings; Violence

Woodson, Jacqueline.

Behind You. 2004. 9780142403907. S J

When fifteen-year-old Miah is killed by cops in a case of mistaken identity, Ellie, his white girlfriend, must go on with life. Miah watches from the afterlife. (BBYA, Quick Picks)

Subjects: Bereavement; Interracial Relationships

Injury

Characters surviving catastrophic injury offer a broad canvas to develop relationships and see growth.

Aronson, Sarah.

Head Case. 2007. 9781596432147. **S**

High school senior Frank Marder is paralyzed from the neck down because of a wreck he caused driving drunk—an accident that killed two other people. Now he must cope with a helpless body and guilt for the deaths he caused. (Quick Picks)

Subjects: Accidents; Guilt; Paralysis; Physical Therapy; Quadriplegics

Bingham, Kelly.

Shark Girl. 2007. 9780763632076. **J**

Fifteen-year-old Jane Arrowood survives a shark attack but loses her arm. This novel is told in verse, clippings, and journal entries.

Subjects: Amputations; Verse Novels

Fahler, Gene.

Beanball. 2008. 9780618843480. **M J S**

When talented baseball player Luke "Wizard" Wallace is hit in the head by a wild fast pitch, it takes away his perfect vision and puts him in a coma. But it also affects twenty-seven other people, who tell their stories about the event in free verse.

Subjects: Baseball; Comas; Verse Novels

Williams, Suzanne Morgan.

Bull Rider. 2009. 9781416961307. **J S**

Living in small town Nevada, Cam O'Meara prefers his skateboard to the family tradition of riding bulls. His grandfather, father, and older brother Ben have all been true to the family avocation. Now that Ben has returned from Iraq, paralyzed by a brain injury, the family is short on money, and Ben is so depressed he won't do his therapy. When Ben promises to work on getting well if Cam can ride Ugly, a bull that has never been ridden, Cam scores a fake ID and heads for the competition.

Subjects: Brothers; Bull Riding; Nevada; Paralysis; Rural Life; Skateboarding; Veterans

Disease

The two dominant types of disease showing up with regularity in teen fiction are cancer and mental illness, including eating disorders.

Anderson, Laurie Halse.

Wintergirls. 2009. 9780670011100. **J S**

Lia, an anorexic cutter, was friends forever with Cassie, a bulimic, and in eighth grade they each vowed to be the skinniest one. However, a falling out before senior year left Lia mystified. One weekend Cassie tried to call her on her cell thirty-three times, but Lia did not pick up the phone. After learning that Cassie died in a motel room, Lia listens to the messages, which were actually calls for help. As Lia moves forward in the days following Cassie's death and becomes sicker herself, readers learn about her life and pain. (BBYA, Quick Picks)

Subjects: Anorexia; Bulimia; Cutting; Death; Eating Disorders

Bray, Libba.

Going Bovine. 2009. 9780385733977. **S**

Weird things are happening to sixteen-year-old Cameron, including inadvertently throwing a tray of shakes and burgers on his big crush, which costs him his job. It turns out he doesn't have behavioral issues; he has mad cow disease, which lands him in the hospital sharing a room with Gonzo, a dwarf. Mentored by a punk angel, Cameron and Gonzo head out to seek a cure, along the way picking up a lawn gnome who is also a Norse god. Is Cam really on a crazy road trip, or is he hallucinating from a hospital bed? (Printz Award, BBYA)

Subjects: Creutzfeldt-Jakob Disease; Don Quixote; Dwarfs; Humor; Mad Cow Disease; Norse Mythology; Physics; Road Trips; Satire

Dessen, Sarah.

Just Listen. 2006. 9780142410974. **S**

A traumatic event misconstrued by her friends turns high school junior Annabel into a pariah at the same time that terrible things happen in her family. (BBYA, TTT)

Subjects: Eating Disorders; Models; Rape

Hautman, Pete.

Invisible. 2005. 9780689869037. **S**

Seventeen-year-old Dougie descends into madness as he builds a model railroad bridge from 22,400 matches. His only friend, Andy, a talented athlete, is his polar opposite. (BBYA)

Subjects: Bereavement; Fires; Mental Illness; Model Railroads

Heuston, Kimberley.

The Book of Jude. 2008. 9781932425260. **M J S**

When fifteen-year-old Jude goes to Soviet-run Czechoslovakia in 1989, her life begins to unravel. As she suffers a psychotic break, her devoutly Mormon parents try to help her.

Subjects: 1980s; Borderline Personality Disorder; Cold War; Faith Healing; Mental Illness; Mormons; Religion; Soviet Union

Johnson, Harriet McBryde.

Accidents of Nature. 2006. 9780805076349. **S**

Seventeen-year-old Jean becomes politicized when she attends the camp for disabled teens that her cabinmate calls Crip Camp. (BBYA)

Subjects: Activism; Camp; Cerebral Palsy

Koja, Kathe.

Going Under. 2006. 9780374303938. **S**

Hilly and Ivan have been homeschooled and are closer than many brothers and sisters, so when Hilly starts working on the local school newspaper and falls into depression, it is up to Ivan to try to save her.

Subjects: Depression; Home School; Journalism; Mental Illness; Newspapers; Siblings; Suicide

Lowenstein, Sallie.

Waiting for Eugene. 2005. 9780965848657. **M** **J**

In the 1960s Sara Goldman, a talented twelve-year-old artist, deals with her holocaust survivor father's mental illness.

Subjects: 1960s; Art; Holocaust Survivors; Mental Illness

Mankell, Henning.

Secrets in the Fire. 2003. 9781550378009. **M**

After her family flees a massacre in their Mozambique village, disaster strikes again when Sofia loses both her legs and her sister when they accidentally explode a landmine. Based on a true story, this novel tells of Sofia's survival and journey to being able to support herself and live on her own.

Subjects: Africans; Amputees; Mozambique; Survival; War

Price, Charlie.

Lizard People. 2007. 9781596431904. **S**

When Ben's mother goes off on a psychotic rampage at his school and is placed in a mental institution, he meets another teen, who tells him a curiously surrealistic story that makes him wonder about his own mental stability.

Subjects: Mental Illness; Mental Institutions; Time Travel

Roe, Monica.

Thaw. 2008. 9781590784969. **S**

Eighteen-year-old competitive cross-country skier Dane finds rehabilitation more challenging than he wants as he tries to recover from the paralysis of Guillain-Barre Syndrome.

Subjects: Florida; Guillain-Barre Syndrome; New York; Paralysis; Rehabilitation; Skiers

Schumacher, Julie.

Black Box. 2008. 9780385735421. **S**

Fourteen-year-old Lena tries to save her older sister, who has attempted suicide and is secretly being treated for depression. (BBYA, Quick Picks)

Subjects: Depression; Mental Illness; Siblings; Sisters

Smith, Jennifer E.

The Comeback Season. 2008. 9781416938477. **M** **J**

On the fifth anniversary of her father's death, fifteen-year-old Ryan ditches school and heads to Wrigley Field, the site of some of her best memories of her dad. There she meets Nick, a new boy at her school, who also loves the Cubs. They begin a romance, but it turns out Nick is fighting bone cancer.

Subjects: Baseball; Cancer; Chicago; Romance

Sonnenblick, Jordan.

Drums, Girls, And Dangerous Pie. 2005. 9780439755191. **J** **M**

Steven, an eighth-grade drummer, finds his life drastically changed when his bratty five-year-old brother is diagnosed with cancer. (TTT, PP)

Subjects: Brothers; Cancer; Musicians

Stratton, Allan.

Chanda's Secrets. 2004. 9781550378351. **S**

Sixteen-year-old Chanda, living in a fictional African country, must arrange for her little sister's burial. The mortuary business is booming due to the AIDS epidemic, but nobody admits to having it. The sequel, *Chanda's Wars*, is annotated in chapter 4. (BBYA, Printz Honor, Film: *Life Above All*)

Subjects: Africans; AIDS; Orphans

Trueman, Terry.

Cruise Control. 2004. 9780064473774. **J** **S**

This companion novel to *Stuck in Neutral* is about high school senior Paul, the talented, athletic, gifted older brother of Shawn, who was the protagonist of *Stuck in Neutral*. Shawn has severe cerebral palsy and is totally uncommunicative. (IRA YAC)

Subjects: Brothers; Cerebral Palsy

Tullson, Diane.

Zero. 2007. 9781550419504. **J** **S**

Kas, a talented artist, is accepted to a prestigious art school, where she will have to live with a family who are also hosting Jacob, a talented musician. Unfortunately, self-loathing Kas has some dangerous proclivities that even those closest to her don't recognize.

Subjects: Anorexia; Artists; Bulimia; Canadian; Eating Disorders; Models; Musicians

Vaught, Susan.

My Big Fat Manifesto. 2008. 9781599902067. **S**

Three-hundred-pound high school senior Jamie Carcaterra, author of "The Fat Girl Manifesto" in the school newspaper, writes about being fat as her boyfriend decides he has to lose weight, even if it entails gastric bypass surgery. (PP)

Subjects: Journalists; Obesity

Trigger. 2006. 9781582349206. **J** **S**

Seventeen-year-old Jersey Hatch can't even remember trying to kill himself, so how can he be expected to know why he wanted to? (BBYA)

Subjects: Brain Injuries; Rehabilitation; Suicide

Vizzini, Ned.

It's Kind of a Funny Story. 2006. 9780786851973. **S**

Paralyzed by achieving his dream of getting into an elite school for the gifted, fifteen-year-old Craig Gilner descends into depression, self-medicating, and eventually thinking of suicide, which lands him in a psych ward. (BBYA)

Subjects: Institutions; Mental Illness; Suicide

Vrettos, Adrienne Maria.

Skin. 2006. 9781416906568. **J** **S**

Starting with fourteen-year-old Donnie trying to revive his anorexic sister, this story tells of the family's descent as the dysfunctional parents, friendless Donnie, who is plagued by ear infections, and Karen, who is starving herself to death, experience a terrible year. (BBYA, VOYA)

Subjects: Anorexia; Siblings

Weaver, Will.

Defect. 2007. 9780374317256. **S** **J**

Fifteen-year-old David is different. He looks strange and lives in foster care. He also has unusual webbing of skin that goes from his rib cage to his arms and enables him to glide down through the air from great heights. David starts attending an alternative school, where he meets Cheetah, a girl who has seizures and is enrolled in an experimental program at the Mayo Clinic in Minnesota. One night when David is flying, he ends up tumbling from the sky, resulting in a hospitalization. Now his secret is out. The cover of this book asks, Monster or miracle? And that is what David must figure out for himself.

Subjects: Birth Defects; Clinics; Flying; Minnesota; Seizures

Wolf, Allan.

Zane's Trace. 2007. 9780763628581. **J** **S**

Suicidal and mentally ill sixteen-year-old Zane Guesswind goes on a journey to his death; along the way, he finds himself through conversations with relatives and ancestors.

Subjects: Hallucinations; Hypergraphia; Mixed Race; Road Trips; Suicide

Zimmer, Tracie Vaughn.

Reaching for Sun. 2007. 9781599900377. **J** **S**

In this verse novel, sixteen-year-old Josie, an avid gardener and nature watcher, lives on a shrinking farm with her mother and grandmother where her cerebral palsy does not define her. (Schneider Family Award)

Subjects: Bereavement; Cerebral Palsy; Farms; Verse Novels

Abuse

Abuse is a difficult issue to read about. Some of the following books involve abuse of teens or children by parents, whereas others deal with relationship abuse. The abuse may be physical, psychological, or sexual. Readers who enjoy titles in this section may also be interested in the section "Violence and Bullying," below.

Felin, M. Sindy.

Touching Snow. 2007. 9781416917953. **J** **S**

In this National Book Award finalist, seventh grader Karina, the middle daughter in a family of Haitian immigrants, deals with a multitude of problems, including an abusive stepfather. (BBYA, NBA Finalist)

Subjects: Haitians; Immigrants; New York; Sisters; Step-Families

Giles, Gail.

What Happened to Cass McBride? 2006. 9780316166393. **S**

Practically perfect Cass McBride also has a nasty side, which shows when she puts down people who are not attractive or popular enough for her. When David, the dweeby younger brother of hunky college student Kyle, asks her out, she writes a note to a girlfriend calling him a loser, and it falls into his hands. David commits suicide, after pinning a note to his shirt blaming "her" for his death. Kyle kidnaps Cass, burying her in a coffin-sized box with a very small pipe for air. As Cass draws Brett's story out, the truth behind who drove David to his death is revealed. This very edgy book is a page-turner even though the characters are not people one would like to meet. (BBYA, Quick Picks, IRA YAC)

Subjects: Kidnappings; Mental Illness; Suicide

Glass, Linzi.

The Year the Gypsies Came. 2006. 9780805079999. **J** **S**

When a visiting Australian family parks their "Gypsy trailer" at her family home in 1960s South Africa, violence enters twelve-year-old Emily's life. (BBYA)

Subjects: 1960s; Australians; South Africa

Hernandez, David.

Suckerpunch. 2008 . 9780061173301. **S**

Seventeen-year-old artist Marcus and his brother Enrique, along with a couple of friends, start off on a road trip, armed with a gun to stop their abusive father from moving back into the family home. (BBYA, Quick Picks)

Subjects: Abuse; Artists; California; Road Trips

Jones, Patrick.

Things Change. 2004. 9780802789013. **J** **S**

Sixteen-year-old Johanna, a good student with strict parents, is thrilled when popular senior Paul shows interest in her, but as their relationship progresses, Paul becomes more controlling and violent. (Quick Picks)

Subjects: Dating Violence

Lipsyte, Robert.

Raiders Night. 2006. 9780060599485. **O**

Matt, co-captain of the football team, will do whatever it takes to win the state title, including taking steroids. But things change and everything falls apart when a teammate is raped by his co-captain. (PP)

Subjects: Football; Rape; Steroids

McDaniel, Lurlene.

Prey. 2008. 9780385734530 . **S**

When his hot teacher, Ms. Settles, starts paying attention to him, class clown Ryan, age fifteen, is thrilled. (IRA YAC)

Subjects: Sexual Abuse; Teachers

Nelson, R. A.

Breathe My Name. 2007. 9781595140944. **S**

Just when she turns eighteen, Frances discovers that her mother, the mother who had smothered her two younger sisters to death, has been released from prison and wants to see her.

Subjects: Adoption; Mental Illness

Scott, Elizabeth.

Living Dead Girl. 2008. 9781416960591. **O**

When Alice was ten years old, Ray kidnapped her during a school field trip. Now age fifteen, even though she is half-starved she is beginning to look like a woman rather than a little girl. So now it is her job to find a new little girl for Ray. (BBYA, Quick Picks, IRA YAC, PP)

Subjects: Kidnapping; Sexual Predators

Werlin, Nancy.

The Rules of Survival. 2006. 9780803730014. **J** **S**

Matt tries to protect his sisters from their dangerously deranged mother over the course of three years as he ages from thirteen to sixteen. (BBYA, NBA Finalist, Quick Picks, PP)

Subjects: Mental Illness; Siblings

Wiess, Laura.

Such a Pretty Girl. 2007. 9781416521839. **S**

Meredith's father, who sexually abused her and her friend Andy, was supposed to be in prison for a long time, but now he has won an early release, and her mother wants him home again. (BBYA, Quick Picks)

Subjects: Incest; Paraplegics; Predators; Sexual Abuse

Williams, Carol Lynch.

The Chosen One. 2009. 9780312555115. **J** **S**

Thirteen-year-old Kyra lives with her large family in a rural Utah compound. She loves to read, but years earlier the prophet of the polygamous cult her family belongs to decreed that all nonscriptural books be burned. Defying the Prophet, Kyra has secretly been meeting the bookmobile every week to feed her reading habit.

When the prophet shows up to announce she has been chosen, her dreams of a happy future collapse. He has promised her to her uncle, an Apostle, who is fifty years her senior, and she is to wed him in only four weeks. Kyra's dilemma is exacerbated by the fact that she loves her family and doesn't want to leave them. (BBYA, Quick Picks)

Subjects: Adventure; Bookmobiles; Child Brides; Murder; Polygamy; Utah

Homelessness and Runaways

Stories dealing with the issues of homelessness and runaways tend to be grim and depressing. In some cases the protagonists are orphans, but more often they have been abandoned or have left home to escape from abuse.

Blank, Jessica.

Almost Home. 2007. 9781423106432. **O**

Seven characters tell about their lives on the streets of Los Angeles. They include a twelve-year-old girl, who has fled her stepbrother's sexual abuse, an addicted porn actress, drug dealers, and prostitutes. (Quick Picks)

Subjects: Drug Abuse; Los Angeles; Prostitution; Sexual Abuse

Booth, Coe.

Tyrell. 2006. 9780439838795. **S**

After Tyrell's father goes back to prison, he, his mom, and his little brother become homeless. All the shelters are full, so they are sent to a disgusting roach-filled hotel. When Tyrell finds out his family won't be moved out of the crummy hotel because his mother has welfare fraud convictions, he decides he has to make enough money to move them into an apartment. Even though his mother wants him to take up drug dealing for the money, he resists. Tyrell has a conservative girlfriend, but he also gets involved with a girl living in the same hotel. (BBYA, Quick Picks, PP)

Subjects: African Americans; DJs; Hotels

Davis, Deborah.

Not Like You. 2007. 9780618720934. **J** **S**

Kayla, who has always taken care of her alcoholic mother, starts up a dog walking business. After they move to a new town in New Mexico, Kayla starts walking a dog that belongs to a musician. When her mother starts drinking again, Kayla runs away.

Subjects: Alcoholics; Dogs; New Mexico

Fusco, Kimberly Newton.

Tending to Grace. 2004. 9780375828621. **M** **J**

Fourteen-year-old Cornelia Thornhill has always taken care of her mother, so what is she to do when Lenore takes off for Las Vegas with a boyfriend, dumping her with Great-Aunt Agatha? (BBYA)

Subjects: Abandonment

Harmon, Michael.

Skate. 2006. 9780375875168. **J** **S**

Ian McDermott, a fifteen-year-old skater with punked out hair, doesn't believe that the administration and coaches at his high school will give him a fair shake. But actually, if he were to cut his hair, lose some of the metal in his ears, and go out for the track team, his life at school would be much easier. On the home front, he is the caregiver and breadwinner for his ten-year-old brother Sammy, who is a little slow. Their mom is hardly ever around, spending weeks at a time away with her drug-dealing boyfriends. When things at school really start going bad and a coach grabs Ian's shoulder, Ian punches him, and the two brothers go on the run from Spokane to Walla Walla, the location of the state prison, looking for the dad who abandoned them before Sammy was even born. (Quick Picks)

Subjects: Prisons; Skateboarding; Survival; Washington

Hyde, Catherine Ryan.

Becoming Chloe. 2006. 9780375832581. ⬛O

After seventeen-year-old Jordan, who has been thrown out of his home for being gay, tries to save diminutive eighteen-year-old Chloe from rape, the two homeless teens leave New York on a cross-country road trip, trying to find beauty and goodness.

Subjects: Gay Boys; New York; Rape; Road Trips

Koertge, Ron.

Strays. 2007. 9780763627058. ⬛J ⬛S

When sixteen-year-old Ted is left an orphan, he goes into foster care, where the lonely teen who has always related to animals better than people finds himself with two foster brothers who begin to build connections to him. (BBYA, Quick Picks)

Subjects: Animals; Foster Brothers; Magical Realism; Orphans

Leavitt, Martine.

Heck, Superhero. 2004. 9781886910942. ⬛J ⬛M

After they are evicted from their apartment and his mentally ill mother wanders off, thirteen-year-old Heck, a talented cartoonist, tries to get his portfolio back and survive on his own while he attempts to change his luck by performing good deeds. (BBYA)

Subjects: Artists; Cartoonists; Depression; Homelessness; Mental Illness; Superheroes

Lowry, Brigid.

Guitar Highway Rose. 2003. 9780823417902. ⬛J ⬛S

When rebel Asher decides to run away after being accused of stealing from a teacher, fifteen-year-old Rosie, who is facing problems at home, goes with him on a journey that takes them far from Perth.

Subjects: Alternate Formats; Australia; Multiple Narratives; Romance

MacCullough, Carolyn.

Stealing Henry. 2005. 9781596430457. ⬛S

After her stepfather tries to hit her eight-year-old brother Henry, seventeen-year-old Savannah smacks him with a hot skillet. Taking Henry with her, she runs away—first to an old boyfriend in New York City, and then to Maine. Savannah's story is entwined with her mother's when she was eighteen.

Subjects: Brothers and Sisters; Maine

Strasser, Todd.

Can't Get There from Here. 2004. 9780689841699. **J** **S**

Living as part of a New York City tribe of homeless teens, Maybe receives help from a young librarian who has the same skin condition she has. (BBYA, IRA YAC, Quick Picks, PP)

Subjects: Librarians; Vitiligo; New York

Van Draanen, Wendelin.

Runaway. 2006. 9780440421092. **M**

Twelve-year-old Holly runs away from her fifth foster home to head to Los Angeles, telling her story in a journal. (VOYA, PP)

Subjects: Abuse; Diaries; Road Trips

Walters, Eric.

Sketches. 2008. 9780670062942. **J** **S**

Dana has found some good friends living on the streets of Toronto, and she is beginning to find self-fulfillment when she finds a drop-in center where she can work on her art.

Subjects: Abuse; Artists; Toronto

Family Situations

Issues revolving around family situations often portray families in transition. Often teen protagonists feel unwanted and unloved as the family problems leave them by the sidelines.

Booth, Coe.

Kendra. 2008. 9780439925365. **S**

Kendra feels like neither her mother, who was fourteen when Kendra was born, nor her Nana, who has raised her, wants her. Her best friend is her same-age aunt, of whom her Nana completely disapproves. Kendra thinks that since her mom is finally graduating from Princeton with a PhD, she will be moving in with her, but her hopes and plans are dashed. (BBYA, Quick Picks)

Subjects: Abandonment

Caletti, Deb.

The Queen of Everything. 2003. 9780689871153. **S**

High school junior Jordan prefers living with her rather bland optometrist father to living in the laid back bed and breakfast run by her hippie-ish mother and artist stepdad. She isn't thrilled when Kale, the attractive school bad boy, decides he is in love with her. Instead, she likes the strange neighbor who plays the bagpipes, but his sister, her best friend, would be appalled because she thinks he is such a freak.

Subjects: Coming-of-Age; Incarcerated Parents; Murder

Ellsworth, Loretta.

In Search of Mockingbird. 2007. 9780805072365. **M** **J**

Just before her sixteenth birthday, Erin discovers her long-dead mother shared her love for Harper Lee's *To Kill a Mockingbird*, so she sets out on a quest to meet the author.

Subjects: Authors; Monroeville, Alabama; Road Trips; St. Paul, Minnesota

Galante, Cecilia.

The Patron Saint of Butterflies. 2008. 9781599902494. **J** **S**

Fourteen-year-old Agnes tries to be a good Believer at the Mount Blessing commune, but her lifelong best friend Honey is always getting in trouble and having to be punished by Emmanuel, the cult's leader. When Nana Pete visits and discovers that Agnes's brother has been injured and isn't getting the medical care he needs, she takes him, Agnes, and Honey away.

Subjects: Abuse; Butterflies; Communes; Cults; Family Secrets; Grandmothers; Road Trips

McCormick, Patricia.

My Brother's Keeper. 2005. 9780786851744. **J** **S**

After his dad leaves the family, thirteen-year-old Toby tries to keep things together as his mother struggles with finances and his older brother starts abusing drugs.

Subjects: Abandonment; Drug Abuse; Humor

Smith, Sherri L.

Sparrow. 2006. 9780385733243. **J** **S**

In orphaned Kendall's last semester of high school, G'ma dies, and Kendall finds that she has an aunt who lives in New Orleans. When the aunt doesn't show up at the funeral, and Kendall can't get the needed signature to keep her apartment, she leaves Chicago on a bus to New Orleans, where she finds that her aunt has left. With shrunken funds and no place to stay, she agrees to stay in the shotgun apartment that had been rented to her aunt, on the condition that she take care of the landlady's seventeen-year-old daughter, who has serious physical disabilities.

Subjects: Chicago; Disabilities; Foster Families; Grandmothers; Homelessness; New Orleans; Orphans

Zarr, Sara.

Story of a Girl. 2007. 9780316014533. **S**

Even though she has never been on a real date, sixteen-year-old Deanna still has the reputation of being a slut. The term was assigned to her after one of her older brother's friends had sex with her when she was thirteen. Her father refuses to talk to her. (BBYA, Quick Picks, IRA YAC, NBA Finalist)

Subjects: Outsiders; Reputation

Fostering Arrangements

Stories about teens who live in homes not their own or with families to which they do not belong hold fascination for many teens. There are many novels featuring teens living in foster homes or group homes listed in other sections of this book. They can be found by looking for "foster care" in the subject index. Some stories featuring teens living in foster living arrangements are poignant and heartwarming; others are horrifying; and some, like *Surviving the Applewhites* by Stephanie S. Tolan, are humorous.

de la Peña, Matt.

Ball Don't Lie. 2005. 9780385902588. **S**

Seventeen-year-old Sticky finds family and acceptance at a Los Angeles recreation center, where his obsessive compulsive disorder helps him hone his basketball skills. (BBYA, Quick Picks)

Subjects: Basketball; Latino; Los Angeles; OCD

Hartinger, Brent.

The Last Chance Texaco. 2004. 9780060509132. **J** **S**

Lucy Pitt desperately wants to make her stay at a foster home called The Last Chance Texaco work out, because if she washes out, her next stop will be a group home with a horrible reputation. However, when an arsonist strikes the neighborhood, suspicion falls on the foster home and Lucy. (Quick Picks, PP)

Subjects: Arson; Romance

James, Brian.

Thief. 2008. 9780545034005. **S**

Kid, a foster teen, lives in New York with an older foster sister and an evil foster mother, who takes in the kids to have them go out and steal for her. (Quick Picks)

Subjects: New York; Thieves

Rash, Ron.

The World Made Straight. 2006. 9780805078664. **O**

When Travis, a high school dropout, is seriously injured after stealing marijuana plants from some growers and being kicked out of the family home, he is taken in by a former teacher turned drug dealer. (Alex Award)

Subjects: Adult Books for Teens; Marijuana; North Carolina; Teachers

Sweeney, Joyce.

The Guardian. 2009. 9780805080193. **J** **S**

Hunter is a scrawny thirteen-year-old, the victim of bullies including his foster mom. At his foster father's funeral, a helmeted man on a motorcycle roars up and waves at him. He remembers that when he was very little, before he first went into foster care, the Angel Gabriel (who despite most depictions had long black hair instead of blond) came to him and told him he would be his guardian. Now with his life a mess and his foster mom, Stephanie, requiring him and his three foster sisters to bring in money, he starts praying out loud to his guardian angel. Then things start happening. An envelope containing the $10. 00 he needs to pay off a bully not to beat him up appears in his locker, and the gorgeous girl in his science class asks him to be her lab partner.

Subjects: Bullying; Romance; Work

Wilson, Jacqueline.

The Illustrated Mum. 2005. 9780385732376. **M**

Ten-year-old Dolphin goes into foster care when her older half-sister moves out and their bipolar mother, who is tattooed from head to toe, goes off the deep end.

Subjects: England; Mental Illness; Tattoos

Wolfson, Jill.

What I Call Life. 2005. 9780805076691. **M**

After being put in a group home because of her mother's mental issues, eleven-year-old Cal waits to get back to her real life as she comes to know the other residents of the Pumpkin House.

Subjects: Group Homes; Knitting; Libraries; Mental Illness

Teen Pregnancy and Parenting

Even though the rate of teen pregnancy has declined in recent years, it is still a serious issue that teens face, and not just girls. The following stories focus on how the protagonist faces pregnancy, makes decisions about the future, and in some cases how he or she parents. The benchmark title for this topic is one of the most award-winning books in teen literature, Angela Johnson's *The First Part Last*.

Buckhanon, Kalisha.

Conception. 2008. 9780312332709. **O**

After Shivana Montgomery, a fifteen-year-old babysitter, is impregnated by her employer's husband, she leaves Chicago for New York with Rasul, a boy who lives in her apartment building.

Subjects: African Americans; Chicago; Magical Realism; Pennsylvania ; Road Trips

Chambers, Aidan.

This Is All: The Pillow Book of Cordelia Kenn. 2006. 9780810970601. **S**

As nineteen-year-old Cordelia Kenn awaits the birth of her child, she chronicles her life from age fifteen on, complete with poems, lists, and her musings on almost everything.

Subjects: Alternate Formats; England; Kidnappings

Draper, Sharon.

November Blues. 2007. 9781416906988. **J S**

November discovers she is pregnant after her boyfriend is killed in an initiation incident. Now his parents want her baby.

Subjects: African Americans; Bereavement

High, Linda Oatman.

Planet Pregnancy. 2006. 9781590785843. **J S**

Sahara relates nine of the most important months of her life in free verse, from when she discovers she is pregnant to when she gives birth.

Subjects: Alternate Formats; Verse Novels

Johnson, Angela.

The First Part Last. 2003. 9780689849220. **J S**

Flashing back and forth in Bobby's seventeenth year is somewhat disorienting, but then so is his life. On his sixteenth birthday his girlfriend Nia tells him she is pregnant. In alternating chapters we see him fathering his baby girl Feather and really being a man and how he got to that point. Bobby was a character in Johnson's *Heaven*. (BBYA, IRA YAC, Quick Picks, Coretta Scott King Award, Printz Award, PP)

Subjects: African Americans; Bereavement; Death

Johnson, Varian.

My Life as a Rhombus. 2008. 9780738711607. **O**

When high school senior Rhonda starts tutoring Sarah, who she discovers is pregnant, she reexamines her own feelings about the abortion she had when she was a freshman.

Subjects: Abortion; African Americans; Mathematics

Knowles, Jo.

Jumping Off Swings. 2009. 9780763639495. **S**

Told from four viewpoints, the pregnancy of Ellie, who wants love so badly she has sex with any boy who makes her feel loved, affects not only her but her best friend Corrine, who is always there for her; Caleb, who has a crush on her; and Josh, who impregnated her but whom she never told. (BBYA, Quick Picks)

Subjects: Multiple Narratives

Olsen, Sylvia.

The Girl with a Baby. 2004. 9781550391428. **J** **S**

Fourteen-year-old Jane was able to hide her pregnancy until the very last minute, but now she is a girl with a baby who is trying to succeed in high school. With the help of her strong First Nations grandmother, Jane succeeds as a mother and a student, even winning the lead in a school play.

Subjects: British Columbia; Canadians; First Nations; Native Americans; Theater

GLBTQ Parents, GLBTQ Teens

In our culture gay, lesbian, bisexual, transgendered, and questioning teens face a multitude of issues with where they fit into the culture and how they are treated by family, friends, and others. Teens who have family members who are members of the GLBTQ community also face unique challenges. Nancy Garden's *Annie on My Mind* is a frequently mentioned classic and could be considered the originator of the genre. Many of the books featuring GLBTQ protagonists don't fit into the issues subgenre, as the characters are not dealing with issues and problems revolving around their sexual orientation but rather are more focused on coming-of-age or relationships, so many of those books are found in chapter 1.

Dole, Mayra Lazara.

Down to the Bone. 2008. 9780060843106. **S**

After her lesbian orientation is discovered, seventeen-year-old Laura is expelled from her Catholic school and kicked out of her family home, but she still manages to create a new sense of family.

Subjects: Cuban Americans; Humorous; Latinas; Miami

Harmon, Michael.

The Last Exit to Normal. 2008. 9780375840982. **S**

Ben's life fell apart when his dad announced that he was gay and his mother took off. Now something worse has happened. In a move to get Ben's life back on track, his father and Edward decide to move the family back to the small Montana town where Edward grew up. (BBYA)

Subjects: Gay Parents; Montana; Small Towns

Koja, Kathe.

Talk. 2005. 9780374373825. **J** **S**

When Kit Webster wins the lead role in a controversial school play, his leading lady, Linsay Walsh, falls for him, and her boyfriend incites trouble.

Subjects: Censorship; Coming Out; Drama; Theater

Peters, Julie Anne.

Between Mom and Jo. 2006. 9780316739061. **J** **S**

Nick's problem isn't that he has two moms. It is that they have split up, and because they are lesbians, one of his moms doesn't have any legal rights to stay in his life, even though she loves him and he loves her. (VOYA)

Subjects: Alcoholism; Cancer; Depression; Divorce; Gay Parents

grl2grl. 2007. 9780316013437. **S**

Ten short stories, told in the first person by girls, explore their thoughts and feelings about sexuality and sexual preferences.

Subjects: Coming-of-Age; Lesbians; Romance; Short Stories; Transgender

Luna. 2004. 9780316733694. **S**

Fifteen-year-old Regan is the only one who knows that her older, super-bright brother Liam is really a girl in a boy's body, but now that he is close to graduating, he is ready to come out and begin transitioning. (BBYA, NBA Finalist, PP)

Subjects: Brothers and Sisters; Transgender

Ryan, P. E.

Saints of Augustine. 2007. 9780060858117. **J** **S**

Formerly best friends Charlie and Sam are brought back together by crises just before their senior year starts.

Subjects: Bereavement; Coming Out; Drug Abuse; Friendship; Gay Parents; St. Augustine, Florida

Crime and Legal Issues

If one is to believe newspaper headlines, teens and crime go hand in hand. In many states teens are tried and sentenced as adults. Novels for adults involving crime usually deal with a protagonist solving a crime, and in caper novels planning and executing a crime. In teen novels the emphasis is more often on the repercussions of the crime and how it affects the characters.

Cassidy, Anne.

Looking for JJ. 2007. 9780152061906. **S**

When seventeen-year-old Jennifer Jones is released from prison, the tabloids are filled with the story of the ten-year-old who murdered her best friend. Using the new identity of Alice Tully, she tries to rebuild her life and reflects on what contributed to who she had become. (BBYA)

Subjects: England; Murder; Redemption; Reporters; Tabloids

Efaw, Amy.

After. 2009. 9780670011834. **S**

Devon, a talented fifteen-year-old soccer star and outstanding student, is arrested for throwing her newborn in a dumpster, but she doesn't even remember ever being pregnant. (BBYA, Quick Picks)

Fields, Terri.

Holdup. 2007. 9781596432192. **J S**

Flirty Sara works at Burger Heaven because she was busted for shoplifting and has to pay a fine. Serious Manuel wants to buy a truck so he can finally get a date. Jordan does everything she is supposed to do, including taking responsibility for Burger Heaven on a Saturday evening when the manager is called away. Elderly Mrs. Wilkins enjoys the company when she comes in to eat—especially Manuel, whom she is trying to convince to go to college. Keith may be chronologically an adult, but he cannot live on his own, so he goes to his favorite restaurant when his mother abandons him. Joe needs some quick cash, so he agrees to act in Dylan's impromptu marriage proposal. Dylan is the mastermind, who has a plan to rob Burger Heaven, a plan that goes horribly awry. (Quick Picks)

Subjects: Fast Food Restaurants; Multiple Narratives; Phoenix, Arizona; Robberies

Grant, Vicki.

I. D. 2007. 9781551436944. **J S**

Chris finds a wallet that changes his entire life. The ID in the wallet is for someone who is his same height, weight, and eye color, but is twenty-five years old and not broke, on the verge of being kicked out of high school, or hated by his stepfather. (Quick Picks)

Subjects: High-Low; Identity Theft

Jones, Patrick.

Stolen Car. 2008. 9780802797001. **S**

When Reid, whom fifteen-year-old Danni has had a crush on forever, notices Danni, she is thrilled and ready to do whatever he wants, no matter what it costs her.

Subjects: Crushes; Manipulation; Revenge

Korman, Gordon.

The Juvie Three. 2008. 9781423101581. **M J**

Three juvenile delinquents are given a second chance when they are paroled to an experimental group home in New York, but when their guardian ends up in the hospital in a coma, it is up to Gecko, Terence, and Arjay to save the program and themselves.

Subjects: Foster Brothers; Group Homes; Hospitals; New York; Parolees

Mazer, Norma Fox.

The Missing Girl. 2008. 9780066237763. **J** **S**

Five sisters, ages eleven to seventeen, are stalked by a predator in their small town. When one is to be sent away to live with an aunt, the youngest disappears. (BBYA)

Subjects: Kidnappings; Predators; Sisters; Small Towns; Suspense

McDaniel, Lurlene.

Hit and Run. 2007. 9780385731614. **J** **S**

Four teens' lives are forever changed after a popular athlete, driving back from a party intoxicated, hits a bicyclist on her way home from babysitting and then drives off.

Subjects: Accidents; Comas

Morgenroth, Kate.

Jude. 2004. 9780689864797. **S**

Kidnapped as a baby and raised by his drug-dealing father, Jude's life abruptly changes when he witnesses his father's murder and is reunited with his mother, a district attorney with high political aspirations. Manipulation by his stepfather sends Jude in a direction that lands him in prison. (IRA YAC)

Subjects: Prison

Myers, Walter Dean.

Shooter. 2004. 9780060295196. **S**

Shooter is the text of the imagined Harrison County School Safety Committee Threat Analysis Report. It features interviews with Cameron Porter and Carla Evens, two teens involved in a school shooting in which the shooter, Leonard Gray, committed suicide after killing another student and wounding several. It also includes Len's journal and other papers that would be found in such a report. One comes to know and empathize with Cam and Carla, who had been friends of Len, but never necessarily liked him. (Quick Picks)

Subjects: Alternate Formats; School Shootings

Nelson, Blake.

Paranoid Park. 2006. 9780670061181. **S**

A preppy type Portland skateboarder goes to a scary skate park under a bridge and ends up taking off with a sketchy kid after he mentions that he's always wanted to try hopping a train. Arriving at a freight yard just blocks from the skate park, they are beset by a security guard, who seems to really want to do them damage. The protagonist strikes the guard with his skateboard, and the guard is caught up by the train and pulled under its wheels. The other kid takes off and the protagonist runs. Told in a series of letters, the story never reveals the name of the skateboarder, but the reader really feels his anguish over the incident, his total confusion about what to do, and his fear when the incident is investigated as a murder. (Quick Picks, Film)

Subjects: Burnside Skate Park; Portland, Oregon; Skateboarders

Reinhardt, Dana.

Harmless. 2007. 9780385746991. **J** **S**

After high school freshmen Anna, Emma, and Mariah make up a story about being assaulted to cover for being someplace they shouldn't have been, a homeless man is arrested. (Quick Picks)

Subjects: Lying

Sonnenblick, Jordan.

Notes from the Midnight Driver. 2006. 9780439757799. **J** **S**

When his parents divorce, sixteen-year-old Alex drinks all the alcohol his dad left behind and takes his mother's car to confront his dad, but being drunk and not knowing how to drive lands him and the car on a neighbor's lawn. Sentenced to 100 hours of community service in a local nursing home, Alex is assigned to act as a companion to curmudgeonly Solomon Lewis, who is full of Yiddish witticisms. (BBYA)

Subjects: Community Service; Drunk Driving; Nursing Homes; Senior Citizens

Strasser, Todd.

Boot Camp. 2007. 9781416908487. **J** **S**

When fifteen-year-old Garrett refuses to end his affair with a teacher, his parents have him abducted and taken to a boot camp, where he faces horrendous mistreatment. (Quick Picks)

Subjects: Abuse; Prison

Tracy, Kristen.

Crimes of the Sarahs. 2008. 9781416955191. **S** **J**

A clique of girls named Sarah commit a variety of crimes under the direction of their ringleader, Sarah A., who seems to be becoming more and more unstable as they start their senior year of high school.

Subjects: Cliques; Humorous; Shoplifting

Volponi, Paul.

Response. 2009. 9780670062836. **S** **J**

When Noah and a couple of his friends head into an Italian American neighborhood to steal a car, they fail, and Noah becomes the victim of a horrific beating. The aftermath pits the two neighboring communities against each other as the trial approaches. (Quick Picks)

Subjects: Hate Crimes; Racism

Watson, Carrie Gordon.

Quad. 2007. 9781595141385. **S**

When shots ring out at their high school, six teens from different cliques end up taking shelter together in the student store. (Quick Picks)

Subjects: Bullying; Cliques; School Shootings

Addiction and Substance Abuse

The issue of addiction to drugs or alcohol is a common theme in young adult literature. In most of the following stories the teen protagonist is addicted to some kind of detrimental behavior, but the toll of addiction and substance abuse on the part of parents also often plays a major role in other types of teen issue novels, such as in *Saint Iggy* by K. L. Going.

Drugs

The drug addiction title that most teens are familiar with is *Go Ask Alice,* a 1971 fictional diary that has fallen into disfavor with librarians because of the duplicity in its publication as a true-life story, but it is still passed hand to hand by teens. Readers may also want to check out *Crank* and *Glass* by Ellen Hopkins, verse novels that deal with the author's own daughter's addiction to methamphetamines, annotated in chapter 10.

Deuker, Carl.

Gym Candy. 2007. 9780618777136. **J S**

Making the football team as a freshman just isn't enough for Mick's dad, who was once a professional player. Trying to be the best, the fastest, and the biggest, Mick starts using and abusing steroids. (IRA YAC, PP)

Subjects: Fathers and Sons; Football; Sports; Steroids

Myers, Walter Dean.

The Beast. 2003. 9780439368421. **S**

Coming home to Harlem for the Christmas break, Spoon, who has been attending a posh prep school as he tries to get into a good university, discovers that his beloved girlfriend Gabi has become addicted to heroin.

Subjects: African Americans; Dominicans; Harlem, New York; Heroin; Poets; Prep Schools

Walters, Eric.

Juice. 2005. 9781551435886. **M J**

High school sophomore Moose starts taking steroids when the longtime coach of his high school football team retires and a new coach and trainer come in with plans to make the team win big.

Subjects: Football; High-Low; Small Towns; Steroids

Alcohol

Alcohol abuse and alcoholism, a popular them in the late 1990s, are not as popular now, but they do continue to appear. Alcoholic parents appear in many of the novels throughout chapter 2.

Hyde, Catherine Ryan.

The Year of My Miraculous Reappearance. 2007. 9780375832574. **J** **S**
Living with her alcoholic mother, thirteen-year-old Cynnie has seen the damage alcohol can cause, but when her three-year-old brother, who has Down syndrome, is taken away, she begins drinking and making bad decisions herself.

Subjects: Alcoholics Anonymous; Brothers and Sisters; Down Syndrome

Tullson, Diane.

Blue Highway. 2004. 9781550051247. **S**
Truth and Skye have been friends since before forever. Now in their sixteenth summer, they work at a pizza place, drink to excess, and play basketball. Truth, a straight A student, has an uncanny ability to find folks who will purchase booze for her and a total inability to gauge how much she is drinking, which leads to reprehensible actions and total blackouts.

Subjects: Accidents; Drunk Driving

Violence and Bullying

Bullying and violence, when carried to murderous extremes, are covered in the "Crime and Legal Issues" section of this chapter, above. School shootings, both in novels and real life, seem to have their genesis in bullying. Unfortunately, bullying is all too often a common occurrence besetting teens, particularly middle school and junior high school students. Benchmark titles dealing with bullying include *The Misfits* by James Howe and *Stargirl* by Jerry Spinelli, which deal with this serious subject in an upbeat way. For older teens, *Whale Talk* by Chris Crutcher is a title to know.

Brugman, Alyssa.

Being Bindy. 2006. 9780385732949. **M**
Starting eighth grade heralds a lot of changes for Bindy, including her best friend since third grade turning into an enemy. (IRA YAC)

Subjects: Australia; Cliques

Harmon, Michael.

Brutal. 2009. 9780375940996. **S**
When her overachieving doctor mom heads off for South America, punk girl Poe Holly is sent to live with the father she never knew in a small town

tourist mecca. Her next door neighbor is a strange kid who calls himself Velveeta, because it is his favorite food. Poe is strong and feisty, while at the same time nursing the deep wounds inflicted by her parents' apparent lack of care for her, so it is not strange that she is willing to step forward to try to right wrongs, especially those perpetrated by a clique at her school who possess a culture of privilege and entitlement. (Quick Picks)

Subjects: Bullying

Marino, Peter.

Dough Boy. 2005. 9780823420964. **J** **S**

Tristan, age fifteen, contentedly alternates weeks spent with his mother with weeks spent with his father, until the daughter of his mother's boyfriend moves in with them and makes him miserable with her digs about his weight.

Subjects: Divorced Parents; Obesity; Plus Size; Step-Siblings

Pixley, Marcella.

Freak. 2007. 9780374324537. **M** **J**

Miriam, a brilliant twelve-year-old, is labeled a freak by the popular girls at her school, who torment her.

Prose, Francine.

Bullyville. 2007. 9780060574970. **J**

Bart Rangely, age thirteen, a scholarship student at an exclusive private school, becomes the victim of bullying, led by the boy who is supposed to be his mentor.

Subjects: Bereavement; Grieving; September 11

Shiraz ,Yasmin.

Retaliation: A Novel. 2008. 9780971817432. **J** **S**

Teshera Odom, a seventeen-year-old girl living in Washington, D.C. , works on her grades, does hair for some extra money, and earns the respect she demands from everyone, including her boyfriend. When she is jumped one day by her boyfriend's ex and winds up in the hospital, both her mother and her brother, a gang member who lost his legs to gang violence, decide to exact revenge on her attackers. (Quick Picks)

Tullson, Diane.

Lockdown. 2008. 9781551439167. **M**

When Josh's hamster is tormented into eating her young, he goes on a rampage through the school. Adam, who was partnered with Josh in a cooking class the previous year, finds himself, along with his crush Zoe and Natalie, a girl who had been in on the bullying, locked out of the locked down classrooms.

Subjects: Guns; High-Low; School Shootings

Wilson, Jacqueline.

Candyfloss. 2007. 9780440866459. **M**

Floss, a middle school girl, stays in London with her divorced father after her mother goes to Australia for six months; and subsequently becomes a target of the mean girls at her school.

Subjects: Divorce; London

Wittlinger, Ellen.

Sandpiper. 2005. 9780689868023. **S**

Sixteen-year-old Sandpiper already has the reputation of being a slut, so nobody steps in when an ex-boyfriend starts harassing her. She finds respite in the friendship of "the Walker," a boy who walks everywhere. (BBYA)

Subjects: Promiscuity

Social and Political Activism

Issues of activism reflect the times in which they are published. When the world is at peace and the economy healthy, activism does not play a major role in the lives of teens. The wars in Iraq and Afghanistan, the presidential election, and the huge meltdown of the American and world economies in 2008 made activism more important to teens. Other topics that can incite activism in protagonists and interest readers include consumerism, conservation, and pollution. A benchmark title dealing with consumerism is *The Gospel According to Larry* by Janet Tashjian, and for conservation, *Hoot* by Carl Hiaasen.

Crutcher, Chris.

The Sledding Hill. 2005. 9780060502430. **J S**

Despite being killed by sheetrock in the school gym, Billy Bartholomew refuses to leave his best friend Eddie Proffit, who has become mute after suffering not only Billy's death but his own father's death as well.

Subjects: Censorship; Elective Mutism; Intellectual Freedom; Ministers; Teachers

Erskine, Kathryn.

Quaking. 2007. 9780399247743. **J S**

Fourteen-year-old goth girl Matt is sent off to another foster home, this time with a family of Quakers who work to end the war in Iraq despite persecution; and she finds new purpose. (BBYA, Quick Picks, VOYA)

Subjects: Antiwar Activists; Foster Care; Quakers

Hiaasen, Carl.

Flush. 2005. 9780375821820. **M** **J**

On Father's Day Noah visits his dad in jail. His dad had sunk a local casino boat because he was sure it was dumping raw sewage in the water. With his dad in jail, it is now up to Noah and a motley group that he assembles to fight the casino. (BBYA, Quick Picks)

Subjects: Casinos; Environmentalism; Florida

Perkins, Mitali.

First Daughter: Extreme American Makeover. 2007. 9780525478003. **J**

The Republican presidential candidate's sixteen-year-old adopted Pakistani daughter, Sameera Righton, fights back against the political flunkies who want to remake her image, by creating her own blog, where she takes on prejudice and real political issues. (PP)

Subjects: Adoptees; Asian Americans; Politics

Petrucha, Stefan.

Teen, Inc. 2007. 9780802796509. **J** **S**

Fourteen-year-old Jaiden Beale is being raised by the NECorp, the corporation responsible for his parents' death when he was a newborn. He has a manager, has regular team meetings, lives in the corporate offices, and eats in the company cafeteria. When the corporate lawyers get involved in his life, Jaiden runs off, ends up in the middle of an altercation at a fast food restaurant, climbs a security fence, is injured, almost drowns, and is taken back to the corporation. He learns that he really does have friends, especially after he discovers that Jenny's dad is an activist trying to expose the mercury dumping being done by NECorp. and the take over plans of a corporate villain.

Subjects: Corporations; Environment; Pollution

Di's Picks

Going, K. L. *Saint Iggy.*

Forman, Gayle. *If I Stay.*

Johnson, Angela. *The First Part Last.*

Morgenroth, Kate. *Jude.*

Pearson, Mary E. *A Room on Lorelei Street.*

Williams, Carol Lynch . *The Chosen One*

Chapter 3

Historical

I love historical fiction because it taught me to love history. I've learned a lot, sure, but mostly I like hearing about these crazy times and thinking "Wow, that really happened!" It makes the spectrum of the likely increase manifoldly when you hear that Houdini might have been a secret spy or Nikola Tesla may have transmitted electricity through the air. The world of fiction is not quite so far away anymore when you throw a little history into the mix. — Andrea, age 17

Through reading historical fiction we can learn a lot, and for many teen fans of this genre the allure is learning about times and places distant from themselves.

The Historical Novel Society defines historical fiction this way: "To be deemed historical (in our sense), a novel must have been written at least fifty years after the events described, or have been written by someone who was not alive at the time of those events (who therefore approaches them only by research)" (www.historicalnovelsociety. org/definition.htm).

Though this definition works well for adults, for teens it is a different story. Teen readers often consider anything that happened before they were born to be ancient history, lost in the mists of time. As I write this in 2010, teen readers I asked considered stories set in the 1980s and prior that pay attention to period detail to be historical fiction.

Readers who like mystery and suspense in their historical fiction may also find books of interest in the "Historical Mysteries" section in chapter 8.

Frequently readers of historical fiction become captivated by a time period or historical event and will want to read nonfiction accounts on the topic or time.

North American Historical Fiction

Reading historical novels set in the United States and Canada can make the history teens study in high school come alive. The popularity of time periods and historical themes changes over years. At the time of this writing, for books set in North America, primarily in the United States, the two major themes or time periods being written about are the nineteenth and twentieth centuries, with slavery and civil rights being frequent themes.

North America Before 1900

The novels in this section are set in what is now the United States and Canada. Unfortunately Mexico has not been the setting for recent teen historical fiction. These books range from the seventeenth century and colonization to the end of the nineteenth century in the "Gilded Era." Historical novels written for teens dealing with precontact Native Americans are few and far between, so the earliest settings are in colonial times.

Anderson, Laurie Halse.

Chains. 2008. 9781416905851. **M** **J** **S**

In 1776, two sisters are sold to a Loyalist family in New York when the mistress who had promised them freedom upon her death dies. Branded with an "I" for insolence after her sister Ruth is sold away, Isabel begins to spy on her master for the Patriots. (Scott O'Dell Award for Historical Fiction, BBYA, NBA Finalist)

Subjects: African Americans; American Revolution; Slavery; Spies

Anderson, M. T.

The Astonishing Life of Octavian Nothing, Traitor to the Nation. **S**

Octavian Nothing, dressed in fine clothes and a good powdered wig, is growing up in a household of scholars who use numbers rather than names. He and his mother, an accomplished princess from a far off land, are the only ones in this house of scholars who are named rather than numbered. As the American colonists veer toward revolution, Octavian discovers he and his mother are not members of the academy, but rather slaves and study subjects.

Subjects: African Americans; American Revolution; Communes; Eighteenth Century; Scholars; Slavery

The Astonishing Life of Octavian Nothing, Traitor to the Nation: The Pox Party. 2006. 9780763624026.

> The first volume of Octavian's story tells about his childhood and coming-of-age as an experimental subject of study in a household of colonial philosophers. (BBYA, Printz Honor, NBA)

The Astonishing Life of Octavian Nothing, Traitor to the Nation: The Kingdom on the Waves. 2008. 9780763629502.

> The second volume details Octavian's life in British occupied Boston when freedom is offered to slaves who take up the British cause. (BBYA)

Avi.

The Seer of Shadows. 2008. 9780060000158. **M**

Horace, an apprentice photographer, discovers a ghost in a portrait he takes; and with Pegg, a black servant girl, uncovers the truth behind the death of his client's daughter.

Subjects: 1872; Ghosts; Nineteenth Century; Photography; Seers

Draper, Sharon.

Copper Sun. 2006. 9780689821813. **S**

Amari, a fifteen-year-old anticipating her wedding, witnesses the slaying of everyone in her African village except the strong young adults, who are taken captive as slaves. After surviving the horrifying middle passage, she is bought at auction as a gift for Clay Derby, the son of a plantation owner in South Carolina. Polly, born in Beaufort, Carolina Colony, is an indentured servant with fourteen years to serve for her parents' debt. This harrowing tale is full of adventure as the two girls and the cook's young son, who had been used as alligator bait, escape and head south toward Spanish Florida. (Coretta Scott King Award)

Subjects: African Americans; Eighteenth Century; Fort Mose, Florida; Indentured Servants; Middle Passage; Runaways; Slavery; South Carolina;St. Augustine, Florida

Duble, Kathleen Benner.

The Sacrifice. 2005. 9780689876509. **M**

Abigail loves to run, even though it is not seemly for a ten-year-old girl. She is sure her day spent in the stocks after being caught racing her cousin will bring the wrath of her grandfather, the preacher in Andover, Massachusetts, in the year of our lord 1692, but instead he preaches about lying because of the witch hunts in nearby Salem. Soon Abigail and her twelve-year-old sister join their young aunt in Salem Town's dismal and deadly jail, accused of witchcraft. This carefully researched book, with an afterword that describes the author's intimate connection to the story, will fascinate readers.

Subjects: Andover, Massachusetts; Jail; Salem, Massachusetts; Seventeenth Century; Witch Hunts

Kelly, Jacqueline.

The Evolution of Calpurnia Tate. 2009. 97808050884100. **M**

Calpurnia Tate, age eleven and three-quarters in 1899, lives in Fentress, Texas, with her immediate family, which includes six brothers; her grandfather, an avid naturalist who was an officer in the Civil War; and a few servants. Her love of reading and science is supported by her grandfather. This comforting slice-of-life tale, told in vignettes, illuminates family life, the role of girls, courting, and science a hundred years ago. (Newbery Honor, BBYA, IRA)

Subjects: 1890s; Fentress, Texas; Science

Lester, Julius.

Day of Tears: A Novel in Dialogue. 2005. 9780786804900. **S**

The biggest slave auction in American history, told in dialogue from multiple viewpoints, gives insight into the lives of African American families torn apart, abolitionists trying to end slavery, slave owners, and others. (BBYA, Coretta Scott King Award)

Subjects: African Americans; Alternate Formats; Multiple Protagonists; Nineteenth Century; Slavery

Time's Memory. 2006. 9780374371784. **S**

On the eve of the Civil War, an African spirit possesses Nat, a slave on a Virginia plantation who loves his master's daughter, Ellen.

Subjects: Nineteenth Century; Possession; Slavery; Virginia

McCaughrean, Geraldine.

Stop the Train. 2003. 9780060507497. **M**

In the 1890s a trainload of homesteaders arrives in Florence, Oklahoma, only to find that there is nothing there, but they are determined to make a town. When the railroad decides to eliminate their stops in Florence, the citizens use creative means to keep their town alive.

Subjects: Florence, Oklahoma; Homesteading; Humorous; Railroads; Westerns

McMullan, Margaret.

When I Crossed No-Bob. 2008. 9780618717156. **M**

A decade after the Civil War, twelve-year-old Addy, a member of the disreputable backwoods O'Donnell clan in Mississippi, is taken in by a young teacher and his bride after her mother abandons her at a wedding. When her pappy shows up, she must return to No-Bob with him, leaving behind the foster parents who have taught her so much. A killing by the Ku Klux Klan presents her with a dilemma. (BBYA)

Subjects: Ku Klux Klan; Mississippi; Reconstruction; Teachers

Miller, Sarah.

Miss Spitfire: Reaching Helen Keller. 2007. 9781416925422. **J** **S**

Annie Sullivan, Helen Keller's teacher, tells her own side of the story in this fictional biography of the troubled girl who became a prolific author and political activist. (BBYA)

Subjects: Biographical Fiction; Blind; Deaf; Handicaps; Keller, Helen; Nineteenth Century; Sullivan, Anne; Teachers; Twentieth Century

Moonshower, Candie.

The Legend of Zoey. 2006. 9780385732802. **M**

A contemporary girl, Zoey is struck by lightning on a school field trip and ends up back in 1811, where she plays a pivotal role in making sure her ancestors survive the New Madrid earthquakes, which created Reelfoot Lake in western Tennessee. Interesting historical details unfold as she befriends Prudence and Pru's heavily pregnant mother, whom Zoey is able to help because she didn't tune out everything her midwife mother had told her.

Subjects: Earthquakes; Field Trips; Lightning; Nineteenth Century; Tennessee; Time Slip

Mosley, Walter.

47. 2005. 9780316110358. **J** **S**

47 is a young slave boy on a Georgia plantation in the 1830s. He is not allowed a name, only the number with which he was branded. His life changes when a mysterious fourteen-year-old runaway slave, Tall John, shows up and teaches him to read.

Subjects: 1830s; Education; Science Fiction; Slavery; Time Travel

Paulsen, Gary.

The Legend of Bass Reeves. 2006. 9780385746618. **M**

Born a slave, Bass Reeves became a deputy U. S. Marshall and one of the most successful and respected lawmen in the old West.

Subjects: Biographical Fiction; Indian Territory; Marshalls; Nineteenth Century; Oklahoma; Slaves; Westerns

Rinaldi, Ann.

The Color of Fire. 2005. 9780786809387. **J** **S**

When an arsonist targets New York City in 1741 during Britain's war with Spain, many believe that a Catholic Spanish sympathizer may be behind the fires, and that the slaves are planning a revolt. Told through the eyes of teenage slave, Phoebe, who sees her teacher come under suspicion and her friend sentenced to be burned alive, this story of "the Great Negro Plot" illuminates a little known bit of history.

Subjects: Arson; Colonial; Eighteenth Century; New York; Slaves

Come Juneteenth. 2007. 9780152059477. **J** **S**

Betrayed by the family she loves, Sis Goose runs away from the Texas plantation where she has always lived after finding out from Union soldiers that she and the rest of the slaves had been freed two years earlier.

Subjects: Nineteenth Century; Sad Stories; Slavery; Texas

The Ever-After Bird. 2007. 9780152026202. **M**

After her father, who worked with the underground railroad, is killed, CeCe McGill accompanies her ornithologist uncle to Georgia as he seeks a rare scarlet ibis. There she discovers the horrors of slavery, and why her father was compelled to help the ragged people who appeared at their door.

Subjects: Abolitionists; Birds; Ornithologists; Slavery; Underground Railroad

Juliet's Moon. 2008. 9780152061708. **M**

In this story about the Civil War in Missouri, twelve-year-old Juliet Bradshaw survives a building collapse that kills several other girls who are related to Quantrill's raiders.

Subjects: Civil War; Missouri; Quantrill's Raiders; Siblings

Or Give Me Death. 2003. 9780152166878. **J**

Patrick Henry's family has problems beyond those brought on by living in a country yearning for freedom. While he is out talking to the populace about the wrongs of British rule, at home his wife Sarah is going insane and endangering their children. The story is told by sixteen-year-old daughter Patsy and nine-year-old daughter Anne, who must deal with a mother locked in the cellar to keep the family safe.

Subjects: Biographical Fiction; Colonies; Eighteenth Century; Mental Illness; Sisters

Sarah's Ground. 2004. 9780689859243. **M J**

Wanting to escape her overprotective siblings, eighteen-year-old Sarah Tracy applies for the job of overseeing Mount Vernon, George Washington's family home, which she must protect through the Civil War.

Subjects: Civil War; Mount Vernon; Nineteenth Century; Virginia

An Unlikely Friendship: A Novel of Mary Todd Lincoln and Elizabeth Keckley. 2007. 9780152055974. **M J**

Raised on an affluent Kentucky plantation, Mary Todd lived a privileged life despite having a harsh stepmother. Lizzy grew up as a slave, the daughter of a slave and her white master, and became an accomplished seamstress, ultimately buying her own freedom. When their paths cross, the two women who seemed so different become best friends.

Subjects: African Americans; Biographical Fiction; First Ladies; Keckley, Elizabeth; Lincoln, Mary Todd; Seamstresses; Slaves

Taylor, Theodore.

Billy the Kid. 2005. 9780152049300. **J**

Nineteen-year-old Billy Bonney finds himself being chased by his partners in crime as well as by his cousin, who is now a lawman in this reimaging of a tale of a real life outlaw.

Subjects: 1880s; Biographical Fiction; Bonney, William; Outlaws; Westerns

Wells, Rosemary.

Red Moon at Sharpsburg. 2007. 9780670036387. **M**

Twelve-year-old India Moody is fascinated by science and medicine, two pursuits not suitable for a proper Southern belle, but when her tutor is killed in the war, her education takes a different turn.

Subjects: Civil War; Medicine; Science; Virginia

Wilson, Diane Lee.

Firehorse. 2006. 9781416915515. **J S**

When her beloved horse is sold and Rachel is forced to move to Boston in 1872, the fifteen-year-old girl finds respite in caring for The Governor's Girl, a firehorse recovering from serious burns. Rachel wants to become a veterinarian, an unsuitable occupation for a girl. As many of the horses that pull the fire engines to fires fall ill, multiple fires strike the city.

Subjects: Boston, Massachusetts; Firefighting; Horses

Wolf, Allan.

New Found Land. 2004. 9780763621131. **J** **S**

This verse novel, told in many voices, including that of Lewis's dog, who accompanied the expedition, chronicles the journey of Lewis and Clark. (BBYA)

Subjects: Lewis & Clark Expedition; Verse Novels

Twentieth Century

The twentieth century features a diversity of topics and types for historical fiction readers. Some teens may feel a connection to some of the events in these titles through their parents and grandparents, who may have witnessed the specific events.

The tumultuous twentieth century, with its many wars including two world wars and the cold war, as well as major activism movements including labor issues, temperance, and opposition to war, is a colorful palate for fiction.

Recent trends have turned the focus of books set during the wars to the home front rather than the battlefield.

Blundell, Judy.

What I Saw and How I Lied. 2008. 9780439903462. **J** **S**

Fifteen-year-old Evie adores her glamorous mother, Bev, and her stepfather, Joe, who recently returned from World War II. When the family suddenly heads to Palm Beach, Florida, after Joe receives repeated phone calls from a former comrade in arms, they wind up in a hotel in the nearly deserted off season town, where a wealthy, attractive couple called the Graysons befriend them. Soon Peter, a gorgeous twenty-three-year-old who served in the war with Joe, turns up, and Evie falls hard for him. (NBA, BBYA)

Subjects: 1940s; Anti-Semitism; Murder Trials; Palm Beach, Florida; Veterans

Cushman, Karen.

The Loud Silence of Francine Green. 2006. 9780618504558. **M** **J**

Thirteen-year-old Francine Green keeps quiet both at home and at All Saints School for Girls because she likes to stay out of trouble, but her new friend Sophie Bowman seems to thrive on trouble. Francine loves metaphors, oxymorons, and most of all irony, using all of them with great regularity. She is glad to live in Los Angeles because of its proximity to Hollywood and the stars whom she so admires, especially Montgomery Clift. When her dad starts building a bomb shelter in the back yard, her six-year-old brother starts walking in his sleep, and Sophie's family friend, an actor, is blacklisted, Francine begins to worry not only about the physical dangers of the world in 1950, but also about the dangers to free speech and community posed by McCarthyism.

Subjects: 1950s; Blacklisting; California; McCarthyism

Dallas, Sandra.

Tallgrass. 2007. 9780312360191. **S**

Rennie Stroud is a young teen growing up on the dusty plains of eastern Colorado during World War II, when a Japanese internment camp is set up near her family's farm. Rennie deals with issues of prejudice, race, cruelty, acceptance, friendship, loyalty, kindness, coming-of-age, and the meaning of family.

Subjects: Adult Books for Teens; Asian Americans; Colorado; Internment Camps; Racism; World War II

Donnelly, Jennifer.

A Northern Light. 2003. 9780152167059. **S**

Mattie Gokey, who has a fascination with words and wants to go to college, takes a job at a resort in the Adirondacks in 1906, where she is on the scene for the murder that inspired Dreiser's *An American Tragedy.* (BBYA, IRA YAC, Printz Honor)

Subjects: Adirondacks; Murder; Resorts; Word Play

Draper, Sharon.

Fire from the Rock. 2007. 9780525477204. **S**

Sylvia Patterson is chosen to be one of the African American students to integrate the high schools in Little Rock in 1957. Now she must decide whether to continue on with her friends or face the dangers in becoming a part of history.

Subjects: 1950s; Integration; Little Rock, Arkansas

Haddix, Margaret Peterson.

Uprising. 2007. 9781416911715. **M** **J** **S**

Three girls become friends in 1909 in New York. Bella immigrated from Italy to try to make enough money to send back to save her starving family. Yetta, a Jewish girl and labor activist, has escaped the pogroms in Russia to come to America with her sister. Jane, a society girl who really wanted to go to college. ends up joining in the picketing of the Triangle Shirtwaist Factory.

Subjects: Fires; Immigrants; Labor Movement; Strikes

Holubitsky, Katherine.

The Mountain That Walked. 2005. 9781551433929. **M**

Fearing he will be accused of murder, sixteen year old "home boy" Charlie Sutherland runs away from an Alberta farm and ends up in the mining town of Frank where he experiences first hand the disastrous 1903 collapse of the mountain that buried half the town.

Subjects: Canada; Mining; Natural Disasters; Orphans; Westerns

Jocelyn, Marthe.

How It Happened in Peach Hill. 2007. 9780375837012. **M**

Fifteen-year-old Annie is forced to act developmentally disabled as part of her mother's clairvoyance scam so she can find information about Madame Caterina's clients. (BBYA)

Subjects: 1920s; Mediums; Scams

Mable Riley: A Reliable Record of Humdrum, Peril, and Romance. 2004. 9780763621209. **M J S**

Fourteen-year-old Mable Riley and her older sister Viola are sent to board with a family in rural Ontario at the turn of the twentieth century. (BBYA)

Subjects: Humorous; Farms; Sisters; Canada; Ontario; Diaries;

Johnston, Tony.

Bone by Bone by Bone. 2007. 9781596431133. **M J**

David's father has always intended for him to become a doctor, which is why he hung a skeleton near David's crib when he was an infant. When David becomes friends with Malcolm, his father can't stop the friendship, but vows, "You ever let that nigger in, by God, I'll shoot him." (BBYA)

Subjects: 1950s; Ku Klux Klan; Racism; Tennessee

Kadohata, Cynthia.

Cracker! The Best Dog in Vietnam. 2007. 9781416906377. **M J**

Cracker, a German Shepherd, is paired with Rick and sent to Vietnam to sniff for bombs. Together they experience the war until they are both wounded and separated.

Subjects: Dogs; Vietnam War

Kira-Kira. 2004. 9780689856396. **M J**

In 1950s Georgia, Japanese American sisters Katie and Lynn are very close. Katie looks up to her older sister Lynn, who guides her as their parents work long grueling hours in a poultry plant. (Newbery Award)

Subjects: 1950s; Asian Americans; Cancer; Georgia; Sisters

Weedflower. 2006. 9780689865749. **M**

Twelve-year-old Sumiko's life changes drastically after the bombing of Pearl Harbor. Her family is forced to leave their California flower farm and live in a dusty, windblown internment camp on an Indian reservation, where she meets a Mohave boy who is not happy with the camp being dumped on the reservation.

Subjects: Asian Americans; Internment Camps; Mohaves; Native Americans; World War II

Karr, Kathleen.

Gilbert & Sullivan Set Me Free. 2003. 9780786819164. **M**

Female prisoners in 1914 Massachusetts, including sixteen-year-old Libby, stage a performance of *The Pirates of Penzance.*

Subjects: Massachusetts; Prisons; Theater

Kerr, P. B.

One Small Step. 2008. 9781416942139. **M** **J**

In 1969, thirteen-year-old Scott is learning how to fly from his father, an Air Force flight instructor, when he is recruited by NASA, because of his size and flying ability, to participate in a secret mission.

Subjects: 1960s; Astronauts; Chimpanzees; Houston, Texas; NASA

Larson, Kirby.

Hattie Big Sky. 2006. 9780385733137. **M** **J**

Yearning for a home of her own, sixteen-year-old Hattie leaves Iowa for Montana to take over her late uncle's homestead as war rages in Europe. (BBYA. Newbery Honor)

Subjects: Homesteading; Montana; Orphans; Twentieth Century; World War I

Lavender, William.

Aftershocks. 2006. 9780152058821. **J** **S**

Fourteen-year-old Jessie Wainwright wants to become a doctor, an ambition that her father, himself a physician, disapproves of. When her friend Mei, a Chinese servant in their home, disappears, Jessie ventures into Chinatown to find her, at the same time that the earthquake strikes.

Subject: Asian Americans; Chinatown; Doctors; Earthquakes; Missing Persons; San Francisco, California

Lawrence, Iain.

The Séance. 2008. 9780385733755. **M**

In the 1920s Scooter King works behind the scenes to feed his mother, Madame King, the information and special effects she needs to make her séances seem legitimate, but when he finds a body the thirteen-year-old is thrust into a mystery investigation.

Subject: 1920s; Houdini; Mediums; Mystery

Lurie, April.

Brothers, Boyfriends & Other Criminal Minds. 2007. 9780385731249. **J** **S**

In 1977, fourteen-year-old April Lundquist lives with her family in a Brooklyn neighborhood filled with mafia types. When she does a favor for "Soft Sal" by making sure his autistic son gets to school OK, hundred dollar bills start showing up in unexpected places, she gets the attention of her bad boy crush, her older brother starts a romance with a girl who has her own mafioso ties, and April's life takes on perhaps too much excitement.

Subject: 1970s; Brooklyn, New York; Humorous; Mafia; Romeo and Juliet

Madden, Kerry.

Maggie Valley series. M

The Weems family may be short on money, but they are long on love, children, and music in the little mountain community of Gentle's Holler in western North Carolina.

Subjects: 1960s; Appalachia; Gentle Reads; Poverty; Mountains; Music; North Carolina

Gentle's Holler. 2007. 9780670059980.

Livy Two, a twelve-year-old songwriter who lives with her eight siblings in the North Carolina mountains, tries to train the family dachshund to serve as a seeing-eye dog for Gentle, her younger sister.

Louisiana's Song. 2007. 9780670061532.

Livy Two's eleven-year-old sister Louise tends to Daddy, who is suffering memory loss and lack of interest in his banjo following time in a coma after a car accident.

Jessie's Mountain. 2008. 9780670061549.

When Livy Two runs off to Nashville trying to make money to buy the family home, things don't work out like she wants, but she finds solace and new purpose from reading her mother's girlhood diary.

Moranville, Sharelle Byars.

A Higher Geometry. 2006. 9780805074703. J S

Fifteen-year-old Anna loves math, but she knows her path in the world is to get married after she graduates from high school. Her life changes when she wins a mathematics competition and her parents let her start dating Mike.

Subjects: 1950s; Cold War; Mathematics; Romance

Murphy, Pat.

The Wild Girls. 2007. 9780670062263. M

A pair of twelve-year-old girls in 1970s California discover a mutual love for exploration, writing, and individuality. (VOYA, BBYA)

Subjects: 1970s; California; Writers

Myers, Walter Dean.

Harlem Summer. 2007. 9780439368438. J S

Sixteen-year-old Mark Purvis gets on the wrong side of mobster Dutch Schultz during the blazingly hot Harlem summer of 1925 and ends up working for W. E. B DuBois's magazine *The Crisis*, a job that takes him into the path of many of the famous people of the Harlem Renaissance.

Subjects: 1920s; Celebrities; Harlem Renaissance; Mobsters; Musicians; New York; Writers

Nuzum, K. A.

A Small White Scar. 2006. 9780060756406. **M** **J**

Fifteen-year-old Will sees himself as a cowboy and plans for a rodeo career, but his life in 1940s Colorado is mostly consumed by taking care of his twin brother, who has Down syndrome. When Will runs away to follow his dreams, Denny follows him, putting them both in danger.

Subject: 1940s; Brothers; Colorado; Cowboys; Developmental Disabilities; Down Syndrome; Rodeo

Peck, Richard.

Here Lies the Librarian. 2006. 9780803730809. **M**

In 1914, fourteen-year-old orphan Peewee McGrath loves doing mechanics with her older brother Jake, and is looking forward to graduating from eighth grade and being done with school forever. The library in their small Indiana town closed after the old librarian died, and that is fine with Peewee, who doesn't have much use for books. Then Irene Ridpath and three other library school students show up in town with big ideas.

Subjects: Cars; Humorous; Indiana; Librarians; Mechanics; Races

The Teacher's Funeral: A Comedy in Three Parts. 2004. 9780803727366. **M**

In 1904, fifteen-year-old Russell Culver sees his teacher's death and the closing of the one-room schoolhouse as the perfect opportunity to leave Indiana for the Dakotas, but the school doesn't close, and even worse, his own sister is appointed as the new teacher. (BBYA)

Subjects: Brothers and Sisters; Farming; Humorous; Indiana; Siblings

Qualey, Marsha.

Too Big a Storm. 2004. 9780803728394. **S**

Eighteen-year-old Brady volunteers at a church that helps the homeless and draft dodgers, where she becomes friends with Sally, a girl from a wealthy family who wants to take further action to stop the war. Meanwhile, Brady's brother is missing in Vietnam, and the military is claiming he is a deserter.

Subjects: 1960s; Activism; Vietnam War

Schmidt, Gary D.

Lizzie Bright and the Buckminster Boy. 2004. 9780618439294. **M** **J**

Turner, a preacher's kid, moves to Phippsburg, Maine, where he becomes an immediate outcast, but does find friendship with Lizzie Bright Griffin, an African American girl. The local leaders have decided their town would be a fine vacation destination if only they can rid the area of the "undesirables" who live on Malaga Island, which is Lizzie's home. (BBYA, Printz Honor, Newbery Honor)

Subjects: African Americans; Baseball; Churches; Eugenics; Minister's Children; Phippsburg, Maine

The Wednesday Wars. 2007. 9780618724833. **M** **J**

As the only Presbyterian in his seventh grade class in 1967, Holling Hoodhood must remain at school on Wednesday afternoons when his Jewish classmates attend Hebrew school and the Catholic ones attend catechism. On those days, his teacher makes him read Shakespeare. It proves to be an eventful year in Holling's life and in the world, with the Vietnam war looming large and the assassinations of Dr. Martin Luther King and Bobby Kennedy. (BBYA, Newbery Honor)

Subjects: 1960s; Long Island, New York; Shakespeare; Vietnam War

Sharenow, Robert.

My Mother the Cheerleader. 2007. 9780061148965. **M** **J** **S**

Thirteen-year-old Louise Collins helps her drunken mother run a boarding house in the Ninth Ward of New Orleans. When the courts order the local school to be integrated, her mother pulls her out of school and becomes one of the protesters called "the cheerleaders" by the Northern press. Louise ends up doing most of the work around the house, including taking care of their one long-term boarder who is bedridden. When Morgan Miller, a man from New York comes to stay, Louise finds new ways to look at the world around her. (BBYA, VOYA)

Subjects: 1960s; Integration; New Orleans; Racism

Smith, Sherri L.

Flygirl. 2009. 9780399247095. **M** **J** **S**

Ida Mae Jones love to fly. She flies her late father's crop duster in Slidell, Louisiana, and works as a maid to earn the money to go to Chicago to test for her pilot's license, because in the 1940s there is no place in the South that will award one to a Negro girl. When war breaks out, her beloved older brother quits medical school and enlists. With all resources going to the war effort, Ida Mae can no longer fly her father's plane, and she begins to pine for the sky. Then the WASP program is announced, a civilian corps of women who ferry planes and perform other flying tasks for the Army Air Force. Ida Mae applies, using her father's altered pilot's license and passing as white. (BBYA)

Subjects: African Americans; Pilots; World War II

Vaught, Susan.

Stormwitch. 2005. 9781582349527. **J** **S**

In 1969 Ruba is sent from Haiti to live with her grandmother in Mississippi, where she experiences firsthand the civil rights movement and Hurricane

Camille. Her Mississippi grandmother, a proper good Christian, has issues with Ruba's connection to her ancestors and their magic. (BBYA)

Subjects: African American; Civil Rights Movement; Unexplained Phenomena; Voodoo

Weaver, Will.

Full Service. 2005. 9780374324858. **S** **J**

In 1965 Paul, a Minnesota farm boy from a tight-knit religious community, goes to work in town at a service station, where he encounters a whole new world. (BBYA)

Subjects: 1960s; Farmers; Hippies; Minnesota; Service Stations; Vietnam War

Welsh, T. K.

The Unresolved. 2006. 9780525477310. **J** **S**

Mallory Meer, who has just received her first kiss, dies along with about another thousand people in the fire that destroys the steamship *General Slocum* while on a church outing in 1904. She is unable to move on from this world to the next because Dustin, the Jewish boy she kissed, is facing suspicion of starting the fire.

Subjects: Disasters; Ghost Story; New York

World Historical Fiction

Although there is more historical fiction being published for teens, and more teens becoming fans of the genre, the focus of the stories has narrowed, with the majority of historical novels not set in North America having European settings and with few exceptions occurring from the Crusades to the end of the twentieth century.

Historical fiction set outside of North America is a huge category, with stories taking place at any time and place in recorded history. This section is starts with general historical novels, followed by those set in the twentieth century, then ancient history, including novels set in biblical settings.

Avi.

The Traitors' Gate. 2007. 9780689853357. **M** **J**

When his father is arrested for selling secrets, fourteen-year-old John Huffman investigates in an attempt to clear him.

Subjects: London; Nineteenth Century

Crispin. **M**

In fourteenth-century England, orphaned Crispin finds he has a secret identity.

Subjects: England; Fourteenth Century; Hidden Identity; Jugglers; Orphans

Crispin: The Cross of Lead. 2002. 9780786808281

After his mother dies, the thirteen-year-old boy who has always just been called "Asta's son" discovers that he has a name, Crispin. When he goes to see the village priest to find out what the writing on his mother's lead cross says, he finds the man murdered. Lord Furnival's steward accuses Crispin of the crime and labels him a "wolf's head"—wanted, dead or alive. On the run, Crispin takes up with Bear, an itinerant juggler who helps him discover his true identity. (Newbery Award)

Crispin: At the Edge of the World. 2006. 9780786851522

When Bear is wounded, he and Crispin find help from Old Aude, who protects Troth, a young girl with a cleft lip. The villagers rise up against them, but Crispin, Bear, and Troth flee to Brittany, where they encounter further danger.

Beauford, Mary Jane.

Primavera. 2008. 9780316016445. **J** **S**

Flora Pazzi is the daughter of an aristocratic Florentine, in a family that finds itself on the wrong side of the Medicis, to deadly effect.

Subjects: Fifteenth Century; Florence, Italy; Girls Dressed as Boys; Goldsmithing; Swordsmanship; Renaissance

Cooney, Caroline B.

Enter Three Witches. 2007. 9780439711562. **J** **S**

Fourteen-year-old Lady Mary witnesses firsthand the events caused by greed and politics in Scotland while she lives as a ward of Lord and Lady Macbeth following the execution of her father as a traitor.

Subjects: Orphans; Scotland; Shakespeare

Cullen, Lynn.

I Am Rembrandt's Daughter. 2007. 9781599900469. **J** **S**

Fourteen-year-old Cornelia van Rijn is left alone with her father, the difficult painter, after her mother dies and her brother marries and moves out. (BBYA)

Subjects: Amsterdam; Seventeenth Century; van Rijn, Rembrandt

Dowswell, Paul.

Adventures of a Young Sailor. **M** **J**

Sam Witchall, thirteen years old in 1800, faces adventures at sea that take him far from England after he is impressed into the navy aboard the ship *Miranda*. On board the ship, he encounters storms, battles, shipwreck, and pirates.

Subjects: Australia; Cornwall; Napoleonic Wars; Nineteenth Century; Norfolk, England; Pirates; Prisoners; Ships; Shipwrecks

Powder Monkey. 2005. 9781582346755.

Sam always wanted to go to sea, but he never expected to be forced into the navy and into battle, running gunpowder from the hold to the cannons.

Prison Ship. 2006. 9781582346762.

> Falsely accused of theft, Sam, who was impressed into the British Navy when he was thirteen, is transported to Australia, where he and his friend Richard fight for survival in the bush.

Battle Fleet. 2008. 9781599900803

> Cleared of theft charges, Sam, who had been transported to Australia for a crime he did not commit, returns to England, where he becomes involved in the war against Napoleon.

Gardner, Sally.

The Red Necklace. **2008. 9780803731004.** **S**

> On the night the magician whom fourteen-year-old orphaned Yann assists is murdered by the evil Count Kalliovski, Yann meets Sidonie, an heiress whose father has promised her to the Count. As the country heads into revolution, Yann and Sidonie's paths cross again. (VOYA, BBYA)

> **Subjects:** Automatons; Dwarves; Eighteenth Century; France; French Revolution; Gypsies; Magicians

Golding, Julia.

Cat Royal Series. **M** **J**

> Feisty, diminutive, red-haired Cat has been raised in the Theater Royal by its owner ever since she was found abandoned there as a baby.

> **Subjects:** 1790s; London, England; Orphans; Theater

The Diamond of Drury Lane. 2008. 9781596433519

> Cat, along with her friends Pedro and Johnny, encounters adventure and danger in the theater, as she tries to protect a much-coveted diamond that was hidden in the theater by her guardian.

Cat Among the Pigeons. 2008. 9781596433526

> Disguised as a boy, Cat goes undercover in an exclusive boy's school, while abolitionists attempt to save Pedro from being taken to Barbados, where he would again live in slavery.

> **Subjects:** Abolitionists; Slavery

Den of Thieves. 2009. 9781596434448

> With the theater where she was raised closed for renovations, Cat, disguised as a ballerina, heads to Paris to spy on the revolution.

Cat O'Nine Tales. 9781596434455. 2009.

> Cat and friends are kidnapped and find themselves aboard a ship headed for the New World.

Grant, K. M.

How the Hangman Lost His Heart. **2007. 9780802796721.** 🇯

When teenage Alice tries to retrieve her executed uncle's head from a pike, the crown's executioner becomes her unlikely ally.

Subjects: Eighteenth Century; England

De Granville Trilogy. 🇲 🇯

Will and Gavin de Granville, descendants of the Sir Thomas who came to England with William the Conqueror, experience the events of the twelfth century along with Eleanor de Barre, a ward of their father.

Subjects: Brothers; Crusades; Horses

Blood Red Horse. 2005. 9780802789600.

Two brothers, Will and Gavin de Granville, head off to the Crusades along with Hosanna, an exceptional horse.

Subjects: Jerusalem; Saladin

Green Jasper. 2006. 9780802780737.

Back from the crusades, brothers Will and Gavin de Granville soon must set out on a new quest, when Ellie is abducted and rumors spread that King Richard is dead.

Subjects: King Richard the Lionhearted

Blaze of Silver. 2007. 9780802796257

William is off to Germany to take a share of treasure to ransom King Richard.

Subjects: Germany

Perfect Fire Trilogy. 🇯 🇸

Set in Occitania in the thirteenth century as conflict heats up between the Cathars and Catholics. Danger comes to Catholic Yolanda and Cathar Raimon, lifelong friends who love each other. The third entry in the trilogy, *Paradise Red*, has not yet been published in the United States, but is available in New Zealand.

Subjects: Cathars; Catholics; France; Inquisition; Occitania; Religion; Thirteenth Century

Blue Flame. 2008. 9780802796943

Yolanda, daughter of the ruling Catholic count and Raimon, son of a Cathar peasant weaver, have been lifelong friends and are falling in love when the Inquisition comes to their region, pitting their two religions against each other as those from both religions strive to keep and protect the blue flame that was ignited at the moment of Christ's death and is a powerful symbol for all Occitans,

White Heat. 2009. 9780802796950.

Even though Yolanda believes Raimon was immolated, she still resists marrying Sir Hugh. Meanwhile Raimon, who has the Blue Flame, is besieged in the mountains above Castelneuf.

Gratz, Alan.

Samurai Shortstop. 2006. 9780803730755. **J** **S**

Sixteen-year-old Toyo Shimada lives in a challenging time as the Emperor has outlawed his family's Samurai traditions and he is sent to a boarding school in Tokyo. (BBYA)

Subjects: 1890s; Baseball; Tokyo, Japan

Hearn, Julie.

Ivy. 2008. 9781416925064. **J** **S**

Life in nineteenth-century London is grim for Ivy, who works by turns to help her relatives with their crimes, as a skinner luring wealthy children into places their clothing can be stolen, and as a painter's model. Along the way she tries to dampen her woes with laudanum.

Subjects: Drugs; England; Nineteenth Century

The Minister's Daughter. 2005. 9780689876905. **J** **S**

Nell, age sixteen, the granddaughter of the village healer, is targeted as a witch by the new minister's daughter. (BBYA)

Subjects: England; Herbalists; Witch Hunts

Hoffman, Alice.

Incantation. 2006. 9780316010191. **J** **S**

Estrella's family hides a deadly secret during the Inquisition, and she finds that assumptions made about friends and family are not always true. (BBYA)

Subjects: Inquisition; Jews; Spain

Hooper, Mary.

Newes from the Dead. 2008. 9781596433557. **S**

In 1650 Anne, a housemaid in a wealthy home, is hanged for infanticide, but she later wakes up just as she is about to be dissected in a medical college.

Subjects: Dissection; England; Maids; Science; Seventeenth Century

The Remarkable Life and Times of Eliza Rose. 2006. 9781582348544. **S**

Traded by her English lady mother for a boy, Eliza Rose is thrust out into the world, and she ends up in prison at age fifteen for stealing food. After she has been taken into a house of prostitution, her fortunes begin to change, and she is befriended by the actress Nell Gwynn, who is a favorite of King Charles II.

Subjects: Actresses; Gwynn, Nell; King Charles II; Mistresses; Prison; Prostitutes

London Disasters. **M** **J**

Hannah and her sisters experience the disasters that hit London during the 1660s, from the plague to the great fire.

Subjects: Disasters; Fires; London; Plague; Seventeenth Century; Sisters

At the Sign of the Sugared Plum. 2003. 9781582346953.

Hannah's visit to London and the sweetmeat shop her older sister Sarah owns is impacted when the bubonic plague strikes. This tale vividly depicts the sights, sounds, and smells of the city in 1665.

Petals in the Ashes. 2004. 9781582349367.

After escaping the plague, Hannah and her younger sister Anne return to London just in time to experience the Great Fire of 1666, in this sequel to *At the Sign of the Sugared Plum*.

Jinks, Catherine.

Pagan series. **M** **J** **S**

In twelfth-century Jerusalem, orphaned Pagan Kidrouk becomes a squire to Lord Roland Roucy de Bram of the Knights Templar.

Subjects: Crusades; France; Jerusalem; Knights Templar; Monasteries; Monks; Twelfth Century

Pagan's Crusade. 2003. 9780763625849.

A failed wager sends streetwise orphan Pagan into service with the Knights Templar.

Pagan in Exile. 2004. 9780763620202.

Pagan accompanies Lord Roland back to France in an effort to enlist aid for a new crusade to wrest the holy land away from the Muslims, but they find themselves in the midst of a battle between secular and religious factions.

Pagan's Vows. 2004. 9780763627546.

Eschewing the life of crusaders, Pagan and Lord Roland enter a monastery as novices, but soon Pagan uncovers a mystery.

Pagan's Scribe. 2005. 9780763629731.

Isadore, a young scribe in service to Pagan, now Archdeacon of Carcassonne, relates what happens when the Pope sends troops into southern France to root out heresy.

Karr, Kathleen.

Born for Adventure. 2007. 9780761453482. **M** **J**

Rechristening himself as Thomas Greenville Ormsby, sixteen-year-old Tom, a pharmacist's assistant, signs on to accompany explorer Henry Morton Stanley on an expedition into Africa, where his pharmaceutical knowledge comes in handy.

Subjects: 1880s; Africa

Fortune's Fool. 2008. 9780375848162. **J** **S**

When orphaned jester Conrad speaks out to Lord Otto on the topic of his unfair taxation of serfs, he is given a horrible beating that precipitates his fleeing along with Christa, who loves him.

Subjects: Fourteenth Century; Germany; Jesters

The 7th Knot. 2003. 9780761451358. **M** **J**

In the waning years of the nineteenth century, fifteen-year-old Wick and his twelve-year-old brother Miles are sent on a tour of Europe with their Uncle Eustace. They end up enmeshed in a mystery involving a missing man and wood-cuts created by Albrecht Dürer.

Subjects: Art; Europe; Nineteenth Century; Secret Societies

Lawrence, Iain.

Curse of the Jolly Stone Trilogy. **J** **S**

With his father serving time in debtor's prison, fourteen-year old Tom Tin takes to the streets of London, where survival is questionable.

Subjects: Adventure; Australia; Convicts; England; Nineteenth Century; Prison Hulks; South Pacific

The Convicts. 2005. 9780385901093.

Fourteen-year-old Tom Tin sees life as he knows it end when his sister drowns, his mother goes mad, and his father is sent to debtor's prison. Forced into a life on the streets, he is wrongly convicted and sentenced to a prison hulk until he is old enough to be transported to Australia.

The Cannibals. 2007. 9780440419334.

Tim escapes from the ship before getting to Australia, only to encounter more dangers and adventures, including headhunters, cannibals, and pirates.

The Castaways. 2005. 9780385730907.

Escaping from slavers, Tim and company make their way back to England, and to the cursed diamond he had hidden at the beginning of his adventures.

Leeds, Constance.

The Silver Cup. 2007. 9780670061570. **M** **J**

Fifteen-year-old Anna, a German Catholic girl, rescues Leah, a Jewish friend who was orphaned when her community was destroyed by Crusaders.

Subjects: Crusades; Eleventh Century; Germany

Libby, Alisa M.

The King's Rose. 2009. 9780525479703. **S**

Catherine Howard, the fifteen-year-old cousin of Ann Boleyn, is a shallow, self-centered girl, who through the machinations of her family weds King Henry VIII and becomes a short-lived queen of England.

Subjects: Biographical Fiction; England; Henry VIII, King; Howard, Catherine; Sixteenth Century

Little, Melanie.

The Apprentice's Masterpiece: A Story of Medieval Spain. 2008. 978-1554511174. **S**

The stories of fifteen-year-old Ramon, who works as a scribe with his father, and Amir, a Muslim slave who lives in their household, entwine as the Inquisition puts them all in danger.

Read-alike: Readers wanting other books dealing with life during the Inquisition may also enjoy Alice Hoffman's *Incantation*.

Subjects: *Conversos*; Fifteenth Century; Jews; Muslims; Scribes; Spain; Spanish Inquisition; Verse Novels

McCaughrean, Geraldine.

Cyrano. 2006. 9780152058050. **J S**

This witty retelling of the classic French play *Cyrano* examines unrequited love and self-image, and includes swashbuckling action.

Subjects: France; Seventeenth Century

Meyer, Carolyn.

Duchessina: A Novel of Catherine de' Medici. 2007. 9780152055882. **S**

Orphaned as an infant, Catherine de' Medici, a wealthy heiress, grows up with relatives (including the pope) and in convents until at age fourteen she is married off to Henri II of France.

Subjects: Catherine, Queen of France; Florence, Italy; France; Henri II, King; Orphans; Sixteenth Century

Loving Will Shakespeare. 2006. 9780152054519. **J S**

Agnes "Anne" Hathaway grows up in Stratford on Avon with a mean stepmother and half-sister. She befriends Will Shakespeare, who is seven years younger and eventually, after a few failed relationships, discovers romance with him.

Subjects: England; Hathaway, Anne; Shakespeare, William; Sixteenth Century

Patience, Princess Catherine. 2004. 9780152165444. **M J**

At the beginning of the sixteenth century, Catharine of Aragon travels to England to marry Arthur, the crown prince, but she is soon widowed, leaving her future in question.

Subjects: Catharine of Aragon, Queen; England; Henry VIII, King; Sixteenth Century; Tudors; Widows

Meyer, L. A.

Bloody Jack. **J S**

As a twelve-year-old orphan living on the streets of London after her family dies of the pestilence, Mary Faber looks for a way out by disguising herself as a boy and shipping out as a ship's boy on H.M.S. *Dolphin*.

Bloody Jack: Being an Account of Curious Adventures of Mary "Jacky" Faber, Ship's Boy. 2002. 9780152167318.

Jacky takes to life on the high seas, chasing pirates, acquiring the nickname Bloody Jack after killing a man, and being taken captive by pirates. As she grows older it becomes harder to hide the fact that she is a girl. Then she falls in love with Jaimy, a fellow sailor. (BBYA)

Curse of the Blue Tattoo: Being an Account of the Misadventures of Jacky Faber, Midshipman and Fine Lady. 2004. 9780152051150.

Put off the *Dolphin* after it is discovered that she is a girl, Jacky Faber ends up at a proper Boston boarding school, where she of course finds trouble. Despite sending letters to Jaimy, she doesn't hear back from him. (BBYA)

Subjects: Boarding Schools; Boston

Under the Jolly Roger: Being an Account of the Further Nautical Adventures of Jacky Faber. 2005. 9780152053451.

Making her way back to England on a whaler, Jacky discovers Jaimy with another girl, and then takes to the street, where she is captured by a press gang and put on a British warship.

Subjects: Privateers

In the Belly of the Bloodhound: Being an Account of a Particularly Peculiar Adventure in the Life of Jacky Faber. 2006. 9780152055578.

Back in Boston at the boarding school, Jacky and her classmates are kidnapped while on a boating excursion, and shipped off to the slave markets of North Africa.

Mississippi Jack: Being an Account of the Further Waterborne Adventures of Jacky Faber, Midshipman, Fine Lady, and Lily of the West. 2007. 9780152060039.

On her way back to Boston after her last adventure, Jacky is arrested by the British on piracy charges, but she escapes and heads for the American frontier.

Subjects: Mississippi River; New Orleans; Riverboats

My Bonny Light Horseman: Being an Account of the Further Adventures of Jacky Faber, in Love and War. 2008. 9780152061876.

Disguised again as a male, Jacky winds up in the French Army, fighting alongside Napoleon.

Subjects: Dancers; Paris; Spies

Rapture of the Deep: Being an Account of the Further Adventures of Jacky Faber, Soldier, Sailor, Mermaid, Spy. 2009. 9780152065010.

Kidnapped just before her wedding, Jacky is off to the Florida Keys to find a lost Spanish treasure and replenish the coffers of the British crown, depleted by the expenses of the Napoleonic War.

Subjects: Diving; Exploration; Pirates; Treasure

The Wake of the Lorelei Lee: Being an Account of the Further Adventures of Jacky Faber, on Her Way to Botany Bay. 2010. 9780547327686.

> Having purchased a passenger ship, Jacky docks in London, only to be arrested and sentenced to be transported to Australia.

Napoli, Donna Jo.

Hush: An Irish Princess' Tale. 2007. 9780689861765. **J** **S**

> Melkorka, a princess, is kidnapped by Russians and sold to an Icelander as a slave. (BBYA)

Subjects: Elective Mutism; Iceland; Ireland; Tenth Century; Vikings

Rinaldi, Ann.

Nine Days a Queen: The Short Life and Reign of Lady Jane Grey. 2004. 9780060549237. **M**

> Jane, who spent nine days as a queen before being beheaded, tells the story of her life from ages nine to sixteen.

Subjects: England; Grey, Lady Jane; Royalty; Tudor Era

Rinaldi, Ann.

The Redheaded Princess. 2008. 9780060733759. **M** **J**

> Elizabeth, at age nine, is out of favor with her father, King Henry VIII, but she eventually ascends to the throne of England.

Subjects: Elizabeth I, Queen; England; Henry VIII, King; Tudor Era

Sturtevant, Katherine.

A True and Faithful Narrative. 2006. 9780374378097. **J**

> When Edward heads off on a sea voyage, sixteen-year-old Meg, who wants to write an exciting story, jokingly asks that he allow himself to be captured by pirates, so that she can write his tale. This is a stand-alone sequel to *At the Sign of the Star.* (BBYA)

Subjects: London, England; Printers; Seventeenth Century

Tingle, Rebecca.

The Edge on the Sword. 2001. 9780399235801. **M** **J** **S**

> Aethelflaed, who at age fifteen is soon to wed one of her father's allies, learns to fight and much more from her body guard. (BBYA)

Subjects: Britain; Ninth Century

Turnbull, Ann.

Quaker Series. M J

Meeting and falling in love with Susanna, a Quaker, makes Will examine his life and faith.

Subjects: Disasters; England; Fire; Plague; Quakers; Religion; Romance; Seventeenth Century

No Shame, No Fear. 2004. 9780763625054.

Susanna, a Quaker teen who works for a printer's widow because her father has been jailed for his faith, falls in love with Will, an Oxford graduate and the only son of a wealthy Anglican merchant. Vivid details of religious persecution in Reformation England bring the era to life. (BBYA)

Forged in the Fire. 2007. 9780763631444.

Three years after their first meeting, Susanna and Will are about to marry, but it is the same year that the plague and the great fire hit London.

Vande Velde, Vivian.

The Book of Mordred. 2005. 9780618507542. J S

Mordred's story is told through the stories of three women: a widow whose child has been kidnapped, a sorceress, and a teenage seer.

Subjects: Arthurian Legend; England; Mordred

Wein, Elizabeth E.

The Mark of Solomon. J S

Telemakos, the grandson of King Arthur and an Ethiopian noblewoman, loses his arm to a lion when Athena, his baby sister, is born.

Subjects: Africa; Arthurian Legend; Ethiopia; Medraut; Mordred; Sixth Century

The Lion Hunter. 2007. 9780670061631.

When political machinations put his family in danger, Telemakos and Athena are sent to a neighboring kingdom.

The Empty Kingdom. 2008. 9780670062737.

Held captive by the ruler who was supposed to be his guardian, aware of actions being planned against his emperor, and separated from his sister, Telemakos tries to get coded messages to his family.

Welsh, T. K.

Resurrection Men. 2007. 9780525476993. S

After witnessing the executions of his parents, twelve-year-old Victor becomes a cabin boy, but he is thrown off the ship after his leg is shattered. Washing ashore in England, he is sold to a pair of "resurrection men," who secure corpses, and sometimes children, for medical research.

Subjects: 1830s; Body Snatchers; Italians; London; Medical Research; Orphans

Twentieth Century

Most of the world historical fiction set in the twentieth century involves either World War I or World War II, but some deals with the Cold War or the move for Indian independence.

Almond, David.

The Fire-Eaters. 2004. 9780385902076. **J** **S**

With the world poised on the brink of war as the Cuban Missile Crisis unfolds, Bobby Burns deals with his father's mysterious illness and meets McNulty, a man who eats fire and pierces his own flesh. (BBYA)

Subjects: 1960s; Cuban Missile Crisis; England; Literary

Bloor, Edward.

London Calling. 2006. 9780375836350. **M**

Seventh grader Martin Conway, who inherited an elaborate antique radio, finds himself falling back in time to London during World War II, where he finds friendship with Jimmy Harker, who is desperate for help. Martin also observes his grandfather, a now revered statesman, when he was young.

Subjects: London; Radios; Time Slip; World War II

Boyne, John.

The Boy in the Striped Pajamas. 2006. 9780385751063. **J** **S**

When his father is appointed as commandant, nine-year-old Bruno is uprooted from his Berlin home and moves to the country, where he sees a huge wire fence and hundreds of people in striped pajamas. As he explores the perimeter, he meets Shmuel, a boy who shares his same birthday, but lives on the other side of the fence. (IRAYAC, VOYA, Film)

Subjects: Auschwitz; Concentration Camps; Germans; Holocaust; Jews; Poland

Dubosarsky, Ursula.

The Red Shoe. 2007. 9781596432659. **J** **S**

In the 1950s, Matilda and her sisters are dealing with their father's mental illness, their mother's strange behavior, and a possible Russian defector staying next door.

Subjects: 1950s; Australia; Cold War; Mental Illness

Fleischman, Sid.

The Entertainer and the Dybbuk. 2007. 9780061344459. **M** **J**

Following World War II, a struggling ventriloquist, The Great Freddie, is possessed by a dybbuk, the ghost of one of the million and a half Jewish children who were killed in the Holocaust. (BBYA)

Subjects: 1940s; Dyybuks; Ghost Story; Holocaust; Paranormal; Performers; Ventriloquists

Hartnett, Sonya.

The Silver Donkey. 2006. 9780763629373. **M**

Two young sisters, Marcelle and Coco, find a blinded World War I deserter starving in the woods near their home. They smuggle food to him, and he tells them stories about a little silver donkey.

Subjects: Deserters; Donkeys; France; Literary; World War I

Lawrence, Iain.

B for Buster. 2004. 9780385730860. **J** **S**

Kak, a sixteen-year-old Canadian, lies about his age and enlists to fight with the RAF in World War II, where he flies bombing missions and ends up caring for the pigeons that carry important messages.

Subjects: Canadians; Europe; Pigeons; World War II

Levitin, Sonia.

Room in the Heart. 2003. 9780525468714. **J** **S**

Stories of many young and old Jews and Gentiles, and how the residents of Denmark tried to save as many Jews as possible during World War II.

Subjects: Denmark; Jews; Multiple Narratives; Nazis; Resistance; Sympathizers; World War II

Mankell, Henning.

Joel Gustafson duet. **M** **J**

In the 1950s, eleven-year-old Joel lives in northern Sweden with his father, who won't talk to him about his late mother

Subjects: Literary; Sweden

A Bridge to the Stars. 2007. 9780440240426.

Joel, obsessed with a dog he sees in the night, starts hanging out with Tore, and their pranks start becoming more serious.

Subjects: Dogs

Shadows in the Twilight. 2008. 9780385734967.

Joel, now almost twelve, is run over by a bus but emerges unscathed, so he decides to perform a good deed as thanks.

Morpurgo, Michael.

Private Peaceful. 2004. 9780439636483. **J** **S**

Tommo Peaceful goes off to World War I with his older brother Charlie, who has married Molly, Tommo's best friend. They leave behind their widowed mother and their developmentally disabled brother. Descriptive of life in the trenches and the unfair treatment of the soldiers at the hands of a sadistic sergeant, this story is told through flashbacks, as Tommo waits for dawn, checking the watch that belonged to Charlie. (BBYA)

Subjects: Brothers; Literary; World War I

War Horse. 2007. 9780439796637. **M**

World War I, told from the viewpoint of Joey, an English farm horse who is sold to the army, then captured by the Germans. Joey always yearns for Albert, the boy on the farm who was too young to join up when Joey first went to war. Like *Private Peaceful*, this book delivers a powerful antiwar message.

Subjects: Animal Protagonists; France; England; Germany; Horses; World War I

Napoli, Donna Jo.

Fire in the Hills. 2006. 9780525477518. **M**

Fourteen-year-old Roberto faces adventure and joins the Italian Resistance while trying to make his way home to Venice after escaping a Nazi prison camp. Sequel to *Stones in the Water*.

Subjects: Italy; Resistance; World War II

Peet, Mal.

Tamar: A Novel of Espionage, Passion, and Betrayal. 2007. 9780763634889. **S**

Tamar was given her name by her grandfather, who worked with the Resistance in Holland during World War II. After he dies, Tamar finds information that leads her back to the story of her namesake. (BBYA)

Subjects: Holland; Literary; Resistance; World War II

Sedgwick, Marcus.

The Foreshadowing. 2006. 9780385746465. **J S**

Seventeen-year-old Alexandra can see when someone is going to die, so when she has a premonition about her brother, who is fighting in the war, she signs up for the nursing corps to try to find and save him. (BBYA)

Subjects: Hospitals; Nurses; Seers; World War I

Sheth, Kashmira.

Keeping Corner. 2008. 9780786838592. **M J**

In 1918 twelve-year-old Leela is widowed before she ever lives with her husband. Now she must shave her head and spend a year confined to a "keeping corner" in the house to mourn him. Meanwhile India is changing, and Gandhi is working toward independence for the country. (BBYA, VOYA)

Subjects: Child Brides; India; Widows

Smith, Roland.

Elephant Run. 2007. 9781423104025. **M**

When the London bombings demolish their apartment, Nick Freestone's mother sends him to live with his father in Burma, but then the Japanese invade and his father is taken prisoner. Pressed into service for the Japanese,

Nick and Mya escape on elephant back, and set out to rescue their loved ones. (BBYA)

Subjects: Burma; Elephants; World War II

Spinelli, Jerry.

Milkweed. 2003. 9780375813740. **J** **S**

An orphan with a succession of names, in World War II Warsaw, Poland, scrounges for survival. (BBYA, IRA YAC)

Subjects: Warsaw, Poland; World War II

Venkatraman, Padma.

Climbing the Stairs. 2008. 9780399247460. **M** **J** **S**

After her father suffers brain damage in a riot that is part of the independence movement, fifteen-year old Vidya and her family must move in with conservative relatives in Bombay, who believe she should marry soon and not go to college. (BBYA)

Subjects: 1940s; Independence; India; World War II

Zusak, Markus.

The Book Thief. 2006. 9780375931000. **S**

The story of Liesel, a foster child living in Munich during World War II, is narrated by Death, who tells of Liesel's theft of books, her foster parents, and the Jewish man the family hides in their basement. (BBYA, Printz Honor, PP)

Books; Death; Foster Children; Germans; Jews; World War II

Ancient History

Readers who like stories set in the ancient world may also enjoy fantasy from the "Myth and Legend" section of chapter 7, as ancient civilizations are often the settings. Many fans of Rick Riordan's mythology-based <u>Percy Jackson and the Olympians</u> series are turning to fiction set in the ancient world.

Ford, Michael.

<u>Spartan Quest.</u> **M**

Lysander, who has grown up as a slave to the Spartans, finds out that his long-dead father was a Spartan and that his grandfather has wealth and influence.

Subjects: Greece; Slavery; Spartans

The Fire of Ares. 2008. 9780802797445.

Lysander, a young Helot slave, leaves the fields for training as a Spartan after his aristocratic grandfather discovers his existence and a pendant left to him by his father is stolen.

Birth of a Warrior. 2009. 9780747593874.

> Lysander and two other boys are sent to the mountains with only a goatskin flask to prove they can survive. When he sees an approaching Persian invasion, Lysander knows he must return to warn of the impending battle.

Legacy of Blood. 2009. 9780802798442

> With Taras under siege, Lysander and his barracks are sent to the remote Spartan outpost, where Lysander discovers a statue wearing The Fire of Ares.

Graham, Jo.

Black Ships. **2008. 9780316068000.** **S**

> At the fall of Troy, the women were taken as slaves, and one of them who was raped gave birth in slavery to a daughter she called Gull. When Gull is crippled in an accident, her mother takes her to Pythia, the oracle who lives in a cave and takes care of the last rites for the dead. Gull becomes Pythia's apprentice and successor, and when Pythia Who Was dies, Gull becomes Pythia, painting her face white and outlining her eyes in black. Then a ship arrives with refugees from her mother's homeland, and Pythia leaves with them to become the Sybil to the Trojan refugees led by Aeneas, who is searching for a new homeland for his people.

> **Subjects:** Adult Books for Teens; Aeneas; Oracles; Seers; Slavery; Trojans

Hand of Isis. **2009. 9780316068024.** **S**

> Three sisters, all daughters of Pharaoh Ptolemy Auletes, are born in the same year to different mothers. Charmain and Iras are the slaves and best friends of their half-sister Cleopatra, who will be queen.

> **Subjects:** Adult Books for Teens; Cleopatra; Egypt; Reincarnation; Rome; Slavery

Lawrence, Caroline.

The Roman Mysteries. **M**

> Flavia Gemima, a Roman sea captain's daughter, and her friends Lupus, Jonathan, and Nubia, find and solve mysteries in several locations in the ancient world, including Ostia, North Africa, Pompeii, Rome, Greece, Turkey, and Egypt.

The Thieves of Ostia. 2002. 9780761315827.

> Twelve-year-old Flavia finds three new friends, Lupus, Jonathan, and Nubia, when she sets out to solve the mystery of why dogs on her street have been slain.

The Secrets of Vesuvius. 2002. 9780761315834.

> When the four sleuths visit Flavia's uncle on a farm near Pompeii, they meet a blacksmith who may help them solve a riddle and find they must escape from the eruption of Mount Vesuvius.

The Pirates of Pompeii. 2003. 9781842550229.

> Living in a refugee camp following the volcanic eruption of Mount Vesuvius, the four sleuths take on a case involving missing children.

The Assassins of Rome. 2002. 9780761319405.

> Jonathan learns that his mother, who he thought had died in the siege of Jerusalem, may actually have been taken as a slave, when his uncle arrives on a mission to warn the emperor of an assassination plot.

The Dolphins of Laurentum. 2003. 9781842550243.

> After Flavia's father's ship is sunk and creditors come demanding their money, the foursome decide to retrieve the treasure from a sunken ship.

The Twelve Tasks of Flavia Gemina. 2004. 9781842550250.

> Flavia is unhappy when her father starts a relationship with a new woman in town and starts looking for a husband for Flavia.

The Enemies of Jupiter. 2005. 9781596430488.

> Flavia, Jonathan, Lupus, and Nubia are summoned to Rome by Emperor Titus to try to find the cause of a plague.

The Gladiators from Capua. 2005. 9781596430747.

> Flavia, Nubia, and Lupus wrangle an invitation to the opening of the Coliseum in the hope they will find their fears for Jonathan unfounded.

The Colossus of Rhodes. 2006. 9781596430822.

> As Lupus searches for his mother, the friends set out for Rhodes, home of one of the seven wonders of the world.

The Fugitive from Corinth. 2006. 9781842555156.

> The companions are off to Greece on a case involving their tutor and a stabbing.

The Sirens of Surrentum. 2007. 9781842555064.

> When the four friends visit a luxurious villa in Surrentum, they find themselves on the trail of a poisoner.

The Charioteer of Delphi. 2007. 9781596430853.

> A missing racehorse draws Nubia into a mystery while the companions are in Rome celebrating the Festival of Jupiter.

The Slave Girl from Jerusalem. 2009. 9781842555729.

> A slave girl is accused of a triple murder, and it is up to the four friends to get to the bottom of the mystery.

The Beggar of Volubilis. 2009. 9781842556047.

> The Emperor Titus sends the four companions on a quest that takes them across northern Africa to find a gem called Nero's Eye.

The Scribes from Alexandria. 2010. 9781842556054.

> The four are shipwrecked near the coast of Alexandria.

Williams, Susan.

Wind Rider. 2006. 9780060872373. **M** **J**

Fern, living on the Asian steppes over 6,000 years ago, finds a trapped wild foal. She keeps it secret because her people eat wild horses. Thunder's life is saved when her existence is discovered, because Fern has trained her to be ridden and to carry far more than a human could.

Subjects: Horses; Prehistoric; Steppes

Biblical

Historical fiction set in biblical times brings an element of familiarity to readers.

Fletcher, Susan.

Alphabet of Dreams. 2006. 9780689850424. **M** **J**

Mitra, disguised as a boy, and her brother Babak, who has prophetic talents, are taken in by Melchoir, a magus who is leaving Persia on a journey to Bethlehem because of the signs he has seen in the stars.

Subjects: Bethlehem; Journeys; Magi; Persia; Psionic Abilities

McCaughrean, Geraldine.

Not the End of the World. 2005. 9780060760304. **J** **S**

This story of Noah's ark is told from the viewpoint of a couple of young stowaways smuggled aboard by Noah's daughter.

Subjects: Arks; Floods; Noah; Stowaways

Myers, Walter Dean. Illustrated by Christopher Myers.

A Time to Love: Stories from the Old Testament. 2003. 9780439220002. **J** **S**

Six biblical stories are retold with teen characters as the narrators.

Subjects: Religion; Short Stories

Provoost, Anne. Translated by John Nieuwenhuizen.

In the Shadow of the Ark. 2004. 9780439442343. **O**

Re Jana's family left the marshes, to the derision of their neighbors, who thought them foolish to go to the desert in search of a city springing up around the building of a huge ship. While her father finds employment as foreman for the Builder's youngest son, Ham, who is in charge of the woodworking facets of the project, Re Jana finds a hidden well of pure water and massages and grooms the Builder's sons. She also discovers that the enormous ark they are building will not save all from the coming devastation of the world promised by the Builder's god.

Subjects: Arks; Floods; Noah; Racism

Di's Picks

Draper, Sharon. *Copper Sun.*

Meyer, L. A. *Bloody Jack.*

Sharenow, Robert. *My Mother the Cheerleader.*

Zusak, Markus. *The Book Thief.*

Chapter 4

Adventure/Thrillers

I read thrillers because my life is not suspenseful enough for my liking.
—Brooke, age 15

Elements of adventure can be found in many of the teen genres, but the books in this chapter focus on it. Readers who enjoy adventure may also enjoy science fiction and paranormal books. Adventure involves danger and often page-turning action.

Action Adventure

This type of adventure, which could also be identified as "thriller," is often described as the type that makes a good movie. The pacing is fast and furious and the plots are often outlandish. The protagonists are larger than life; sometimes they are criminals. Artifacts and ancient cultures often play a role.

Cole, Stephen.

Thieves. J S

Fast-paced action and James Bond–like gadgets abound in this series that features a team of teens working under the direction of Nathaniel Colhardt to steal ancient artifacts.

Subjects: Gadgets; Geniuses; Teams; Thieves

Thieves Like Us. 2006. 9781599900414.

When Jonah Wish, age seventeen, is taken out of a juvenile correctional facility in the dark of night, he finds he has now become a member of a gang of thieves who need his special computer abilities in their globe-spanning capers.

Thieves Till We Die. 2007. 9781599900827.

On the trail of the Sword of Cortes, Tye, part of a teenage gang of thieves, is kidnapped by murderous worshipers of the goddess Coatlicue, as the teen geniuses turned outlaws find an ancient Aztec temple and an apocalyptic cult. (PP)

Subjects: Aztecs

Docherty, Jimmy.

The Ice Cream Con. 2008. 9780545028851. **M**

After Jake, a twelve-year-old living in the Glasgow housing projects, is mugged for the last 20 quid his gran and he have to their names, he decides something must be done. He contacts the local mob boss for help, but after discovering he isn't going to get any help on that front, he creates a new mob boss and runs a big con of his own. Jake's con involves inflatable sumo suits, diamonds, an ice cream truck, and scads of violence.

Subjects: Humorous; Organized Crime; Scotland

Gilman, David.

The Devil's Breath. 2008. 9780385735605. **M**

After escaping an assassin and being told his dad is dead, fifteen-year-old Max Gordon leaves his British boarding school and heads to Namibia, Africa, where he uncovers a plot that could kill multitudes.

Subjects: Assassins; Ecology; Namibia

Johnson, Maureen.

Girl at Sea. 2007. 9780060541453. **J** **S**

Seventeen-year-old Clio has her summer all planned out. She is going to work with her art store crush. But those plans come crashing down when she is sent to Europe to stay with her dad. Upon arriving she discovers that he now has a yacht, and that she is going to be spending the summer on it sailing the Mediterranean in search of treasure along with her dad's best friend; her dad's girlfriend, who is an academic researcher; the girlfriend's daughter; and a hunky assistant. (PP)

Subjects: Mediterranean; Pirates; Romance; Yachts

Miller, Kirsten.

Kiki Strike. **M** **J**

After a mysterious very tiny girl named Kiki Strike shows up, a group of girls from an elite New York school who call themselves "the Irregulars" embark on an eventful adventure involving the city under the city, lost treasure, rats, and explosions.

Subjects: New York; Private Schools; Underground Cities

Kiki Strike: Inside the Shadow City. 2006. 9781582349602.

When twelve-year-old Anaka Fishbein discovers a sinkhole and meets the diminutive but mighty Kiki Strike, a friendship forms and soon extends to a group of talented and adventurous girls who explore the shadow city under New York. There they find treasure and a defense against marauding rats, and solve a kidnapping, in this quirky and unusual novel. (BBYA, PP)

Subjects: Inventions; Kidnappings; Rats

The Empress's Tomb. 2007. 9781599900476.

Kiki Strike and the Irregulars, now fourteen years old, encounter new dangers. Oona's father decides to change his criminal ways, and the Irregulars don't believe him. In this adventure they deal with art theft, smugglers, the mummy of a Chinese empress, illegal immigrants, Russian criminals, a haunted mansion, and angry squirrels.

Subjects: Art Theft; Gadgets; Kidnappings; Museums

Smith, Alexander Gordon.

Furnace series. 🇯 🇭

Furnace is a prison built a mile under the surface of the earth, where teens sentenced to life at hard labor face monstrous guards, horrifying torture, and nasty food.

Lockdown: Escape from Furnace. 2009. 9780374324919.

Framed for killing his best friend, fourteen-year-old Alex Sawyer is determined to escape from the supposedly inescapable prison called Furnace. (Quick Picks)

Furnace: Solitary. 2010. 9780374324926.

Despite being in solitary confinement, Alex and Zee, in separate vaults in the floor of one of the tunnels a mile underground in Furnace, an "escape-proof" prison, manage to communicate with each other. In concert with a group of escapees who are still marooned in the network of tunnels where horrific surgical procedures are taking place, they try to find a way to get completely out of Furnace.

Varrato, Tony.

Fakie. 2008. 9781897073797. 🇯 🇸

Fifteen-year-old Alex and his mother have been on the run in the Witness Relocation Program for a long time, and they've managed to stay alive by being ready to move on to a new place and identity without notice. This time Alex has decided to switch from football player to skateboarder with the move, but he finds that his new acquaintances are becoming friends, which puts them at risk. (Quick Picks)

Subjects: Skateboarding; Witness Protection

Wasserman, Robin.

Chasing Yesterday. 🇲

Waking up in a hospital with no memories, thirteen-year-old JD (Jane Doe) tries to find out who she really is.

Subjects: Amnesia; Psionic Powers

The Awakening. 2007. 9780439933384.

After an explosion, thirteen-year-old JD, or Jane Doe, wakes up in a hospital with no memory of who she is. After she physically recovers, she is sent to a large group home, where she becomes friends with Daniel, another outcast. Her face is splashed all over the news, and a woman claims JD is her daughter Alexa. Something just doesn't seem right, especially after her mother starts taking her to a psychiatrist who seems hauntingly familiar. Bedeviled by nightmares and strange waking dreams, JD contacts Daniel and discovers that nothing is as it seems. This is actually one novel published in three short volumes. None of the books stand alone, and they should be read one right after the other. (Quick Picks)

Betrayal. 2007. 9780439933414.

JD goes on the run with Daniel but can't completely escape the memories implanted in her brain by Dr. Styron. Are they real or not? Will she ever find out who she really is?

Truth. 2007. 9780439933421.

Realizing her powers are too dangerous for her to control, JD decides to return to the Institute, knowing she may never come out again. There she finds more people like her. When Daniel shows up she realizes that she is actually a weapon and must escape those who want to use her.

Survival Stories

Teens fighting for their lives are the common thread in survival stories, whether their peril is freezing cold, natural disasters, harsh terrain, or deadly predators. The protagonists in these stories are characterized by perseverance and ingenuity, especially when facing danger as they fight their fears.

Doyle, Roddy.

Wilderness. 2007. 9780439023566. **M** **J**

When Irish brothers, Johnny, age twelve, and Tom, age ten, lose their mother while on a dogsledding tour in Finland, they try to find and rescue her and face many dangers. Meanwhile, back home in Dublin, their eighteen-year-old half-sister must face her own long-absent mother.

Subjects: Dogs; Dogsledding; Dublin, Ireland; Finland; Literary; Parallel Narratives

Hobbs, Will.

Crossing the Wire. 2006. 9780060741389. **J** **S**

Fifteen-year-old Victor Flores starts on a perilous journey to El Norte, where he hopes he can make enough money to keep his family alive after his tiny corn-farming enterprise is put out of business by cheap imports. Along the way he is almost deported to Guatemala, meets a man almost crippled by vigilantes, and falls into a drug-smuggling scheme.

Subjects: Drug Smuggling; Immigrants; Mexico; Undocumented Immigrants

McCaughrean, Geraldine.

The White Darkness. 2007. 9780060890353. **J** **S**

When her deranged Uncle Victor takes her along on his quest to make it to the South Pole, fourteen-year-old Sym fights for survival on the ice. Sym's life-saving mentor is the voice of Captain Laurence Titus Oates, of Robert Scott's ill-fated, historical expedition. (BBYA, Printz Award)

Subjects: Antarctica; Bereavement; South Pole

McNamee, Graham.

Bonechiller. 2008. 9780385746588.

On his way home from a disturbing night out with three other teens from the tiny town of Harvest Cove in the big empty spaces in Canada, Danny is attacked and stung by a horrifying creature, who then invades his dreams. As he and his friends, including an Ojibwa girl boxer, investigate, they discover that the beast has been preying on teens in their area for centuries; and they devise a plan to take it out. Though the danger faced may be paranormal, the focus of this tale is on the adventure elements. (BBYA, IRA YAC)

Subjects: Canada; Caves; Explosions; Folklore; Mythic Creatures; Ojibwas

Morpurgo, Michael.

Kensuke's Kingdom. 2007. 9780439382021. **M**

When eleven-year-old Michael and his dog are swept overboard, off the yacht his British family has been living on since his father lost his job, they wash up on a seemingly deserted jungle island. A Japanese doctor who has been marooned there for forty years, since World War II, becomes Michael's mentor, teaching him much more than survival skills.

Subjects: 1980s; British; Castaways; Dogs; Islands; Japanese

Salisbury, Graham.

Night of the Howling Dogs. 2007. 9780385901468. **M** **J**

In this tale based on a true story, Dylan's Boy Scout troop goes to a remote part of an island for a camp out. When an earthquake rocks the night, followed by a huge wave, Dylan, an eighth grader, must team up with Louie, with whom he shares a mutual dislike, to help rescue their fellow campers and find help for their injured leader.

Subjects: Boy Scouts; Camping; Earthquakes; Hawaii; Tsunamis

Smith, Roland.

Peak. 2007. 9780152024178. **M** **J** **S**

Peak Marcello, age fourteen, the son of a famous mountain climber, finds himself on an expedition to climb Everest after he is busted in New York for climbing and tagging skyscrapers. About to spend the rest of his teen years in juvie, he is rescued by the dad he never sees, who runs a climbing business in Tibet and wants the publicity of his son being the first teen to ascend Everest. (BBYA, Quick Picks, IRA YAC)

Subjects: Everest; Mountain Climbing; Sherpas; Tibet

Trueman, Terry.

Hurricane. 2008. 9780060000196. **M**

When Hurricane Mitch strikes Honduras, thirteen-year-old José is in one of only two structures that are not buried by the horrific mudslide during the storm. With his father and older siblings away from home, it is up to Jose to ensure the survival of his remaining family and help the villagers dig through the wreckage and mud for supplies, as well as the bodies of those killed in the storm.

Subjects: Honduras; Hurricanes; Mudslides; Siblings

Tullson, Diane.

The Darwin Expedition. 2007. 9781551436760. **J S**

High school seniors Tej and Liam don't want to miss any hours of snowboarding at Whistler, so when the highway is closed due to a wreck, they take a back country logging road and end up rolling Tej's truck. As they try to hike out, they encounter a couple of grizzly bears, a deadly scree slope, and many other dangers. (Quick Picks)

Subjects: Accidents; Bears; High-Low; Snowboarders

Red Sea. 2005. 9781551433318. **J S**

Fourteen-year-old Libby's passive/aggressive behavior causes her family to be late setting out for a year-long sail and leaves them alone to try to catch up with the flotilla. Then contemporary pirates attack, a storm hits, her stepfather is killed, and her mother is gravely injured. It is up to Libby to sail for help. (BBYA)

Subjects: Pirates; Sailing

Volponi, Paul.

Hurricane Song. 2008. 9780670061600. **J S**

High school sophomore Miles Shaw moved to New Orleans to live with his jazz musician father just before Hurricane Katrina. When his uncle's car becomes stranded during the evacuation, they head to the Superdome, where food, water, and sanitation are lacking and they have to deal with abusive soldiers and dangers from marauding gangs. (PP)

Subjects: Fathers and Sons; Hurricanes; Jazz; Katrina; New Orleans

Espionage and Terrorism

Teenage spies dealing with terrorist threats may seem like a preposterous proposition, but they are vital components of a growing subgenre of adventure. The Alex Rider series by Anthony Horowitz was at the forefront of this trend when *Stormbreaker* was published in 2001 and continues to be popular, now even published in graphic novel format. Most of the books in this section feature teens who are recruited to perform as spies, but some also feature protagonists who have run afoul of terrorists or intelligence agencies.

Bloor, Edward.

Taken. 2007. 9780375836367. **M** **J**

Less than thirty years from now, the division between rich and poor has grown. Charity Meyers, the daughter of an inventor and stepdaughter of a media celebrity, lives in the Highlands, a gated community in Florida. Her school consists of a small classroom filled with other rich kids, who are virtual students of an exclusive New York prep school. Every rich kid is taught early on what to do if kidnapped. Now Charity must use that knowledge. Though this is set in the near future, the emphasis is on political intrigue.

Subjects: Celebrities; Florida; Future; Kidnapping; Virtual Learning

Greenland, Shannon.

The Specialists. **M** **J**

A secret government agency recruits teens to work undercover as models while trying to fulfill their covert missions.

Model Spy. 2007. 9780142408490.

Sixteen-year-old Kelly hacks into a top secret government computer and is caught. She ends up becoming a spy with the code name GiGi, for girl genius. (PP)

Down to the Wire. 2007. 9780142409176.

Frankie, a teen who can penetrate almost any security system, is nicknamed Wirenut, and sent on a mission to recover some stolen neurotoxin.

The Winning Element. 2008. 9780142410523.

Going undercover at a cheerleading competition, sixteen-year-old GiGi teams up with chemistry expert Beaker to stop the smuggler who killed her parents.

Native Tongue. 2008. 9780142411605.

GiGi, and Parrot are off to South America, where language expert Parrot's skills are needed to settle a dispute over ownership of an ancient artifact. GiGi is asked to decode some ancient hieroglyphics that should reveal the true owners.

Fight to the Finish. 2009. No ISBN.

In the conclusion to the series, GiGi, Bruiser, and Mystic jump into the fray when someone close to TJ is taken. The book is not available in print, but a free download of the text is available at www.shannongreenland.com/fight.php.

Horowitz, Anthony.

Alex Rider series. M J S

Alex Rider goes from fourteen-year-old schoolboy to superspy after his guardian is killed under mysterious circumstances and he is forced to join the secret spy organization MI6. Alex Rider can be though of as a teenage James Bond, battling to stop megalomaniacs set on world domination. This series is so successful that it has been adapted to film and graphic novel formats.

Subjects: Espionage; Gadgets

Stormbreaker. 2001. 9780399236204.

> In his first mission Alex, age fourteen, after discovering his uncle was a secret agent, takes on the job himself and must stop a diabolical scheme targeting Britain's schoolchildren with free computers that are scheduled to unleash a horror that will kill an entire generation. (Quick Picks, PP)

Point Blank. 2002. 9780399236211

> Alex is sent off to the French Alps to find out what is happening in an exclusive boarding school, where bad boy sons of the wealthy are sent and become surprisingly docile.

Skeleton Key. 2003. 9780399237775.

> Whisked away from Wimbledon, fourteen-year-old British secret agent Alex ends up in Cuba, where he must stop a general armed with a nuclear bomb who wants to reinstate the Soviet Union. (Quick Picks)

Eagle Strike. 2003. 9780399239793.

> A vacation with his girlfriend's family in the south of France ends when fourteen-year-old Alex, a reluctant member of the British intelligence agency MI6, spots an assassin, has to survive a real-life computer game, and has to stop an insane rock star who is willing to annihilate anyone in his quest to rid the world of drugs. (BBYA, Quick Picks)

Scorpia. 2006. 9780399241512.

> While trying to decide which side of good or evil his late father was operating on, fourteen-year-old Alex infiltrates Scorpia, a secret organization that is planning to destroy the relationship between Britain and the United States by killing off all twelve- and thirteen-year-old British children. (Quick Picks)

Ark Angel. 2007. 9780399241529.

> Recuperating from a gunshot wound, Alex stymies a kidnapping of a fellow patient, the son of a rich hotelier targeted by eco-terrorists who want to stop him from building a luxury hotel in space.

Snakehead. 2007. 9780399241611.

> After crash landing off the coast of Australia, Alex is recruited to help stop a band of smugglers while still trying to uncover his parents' secrets. (VOYA)

Jinks, Catherine.

Evil Genius. 🇯 🇸

Expert hacker Cadel Piggott, age ten, is taken by his adopted parents to see a therapist, who manipulates his skills for evil purposes.

Subjects: Australia; Geniuses; Hackers

Evil Genius. 2007. 9780152059880.

Young Cadel Piggott, a child genius who has been banned from using computers due to his expert hacking, is taken to see Dr. Thaddeus Roth, who turns out not to really be a therapist helping him with his problems, but rather a minion of Cadel's evil genius biological father, who has a diabolical plan for Cadel. (PP)

Genius Squad. 2008. 9780152059859.

Now fifteen, Cadel leaves the Sydney foster home where he is living for a group home of geeks who are trying to stop an evil genetic engineering corporation.

Subjects: Genetic Engineering; Sydney, Australia

Korman, Gordon.

On the Run series. 🇲

Fifteen-year-old Aiden and eleven-year-old Meg Falconer escape from a juvenile correctional facility to try to clear their parents, who are facing life in prison after being framed for treason.

Chasing the Falconers. 2005. 9780439651363.

Aiden and his sister Meg escape from a juvenile correctional facility and are followed not only by the law, but also by an evil assassin.

The Fugitive Factor. 2005. 9780439651370.

As Aiden and his sister Meg try to exonerate their parents, they find they can't even trust old family friends when both the FBI and an assassin are pursuing them.

Now You See Them, Now You Don't. 2005. 9780439651387.

Still trying to find Frank Lindenauer, who can clear their parents, Meg and Aiden head for California, where they team up with one gang leader, only to add a gang member to the growing number of people trying to hunt them down.

The Stowaway Solution. 2005. 9780439651394.

Still hunting for Frank Lindenauer, Aiden and Meg end up leaving Los Angeles by stowing away on a ship, which thrusts them into even more danger.

Public Enemies. 2005. 9780439651400.

Hairless Joe, the assassin who has been chasing them through their adventures, gets closer to Meg and Aiden as they crisscross the nation trying to find a man who may have the information they need to clear their parents of a treason conviction.

Hunting the Hunter. 2006. 9780439651417.

Aiden and Meg decide to turn the tables on assassin Hairless Joe, who has been following them across the country. They decide to capture him and make him divulge the information that will free their wrongfully convicted parents.

Kidnapped. M

Aiden and Meg, the brother and sister from the On the Run series, live a normal life for too short a time after clearing their parents, because Meg is kidnapped.

Abduction. 2006. 9780439847773.

On their way home from school one day, eleven-year-old Meg is kidnapped, so fifteen-year-old Aiden must team up with his former nemesis, the FBI, in an attempt to get her back. Meanwhile, ever-resourceful Meg attempts to extricate herself.

The Search. 2006. 9780439847780.

With the new FBI agent assigned to their family refusing to search for Meg, Aiden realizes he has to assume a friend's identity to follow the clues Meg is leaving in her wake as the kidnappers take her across the country.

The Rescue. 2006. 9780439847797.

Meg escapes from her kidnappers just as Aiden is about to rescue her, and now she has to face the dangers of trying to survive a blizzard in the mountains of western Virginia while staying clear of her former captors and trying to link up with Aiden.

Marsden, John.

The Ellie Chronicles. J S

In the Tomorrow series, Ellie survived a war that saw contemporary life in Australia totally changed after an invading force conquered most of the continent. The war may be over, but life will never be the same for teenager Ellie and the other kids who survived in the Tomorrow series as they face a new slew of problems in an Australia divided.

Subjects: Australia; Deaf Characters; Terrorists

While I Live. 2007. 9780439783231.

With the war over, sixteen-year-old Ellie Linton is glad to be back at home on the farm with her parents and Gavin, her adopted deaf brother, but after all she did and saw as a guerrilla fighter in the war, adapting to civilian life is a challenge. After her parents are killed by people coming over the new border, Ellie faces new battles as she tries to run the farm and keep from losing it to the bank.

Incurable. 2008. 9780439783224.

As the border clashes worsen, Ellie tries to keep Gavin safe and find out who among those she knows is involved with the underground Liberation Front movement.

Circle of Flight. 2009. 9780439783217.

In the concluding volume of the series, Ellie faces down her enemies once again and comes to discover more about herself and the unnamed invaders who have changed her life.

McNab, Andy, and Robert Rigby.

Danny Watts series. **J S M**

Seventeen-year-old orphan Danny Watts want to join the military, but he is refused on the grounds that his grandfather was a traitor.

Traitor. 2005. 9780399244643.

When Danny Watts is refused for British military service on the grounds that his grandfather, Fergus, was a traitor, he enlists the help of his friend Elena, a computer whiz. He hunts down Fergus and discovers he is innocent, but now someone is after all three of them, and Fergus is abducted. (PP)

Payback. 2006. 9780399244650.

Danny and his grandfather Fergus leave Spain after spending six months there when British agents hunt them down. Danny, home in London and reunited with his girlfriend Elena, a computer wiz, comes under suspicion as a terrorist when suicide bombers start attacking London sites.

Avenger. 2007. 9780399246852.

Having fulfilled a personal mission, Danny and Elena are recruited by the British government. Elena goes undercover as a suicide bomber, pretending to buy into master hacker Black Star's big plan, and is sent to New York with Danny and Fergus secretly backing her up. (Quick Picks)

Meltdown. 2008. 9780399246869.

In Danny and Fergus's concluding adventure, they infiltrate a drug ring to keep terrorists from using a new drug called Meltdown as the next weapon of mass destruction.

Walden, Mark.

H.I.V.E. **M J**

Because of his inherent evil genius proclivities, thirteen-year-old orphan Otto Malpense is kidnapped and taken to a secret academy, where super villains are trained with the goal of world domination. He befriends Wing Fanchu, a martial arts expert; Laura Brand, an electronics expert; and Shelby Trinity, a talented jewel thief. They all have been brought to H.I.V.E. because of their potential as villains.

Subjects: Islands; Schools; Volcanoes

H.I.V.E.: Higher Institute of Villainous Education. 2007. 9781416935711.

Otto, Wing, Laura, and Shelby become friends when they are all abducted and taken to a secret school that has the objective of turning the offspring of super villains and promising orphans who look like they have the abilities to be master bad guys into the next generation of super villains. The academy is hidden in a volcano from which escape seems unlikely if not impossible, but Otto, Wing, Laura, and Shelby are willing to give escape a try. (PP)

H.I.V.E.: The Overlord Protocol. 2008. 9781416935735.

When word comes that Wing's father has been killed, Otto, now fourteen, accompanies him to Japan for the funeral, but along the way they are attacked by ninjas who seem impervious to injury. During their escape Otto and Wing uncover a plot by a nefarious villain who is set on annihilating H.I.V.E. using an evil artificial intelligence.

Yancey, Rick.

Alfred Kropp. Ⓜ Ⓙ Ⓢ

Alfred Kropp, age fifteen, is "an over-sized kid whose hobby happens to be riding to the world's rescue," and who is "the only hero ever born who saves the day by screwing up." He is roped into world-saving adventures by the agents of OIPEP (Office of Interdimensional Paradoxes and Extraordinary Phenomena), and he wields the famous sword Excalibur.

The Extraordinary Adventures of Alfred Kropp. 2005. 9781599900445.

After his mother dies, Alfred Kropp is living with his uncle, a night watchman in an office building, who agrees to steal something from an executive's office in exchange for a million dollars. Roped into the scheme, Alfred finds the legendary sword Excalibur and unwittingly turns it over to the forces of evil. (PP)

Alfred Kropp: The Seal of Solomon. 2007. 9781599900452.

When Alfred Kropp, the last descendant of Lancelot, is informed that he has just inherited a fortune, and finds out that his weasel of a foster father wants to adopt him, he plans an escape. But before it can happen, rogue OIPEP agent Mike Arnold kidnaps him. Mike has also stolen the two Seals of Solomon from OIPEP, one a ring that belonged to King Solomon and the other a sacred vessel that has kept the millions of demons, the fallen angels who joined Lucifer, contained for thousands of years. Alfred's blood may be the only salvation for the world.

Alfred Kropp: The Thirteenth Skull. 2008. 9781599903637.

As Alfred questions his safety with OIPEP, he becomes involved with a new mystery, as he searches for the connection between Sofia and elusive Thirteenth Skull. After surviving death, Alfred's blood can now be used as a cure, which makes him, the last descendant of Lancelot, a more enticing prize than ever.

Young, E. L.

STORM. **M** **J**

Andrew, a fourteen-year-old software millionaire, teams up with Will, a gadget inventor, and Gaia, a chemistry and language whiz, to start a secret organization called Science and Technology to Over-Rule Misery (STORM).

Subjects: Chemists; Gadgets; Geniuses; Inventors

The Infinity Code. 2008. 9780803732650.

After his father dies and his mother drops him off with a friend, fourteen-year-old Will, a gifted inventor, is recruited by Gaia, whose chemistry expertise makes her great at explosives, to become a member of STORM, a secret organization founded by Andrew.

The Ghost Machine. 2008. 9780803732674.

The STORM trio of fourteen-year-old geniuses is off to Venice, where a string of burglaries appear to involve an actual ghost. With their expertise they discover that much more is going on and the burglaries involve technology rather than the paranormal.

The Black Sphere. 2009. 9780803732681.

With five of the world's leading scientists killed and the sixth on the run, the STORM crew is trying to find him before a maniac can get the world-changing technology he is carrying.

War Stories

Stories of war often involve action, survival, and espionage, as well as battles. This type of adventure novel tends to be more serious than many of the other types. Often they feature authentic historical detail. Readers who enjoy war stories will find additional war stories in chapter 3 and by checking "war" in the subject index.

Durbin, William.

The Winter War. 2008. 9780385746526. **M** **J**

When Finland is invaded by the Russians in 1939, Marko, age fourteen, who refuses to allow his polio-crippled leg to stop him, helps the war effort by skiing through the woods to deliver messages and participating in other guerrilla actions against the Russians.

Subjects: Finland; Historical Fiction; Resistance; Skiing; World War II

Myers, Walter Dean.

Sunrise Over Fallujah. 2008. 9780439916240. **J** **S**

In the wake of 9/11, eighteen-year-old Robin Perry decides to forgo college to enlist in the army. He ends up experiencing war in Iraq in the Civil Affairs unit, a diverse unit made up of men and women of various races and backgrounds. Through his experiences Robin comes to understand why his

Uncle Richie, the protagonist in Myers's classic *Fallen Angels*, does not talk about war.

Subjects: African Americans; Iraq

Rosoff, Meg.

how i live now. **2004. 9780553376050.** [S]

When Daisy goes from contemporary Manhattan where her father and step-mother want be rid of her to visit her aunt and cousins in England, she has no idea that terrorist will attack while her aunt is away at a peace conference, that war will break out, and that she will have to fight for survival in an occupied land. (BBYA, Printz Award)

Subjects: Cousins; Farms; Romance; Survival

Stratton, Allan.

Chanda's Wars. **2008. 9780060872625.** [S]

In a fictional sub-Saharan African country, the events orphaned Chanda faces echo true life, as she takes her younger siblings to reconcile with relatives, only to find out that they have arranged a marriage for her that she does not want. When war in a neighboring country explodes over the border, it is up to Chanda to rescue Soly and Iris, who have been stolen to be child soldiers.

Subjects: Africa; Child Soldiers

Di's Picks

Hobbs, Will. *Crossing the Wire.*

Miller, Kirsten. *Kiki Strike.*

Smith, Roland. *Peak.*

Varrato, Tony. *Fakie.*

Chapter 5

Paranormal and Horror

I LOVE vampire books. I love the whole vamp/human love stuff and I just love everything about vamps. I guess I just like bloodsucking weirdos!!!—Shelby, age 12

Scary stories have long been popular with teen readers, but Stephenie Meyer's <u>Twilight</u> saga has turned tales of vampires and werewolves into a publishing phenomenon. In 2008 Meyer was named one of the 100 most influential people in the world and United States, and the release of the movie based on *Twilight* had some fans waiting in line for days to be the first to see it. But the <u>Twilight</u> series is just the tip of the iceberg when it comes to paranormal and horror literature.

Horror, though often having paranormal elements, focuses on the scary or horrifying. The paranormal beings are often malevolent; and its purpose is to frighten. One of the appeals of the genre is that the stories engender fear or uneasiness in the reader. In contrast, though paranormal often shares many of the same creatures found in horror, in these stories the vampires, werewolves, and demons are often romantic heroes, humorous characters, or just misunderstood ordinary paranormals. Whether a story falls more into the horror arena or the paranormal camp is largely up to the individual reader. One reader's romantic tortured hero may be another reader's threatening and horrific bloodsucker. Often readers who like the horrific vampire stories also enjoy the romantic or funny ones. Some readers just can't get enough of the fanged ones.

While fangs and fur or vampires and werewolves come immediately to mind when thinking of the paranormal, the genre has grown to encompass everything from mythological creatures to superheroes. Paranormal powers also figure in making rather ordinary people, who find they have telepathic powers, telekinetic abilities, or other unusual quirks, part of this genre. As the genre grows, writers extend its reach (as in paranormal fiction written for adults), encompassing many types of paranormal beings and abilities.

This chapter is organized topically according to popular areas of reading interest. Because readers of this genre tend to identify the books they like by the type of paranormal creature that is featured, the two types of stories—horror and paranormal—are integrated into thematic lists. Reading the annotations may help you (or your reader) determine whether a particular book is "scary enough" or "too scary."

Occult

Novels of the occult deal with the unknown and usually have a spooky feel and feature a sense of foreboding. Horror predominates in this area.

Fahy, Thomas.

The Unspoken. 2008. 9781416940074. **J** **S**

In this creepy horror story, six kids who were the survivors of a cult that went up in flames meet again as teens at the funeral of one of them. The cult leader had promised them that they would all die in five years from what they fear most, and now the time has arrived.

Subjects: Cults; Drownings; Orphans

Gantos, Jack.

The Love Curse of the Rumbaughs. 2006. 9780374336905. **S**

In this horrifying and darkly gothic tale, when sixteen-year-old Ivy finds out that her father is one of the aged Rumbaugh twins, the septuagenarian pharmacists who share an obsessive love for their taxidermy hobby and their mother, she also discovers that there is an inherited curse that links them to their mother and her to her mother. (BBYA)

Subjects: Albinos; Genetic Engineering; Taxidermy; Twins

Golden, Christopher.

The Boys Are Back in Town. 2004. 9780553586152. **O**

Will James is pretty satisfied with his life. Having remained friends with his old high school buddies, he sees no real reason to return to his old hometown for the ten-year high school reunion, but he ends up going anyway. His old home looks radically different, morphed by the current owners into an ugly house devoid of the rampant greenery that Will remembers. Then, at a reunion function, he begins to realize that his memories don't jive with the current reality. A week previously he made plans with old bud Mike Lebo to meet away from the reunion, but now he is told, and memories start falling into place that let him know, that Lebo was killed just before homecoming their senior year. His best friend Ashleigh also undergoes a terrifying change in his memories, from the confident lawyer and mother of twins to an embittered and hardened childless woman. Something is changing the fabric of history, and now Will must go back in time to stop terrible things from happening.

Subjects: Adult Books for Teens; Revenge; Time Travel

Poison Ink. 2008. 9780385734837. **O**

High school junior Sammi and her four best friends decide to get matching tattoos to always remember their solidarity, but when Sammi backs out, her friends turn on her. She must go to extreme lengths to save them all after their tattoos seem to take over their lives. (Quick Picks)

Subjects: Friends; Possession; Tattoos

Horowitz, Anthony.

The Gatekeepers. **M** **J**

Foster child Matt Freeman, age fourteen, discovers that devil worshipers are trying to bring back evil beings who had been banished long ago by five children, and that he may have the unique talents to stop them as one of five Gatekeepers who have been prophesied.

Subjects: Adventure; England; Portals; Witchcraft

Raven's Gate. 2005. 9780439679954.

Fourteen-year-old Matt is sent to live with old Mrs. Deverill in the small village Lesser Malling as punishment for a crime he did not commit. There he discovers sinister forces at work and finds out that he may be intended as a blood sacrifice to open Raven's Gate, a portal to evil. (Quick Picks, PP)

Evil Star. 2006. 9780439679961.

Matt travels to Peru with journalist Richard, because a second gate to evil may be on the verge of opening. There he meets Pedro, another Gatekeeper.

Subjects: Peru

Nightrise. 2007. 9780439680011.

Orphaned identical twins Jamie and Scott have a psychic bond that becomes essential to their survival after Scott is kidnapped by the evil Nightrise Corporation, and Jamie must travel back into the past.

Subjects: Native Americans; Time Travel; Twins

Necropolis. 2009. 9780439680035.

Puddles turn to blood in Necropolis, the onetime city of Hong Kong, where Matt, Richard, Jamie, and Scott go to find Scarlett, the fifth Gatekeeper and the only female in their quintet.

Subjects: Adoption; China; Hong Kong, Indonesians

Nance, Andrew.

Daemon Hall. 2007. 9780805081718. **J** **S**

After they win a contest to meet a famous author, five aspiring teenage writers spend a horrifying night in a haunted mansion. The stories are told in prose, newspaper clippings, e-mails, and stories within the story. (Quick Picks)

Subjects: Alternate Formats; Haunted Houses; Writers

Sleator, William.

Hell Phone. 2006. 9780810993600. **M**

When seventeen-year-old Nick buys a used cell phone so he can keep in touch with his girlfriend Jen, he starts receiving phone calls directing him to do things he would never do on his own, including murder. (IRA YAC)

Subjects: Hell; Torture

Ghosts

Avi.

The Seer of Shadows. 2008. 9780060000158. **M**

When science-minded apprentice photographer Horace Carpetine develops his first professional portrait, it includes the image of a ghost. In 1872 New York City, Horace teams up with a servant, who works for the family of the ghost, to discover what actually happened to the young socialite.

Subjects: Historical Fiction; New York; Photography

Gaiman, Neil.

Graveyard Book. 2008. 9780060530921. **M J S**

Nobody Owens, a precocious toddler, wanders away from his house and into a mostly abandoned cemetery just as an assassin breaks in and slays his parents and older sister. The ghostly residents of the cemetery take him under their wing. A living child being raised by ghosts presents some logistical problems, which are solved by a vampire guardian who is neither alive nor dead and can obtain food for Bod. As Bod grows up he learns many of the ghostly skills such as fading and scaring, and human skills such as reading, and finds a living friend whose family figures him for an imaginary companion. As an adolescent he learns that the assassin who killed his original family is still seeking him and he must save himself. (Hugo, Newbery, BBYA, TTT)

Jenkins, A. M.

Beating Heart: A Ghost Story. 2006. 9780060546076 **S**

After seventeen-year-old Evan moves with his family into a ramshackle Victorian house, he starts having erotic dreams about a strange light-haired girl, who died in his bedroom about a hundred years earlier. Told in alternating sections of prose and verse.

Subjects: Alternate Formats

Joyce, Graham.

TWOC: Taken Without Owner's Consent. 2007. 9780670060900. **S J**

Matt, age sixteen, loves to steal cars and drive them fast. He learned that from his brother Jake, who was killed in a fiery crash and now haunts him, as Matt may have been to blame. In therapy Matt meets Amy, an arsonist, and Gilb, a tagger.

Subjects: Accidents; Burns; Crime; Psychological Suspense

Levithan, David.

Marly's Ghost. 2005. 9780142409121. **J** **S**

Mourning the death by cancer of his girlfriend Marly, sixteen-year-old Ben experiences *A Christmas Carol* type of experience when Marly's ghost visits him, followed by the spirits of Valentine's past, present, and future.

Subjects: Death; Valentine's Day

Noyes, Deborah.

The Ghosts of Kerfol. 2008. 9780763630003. **S**

A novella inspired by Edith Wharton's short story "Kerfol" and set in 1613 at a country estate in France is followed by four short stories, each set in subsequent later time periods, in which the echoes of the past (and in one instance a vision of the future) reverberate.

Subjects: Art; Historical Fiction; Literary; Short Stories

Price, Charlie.

Dead Connection. 2006. 9781596431140. **S**

High school student Murray Kiefer hears dead people. He likes to hang out in the cemetery and visit with the dead. When a new voice starts talking to him, he suspects that it may be missing cheerleader Nikki Parker. With Pearl, the cemetery caretaker's daughter, he tries to solve the mystery that many others are working on. (BBYA, PP)

Subjects: Cemeteries; Drugs; Multiple Narrators; Murder

Soto, Gary.

The Afterlife. 2003. 9780152047740. **J** **S**

Chuy, the cousin who was murdered in Soto's *Buried Onions,* is the main character here. First he tries to figure out life as a ghost by learning how to navigate the world without being blown hither and yon by random winds. Now that he is dead, he begins to see what is really important and what isn't, especially as he tries to keep his cousin from ruining his life when his mother begs him to kill the guy who killed Chuy. Chuy even meets a girl, a girl he can help adjust to life as a dead person. Meanwhile, he begins to fade, as part after part of himself disappears. (IRA YAC, Quick Picks)

Subjects: California; Cousins; Revenge

Welsh, T. K.

The Unresolved. 9780525477310. 2006. **S** **J**

After fifteen-year-old German American Mallory Meer is killed in the horrendous *General Slocum* steamboat fire in 1904, her Jewish boyfriend is accused of starting it. Even though Mallory is a ghost, she tries to clear his name and save him from the community that wants to blame him for the disaster.

Subjects: Disasters; Early Twentieth Century; Fires; Historical Fiction; New York; Steamboats

Monsters

Monsters can take many forms and range from silly to horrifying. Some are benign; some the epitome of evil. A recent trend has seen a rise in the popularity of zombies, but demons and golems also find their place here.

Almond, David.

Clay. 2006. 9780440420132. **M** **J**

Fourteen-year-old altar boys Davie and Geordie sculpt a life-sized golem that comes to life under the direction of the very strange Stephen, an older boy who has recently moved to the community in the English north country. When the bully who has been harassing Davie and Geordie dies in a suspicious fall, they begin to wonder if they have actually created a monster. (BBYA)

Subjects: Altar Boys; Bullies; Golems

Buckingham, Royce.

Demonkeeper. 2007. 9780399246494. **J**

Orphaned Nat was taken in by Daliwahl as an apprentice demonkeeper. Now, with his mentor gone, Nat, a young teen, is in charge of a rambling house in Seattle that is home to a myriad of demons. Some of the demons, which are Nat's minions, aren't too bad, but there is a terrible demon in the basement. When Nat goes to the library, he meets Sandy, a sixteen-year-old who works there. She boldly gives him her phone number. When they go out on a date, Nat accidentally leaves a window open. Two homeless skateboarders sneak in and unleash the demon in the basement. The kid who isn't eaten by the demon escapes with the journal that holds all written knowledge of demons, kept from time immemorial. As Nat and Sandy try to find the kid who took the book, they face not only dangerous demons, but also a strange, thin man who has a plan.

Subjects: Demons; Orphans

James, Brian.

Zombie Blondes. 2008. 9780312372989. **J** **S**

Hannah Sanders, age fifteen, is used to moving frequently, so she isn't worried when she and her father move to Maplecrest, Vermont. Her new friend Lucas warns her that the town is full of zombies, but she doesn't really believe it—until the uniformly thin and blond cheerleaders take an interest in her.

Subjects: Vermont; Zombies

Ryan, Carrie.

Dead-Tossed Waves. 2010. 9780385906326. **S**

Gabry lives in a town between the forest and the ocean, but when she has a chance for a first kiss with her crush, Catcher, she follows her friends over the barrier that protects the town from the Mudos, the virus-infected zombies who, when her mother was her age, were called the Unconsecrated. This companion novel to *Forest of Hands and Teeth* stands alone.

Subjects: Post-Apocalyptic; Religion; Zombies

Forest of Hands and Teeth. 2009. 9780385736817. **S**

Teenage Mary lives in a village surrounded by a high fence that keeps the Unconsecrated out. A zombie virus has struck the world, and the infected catch and eat anyone they can. Anyone who is bitten but not devoured turns into one of the Unconsecrated. Shortly after both her parents have been turned, the village is overrun, and Mary, along with Travis, whom she loves, and his brother Harry, to whom she is promised, set out on a perilous quest for survival.

Subjects: Post-Apocalyptic; Quests; Religion; Survival; Zombies

Sleator, William.

The Boy Who Couldn't Die. 2004. 9780810987906. **J**

After his best friend is killed in a plane crash, Ken, age sixteen, undergoes a ritual to achieve immortality; but he discovers that he is now a zombie whose soul is being used for evil. He experiences nightmares in which he kills people, and when he is awake he discovers that the murders he's dreamed have actually happened. (IRA YAC, Quick Picks)

Subjects: Nightmares; Voodoo; Zombies

St. Crow, Lili.

Strange Angels. **S**

Sixteen-year-old Dru Anderson knows about things that go bump in the night. She has moved every couple of months with her widowed father, who chases down poltergeists, scuttling roachlike things of the night, wulfen, and other denizens of the dark.

Strange Angels. 2009. 9781595142511.

Now living in the frigid northern Midwest, all the training her father put sixteen-year-old Dru through to keep her safe seems inadequate, because he has returned home as a zombie that she has to kill. Taking refuge in the local mall, the terrified Dru meets up with the interesting half-Asian-looking goth geek from her history class, who has a hidden room where she can recuperate from the trauma, but trouble follows hard and fast.

Betrayals. 2009. 9781595142528.

Dru ends up at an isolated school full of vampires and werewolves, where she is the only girl. As she processes her grief over her father and her relationships with Graves and Christophe, she also begins to realize her powers. Plot threads are not tied up at the end, leaving this very much a middle book in a series.

Jealousy. 2010. 9781595142900.

Dru, having discovered she is half-vampire, trains to take her place in The Order, but the training may be the death of her.

Stahler, David, Jr.

Doppelganger. 2006. 9780060872328. ⑤

When a doppelganger, a monster who kills a human to take his place, kills Chris, he finds that the football star had a complicated life. The doppelganger, trying to be Chris, has to face a football coach he fails, an abusive father, an abused family, and a girlfriend who is beginning to fear Chris. (BBYA)

Subjects: Abuse; Doppelgangers; Football Players; Peer Pressure; Shape-shifters

Waters, Daniel.

Generation Dead. ⑤

When teenagers who have died stop staying dead, everyone must make adjustments to what is acceptable—especially in high schools, where political correctness dictates reactions to the "living impaired" or "differently biotic."

Subjects: Football Players; Humor; Prejudice; Romance; Zombies

Generation Dead. 2008. 9781423109228.

Phoebe is a goth girl whose identity stops working when some teens start coming back from the dead. Her best friend and next door neighbor, Adam, ends up being one of the only ones on the football team who is willing to work with a living-impaired teammate, while one of his former crowd is willing to rekill any of the undead he can.

Kiss of Life. 2009. 9781423109235.

As the numbers of the "differently biotic" continue to grow, more of the living begin to view them unkindly, and incidents of intolerance rise. Meanwhile, goth girl Phoebe is torn between two dead boys that she likes.

Passing Strange. 2010. 9781423121992.

Karen, passing as someone who is still alive, attempts to clear her zombie friends of murder charges.

Wooding, Chris.

Haunting of Alaizabel Cray. 2004. 9780439546560. ⑤

A parallel Victorian London is terrorized by horrible monsters of many types, and seventeen-year-old wych-hunter Thaniel fights them. When he treats a young amnesiac woman, Alaizabel Cray, he realizes she is possessed by a wych who is about to unleash unprecedented horror on the world. (BBYA)

Subjects: Alternate Worlds; London; Possession

Vampires

The Twilight phenomenon has made vampires the rock stars of the current paranormal boom. Today's vamps tend to be sexy, and the stories romantic.

Brewer, Heather.

The Chronicles of Vladimir Tod. 🅜 🅙

Vlad, a half-vampire orphan, shares a telepathic bond with Henry, the best friend he once bit accidentally. His guardian, a nurse, obtains blood for him from the hospital.

Subjects: Bullies; Crushes; High School; Middle School; Romance; Slayers; Telepathy

Eighth Grade Bites. 2007. 9780525478119.

As if eighth grade weren't bad enough Vlad is the favorite target of the school bullies, his beloved homeroom teacher has gone missing, he has a major crush on an awesome girl, and the new substitute teacher is very strange and seems to know Vlad's secret. (Quick Picks)

Ninth Grade Slays. 2008. 9780525478928.

Vlad makes it to high school, but a determined vampire slayer has him in his sights. Vlad, who seems to be the Pravus of vampire prophecy, a vampire destined to rule all vampires and enslave humans, heads to Siberia for some vampire training in mind control.

Tenth Grade Bleeds. 2009. 9780525421351.

In love with Meredith, Vlad resists feeding on her; tries to maintain his friendship with Henry, who seems to have abandoned him for the popular clique; and tries to avoid the evil vampire D'Ablo, who is looking for a ritual to strip Vlad of his powers.

Eleventh Grade Burns. 2010. 9780525422433.

Mere survival becomes a major issue for vampire Vlad, as an old friend turned slayer comes back to try to finish him off, a new vampire comes to town, and D'Ablo continues his plan to defeat him.

Cary, Kate.

Bloodline. 🅙 🅢

John Shaw, a nineteen-year-old British soldier during World War I, witnesses his commanding officer's vampire proclivities.

Subjects: Diaries and Journals; Epistolary Novels; Historical Fiction; World War I

Bloodline. 2005. 9781595140784.

Back in England after being wounded in World War I, John Shaw is visited by his supernatural commander, Captain Quincy Harker, a descendant of Dracula, who falls for John's sister, Lily, and takes her back to Transylvania. John and his fiancée, nurse Mary Steward, follow them to try to save Lily. (IRA YAC, PP)

Reckoning. 2007. 9781595140135.

Mary Seward, a nurse who had traveled to Transylvania with her fiancé in an attempt to save his sister from Quincy Harker, a descendant of Dracula, returns to England after her fiancé becomes a vampire. Two years later Quincy Harker finds her, claiming he wants to reform.

Cast, P. C., and Kristin Cast.

House of Night. ⬛

In a world where seemingly random teenagers suddenly show signs they are turning into vampyres, they must immediately move into one of the boarding schools, called House of Night, for any hope to survive. The time of change is dangerous and lengthy, sometimes resulting in death.

Subjects: Boarding Schools; Cherokees; Goddess Worship; Grandmothers; Tattoos; Tulsa, Oklahoma; Zombies

Marked. 2007. 9780312360252.

Sixteen-year-old Zoey Redbird, who hates her stepfather and the way her mother now always sides with him, is marked as a vampyre; and must get to the House of Night soon or die. Her mentor is Neferet the High Priestess, who leads ceremonies in honor of the Goddess Nyx. Strangely enough, Zoey's faint moon mark has filled in like those on the brows of adult vampyres. She feels the rituals of the school with an intensity unknown in other third years, and now seems to be acquiring vampyre talents and proclivities way ahead of schedule. Of course, she will be tested, and will have to rely on her friends and her own ethical compass if she is to survive. (Quick Picks)

Betrayed. 2007. 9780312360283.

Zoey has been gifted with great powers by the vampyre goddess Nyx. Now as the Leader of the Dark Daughters, it is her responsibility to use those gifts wisely. When ordinary teens from her life before she was Marked are murdered, Zoey begins to fear that someone from the House of Night is responsible. (Quick Picks)

Chosen. 2008. 9780312360306.

With three potential boyfriends, Zoey's life just keeps getting more complicated. Her friend and former roommate Stevie Rae is now undead, and other vampyres start turning up dead. Could Zoey's horrible stepfather or his church have something to do with it?

Untamed. 2008. 978-0312379834.

One week after the events in *Chosen*, Zoey suddenly finds she is a total outsider. Neferet's plans, including war on humans in retribution for the vampyre deaths, spell a future of death and destruction. (TTT)

Hunted. 2009. 9780312379827.

Taking refuge in the hidden Prohibition era tunnels under Omaha that Stevie Rae and the red fledglings have cleaned up may not keep Zoey and her friends safe from Neferet and her gorgeous immortal consort Kalona, a fallen angel who hides immense evil.

Tempted. 2009. 9780312567484.

In training as a High Priestess, Zoey begins to suspect Stevie Rae of hiding something involved with the dark force that is spreading out from under the Tulsa depot. Meanwhile the number of guys in Zoey's life is up to three again, and maybe even more, as she finds herself attracted to Kalona, whom she loved in a previous life.

Burned. 2010. 9780312606169.

> Zoey's heart is shattered, and she doesn't want to leave the Otherworld. Stark may be the only one who can bring her back, but he may have to die to do it. Stevie Rae is facing major problems with the Red Fledglings, and the horrible seer Aphrodite is now speaking with Nyx's own voice.

Jablonski, Carla.

Thicker Than Water. 2006. 9781595141231. **O**

> As sixteen-year-old Kia's life goes from bad to worse, with her mother battling cancer and her father never home, she hooks up with some wannabe vampires and meets someone she believes may really be one.

Subjects: Cancer; Cutting; New York

Jenkins, A. M.

Night Road. 2008. 9780060546045. **S**

> Cole, who looks like a teenager but is hundreds of years old, is summoned back to the New York apartment building that is hemovore headquarters. Another teenager, Gordon, has been accidentally turned by his old friend Sebastian and is going to need some careful training to avoid turning bad. Life is easy in the apartment, with plentiful omnis, who love contributing sex and blood to the hemovores. Johnny, the owner of the Building and hemovore leader, wants Cole and Sebastian to take Gordon on a road trip, so he can learn how to feed without killing or turning anyone. On their journey, they encounter a goth-like vampire who has obviously never received any training and starts trailing them in a very menacing way. If hemovores are to survive, their existence must be kept secret. (BBYA)

Subjects: Hemovores; New York; Road Trips

Jinks, Catherine.

The Reformed Vampire Support Group. 2009. 9780152066093. **J** **S**

> Perpetually fifteen, Nina has spent the last thirty-six years living the grim life of a vampire, feeling sick all the time, having to attend weekly AA-style meetings, and subsisting on hamster blood. She finds some adventure when a member of the support group is staked. This unique take on vampires won't appeal to <u>Twilight</u> fans and those who like their vamps gorgeous, irresistible, and sexy, but those who like quirky, off-the-wall stories will enjoy it. (BBYA)

Mead, Richelle.

<u>**Vampire Academy.**</u> **O**

> Moroi, living vampires, and dhampirs, Guardians who are offspring of human and Moroi with a combination of strong traits from both, survive against attacks by Strigoi, dead vampires with great powers and no morals. This story is set mostly in an exclusive and remote Montana boarding school for Moroi and dhampir teens.

Subjects: Dhampirs; Moroi; Strigoi

Vampire Academy. 2007. 9781594141743.

> Rose is the dhampir Guardian of her best friend Lissa, a Moroi vampire princess. When the two of them are returned to St. Vladimir's Academy after running away, Rose must continue her training so she can continue to protect Lissa from the evil undead vampires called the Strigoi. (Quick Picks, TTT)

Frostbite. 2008. 9781595141750.

> Under attack by the Strigoi, the Moroi and dhampirs decide that a remote Moroi ski resort is just the place to relax in safety for the holidays. Torn between her attraction for Dimitri, who is seven years older and her tutor, and Mason, who is an appropriate love interest who is head-over-heels in love with her, Rose gets confused, and she acts badly when her estranged mother shows up.

Shadow Kiss. 2008. 9781595141972.

> It is spring time at the Academy, but the Moroi are on edge due to the Strigoi threat. Rose, who is feeling strange after killing Strigoi, is conflicted by her attraction to Dimitri and her responsibility to Lissa.

Blood Promise. 2009. 9781595141989.

> An attack has left many Moroi dead, and a fate far worse faces those abducted by the Strigoi. Rose made a promise to Dimitri, and now that he has been taken to Siberia by the Strigoi, she must abandon Lissa and follow Dimitri's wishes.

Spirit Bound. 2010. 9781595142504.

> Back at St. Vladimir's and ready for graduation, Rose finds that she is being stalked after her failure in Siberia and that graduation may not be a new beginning after all.

Meyer, Stephenie.

Twilight. **S**

What's a girl to do? When Bella moves to Forks, Washington, she meets two very attractive boys: Edward, a gorgeous white vampire, and Jacob, a gorgeous Native American werewolf. The best-selling <u>Twilight</u> series, like <u>Harry Potter</u>, has had a huge impact, not only on teen readers but on adult readers as well. It has become an icon of popular culture, with Bella and Edward becoming recognizable names and people claiming either "Team Edward" or "Team Jacob."

Twilight. 2005. 9780316015844.

> When her mother remarries, seventeen-year-old Bella leaves the sunshine of Phoenix for the omnipresent rain and gloom of the Olympic peninsula where her dad lives. In her new school she is forced to sit next to Edward, a gorgeous member of the elusive and stand-offish Cullen family, who acts like he hates Bella. When he uses preternatural speed to save Bella's life in the school parking lot, she discovers that they have a mutual fascination with each other. (BBYA, IRA YAC, TTT, Quick Picks, Film)

New Moon. 2006. 9780316160193.

After Edward and the rest of the vampire Cullen family leave Forks, Washington, after realizing how very tempting seventeen-year-old Bella's blood is, Bella sinks into depression. To soothe her loneliness, she starts hanging out with Jacob, but soon uncovers his secret and finds a hidden link to Edward that manifests when she is in danger. (TTT, Quick Picks, IRA YAC, Film)

Eclipse. 2007. 9780316160209

Bella is looking forward to graduation, when vampire Edward will marry her and she can become a vampire, which does not sit well with werewolf Jacob. As a string of murders torments the city of Seattle, Edward and Jacob vie for Bella's love. (TTT, Film)

Breaking Dawn. 2008. 9780316067928.

Bella and Edward finally marry. The sexual consummation of their union results in an unforeseen circumstance, which delays her turning into a vampire until after a special delivery. The culmination of the <u>Twilight</u> saga brings big changes to all and wraps up diverse plot threads. (TTT)

Schreiber, Ellen.

Vampire Kisses. 🇯 🇸

Sixteen-year-old goth Raven is an outsider in Dullsville. She doesn't fit in at school or at home, is bullied by Trevor an attempted rapist, and is obsessed with vampires.

Vampire Kisses. 2003. 9780060093341.

Raven is fascinated by Alexander, the new boy who moved into the local "haunted" mansion on her sixteenth birthday. Rumor has it that he is a descendent of the Romanian baroness who built the mansion and that he is a vampire. When Raven starts sleuthing around the mansion, she manages to land a date with Alexander. (IRA YAC)

Kissing Coffins. 2005. 9780060776244.

No sooner has Raven discovered that Alexander is actually a vampire than he disappears. Raven tracks him down to Hipsterville, a nearby town where she can go to stay with her aunt during spring break and find Alexander, who it turns out is being menaced by vampire Jagger.

Vampireville. 2006. 9780060776251.

Jagger, Alexander's rival, and Jagger's twin sister Luna seem intent on turning Dullsville into Vampireville, starting with Trevor, who has always bullied Raven.

Dance with a Vampire. 2007. 9780061132230.

Jagger and Luna have left, but their younger brother, Valentine Maxwell, turns up and befriends Raven's 'tween brother Billy. Raven and Alexander know Valentine is up to no good and must save Billy.

The Coffin Club. 2008. 9780061288845.

> School's out for summer, and Alexander has gone to Hipsterville, but when he stays away too long Raven decides to pay another visit to her aunt. She discovers a secret door leading to the depths of the Coffin Club and a place where real vampires hang out.

Royal Blood. 2009. 9780061288890.

> Back at school, Raven is forced to work on a project with bully Trevor. Alexander's parents have finally arrived from Romania, but Raven seems to be the only one in Dullsville who hasn't yet met them. Is Alexander keeping her away from them on purpose?

Love Bites. 2010. 9780061689420.

> After Alexander's parents return to Romania, he and Raven can resume their romantic interludes, but then his best friend Sebastian shows up. Raven hopes that she can find out more about the love of her life from Sebastian while she waits to be turned into a vampire.

Sedgwick, Marcus.

My Swordhand Is Singing. **2007. 9780375846892.** **S**

Teenage Peter and his father Tomas are woodcutters in an eastern European medieval village beset by zombie-like vampires. Tomas may have a sword that will stop this scourge of the undead. (BBYA)

Subjects: Gothic; Historical Fiction; Seventeenth Century; Vampires

Shan, Darren.

Cirque du Freak. **M** **J**

Darren Shan's adventures with vampires and other denizens of the weird start when he and his friend Steve, both age twelve, visit a very unusual freak show called Cirque du Freak, and continue on for several years. The Cirque du Freak series is also available in a manga graphic novel format.

Cirque du Freak: A Living Nightmare. 2001. 9780316605106.

> After Darren sneaks out to go to Cirque du Freak, a bizarre traveling freak show with his friend Steve, he ends up becoming a half-vampire. (Film: *The Vampire's Assistant*)

The Vampire's Assistant. 2001. 9780316606844.

> Darren, having unwillingly joined Cirque du Freak, a traveling freak show, as Mr. Crepsley's assistant, becomes roommates with Evra, the snake boy. Even though he has been turned into a vampire, he refuses human blood, which makes him weaker and weaker. (Film)

Tunnels of Blood. 2002. 9780316606080.

> Even though Darren, Evra, and Mr. Crepsley have left the Cirque du Freak, horrifying events won't leave them alone. After they move to the city, corpses completely drained of blood start turning up, and Darren and Evra begin an investigation. (Film: *The Vampire's Assistant*)

Vampire Mountain. 2002. 9780316605427.

Six years after the events in *Tunnels of Blood*, Darren accompanies Mr. Crepsley on a torturous trek to Vampire Mountain, where Darren meets the Vampire Princes and Generals and learns vampiric history.

1

Trials of Death. 2003. 9780316603959.

Inside Vampire Mountain, Darren is coming to terms with his vampiric nature. While trying to complete five deadly, dangerous trials, Darren uncovers a diabolical conspiracy.

The Vampire Prince. 2003. 9780316602747.

2

Even though he is sentenced to death, Darren, who was thrown out of Vampire Mountain after failing his "trials of death" and subsequently nursed back to health by a pack of wolves, journeys to the center of Vampire Mountain. He is attempting to stop the annihilation of the vampire clan by the evil vampaneze.

3

Hunters of the Dusk. 2004. 9780316602112.

Vampire Prince Darren Shan is one of three hunters who must try to stop the Vampaneze Lord, who has now created a new vampire hybrid, called Vampets, that could help the vampaneze wipe out the vampires.

Allies of the Night. 2004. 9780316155700.

4

Now in his thirties, Darren, who still looks like he is fifteen years old, goes to Mr. Crepsley's hometown, where he is hunting vampaneze at night, and corpses drained of blood have been turning up. Darren is forced to go to high school when caught by a truant officer.

Killers of the Dawn. 2005. 9780316156264.

Darren and his allies are on the run, having escaped from a police station, pursued by a mob of humans and the vampaneze. Darren and company face the Lord of the Vampaneze in an underground confrontation.

5

The Lake of Souls. 2005. 9780316156271.

Darren and Harkat encounter fantasy-game-like dangers on their quest to reach the Lake of Souls, in a slight detour on their mission to destroy the Lord of the Vampaneze and end the war between vampires and vampaneze.

6

Lord of the Shadows. 2006. 9780316156288.

Now Darren knows the true identity of the Lord of the Vampaneze and that to end the deadly war one of them will have to become the Lord of Shadows. Traveling again with the Cirque du Freak, Darren revisits his old hometown, where the whole mess started.

7

Sons of Destiny. 2006. 9780316156295.

"Dead if he loses. Damned if he wins." In the climax of the series, Darren Shan faces his onetime friend and longtime nemesis, Steve Leopard, in a deadly fight that will decide the fate of the vampires.

8

Smith, Cynthia Leitich.

Eternal. 2009. 9780763635732.

Annotated in the "Angels" section of this chapter.

Tantalize. **2007. 9780763627911.** **J** **S**

Seventeen-year-old Quincie Morris is in love with her lifelong best friend Kieren Morales, who just happens to be half-werewolf. She is, to a minimal extent, being raised by her young uncle since her parents died, leaving her an Italian restaurant that had been in her family for years. With the restaurant in danger of going under, Uncle D has decided that it should sport a vampire theme, and Sanguini's is born. A few weeks before the grand reopening, while they are still working out the menu, the chef, who has been a grandfather figure to Quincie, is savagely murdered in the kitchen in what appears to be a wolf attack. A new chef is hired, and Quincie works on making him appear vampire-like. While her life spirals out of control, the new chef takes her under his wing, and they start drinking wine together. She begins to suspect Kieren of the attacks, and she allows both her meticulously kept day planner and school to fall by the wayside. Although werewolves play a role, this is a creepy vampire novel.

Subjects: Austin, Texas; Restaurants; Werewolves

Somper, Justin.

Vampirates. **M** **J**

Combining the popular themes of vampires, pirates, twins, and orphans, this series presents the adventures of fourteen-year-olds Connor and Grace and is full of swashbuckling action.

Subjects: Pirates; Twins

Demons of the Ocean. 2005. 9780316014441.

When fourteen-year-old twins Grace and Connor's father, a lighthouse keeper, dies, they set out to sea, but a shipwreck separates them. Connor is picked up by pirates, while Grace is rescued by the captain of a ship crewed by vampire pirates.

Tide of Terror. 2007. 9780316014458.

The twins are reunited at the Pirate Academy, where they have been invited to spend a week after an attack aboard the pirate ship *Diablo* results in the death of one of Connor's friends. Connor loves being at the academy, but Grace longs for her old life on the vampirate ship and misses her friend, Lorcan. Using a ring Lorcan gave her, Grace is able to visit the vampirates through astral projection.

Blood Captain. 2008. 9781416901020.

Grace begins to study healing after making a journey and trying to help her vampirate friend Lorcan get his vision back. Meanwhile her twin, Connor, and the crew of the pirate ship *Diablo* are out to avenge the death of Captain Wrathe.

Black Heart. 2009. 9780316020879.

> Following the slaying of a high-profile pirate, the pirate federation fields a ship of highly trained vampire hunters, including Connor, to stop a crew of female vampires.

Empire of Night. 2010. 9780316033220.

> Grace and Connor have discovered they have vampirate roots as they face further dangers at sea, when Sidorio continues his conquests.

Westerfeld, Scott.

Peeps. **S**

Vampirism with a scientific background gives a unique twist to this duology. Peeps, people who are parasite positive, infected by the exchange of bodily fluids, find all that they loved anathema. However, some who are infected do not turn into ravening monsters who live with an entourage of rats but become carriers who can easily infect others. A secret city agency keeps tabs on the Peeps and enlists the carriers to hunt down the infected who have become vampires.

Subjects: Apocalypse; New York; Parasites; Rats; Science Fiction

Peeps. 2005. 9781595140319.

> Cal, a college freshman living in New York, is parasite positive, a carrier for vampirism caused by a parasite vectored infection, and must hunt for the girls he kissed and unknowingly infected. The factual information about parasites that starts alternating chapters is chilling. (BBYA, TTT)

The Last Days. 2006. 9781595140623.

> Five teen band members try to stave off an apocalypse that will engulf New York, as the parasite-infected vampires mutate and grow in numbers and giant worms break through the streets to consume people. (Quick Picks)

Werewolves

The transformative experience of shifting shape, changing from human to something else entirely and then changing back, is an alluring premise. Werewolves seem to be second only to vampires in the paranormal popularity competition. Many Twilight fans consider themselves "Team Jacob," in honor of the Native American werewolf in the series.

Jennings, Patrick.

The Wolving Time. 2003. 9780439395557. **M** **J**

In sixteenth-century France, the Inquisition is looking for werewolves. A shepherd family, the Embereks, and their teenage son Lazlo are gentle, kind werewolves who must flee after rescuing a young servant girl from the evil village priest.

Subjects: France; Historical Fiction; Inquisition; Sixteenth Century

Millar, Martin.

Lonely Werewolf Girl. 2008. 9780979663666. **O**

Kalix MacRinnalch, a seventeen-year-old, suicidal, drug-addicted werewolf girl, is taken in by a couple of London university students, who subsequently encounter her sorceress sister, a queen of the fire elementals obsessed with her wardrobe, as well as scores of other darkly wacky characters. Kalix's story continues in *Curse of the Wolf Girl* (2010, 9780980226058).

Subjects: Adult Books for Teens; Drug Addicts; London; Scotland; Sorceresses

Reisz, Kristopher.

Unleashed. 2008. 9781416940012. **S**

High school junior Daniel Morning hangs out with the "right" crowd, and due to his parents pushing for him to be classified as having ADD, he has improved his SAT scores enough to be accepted at Cornell. When an outcast girl in one of his classes rescues an injured dog, Daniel becomes fascinated with her. She draws him into her circle, where magic mushrooms and ritual turn the teens into wolves to prowl the city at night.

Stiefvater, Maggie.

Wolves of Mercy Falls. **S**

Shiver. 2009. 9780545123266.

When seventeen-year-old Grace was a young child, she was dragged away from her family by wolves, but one wolf stopped the pack from killing her. Ever since, she has been fascinated by wolves, rather than afraid of them. Every winter a gorgeous yellow-eyed wolf appears near her house. Meanwhile, Sam has always had a crush on Grace, and he is hoping she will notice him at the bookstore where he works—especially because it may be his last summer as a human. (BBYA, Quick Picks)

Linger. 2010. 9780545123280.

Told from four different viewpoints, the story of Sam and Grace continues as their relationship changes in response to the changes in their lives; Cole, a new werewolf who may not really want to retain his humanity, and Isabel, a human, fall in love.

Witchcraft

Stories about witches have historically explored female relationships, bonds of friendship, and rivalry, but recently the subgenre has started featuring more boys who become involved in magic. Witches, like so many other beings in current paranormal novels, are sometimes on the side of goodness and light and sometimes on the side of evil.

Delaney, Joseph.

The Last Apprentice (also called The Wardstone Chronicles). **M**

The Spook keeps villagers and farmers safe from witches, boggarts, and other wicked beasties, but he is shunned by those he protects. Twelve-year-old Thomas Ward, the seventh son of a seventh son, becomes his apprentice. Delaney has also written two collections of short stories set in this world, which are annotated in the "Short Stories" section of this chapter.

The Revenge of the Witch. 2005. 9780060766184.

When twelve-year-old Tom is tricked by Alice, a young witch whom he is desperately trying to befriend, he releases her evil ancestor Mother Malkin, who has been imprisoned in a pit. (BBYA, Quick Picks)

Curse of the Bane. 2006. 9780060766238.

Now thirteen and settling into his duties as apprentice to Mr. Gregory, the Spook, who fights the supernatural evils that threaten the County, Tom goes up against the Bane, a horrifically evil creature that lurks in the labyrinthine catacombs under the cathedral in Priestown. (VOYA)

Night of the Soul Stealer. 2007. 9780060766245.

After moving to Anglezarke, a dismal spot across the county, for the winter, Thomas, Alice, and the Spook encounter even more evil, including Morgan, a failed apprentice with plans to awaken an ancient god who could bring on an eternal winter.

Attack of the Fiend. 2008. 9780060891275.

When three powerful covens of witches unite to summon the Devil himself, Tom, Mr. Gregory, and Alice travel to Pendle, where Tom uncovers secrets involving trunks his mother left for him. With his family in danger, Tom is unsure whom to trust.

Wrath of the Bloodeye. 2008. 9780061344596.

Two years into his apprenticeship, Thomas is sent off to learn from one of the Spook's former students and finds himself conflicted over Alice, his friend who may be good or evil.

Clash of the Demons. 2009. 9780061344626.

Tom's Mam returns to the County to ask him to return to Greece with her for help in banishing an old god, the Ordeen. She also recruits Alice, witches from Pendle, and the Spook to go along.

Rise of the Huntress. 2010. 9780061715105.

Fleeing to the island of Mora, Tom, Alice, and the Spook face a new fight against a now-more-powerful old enemy.

Garcia, Kami, and Margaret Stohl.

Beautiful Creatures. 2009. 9780316042673. **J** **S**

Fifteen-year-old Ethan Wate lives a life of quiet boredom in Gatlin County, South Carolina, until a mysterious girl named Lena moves to town. Suddenly, Ethan finds himself in a world where magic is real.

Subjects: South Carolina

Myracle, Lauren.

Rhymes with Witches. 2005. 9780810992153. **J** **S**

When high school freshman Jane Goodwin is invited to join the most exclusive clique at her school, she discovers that they have a diabolical secret that contributes to their popularity. This combination of mean girl contemporary fiction and witchcraft is eerie and creepy.

Demons

With the huge interest in paranormal tales, all kinds of creatures are being featured. Demons, though still far behind vampires and werewolves in popularity, are gaining some steam. Faustian bargains often play a role in these tales.

Desrochers, Lisa.

Personal Demons. 2010. 9780765328083. **S**

When new kid Luc, short for Lucifer starts at her school, Frannie is quite attracted to him. Luc and Gabe are both vying for her soul because she is one of the unique people (the only other ones mentioned are Moses and Hitler) who have "Sway," the ability to make world-changing shifts in what people do. Luc, a demon, wants to win her soul for hell, whereas Gabe wants to makes sure she is firmly on the side of good before she dies. Could her "Sway" influence even the emissaries of heaven and hell?

Subjects: Angels; Romance

Gill, David Macinnis.

Soul Enchilada. 2009. 9780061673016. **S**

Bug Smoot, an orphaned mixed-race teen in El Paso, uses the vintage Cadillac she inherited from her grandfather to deliver pizzas—until the day she meets hunky Pesto and creepy Mr. Beals. Seems her granddaddy made a deal with the devil, and she cosigned at the tender age of thirteen. Now, in sixty hours, the car and her soul will be repossessed. Fortunately Pesto works for an agency that fights evil, and his mother has a few tricks of her own.

Subjects: Cadillacs; El Paso, Texas; Romance

Jenkins, A. M.

Repossessed. 2007. 9780060835705. 🄹 🅂

Kiriel, a demon in need of a vacation after an eternity of reflecting back shame, guilt, and sorrow on the condemned, steps into the body of Shaun Simpson, a teen slacker who is about to depart the world and experiences human life. (BBYA, IRA YAC, Printz Honor)

Subjects: Demons; Possession

Johnson, Maureen.

Devilish. 2006. 9781595141323. 🄹 🅂

High school senior Jane Jarvis is mystified when her friend Allison begins acting strangely and discovers that Allison believes she has sold her soul to Lanalee, a junior devil, in exchange for popularity. Determined to save her friend, Jane, who does not believe in this kind of evil, offers her own soul in exchange, then must fight for her life and her soul. (BBYA, PP)

Subjects: Devil; Faustian Bargains; Possession

Kaye, Marilyn.

Demon Chick. 2009. 9780805088809. 🄹 🅂

On her sixteenth birthday, Jessica Hunsucker discovers that her soul was sold to the devil by her mother in a quest for political power and world domination. With the help of a demon named Brad, Jessica attempts to put a halt to her mother's diabolical plan.

Subjects: Boarding Schools; Deal with the Devil; Demons; Faustian Bargains; Politics

Shan, Darren.

<u>The Demonata.</u> 🄹 🅂

Three different protagonists experience horror as they come up against demons who travel through different universes wreaking gruesome havoc. Each story in the series is meant to also stand alone, so reading order is not important.

Subjects: Demons; Horror; Parallel Worlds; Time Travel; Werewolves

Lord Loss. 2005. 9780316012331.

Grubbs Grady discovers true evil exists when his family is ripped to shreds by a demon called Lord Loss, who feeds on human suffering. Afterward he is sent to a mental institution and eventually released to his Uncle Dervish, who tells him gruesome stories about the house he now lives in. (PP)

The Demon Thief. 2006. 9780316012386.

Teenager Kernel Fleck opens a window into another universe and loses his memories. When demons come through, slaughter many of the local children, and kidnap his brother, Kernel must go through the window to try to save him.

Slawter. 2006. 9780316013871.

> While trying to keep Grubbs safe, Dervish takes him along to where he is working as advisor on a horror movie. Suddenly many members of the cast, crew, and town begin disappearing, and Grubbs must convince the residents of Slawter that real demons have been unleashed.

Bec. 2007. 9780316013895.

> Orphaned Bec, a priestess in training in Celtic Ireland, befriends a simple-minded stranger, who may hold the key to helping them when demons invade and she tries to find a way to close the portal that is spewing the demons into this world.

Blood Beast. 2007. 9780316003773.

> Teenage Grubbs becomes friends with a school bully who is targeting Bill-E, Grubbs's half-brother, but he has horrifying dreams that make him think he may really be turning into a werewolf.

Demon Apocalypse. 2008. 9780316003797.

> With the world poised on the point of apocalypse, teenage Grubbs becomes an assistant to a magician, knowing he is probably going to have to devote his life to fighting demons, after he is betrayed by Juni while on an airplane flight invaded by voracious demons.

Death's Shadow. 2008. 9780007260379.

> After centuries of imprisonment, Bec is brought to modern times, where she becomes a ward of Dervish, but a new threat has come forward in time with her.

Wolf Island. 2008. 9780007260409.

> Upon discovering that Dervish has been attacked by werewolves, Grubbs, who continues to fight changing into a werewolf, returns to Earth with Kernel and Beranabus, then must visit an island overrun by werewolves.

Dark Calling. 2009. 9780007260430.

> Kernel, after being dragged across the universe, discovers our world isn't the only one in peril and that the Disciples are being manipulated.

Hell's Heroes. 2010. 9780316048958.

> Long-standing relationships and alliances are torn asunder after Beranabus and Dervish are gone. With Bec teaming up with Lord Loss, the Disciples failing, and Grubbs out of control, the future looks even more bleak than usual.

Angels

Angels are the opposite of demons, but the stories featuring them are often as dark and sometimes even darker than their evil counterparts. Angels also appear in Cassandra Clare's popular <u>Mortal Instruments</u> series, annotated in the "Urban Fantasy" section of chapter 7.

Fitzpatrick, Becca.

Hush, Hush. 2009. 9781416989417. S

High school sophomore Nora Grey finds her new bad boy science lab partner, Patch, alluring but also creepy. He seems to invade her thoughts. Could it be that Patch is actually a fallen angel trying to become human? The sequel, *Crescendo* (2010, 9781416989431), continues the story of Nora and Patch.

Kizer, Amber.

Meridian. 2009. 9780385736688. **J S**

Things around Meridian have always died. Since Meridian was an infant, the area around her has been littered with the corpses of insects. As she gets older, the dead grow, too. On her sixteenth birthday, her parents send her off to the ancient Auntie who lives in Colorado, and they go into hiding. She arrives at the bus station, but is not met, so after hours of waiting, she takes a cab as far as she can, then trudges through a howling snowstorm to Auntie's house. It turns out that like Auntie, Meridian is a Fenestra, a human/angel hybrid who serves as a conduit for souls to move on to the next place. Auntie's assistant is Tens, a gorgeous psychic teen who treats Meridian with disdain, but it is obvious that there is a mutual attraction. Frequent vandalism shows that the cult who have moved into town are accelerating their campaign against Auntie, whom they see as a witch.

Subjects: Colorado; Persecution

Laurens, Jennifer.

Heavenly. 2009. 9781933963846. **J S**

With an autistic sister, a pothead brother, and a couple of overwhelmed parents, teenager Zoe copes by partying—until she meets Matthias, her sister's guardian angel. That's when she falls in love.

Subjects: Autism; Substance Abuse

McNish, Cliff.

Angel. 2008. 9780822589006. **J S**

Fourteen-year-old Freya, with her obsession for angels, has spent several years undergoing psychiatric care for what her parents think are delusions. Now in high school, she becomes friends with Stephanie, a new girl who also believes in angels.

Subjects: Bullying; Schools

Smith, Cynthia Leitich.

Eternal. 2009. 9780763635732. **J S**

Told in alternating points of view by Zachary and Miranda. Zachary is a guardian angel who was de-winged after he made himself visible when trying to save the teenage girl he not only watches over but loves. Miranda, the girl in question, has been turned into a vampire princess. This novel examines issues of right and wrong.

Subjects: Vampires

Whitcomb, Laura.

The Fetch. 2009. 9780618891313. **S** **J**

Calder, a Fetch, may be a reaper, an angel who has the job of taking people from the scenes of their deaths to heaven; but when he goes to early twentieth-century Russia, he falls in love and breaks a vow, which leads to deadly repercussions.

Subjects: Historical Fiction; Romanovs; Russian Revolution

Humorous Paranormal

Paranormal stories, though often gruesome and gory, such as in the <u>Demonata</u> series by Darren Shan, have their counterpoint in humorous tales that feature beings such as skeletons, ghosts, vampires, witches, and monsters.

Hurley, Tonya.

Ghostgirl. **J** **S**

Despite choking to death on a gummy bear the first day of school, teenager Charlotte Usher still wants to be popular at Hawthorne High and win the heart of Damen Dylan.

Subjects: Ghosts; High School; Possession

Ghostgirl. 2008. 9780316113595.

Charlotte, who is willing to do almost anything to win Damen, is determined to not let death deter her, so she possesses Scarlet, the coolest girl at Hawthorne High, switching places so that Scarlet must now attend Dead Ed in her place.

Ghostgirl: Homecoming. 2009. 9780316113595.

Charlotte and Scarlet are back, Charlotte working a hotline for troubled teens and Scarlet trying to save her sister, who has gone into a coma due to a pedicure mishap.

Kenner, Julie.

Good Ghouls. **J**

This Chick Lit vampire series features sixteen-year-old Beth Frasier, who is way too busy with school, but nonetheless ends up having to deal with life as a vampire.

Subjects: Cheerleaders; Football Players; Humorous; Science; Vampires

The Good Ghouls' Guide to Getting Even. 2007. 9780441017041.

Beth Frasier's sixteenth birthday goes from bad to worse after she is recruited for the cheerleading squad and asked out by the school football stud, who turns her into a vampire.

Good Ghouls Do. 2007. 9780425217030.

What's a vampire to do? Between yearbook duties, figuring out a formula to allow vamps to go out in daylight, and trying to find her master to kill him, high school freshman Beth barely has time for anything.

Landy, Derek.

Skulduggery Pleasant. M J

After inheriting a huge estate from her famous author uncle, Stephanie, age twelve, who changes her name to Valkyrie, teams up with his fire-flinging skeleton friend for adventures.

Subjects: Heiresses; Horror Authors; Humorous; Skeletons

Skulduggery Pleasant. 2007. 9780061231155.

When Stephanie inherits her famous author uncle's estate, she also inherits his friend Skulduggery Pleasant, a fire-flinging skeleton who wants to help her solve her uncle's murder. (BBYA, IRA YAC, VOYA)

Subjects: Mystery

Playing with Fire. 2008. 9780061240881.

Thirteen-year-old Valkyrie Cain, formerly known as Stephanie Edgley, again teams up with her mentor, the fire-flinging skeleton, Skulduggery Pleasant, to combat an ancient evil in the form of the Grotesquery, a horrendous combination of monstrous parts that the evil Baron Vengeous is trying to bring to life.

The Faceless Ones. 2009. 9780007302147.

The fire-flinging detective Skulduggery Pleasant and his fourteen-year-old sidekick Valkyrie, the girl formerly known as Stephanie Edgley, must stop the group called the Diablerie, who are trying to find a person who is a teleporter to bring the Elder Gods and all their destruction through a portal into this world.

Mlynowski, Sarah.

Magic in Manhattan series. J

Living in Manhattan with a mother who is a witch, fourteen-year-old Rachel can't wait for her own powers to kick in, but things keep going wrong for her. This contemporary blend of Chick Lit and magic is light and humorous.

Subjects: Humor; Manhattan; Mothers and Daughters; Sisters; Witches

Bras & Broomsticks. 2005. 9780385731843.

Rachel wants magical witch powers, but it is her younger sister Miri who ends up with them. Even though Miri isn't supposed to use her powers until she's had a year of training, Rachel gets her to cast spells to turn her into a great dancer and win the boyfriend she wants.

Frogs & French Kisses. 2006. 9780385731850.

> With Miri trying to save the world with magic and their mother going overboard with magic transformations to find romance, Rachel tries to put on the brakes and keep things together.

Spells & Sleeping Bags. 2007. 9780385733885.

> Rachel and Miri are off to summer camp in the Adirondacks. Fortunately, Rachel's witch powers have finally kicked in, but now she has to keep them hidden from the other girls as she tries them out.

Parties and Potions. 2008. 9780385736459.

> Rachel and Miri join a class for witches and start preparing for a Samsorta ceremony, a witchly debutante ball. Meanwhile their dad and stepmother have no idea that the sisters are witches.

Robar, Serena.

Half-Blood Vampire series also called Colby Blanchard series. **J** **S**

In this lighthearted series, Colby Blanchard, a cheerleader and high school senior, must adapt to life as a vampire.

Subjects: Braces; Cheerleaders; Humor; Prophecies; Vampires

Braced 2 Bite. 2006. 9780425209769.

> Popular cheerleader, high school senior Colby Blanchard is at a distinct disadvantage when she becomes a vampire, because her orthodontist dad has removed her canine teeth to perfect her smile. This book is being reissued in 2010 with the title *Braced to Bite*.

Fangs 4 Freaks. 2006. 9780425211953.

> Colby is off to college and the Psi Phi sorority, which is exclusively for half-vampires, where she emerges as the Protector of the half-blood vampires. This book is being reissued in 2010 with the title *Fangs for Freaks*.

Dating 4 Demons. 2007. 9780425215142.

> Something is wrong when Colby's best friend Piper undertakes being tutored in a cemetery and it turns out she is a demon slayer. This book is being reissued in 2010 with the title *Dating for Demons*.

Psionic Powers and Unexplained Phenomena

Out-of-the-ordinary powers, including telepathy, telekinesis, and teleportation, can make life very interesting for teens, as well as imposing some difficulties. In addition to stories about extraordinary powers, titles in this section also include out-of-body experiences and unexplained phenomena, as well as about individuals with superpowers that make them superheroes.

Psionic Powers

The possession of paranormal powers is an enticing subject. Psionic powers can include telepathy, the power to communicate mind to mind; teleportation, the ability to transport the body from place to place; telekinesis, the ability to move objects with the mind; precognition, the ability to see the future; and many more. Psionic powers appear in all the speculative fiction genres: science fiction, fantasy, horror, and paranormal.

Barnes, Jennifer Lynn.

Tattoo. 2007. 9780385733472. **J** **S**

When fifteen-year-old Bailey and three friends apply temporary tattoos, they all acquire unusual powers that herald the arrival of a deadly danger, which they must overcome before their temporary powers wear off along with the tattoos. (Quick Picks, PP)

Cabot, Meg.

Jinx. 2007. 9780060837648. **M** **J** **S**

When Jean was born, the electricity in the hospital went out. That was only the first mishap of thousands that resulted in her being called Jinx. Now at sixteen she has been sent to New York to live with her aunt's family and attend a tony private school. Her cousin Tory, with whom she had great fun when they were younger, is now sullen and unfriendly. Tory believes that she has inherited their many times great-grandmother's talent for witchcraft and tries to draw it out of Jean, but Jean, who has left her Iowa hometown because of a stalker, wants nothing to do with witchcraft. The hunky next-door neighbor who is Tory's crush is very friendly to Jinx, and that creates additional problems. (IRA YAC)

Dogar, Sharon.

Waves. 2007. 9781905294602. **S**

A year after his sister washed up on the beach in a coma, fifteen-year-old Hal revisits the scene. Suddenly he has Charley's memories, and now maybe he can discover the truth about what happened to her that put her in the coma.

Subjects: Comas; Cornwall; Siblings; Telepathy

Harper, Suzanne.

The Secret Life of Sparrow Delaney. 2007. 9780061131585. **J** **S**

High school sophomore Sparrow, the seventh daughter of a seventh daughter, has kept her psychic abilities secret. She doesn't want to see ghosts, but the truth is, she does.

Subjects: Ghosts; Mediums; Psychics

Jacobs, Deborah Lynn.

Powers. 2006. 9780312377564. **J** **S**

Gwen has dreams, dreams that scare her, so she is very afraid when the boy in her dreams shows up as the new kid at her school. Adrian always knows the right things to do and say, but Gwen is not charmed. There is something about her, though, that enables him to read people's minds when they are close to each other. When they start dating, Gwen starts having dreams of disaster that together they can stop—but not with the expected outcomes.

Subjects: Dreams; Ontario, Canada

Kaye, Marilyn.

Gifted. **M** **J**

Meadowbrook Middle School has one unusual gifted class with a diversity of unusual students, who all have different abilities and powers.

Out of Sight, Out of Mind. 2009. 9780753416495.

Amanda, eighth-grade queen of mean at Meadowbrook Middle School, is always cruel, because whenever she starts feeling sorry for someone she finds herself looking out at the world from behind that person's eyes. When she finds herself inside Tracey Devon, an unattractive, totally forgettable girl, she isn't worried, because she knows she'll be back to herself before long, but she wakes up the next morning still in Tracey's life. Nobody notices Tracey. The bus driver closes the door in her face. Her mother, who is focused on the family's sextuplets, doesn't even seem to know she exists, and no matter how much she waves her arm in the air in class, the teachers never call on her. (Quick Picks)

Subjects: Out-of-Body Experiences

Better Late Than Never. 2009. 9780753463000.

Goth girl Jenna Kelley knows what people are thinking by reading their minds. When someone claiming to be her long-lost father shows up while her alcoholic mother is hospitalized, Jenna yearns for a normal life. (Quick Picks)

Subjects: Psychics

Here Today, Gone Tomorrow. 2009. 9780753463109.

When kids start disappearing from the "Gifted" class, Emily wants to do something. She is frightened when she has a vision of going to a bad part of town and getting in a car with strangers, but she ends up doing it anyway. She and several of the other gifted teens have been kidnapped to help stage a bank robbery, but Emily knows that is only the tip of the iceberg. (Quick Picks)

Subjects: Clairvoyance; Seers

Finders Keepers. 2010. 9780753419533.

After a serious accident on the football field, Ken discovers he can hear the dead, but he needs tp save the others from the "Gifted" class at Meadowbrook Middle School from terrible danger.

Subjects: Mediums

Out-of-Body Experiences

Teens often wonder what life is like for someone else. The characters in the following stories find out firsthand when they end up living in someone else's body. *Out of Sight, Out of Mind* by Marilyn Kaye, annotated in the "Psionic Powers and Unexplained Powers" section of this chapter (above), also features an out-of-body experience.

Harrison, Kim.

Madison Avery series. 🅹 🆂

Madison, age seventeen, was scythed after a car crash on her prom night, but she grabbed the amulet from her slayer, which has put her in a unique position. Now she is dead, but most people don't know it.

Once Dead, Twice Shy. 2009. 9780061718168.

Madison is teamed with Barnabas to save others, but they can't establish the telepathy they need, so things go awry. Could it be because she really isn't intended to be a reaper, but something different? Can she ever be reunited with her body? And what is the deal with her limerick-spouting cherub of a guardian angel?

Early to Death, Early to Rise. 2010. 9780061718175.

Never good at following rules, Madison Avery, discovering she is the dark timekeeper, goes her own way and brings together a group of rogue reapers.

Singleton, Linda Joy.

The Dead Girl Series. 🅼 🅹 🆂

After being hit by a mail truck and ending up in a coma, sixteen-year-old Amber is sent into other people's bodies to give them a break and try to resolve their issues.

Dead Girl Walking. 2008. 9780738714059.

Amber has big ambitions, but she needs a big scholarship to meet her preliminary goals. After leaving a party where she overhears the popular crowd saying awful things about her, she receives her admission letter for university, along with the news that she's won a big scholarship—but just then the mail carrier's truck runs amok and mows her down. As she goes toward the light, she sees her dead grandmother and dog. Her Gran tells her to go back, but she makes a wrong turn and wakes up in the body of rich, gorgeous, popular, and oh-so-fake Leah. As she tries to make it back into her own body, she has to deal with myriad serious issues in Leah's life. (Quick Picks, PP)

Dead Girl Dancing. 2009. 9780738714066.

Amber wakes up not in her own sixteen-year-old body, but in that of Eli's twenty-one-year-old college sister, who is suffering a massive hangover and about to embark on a spring break road trip with a couple of friends. Unfortunately Sharayah is haunted by both a stalker and a recurring nightmare, and somewhere along the line she has turned from a conscientious premed student into a wild party girl. (Quick Picks)

Dead Girl in Love. 2009. 9780738714073.

Now working for her dead grandmother, Amber lives in the bodies of people who need a break from their reality. This time she finds herself in the body of her best friend, who just happens to be in a coffin instead of her own body, which is now the lodging place of her grandmother. (Quick Picks)

Snow, Carol.

Switch. 2008. 9780061452086. **J** **S**

When lightning is near, Claire Martin, age fifteen, switches places with any nearby girl who was born under the same moon she was. After falling asleep she usually wakes up again in her own body, but when a static electricity shock switches her into the body of a gorgeous summer visitor, something goes wrong and she doesn't switch back. Even the ghost of her grandmother, who died before she was born, can't seem to help her. Being in the wrong body does draw the attention of her crush, but it also shows her that what looks like a perfect life may be far from it.

Unexplained Phenomena

All kinds of unexplained things happen in teen paranormal novels. The following tales see characters transported to other places, experiencing paranormal phenomena, or facing a variety of paranormal situations.

Matthews, L. S.

The Outcasts. 2007. 9780385733670. **J** **S**

After a group of five high school outcasts are chosen to go on a fieldtrip, they find themselves facing danger in another dimension.

Subjects: England; Fieldtrips; Legends

Denman, K. L.

The Shade. 2008. 9781551439310. **M**

Young teen Safira wakes up one night at summer camp, and she sees the apparition of a girl with ragged black hair wearing a striped shirt. When she returns home in the midst of her sister's wedding preparations, her friend Trinity talks her into trying to get to the root of what she saw, using a Ouija board.

Subjects: Apparitions; High-Low; Weddings

Jablonski, Carla.

Silent Echoes. 2007. 9781595140821. **J** **S**

Sixteen-year-old Lindsay thinks she may really be going schizophrenic after she starts hearing the voice of Lucy, who lives as a medium in 1882, and Lucy begins to believe that she may have actually contacted a spirit.

Subjects: Manhattan; Mediums; Mental Illness; New York; Séances;

Jonsberg, Barry.

Dreamrider. 2008. 9780375844584. **S**

Michael, a high school student who has changed schools multiple times, has always been bullied about his weight, and now once again he is the new kid in school. His respite is in lucid dreaming, but then he starts using it to get even with his tormenters.

Subjects: Australia; Bullying; Lucid Dreaming; Overweight

Lubar, David.

Talents Series. **M** **J** **S**

Edgeview Alternative School is the end of the line for kids who can't cut it in regular schools because of behavioral problems. However, the talents the kids who are sent there have sometimes go far beyond getting in trouble.

Hidden Talents. 1999. 9780765342652.

Thirteen-year-old Martin Anderson has an uncanny knack for irritating everyone he comes in contact with, until he hooks up with the misfits in a boarding school full of misfits, including his roommate Torchie and other kids, called Trash, Lucky, Cheater, and Flinch. Martin soon discovers that they all have hidden talents. (BBYA, Quick Picks)

True Talents. 2007. 9780765309778.

Trash's telekinetic powers bring him to the attention of someone very powerful, who kidnaps him and keeps him drugged; his family and pals from Edgeview Alternative School think he is dead. As if that wasn't horrible enough, the bad guy has also created a machine that negates the powers of Trash, Cheater, Lucky, Flinch, Torchie, and Martin. When Trash escapes, all the gang are mysteriously drawn together again. (Quick Picks, VOYA)

Matas, Carol.

The Freak. **M** **J**

Following a raging meningitis-induced fever, Jade, age fifteen, acquires some unusual abilities, including the ability to see auras and experience prophetic dreams.

Subjects: Auras; Dreams; Racism

The Freak. 2002 Reissued 2008. 9781552639306.

After a serious illness, fifteen-year-old Jade wakes up to discover that she knows things about friends and family that she shouldn't know and can tell that her aunt's boyfriend is in danger in time to save him from a car bomb.

Visions. 2007. 9781552639320.

When Jade dreams about some women who end up murdered, she must try to solve the mystery and stop the killer before he can kill her friend's mother.

McMann, Lisa.

Dream Catcher. **J S**

Janie Hannagan, a high school senior, experiences the dreams of those around her, which has caused her to keep her distance from others as she cares for her alcoholic mother.

Subjects: Dreams; Lucid Dreaming; Romance

Wake. 2008. 9781416953579.

Seventeen-year-old Janie Hannagan often finds herself pulled unwillingly into other people's dreams and nightmares, but when she dreams the murder dreams of an interesting boy, her life takes quite a turn, and she discover that she is a dream catcher. (TTT, Quick Picks, IRA YAC)

Fade. 2009. 9781416953586.

Janie and Cabel discover that a sexual predator is going after the students of their high school, and they decide they must do something about it, using Janie as bait.

Gone. 2010. 9781416979180.

Now eighteen, Janie is spending the summer before college trying to decide if she is going to continue to help solve crimes, which will eventually cripple her, or if she should isolate and protect herself, when she discovers the father she has never known is also a dream catcher and is dying in a hospital nearby.

Mitchard, Jacquelyn.

The Midnight Twins. **J**

Thirteen-year-old twins Mally and Merry were born in two different calendar years. After a devastating fire, they discover that Merry has the psychic ability to see into the past, whereas her mirror twin can now see into the future.

Subjects: Dreams; Twins

The Midnight Twins. 2008. 9781595141606.

Twins Mally and Merry, who have lost their psychic connection to each other, discover that they can combine their talents to pursue a teen psychopath, who is torturing animals and attempting rape.

Look Both Ways. 2009. 9781595141613.

Mally's friend Eden is unhappy with the role she is to play as a medicine woman for her Native American tribe, but her major problem is that she is a shape-shifter.

Watch for Me by Moonlight. 2010. 9781595142771.

With their mother in medical school, Meredith and Mallory investigate why their baby brother keeps getting sick while in the care of various babysitters. Merry grieves over falling in love with a boy who died in the Vietnam War.

Singleton, Linda Joy.

The Seer. 🅜 🅙

Sabine Rose, a high school student, tries to use her powers to stop disasters from happening; but it turns out that seeing what is going to happen doesn't mean she can stop it from happening.

Subjects: Astral Projection; Dreams; Grandmothers; Magic

Don't Die Dragonfly. 2004. 9780738705262.

> Living with her grandmother, Sabine is finding acceptance at her new high school, but when she sees a vision of a bloody dragonfly, she knows she must act or someone will die.

Last Dance. 2005. 9780738706382.

> While trying to find a remedy book to help her grandmother, Sabine and Thorn, her goth friend, travel to a small California town, where they find themselves in the middle of a fifty-year-old mystery.

Witch Ball. 2006. 9780738708218.

> When a real witch ball is substituted for the fake crystal ball Sabine is using for a school carnival fortune-telling booth, new dangers abound as she sees future death and destruction.

Sword Play. 2006. 9780738708805.

> Sabine is forced to leave her friends and grandmother and go back to live with her mother. She becomes an assistant to her former fencing teacher and reconnects with some old friends, but is haunted by the ghost of Kip, the football player she had tried to warn, whose death led to her expulsion from school and estrangement from her friends. Kip wants her to save someone, but first she must discover whom.

Fatal Charm. 2007. 9780738711539.

> While using astral projection to spy on her secret half-sister Sabine witnesses a gruesome murder, but the next day she discovers that the victim is still alive.

Vrettos, Adrienne Maria.

Sight. 2007. 9781416906575. 🅙 🅢

> Fifteen-year-old Dylan, who lives in a small mountain town above the California desert, can see dead people. More specifically, she can see moments in the lives of children who are kidnapped and murdered, but never in time to save them. Her ability has been kept secret from all but the sheriff and his deputy. They have depended on her ever since she found the body of a kindergarten classmate and her ability freaked her dad out so much that he left, never to be seen again. Now, ten years later, with more young children going missing, rumor has it that the Drifter has returned. The tight-knit group of teens who have been friends forever face a challenge when a new girl starts at their school, and relationships change as she picks at the scab that is the tale of the Drifter. (Quick Picks)

Westerfeld, Scott.

Midnighters. **J** **S**

Bixby, Oklahoma, is one of the strange places on the earth, where ley lines come together, allowing people who were born in the secret twenty-fifth hour of the day to see the hidden monsters that manifest in that one hour.

The Secret Hour. 2004. 9780060519513.

Specific spots on the earth, including one in Bixby, Oklahoma, are places that the darklings and slithers come out in the mysterious twenty-fifth hour of the day when time freezes and the only humans active are those who were born at exactly midnight. New girl at Bixby High Jessica Day is befriended by the midnighters, those other teens who are alive during the twenty-fifth hour, but she doesn't know what her talent is. Jonathan, Rex, Melissa, and Dess, the other midnighters, have talents such as flying, psychic abilities, and incredible computation skills that help them fight the terrors of the twenty-fifth hour. (IRA YAC, Quick Picks, PP)

Midnighters: Touching Darkness. 2004. 9780060519544.

As the five Midnighters learn more about the Secret Hour and the darklings, they face greater dangers as they discover they aren't the only ones who know about the darklings.

Midnighters: Blue Noon. 2006. 9780060519582.

If the Midnighters can't stop the darklings, they may destroy the daylight world. They have discovered how to expand the twenty-fifth hour to the middle of the day, which leaves humans as prey.

Wood, Jamie Martinez.

Rogelia's House of Magic. 2008. 9780385734776. **J** **S**

Marina and Fern ask Rogelia, the maid in Marina's house who is a curandera, to teach them the magic of their Hispanic ancestors. Rogelia's granddaughter, Xochitl, who is still mourning her sister, doesn't like the idea, but the three fifteen-year-olds find that together they can use magic for good.

Subjects: Auras; Curanderas; Invisibility; Latinas; Mexicans

Superheroes

Superheroes are familiar, perhaps because of their long history of appearing in comic books, graphic novels, and television series. They take on the role of protecting humankind from villainous plots. The following books take them beyond caricature and look at how superpowers can impact the life of a teen.

Campbell, Chelsea.

The Rise of Renegade-X. 2010. 9781606840603. **S**

Damien Locke, the son of a supervillain, stages a big event for his sixteenth birthday, when the V indicating his status as a supervillain will appear on his fingerprints, but the worst thing that can happen does, and instead of a V he develops and X. An X means that his status as supervillain or superhero is undetermined. It can only mean that his mother conceived him with a superhero, but who? Damien's investigation leads him to three possible dads and what he feels is an untenable living situation.

Carroll, Michael.

Quantum Prophecy. M J

Ten years before the series story starts, all the superhumans disappeared in a battle—both superheroes and supervillains. It turns out that on that fateful day, superheroes and supervillains alike lost their superpowers and began living mundane lives.

The Awakening. 2007. 9780399247255.

Thirteen-year-old Danny Cooper saves the life of a little girl about to be struck by a bus, but in order to do it he had to have moved at super speed. He confides in his best friend Colin Wagner, who soon discovers that he himself has acquired the ability of super hearing and super strength; but that doesn't save him when he and his parents are abducted. Escaping their captors in Jacksonville, Florida, Colin has amazing adventures on his way to find former superhero Solomon Cord. Meanwhile Renate, aka Diamond, a teenage girl who can turn solid and impervious to damage, has woken from a ten-year sleep. (PP)

The Gathering. 2008. 9780399247262.

Danny, Colin, and Renate go into hiding when their identities are exposed and end up in a secret location, where they can learn how to use their powers, but there is a traitor in their midst.

The Reckoning. 2009. 9780399247279.

With the world on the brink of World War III, the young superheroes must make some major decisions, but knowing whom to trust is one of their biggest dilemmas.

Moore, Perry.

Hero. 2007. 9781423101956. J S

Thom Creed, the son of a disgraced superhero, is keeping two big secrets: that he is developing superpowers and that he is gay. After saving a woman's life, he is invited to compete for a spot in the League of superheroes. (BBYA)

Subjects: Cancer; Gay Boys; Healers

Sniegoski, Thomas E.

Legacy. 2009. 9780385737142. S

Eighteen-year-old high school dropout/auto mechanic Lucas lives with his waitress mother in a trailer park and has never known who is deadbeat father was. After Lucas discovers amazing healing powers when he is knifed in the garage, the richest resident of Seraph City turns up claiming to be his father and the alter ego of superhero Raptor. Lucas wants no part of what he is offering, until the trailer park is attacked and his mother is killed. Wanting to avenge his mom, Lucas agrees to apprentice as the next Raptor, but things are not as they appear. (Quick Picks)

Short Stories

Short stories are a wonderful way of "tasting" several different authors. They are also great for when the reader wants something to read but does not have enough time for a novel.

666: Number of the Beast. 2007. 9780545021173. **S**

Eighteen stories dealing with vampires, werewolves, and evil faeries by authors, some known for writing for teens and others who usually don't write for teens. The authors included are Peter Abrahams, Laurie Faria Stolarz, Christopher Pike, Joyce Carol Oates , Heather Graham, Bentley Little, Chet Williamson, Jane Mason, Amelia Atwater-Rhodes, Joshua Gee, Robin Wasserman, T. E. D. Klein, David Moody, Melissa de la Cruz, P. D. Cacek, Isobel Bird, Ellen Schreiber, and Sarah Hines Stephens.

Cabot, Meg, ed.

Prom Nights from Hell. 2007. 9780061253102. **S**

Five paranormal tales of prom nights gone seriously wrong. In Meg Cabot's "The Exterminator's Daughter," a teen finds romance while trying to take out the vampire her best friend is dating. A wish for a prom date sends Will to a gruesome death in Lauren Myracle's " The Corsage." Kim Harrison tells the story of a girl who dumps the date her father found for her for the prom and takes a ride home with a handsome stranger who has plans to kill her, in "Madison Avery and the Dim Reaper." In "Kiss and Tell" by Michele Jaffe, Miranda, a high school senior and limo driver, picks up a young girl with oracular powers and uncovers a deadly supernatural plot. Can a demon and an angel find love together in Stephenie Meyer's "Hell on Earth"?

Delaney, Joseph.

A Coven of Witches. 2010. 9780061960383. **M**

Four tales of witches include one that gives some more insight into Tom Ward's friend Alice. Stories included are "Meg Skelton," "Dirty Dora," "Alice and the Brain Guzzler," and "The Banshee Witch. "

The Spook's Tale: And Other Horrors. 2009. 9780061730283. **M**

In addition to several delightfully scary stories, this collection also provides a look into the past of Mr. Gregory. Stories included are "Horrors Begin," "Spook's Tale: Dead Apprentice," "Witch's Lair," "Spook's Bones," "Blood Dish," "Silver Chain," "Alice's Tale: Mouldheels And Maggots," "Grimalkin's Tale: Witch Assassin," and "Gallery of Villains. "

Horowitz, Anthony.

More Horowitz Horror. 2007. 9780399245190. **M** **J**

This collection of nine short stories features fast-paced, gruesome stories that revolve around teens who encounter horror in the midst of the mundane, from cell phones to elevators. Stories include "The Hitchhiker," "The Sound of Murder," "Burned," "Flight 715," "Howard's End," "The Elevator," "The Phone Goes Dead," "Twist Cottage," and "The Shortest Horror Story Ever Written."

Lubar, David.

Weenies Short Stories. **M**

Lubar's very short, very warped, creepy, and sometimes funny stories have high appeal for middle school readers. Many have the feel of urban legends.

Subjects: Horror; Humorous

In the Land of the Lawn Weenies and Other Misadventures. 2003. 9780765345707.

Invasion of the Road Weenies and Other Warped and Creepy Tales. 2005. 9780765314475.

The Curse of the Campfire Weenies: And Other Warped and Creepy Tales. 2007. 9780765357717.

The Battle of the Red Hot Pepper Weenies and Other Warped and Creepy Tales. 2009. 9780765320995.

Shusterman, Neal.

Darkness Creeping: Twenty Twisted Tales. 2007. 9780142407219. **M**

Twenty sinister scary stories, including "Catching Cold," "Who Do We Appreciate?," "Soul Survivor," "Black Box," "Resting Deep," "Security Blanket," "Same Time Next Year," "River Tour," "Flushie," "Monkeys Tonight," "Screaming at the Wall," "Growing Pains," "Alexander's Skull," "Connecting Flight," "Ralphy Sherman's Root Canal," "Ear for Music," "Riding the Raptor," "Trash Day," "Crystalloid," and "Shadows of Doubt."

Subjects: Horror; Paranormal

Vande Velde, Vivian.

All Hallows' Eve: 13 Stories. 2006. 9780152055769. **J** **S**

Creepy horror stories with a Halloween theme, including "Come in and Rest a Spell," "MARIAN," "Morgan Roehmar's Boys," "Only on All Hallows' Eve," "Cemetery Field Trip," "Best Friends," "Pretending," "I Want to Thank You," "When and How," "When My Parents Come to Visit," "Edward, Lost and Far from Home," "My Real Mother," and "Holding On." (TTT, VOYA)

Subjects: Ghosts; Vampires

Di's Picks

Gill, David Macinnis. *Soul Enchilada*.

Smith, Cynthia Leitich. *Eternal*.

Stiefvater, Maggie. *Shiver*.

Vrettos, Adrienne Maria. *Sight*.

Westerfeld, Scott. *Peeps*.

Chapter 6

Science Fiction

I love science fiction. It's so entertaining to see the twists on modern life and technology that sci-fi writers come up with, especially since some of the out there concepts might soon become reality. (I especially look forward to traveling through wormholes.) Ever since I read Ender's Game by Orson Scott Card in seventh grade, I've been hooked.—Alice, age 15

The science fiction genre is experiencing a resurgence in popularity with teen readers. *Hunger Games*, a dystopic survival novel and one of the most talked about books of 2009 and 2010, also made the 2009 Teens Top Ten List. Four of the twenty-five finalists for Teens Top Ten 2009 were science fiction. On a more personal level, the very active teen book clubs that this author conducts in Grand Junction, Colorado, have nominated eighteen science fiction titles for the Teens Top Ten list in the second half of 2010.

Many of today's adults who grew up in the 1960s and 1970s became interested in the genre around age twelve, the age that has often been called the "golden age of science fiction," as so many fans discovered science fiction at that age. Once hooked, readers continue reading SF as long as they can find stories that interest them and create a sense of awe, which, with today's rich offerings, can last a lifetime.

Nonreaders of the genre often have a hard time identifying science fiction or differentiating it from fantasy, especially since the two genres are often shelved together. Of course, each reader makes up his or her own mind about where a book fits. Orson Scott Card, one of the best known science fiction authors read by teens, once stated at a YALSA preconference on genre fiction that if rivets are pictured on the cover, a book is science fiction; if foliage is present, it belongs in fantasy.

The age for which a book is intended is not much of an issue for science fiction readers (nor fantasy readers). I have found that teen readers are more than happy to read science fiction published for adults, and adult readers of science fiction are happy to find great reads in the teen section. Recently, *The Roar* by Emma Clayton, originally designed for and marketed to readers ages nine to twelve, has been quite popular with teen readers.

The main appeal of science fiction revolves around the question "what if?" What if everyone over the age of fourteen disappeared? What if scientific discoveries a century ago shaped a very different world than the one we live in now? What if genetic engineering could create people with extraordinary powers? Science fiction is a genre that allows readers to look at all the possibilities.

Action Adventure

Action adventure science fiction is plot driven. The pacing is fast, the pressure is high, and the protagonists experience danger on many levels, often in the course of their own explorations of places where they should not have been to begin with. Readers who enjoy page-turners and "fast reads" would be best served by these titles.

Bechard, Margaret.

Spacer and Rat. 2005. 9781596430587. **M** **J** **S**

> Jack has always lived on Freedom station, but is close to leaving when he encounters Kit, an Earthie Rat in possession of an illegally modified robot. Now he is drawn into problems he never anticipated.
>
> **Subjects:** Robots; Space Colonies

Buckell, Tobias.

Sly Mongoose. 2008. 9780765319203. **S**

> Fourteen-year-old Timas belongs to an elite class of residents of Yatapek, a city that floats above the crushing pressure, heat, and toxic air of the planet Chilo. His family lives on high level because he is small and smart, able to fit into the antique pressure suits needed to perform work on the deadly surface of the planet. Pepper, a sly old man, lands on Yatapek after catapulting himself through space without a parachute to escape a disaster, but he is wanted for slaying all his shipmates and creating the disaster that may result in the zombification of all humankind if not stopped. A teen girl is sent to Chilo as an emissary from a community of people who link consciousnesses for instant communication and operate on consensus.
>
> **Subjects:** Adult Books for Teens; Eating Disorders; Space Colonies; Zombies

Carroll, Michael.

Quantum Prophecy. **M** **J**

> This series dealing with superpowers is annotated in chapter 5.

Daley, Michael. **J**

Shanghaied to the Moon. 2007. 9780399246197. **M**

> In an action-packed adventure, thirteen-year-old Stewart Hale, who wants to go to space more than anything, meets a drunken old spacer who is delighted with Stewart's short stature. The spacer grabs Stewart, and soon they leave the earth,

heading to the moon in a derelict craft on a mysterious quest. On the perilous journey Stewart discovers things about himself, the spacer, his hero, and his family.

Subjects: Space Travel

Doctorow, Cory.

Little Brother. **2008. 9780765319852.** 🇯 🇸

"Those who would give up Essential Liberty to purchase a little Temporary Safety, deserve neither Liberty nor Safety" (Benjamin Franklin). Marcus Yallow and three of his friends skip out of school to participate in a game, and in a horrible case of being in the wrong place at the wrong time, they witness the San Francisco Bay Bridge being blown up, perhaps by terrorists. When the quartet tries to go to ground in a BART station, the press of the crowd proves deadly, and Marcus's friend Darryl is stabbed. Up on the street, trying to flag down help to get Darryl to a hospital, the four are picked up as suspected terrorists by the Department of Homeland Security and taken to a secret prison, where Marcus is tortured and interrogated. Days later he is allowed to go home, but threatened with retribution if he reveals that he had been imprisoned and tortured. An accomplished hacker, Marcus figures out a way to fight back. (BBYA)

Subjects: Espionage; Freedoms; Hackers; Surveillance

Haarsma, P. J.

The Softwire. 🇲 🇯

Nearly 200 orphaned kids arrive in the Orbis system to find that they are now slaves to pay for the passage of their parents, who died before the children were born. Twelve-year-old JT turns out to be a "softwire," a human who can interface mentally with computers.

Subjects: Aliens; Orphans; Psionic Powers; Slavery; Space Colonies

The Softwire: Virus on Orbis 1. 2006. 9780763636388.

When all the adults on the *Renaissance* died en route to Orbis, a multicultural world orbiting a wormhole, the ship incubated their embryos and raised the children, who upon arrival discover they are now indentured to pay for their passage. Being a softwire places JT, who can interface mentally with computers, under suspicion and in peril.

Betrayal on Orbis 2. 2008. 9780763627102.

Relocated to the second planet in the Orbis system, the children find their new masters even more cruel. JT is able to communicate with the giant aquatic creatures who are also slaves.

Wormhole Pirates on Orbis 3. 2009. 9780763627119.

Sent to Orbis 3, the children are happy to have a human master who sends them to school, but it, too, is brutal. They find respite that leads them further into danger when they begin to play a game that culminates in a gladiatorial-like competition.

Awakening on Orbis 4. 2010. 9780763627126.

> In this conclusion to the series, with new troubles on a new planet, JT, now seventeen, discovers that he actually is a Tonant, the one who must protect the Scion, the individual who will save the universe.

Zahn, Timothy.

Dragonback Adventures. 🅼 🅹 🆂

Jack Morgan, a fourteen-year-old orphaned thief, becomes the symbiotic host of Draycos, an alien warrior poet who is trying to save his people from genocide.

Subjects: Aliens; Artificial Intelligence; Dragons; Genocide; Orphans; Poets; Symbiots; Thieves; Warriors

Dragon and Thief. 2003. 9780765342720.

> When fourteen-year-old Jack Morgan, who is hiding on a deserted planet, finds a crashed ship, he finds one survivor, Draycos, a dragon-shaped K'da who must bond with a host to stay alive. When he does attach to Jack, he has the appearance of a huge dragon tattoo. Draycos, extremely honorable, enlists Jack's help in trying to save his people, who are on the verge of being annihilated by another alien race, and promises to help Jack clear his name. (BBYA)

Dragon and Soldier. 2004. 9780765350176.

> Jack enlists as a mercenary in his quest to find out more about those who attacked Draycos's ship and meets Alison Kayna another teen mercenary.

Dragon and Slave. 2005. 9780765340412.

> Needing to infiltrate the computer system on the planet Brum-a-dum, Jack arranges to be captured and become a slave at the estate, where he will be able to get the information he needs.

Dragon and Herdsman. 2007. 9780765352767.

> Fleeing to the planet Rho Scorvi, Jack and Draycos find a population of Phookas, a herd of beasts much like the K'da that they must herd to safety when the Malison Ring turns up, chasing Jack for his activities on Brum-a-dum.

Dragon and Judge. 2007. 9780765352774.

> Even though his parents died when Jack was only three, a race of aliens for whom they worked want Jack to serve as a judge for them. Meanwhile, he and Draycos strive to stop the plot to eliminate the last of K'da survivors still en route to what they believe is safety.

Dragon and Liberator. 2008. 9780765314192.

> As the last of the K'da approach, Jack and Draycos have allies in the symbiotic partnership of Alison and Taneem, to stop their enemies and prevent the Death machine from being used.

Bioengineering

Bioengineering themes have expanded from the idea of cloning to altering human DNA to create humans with special abilities. It also includes medical advances that allow human parts to be regrown to replace those lost in accidents, techniques that wreak havoc instead of cures, and techniques that cause animals to become more human-like.

Readers who enjoy the bioengineering theme may also enjoy books like Meg Cabot's *Airhead*, which on the surface looks like Chick Lit that deals with identity, but is actually science fiction about medical advances that can impact identity. One of the best known teen novels dealing with bioengineering, *House of the Scorpion* by Nancy Farmer, a novel about cloning, won both Printz and Newbery honor awards, as well as being chosen an IRA Young Adult Choice.

Cooper, Brenda.

Silver Ship. 🅾

The planet Fremont, with its multitude of moons and hostile flora and fauna, was settled by a colony that abhorred genetic manipulation. Two centuries after its establishment, a new ship of colonists, all with genemods (gene modifications), arrives, but the two groups find it impossible to live together and a war breaks out, leaving six genemodified orphans behind after the few surviving new colonists depart.

Subjects: Adult Books for Teens; Orphans

The Silver Ship and the Sea. 2007. 9780765355096.

Adopted by settlers, teens Chelo, Joseph, Bryan, Liam, Alicia, and Kayleen try to use their biological advantages to help the community, but struggle against discrimination. Alicia, adopted by one of the two wandering bands on the planet, is treated as a prisoner of war. Kayleen has a loving adoptive mother. Liam is expected to succeed his adoptive father as leader of the other roving band. Chelo and Joseph, siblings by birth, are very happy as the adopted children of the leaders of Aristos, the only city on the planet, but when those parents die, forces prove that none of the six gene-modified teens is safe.

Reading the Wind. 2008. 9780765315984.

War comes to Fremont, and Chelo, thought dead, may be the salvation of the planet. She, Liam, and Kayleen stayed on Fremont when her brother Joseph, Alicia, Bryan, and Jenna went to a planet where all are genmods.

Wings of Creation. 2009. 9780765320957.

In this increasingly complex series, Celo, Joseph, and their "family" go to the planet Lopali, where the genetically engineered residents can fly but no longer walk with ease or reproduce. They are counting on Joseph to help them.

Daley, Michael J.

Rat. [M]

Rat, a lovely lavender rat, lives on a space station; her artificial enhancements allow her to do many un-ratlike things.

Subjects: Rats; Robots; Space Stations

Space Station Rat. 2005. 9780823421510.

Jeff teams up with Rat, a genetically modified and artificially enhanced rodent, to save the space station, and evades the horrific robotic Nanny his parents have entrusted him to.

Rat Trap. 2008. 9780823420933.

Jeff and Rat team up again when the scientist who engineered Rat visits the space station, and Rat tries to return to Earth.

Halam, Ann.

Taylor Five. 2004. 9780440238201. [J]

Fourteen-year-old Taylor Walker, the clone of Pam Taylor, founder of Lifeforce, the corporation her parents work for, is exploring a cave system with her brother near their home in Borneo when a wildfire sweeps overhead. They return home to total devastation. The primate reserve has been destroyed, and all the scientists, including their parents, have been taken hostage by insurgents.

Subjects: Adventure; Biotechnology; Borneo; Cloning; Orangutans; Primate Research

Levitin, Sonia.

The Goodness Gene. 2005. 9780525473978. [S]

In the twenty-third century, a benign dictator's identical twin sons, Will and Berk, are very different from each other in temperament and personality. When Will is sent on a goodwill mission to a remote area, he finds that he and Berk are actually clones of a historical personage know for evil.

Subjects: Clones; Dictators; Twins

Patterson, James.

Maximum Ride. [J] [S]

A group of six children, ages six to fourteen, escape from the bioengineering lab where they were created from a mixture of human and bird DNA, which enables them to fly.

Subjects: Ecology; Espionage; Flying ; Mad Scientists

Maximum Ride: The Angel Experiment. 2005. 9780316067959.

Max, Maximum Ride, a fourteen-year-old flying girl, leads the "flock" on a quest across the country to rescue Angel, the youngest of the flying children, who has been taken back to the "School" by Erasers, a bioengineered combination of human and wolf. (TTT, IRA YAC)

Maximum Ride: School's Out—Forever. 2006. 9780316067966.

> A flying fight with Erasers leaves Fang so gravely injured the "Flock" must take him to a hospital, which makes their existence known to the FBI. Taken in by an FBI agent, the six flying children enjoy a normal life—for a short time. (TTT, VOYA, IRA YAC, PP)

Maximum Ride: Saving the World and Other Extreme Sports. 2007. 9780316154277.

> The flock face various enemies, and their travels take them to Germany and Venice Beach. Some of the mad scientists who created them are planning genocide for the world. (TTT)

The Final Warning. 2008. 9780316002868.

> While on a mission to Antarctica in an attempt to stop global warming, the flock encounter the plans hatched by the scientist who created them to auction them off.

Max. 2009. 9780316002899.

> Flying exhibitions to publicize an environmental group prove dangerous to Max and the flock. They also must stop an evil businessman who has been dumping radioactive waste into the ocean.

Fang. 2010. 97803160361901.

> In Africa for a photo shoot, Max and the flock meet Dr. Gunther-Hagen, who is obsessed with them and tries to match Max up with Dylan, a bird kid, only eight months old, who has been aged to be her perfect mate. Meanwhile Max is fearful for Fang because Angel has predicted his death.

Pearson, Mary E.

The Adoration of Jenna Fox. 2008. 9780805076684. **J S**

When seventeen-year-old Jenna Fox awakens from a coma with amnesia, she is told that she has been in a terrible accident. She is living in California with her mother and grandmother while her father commutes to Boston. As she convalesces, she watches video discs of her life. It seems her parents recorded almost her entire life, but some of the things she sees there make her question what is going on. Her grandmother, who loved her in the vids, seems to hate her now. She had close friends in the vids, but now nobody visits, calls, or writes. Then she meets a neighbor and discovers that her family had only recently moved to California. Why would a family move a daughter who was in a coma away from the great hospitals in a city where her father still works? When Jenna starts attending a small charter school, she becomes friends with a girl crippled by a biomedical disaster, which has turned her into an activist. (BBYA, VOYA, IRA YAC, PP)

Subjects: Biomedical; California; Charter Schools; Near Future

Sawyer, Robert J.

WWW. S

Subjects: Adult Books for Teens; Artificial Intelligence; Blindness; Sentience

WWW: Wake. 2009. 9780441016792.

Fifteen-year-old Caitlin, a brilliant math student and Web surfer who happens to have been blind since birth, receives an e-mail from a researcher in Japan who believes he has a way to cure her blindness. All does not go as expected, and instead of being able to see after the surgery, she achieves the ability to see the Web, where she encounters what may be an emerging intelligence. Two subplots involving a chimpanzee and a Chinese hacker relate to freedom of information and evolving sentience.

WWW: Watch. 2010. 9780441018185.

When the U.S. government discovers Webmind, it is in danger, as is its friend Caitlin, who has also come to the attention of the government agency that monitors the Internet for dangers to the country.

Scalzi, John.

Zoe's Tale. 2008. 9780765316981. S

Told from the viewpoint of a teenage girl, this adventurous tale takes Zoe, who has had a very event-filled life, to a new world with her adoptive parents, who are to lead the colony. En route something goes wrong, and they end up orbiting the wrong planet but must make do. Because they are the targets of a conclave of spacefaring races that want to regulate human colonization, they must eschew all technology that could possibly emit a signal and give away their location.

Subjects: Adult Books for Teens; Immortality; Space Colonies

Stahler, David.

Truesight Trilogy. M J

On a colony settled and inhabited by the blind, a group who chose to genetically select blindness for their babies espouse a doctrine that claims vision keeps people from seeing the truth.

Subjects: Blindness; Colonization; Dreams; Dystopia

Truesight. 2004. 9780060522872.

Twelve-year-old Jacob finds his life thrown into turmoil when he begins to be able to see, which shows him not all is well in Harmony, the town of the blind where he lives.

The Seer. 2007. 9780060522889.

Exiled from Harmony, thirteen-year-old Jacob sets out to find the city of the seers, where he searches for Delaney, who had run away. Rescuing her from bondage as an entertainer, they escape to the desert with Xander, an ex-mercenary.

Otherspace. 2008. 9780060522919.

> Fourteen-year-old Jacob, born into the community of Harmony, where the genetic engineering routinely done to insure blindness was not successful on him, leaves his friends to go to another planet where other seers are in hiding, as he tries to discover why he is having visions.

Thompson, Kate.

Missing Link. 🅼 🅹

As the world comes to a grinding halt due to an energy crisis, Christie, age thirteen, and his fifteen-year-old developmentally disabled stepbrother Danny make their way to Scotland to Danny's mother, who has a compound much like the island of Dr. Moreau.

Subjects: Apocalypse; Geneticists; Himalayas; Scotland; Talking Animals

Fourth World. 2005. 9781582348971.

> When Danny decides to run away to see his scientist mother in Scotland, his stepbrother Christie, who feels responsible for him, goes along to protect him. Along the way they add a homeless girl, a talking dog, and a talking bird to their company.

Only Human. 2006. 9781582346519.

> Christie and a group of diverse genetically engineered teens who are part human and part animal go to the Himalayas in search of a yeti and answers about their own creation.

Origins. 2007. 9781582346526.

> Alternating between Christie's journal of his life at Fourth World with his genetically altered stepbrother and his stepbrother's half-siblings, and a part-cat girl and part-dog boy who are living in a post-apocalyptic world, the secrets of the Fourth World and the missing link are finally revealed.

Vizzini, Ned.

Be More Chill. 2004. 9780786809950. 🆂

> Geeky high school student Jeremy Heere swallows a supercomputer in pill form that lodges in his brain to tell him how to be cool and attract girls. (Quick Picks, PP)

Subjects: Computers; Sex

Virtual Reality

Virtual reality is a computer-generated world in which people can interact. Second Life (http://secondlife. com) is a primitive version of virtual reality. In the following novels, the worlds encountered, usually in games, are so vivid and real they cannot be distinguished from reality. These stories are great for readers who enjoy an "immersion" experience.

Hamilton, Peter F.

The Web: Lightstorm. 2005. 9780765349422. **M**

Thirteen-year-old Aynsley and his virtual reality game-playing cohorts uncover a corporate conspiracy that has created a horrendous danger in a nearby swamp.

Subjects: Gaming; Physically Challenged; Pollution

Kostick, Conor.

Epic. **J** **S**

The series starts on a world where the economy is determined by the inhabitants' standing in a virtual reality game, and continues into a world in which the inhabitants live in a game.

Subjects: Avatars; Gaming

Epic. 2007. 9780670061792.

Violence is an unforgivable crime on the planet New Earth, which was settled by those fleeing the violence of Earth. The planet is ruled by a committee that allocates resources and jobs based on how people perform in an online game called Epic. Erik's family and community are in great need, so they enter a tournament that gives them a slim chance of winning a new tractor that will mean their survival or ending up being moved to an even poorer community with worse lives. (IRA YAC)

Saga. 2008. 9780670062805.

Ghost, a fourteen-year-old airboarder, has no memory of her first nine years. She lives in a city oppressed by a 2000-year-old queen. When Cindella Dragonslayer, Erik's gaming avatar, shows up, Ghost and Cindella combine forces to try to stop the queen's diabolical plots, which have enslaved the inhabitants of New Earth to a new game and will annihilate the population of Ghost's world.

Lubar, David.

Flip. 2003. 9780765340481. **M**

When eighth grader Ryan sees a flash in the night and discovers a crashed spaceship, he salvages some alien virtual reality entertainment disks, which temporarily give him the personalities, knowledge, and skills of various people throughout history, including Queen Victoria and Spartacus.

Subjects: Alien Technology; Historical Persons

Vande Velde, Vivian.

Heir Apparent. 2003. 9780152053413. **M** **J**

A protest at the gaming center is not going to stop Giannine from using the certificate she received for her fourteenth birthday. Unfortunately the protesters sabotage the equipment when she is in a game, keeping her in the game until she can win a swashbuckling medieval adventure, or she will die in real life. (BBYA)

Subjects: Gaming; Historical Fiction; Protests

Alternate Worlds and Parallel Worlds

The idea of different versions of the world all existing simultaneously is a common one in science fiction. Sometimes the worlds are created when different decisions are made. Some of the stories in this section are about worlds that diverged from ours when their history took a slightly different tack. Another subgenre that immerses readers in other worlds.

Davidson, Jenny.

The Explosionist. 2008. 9780061239755. **J S**

Fifteen-year-old orphan Sophie attends an academy where she comes to suspect that a teacher she really likes may be a terrorist. A murdered medium and a run-in with a former schoolmate, who has been radically transformed after joining the branch of service started by Sophie's feminist aunt, start her on a quest to solve the mysteries. Set in a Scotland on the eve of World War II, countries are aligned quite differently than in our time, because of a divergence in 1815, when Wellington was defeated at Waterloo. Scotland is independent of England and allied with the Scandinavian countries. Spiritualism is a fact and a science. Countries without oil or coal reserves have affected new technologies, including running cars on fuel cells.

Subjects: Alternate History; Scotland; Terrorists

Gaiman, Neil, and Michael Reaves.

InterWorld. 2007. 9780061238963. **M**

Fourteen-year-old Joey Harker is a Walker, someone who can travel between all the parallel realities. He finds himself in several worlds as he works against two forces who are fighting for universal domination.

Hartinger, Brent.

Grand & Humble. 2006. 9780060567279. **J S**

Harlan has a quip for every situation and is at ease everywhere; after all, he's been being groomed for high political office all his life. He has a girlfriend he doesn't really like and is popular not only with his classmates, who elected him president of the student body, but also with his teachers. Unfortunately his overbearing mother plans his entire life for him, requiring him to attend functions that will make his father, the senator, look good. Meanwhile, he has also been experiencing terrifying premonitions. Harlan's story alternates with that of Manny, a theater geek, who lives with his single dad and hangs out with his best friend, who is a deaf girl. Manny suffers from horrific nightmares that make him start thinking his dad is hiding something, which, coupled with the fact that there are no photos of his first three years, makes him very suspicious.

Subjects: Deafness; Dreams; Nightmares; Politicians

Jacobs, Deborah Lynn.

Choices. 2007. 9781596432178. **J** **S**

What if? What if Kathleen hadn't gone to the party with her best friend? What if her brother hadn't been killed coming to pick her up? What if she wasn't afraid to drive? Could every "what if?" actually cause a new universe to form? What if one could move from one world to the next, and the next, and the next? Luke, whom Kathleen meets at her brother's funeral, also has the ability to shift from one reality to another; but he has a secret that may alienate her forever. (Quick Picks)

Jeapes, Ben.

The New World Order. 2005. 9780385750134. **J** **S**

When aliens from a parallel world jump into the civil war between King Charles I and Cromwell's Parliament, they use their superior weapons in a bid to turn England into a colony. One of the people observing this time is Daniel, the fifteen-year-old son of an alien.

Subjects: Aliens; Alternate History; Seventeenth Century

Lawrence, Michael.

Aldous Lexicon trilogy. **J** **S**

Sixteen-year-old Alaric Underwood lives in Withern Rise. In a parallel world, Naia Underwood, who was born on the same day at the same time as Alaric, lives in Withern Rise. There are multiple Withern Rises and multiple Alarics and Naias.

Subjects: Estates; Family Secrets; Parallel Worlds; Quantum Physics; Time Travel

A Crack in the Line. 2004. 9780060724795.

Alaric, not surviving well in the aftermath of his mother's death, lives in the crumbling and increasingly dirty and rundown Withern Rise with his father, who has just taken off to bring his girlfriend Kate back to live with them. At sixteen he is too old for a babysitter but is stuck with his inept Aunt Liney, who has come to stay with him. When prowling through the freezing house he comes across Alex's Folly, an exact model of Withern Rise carved from a fallen branch of the whimsically named Family Tree. As he touches it he sees the snow outside the window reflected in it and experiences severe pain, then finds he is mysteriously outdoors. Wishing to be inside, he is, but it isn't his Withern Rise. He is in a home just like his (but far cleaner and better maintained), looking at a girl who looks almost exactly like him. In this world his mother did not die in a horrible train wreck.

Small Eternities. 2005. 9780060724801.

Alaric and Naia, living in each other's realities, both experience flooding at Withern Rise and travel back in time separately and together, experiencing the history of their home and meeting their dead great-uncle Aldous.

The Underwood See. 2007. 9780060724832.

Naia returns to Withern Rise as a pregnant adult, where she again visits the time when she was sixteen. Aldous tries to save members of the family in different realities.

Sleator, William.

The Last Universe. **2005. 9780810992139.** **J**

This fascinating story revolves around quantum mechanics as four-teen-year-old Susan tries to push her wheelchair-bound, sixteen-year-old brother Gary through a garden maze into a parallel universe where he can walk.

Subjects: Gardens; Massachusetts; Quantum Mechanics

Stead, Rebecca.

First Light. **2007. 9780375840173.** **M**

Thea, a fourteen-year-old girl from a civilization that is built under the ice of Greenland, comes topside and meets Peter, the twelve-year-old son of a gla-ciologist and a geneticist who are there studying global warming.

Subjects: Global Warming; Greenland; Utopias

Voake, Steve.

Dreamwalker's Child. **M** **J**

Sam Palmer, a fifteen-year-old amateur entomologist, is hit by a car, leaving his body in a coma, but he travels to a parallel world where insects are used as aircraft.

Subjects: Insects; Parallel Worlds

The Dreamwalker's Child. 2006. 9781582346618.

When Sam finds himself in Aurobon, he discovers that his presence is no mere accident and that his arrival was prophesied. Unfortunately the leader of the city to which he is taken is set on obliterating human life on Earth. Fortunately a girl named Skipper, who flies genetically engineered wasps, comes to his rescue.

The Web of Fire. 2007. 9781582347370.

Sam is returned to Aurobon four years after his first adventure there, to find Skipper again and to help the Resistance fight Emperor Odoursin, who is set on waging war against the Earth.

Steampunk

Steampunk, a science fiction subgenre that came to the fore in the late 1980s and early 1990s, is coming back into popularity with teen audiences today. It features science fiction stories set in previous, often Victorian, times, making these titles appealing to some historical fiction fans.

Oppel, Kenneth.

Matt Cruse series. J S

In an alternate world where Edwardian mores are the norm, an element called Hydrium, a lighter-than-air gas, was discovered, leading to a world where air travel is the norm and great airships sail the sky.

Subjects: Flight; Pirates; Scientific Exploration

Airborn. 2004. 9780060531829.

> Teenage cabin boy Matt Cruse, on the airship Aurora, and wealthy passenger Kate de Vries find adventure as they track an unknown species, survive a shipwreck, and flee from pirates. (BBYA, Printz Honor, Quick Picks, PP)

Skybreaker. 2005. 9780060532291.

> Matt, now attending the Airship Academy, is on his two-week training tour on a dilapidated and poorly captained freighter. He barely escapes death when the airship escapes disaster and ends up far above where it should be flying, and he catches sight of a fabled lost ship. (BBYA)

Starclimber. 2009. 9780060850579.

> Matt and Kate are chosen to be members of the first crew of Astralnauts, who travel into outer space aboard the *Starclimber*, Kate as a biologists and Matt as crew member.

Reeve, Philip.

Larklight. M J

In a world reminiscent of Jules Verne, Art and Myrtle Mumby live with their parents in Larklight, a house that orbits the Earth.

Subjects: Aliens; Humor; Nineteenth Century; Space Travel; Steampunk; Time Travel

Larklight: A Rousing Tale of Dauntless Pluck in the Farthest Reaches of Space. 2006. 9781599901459.

> One day in 1851, Larklight is attacked by spiderlike creatures, setting Art and Myrtle on the path of adventures that will take them to the Moon and into the orbit of extraterrestrial pirates.

Starcross: A Stirring Adventure of Spies, Time Travel, and Curious Hats. 2007. 9781599902968.

> With Larklight being redecorated, Art and Myrtle accompany their mother to an asteroid resort, where they find a pirate and some intelligent hats that plan on invading the British Empire.

Mothstorm: The Horror from Beyond Uranus Georgium Sidus! 2008. 978-1599903033.

> As the Mumby family celebrates Christmas with Jack and his crew at Larklight, they are alerted to a new menace, a "great danger" that has emerged on the edge of the galaxy in the form of giant cloud of enormous moths, and they must immediately head to Georgium Sidus, also known as Uranus.

Slade, Arthur.

The Hunchback Assignments. 2009. 9780385737845. **M J**

Fourteen-year-old Modo was rescued as a baby from a traveling freak show by Mr. Socrates, who along with his Indian servant has trained him to be an extraordinary agent. Modo is incredibly ugly, but as part of his training he has achieved the ability of altering his appearance, actually changing his face and form for a few hours. After being abandoned in London by Mr. Socrates, he sets himself up as a private investigator and is hired by a young woman claiming to be Miss Featherstone, who involves him in a case involving the crown prince, a number of politician's sons, a diabolical plan involving kidnapped children, and a horrendous automaton that could destroy the British Empire. Set in 1873, this creepy story mixes steampunk with espionage and *Matrix*-like horror. A sequel, *The Dark Deeps* (978-0385737852), was published in 2010.

Subjects: Detectives; London; Nineteenth Century; Robots; Shapeshifters

Westerfeld, Scott.

Leviathan. 2009. 9781416971733. **M J S**

Alek, the son of Archduke Ferdinand, is awakened in the middle of the night by two trusted advisers to go out in one of the armored walking war machines. It is the night his parents were assassinated, starting the Great War. Deryn Sharp, a girl from Glasgow, loves to fly, so she has assumed a male identity and the name Dylan and enlisted in the Air Service. The major division in the world is between the Clankers and the Darwinists: those who build complex, powerful machines and those who tweak DNA to engineer fantastical beasts. (BBYA)

Subjects: Alternate History; Bioengineering; Machines; World War I

Time Travel

Traveling through time takes characters to exotic or remote settings in the past or future. Sometimes it is merely a segue for a historical novel. In science fiction, the travel usually reveals a technological problem with far-reaching effects. Contemporary teens are sometimes better able to envision the past through the eyes of a contemporary who is traveling there. The stories found here use some scientific or pseudo-scientific ploy to explain the mechanics of time travel. Science fiction readers who enjoy evocative settings will likely enjoy these books.

Falkner, Brian.

The Tomorrow Code. 2008. 9780375843655. **J S**

Tane and Rebecca have been best friends forever. Rebecca, at fourteen, is an outstanding scholar in math and science. Tane, a talented artist who thinks outside the box, is the son of a famous Maori artist. One night when Tane and Rebecca are watching the stars, they start discussing time travel and how even though it may be impossible, communication between different times may work. They decide to build a receiver in case anyone from the future is trying to communicate with them, and soon they discover hidden messages being transmitted to them. Ultimately, they discover that they themselves, at some time in the future, are sending the messages warning of a peril that could destroy their world.

McNamee, Eoin.

Navigator trilogy. M

Fifteen-year-old Owen is whisked into a world where the Resisters fight to keep time moving forward while the Harsh cause time to run backward.

Subjects: Time

The Navigator: Chosen to Save the World. 2007. 9780375839108.

When fifteen-year-old Owen leaves his secret den, he finds he has entered a time vortex where he meets Cati, one of the Wakeful, and discovers that he, like his father before him, is a Navigator.

City of Time. 2008. 9780375839122.

Cati and Owen embark on an adventure-filled quest to the City of Time to try to stop a new threat from the Harsh as the moon heads on a crash course toward their world, wreaking havoc in the form of natural disasters.

Frost Child. 2009. 9780385735636.

As the Harsh seek revenge on Owen for killing their king, he finds help from his father and grandfather in stopping them from turning the world into a frozen wasteland.

Mosley, Walter.

47. 2005. 9780316016353. J S

Annotated in chapter 3.

Paulsen, Gary.

The Time Hackers. 2005. 9780553487886. M

Twelve-year-old Dorso Clayman, after finding many different dead things including a cadaver that disappear within seconds, and his pal Frank set out on a quest through time to find out who has been pranking them and why.

Subjects: Computers; Future; Gold; Pranks

Winterson, Jeanette.

Tanglewreck. 2006. 9781582349190. M J

Time tornadoes are wreaking havoc on the world, snatching people from one time and depositing them in another, which is how Silver lost her family and gained the thoroughly unpleasant Mrs. Rockabye as a guardian. Able Darkwater wants the timekeeper that he thinks Silver has or can find, so he locks Silver in a cage. Assisted in her escape by Gabriel, who is from another time and lives underground, the two embark on a quest to find the timekeeper and keep the Earth safe from two villains who have plans for world domination.

Subjects: London; Storms; Tornadoes

Aliens

Aliens are conscious beings from other worlds. They may be loveable or loathsome, but what they may be like and how they might interact with humans offer countless possibilities. The character of the alien plays a central role in these stories.

Meyer, Stephenie.

The Host. 2008. 9780316068048. **S**

When an alien race invades Earth and takes up residence in the bodies of humans, teenager Melanie avoids capture along with her younger brother, but is eventually implanted with the consciousness of Wanderer. As the two vie for control of Melanie's body, something unprecedented happens. (BBYA)

Subjects: Adult Books for Teens; Invasions; Love Triangles

Nelson, Blake.

They Came from Below. 2007. 9780765314239. **J** **S**

Seventeen-year-olds Emily and Reese, vacationing on Cape Cod, meet a couple of fascinating boys who continually seem to change and have a hidden agenda that may help save the world after an underwater nuclear explosion sets the scene for ecological disaster.

Subjects: Cape Cod; Ecology; Oceans

Pratchett, Terry.

Johnny Maxwell trilogy. **M**

Twelve-year-old Johnny Maxwell is familiar with conflict, having seen the Gulf War on TV and his parents always fighting.

Subjects: Gaming; Humor; War

Only You Can Save Mankind. 2005. 9780060541873.

When twelve-year-old Johnny tries to play the hot new video game he just got, he is surprised that the alien leader surrenders to him, asking for safe conduct through the gaming world. Suddenly the aliens disappear from games being played all over the world.

Subjects: Gaming

Johnny and the Dead. 2006. 9780060541903.

Johnny becomes involved with "post-senior citizens," the residents of a cemetery who are concerned with corporate plans to relocate their final resting place, and teams up with three living friends to keep his "breathily challenged" friends from losing their homes.

Subjects: Ghosts

Johnny and the Bomb. 2007. 9780060541934.

Now thirteen, Johnny and friends travel back in time to 1941 and try to save the residents of his village from a Nazi bomb.

Subjects: Historical Fiction: Time Travel

Rex, Adam.

The True Meaning of Smekday. 2007. 9780786849000. **M**

Tip and the other kids in her class are assigned to write an essay on the "true meaning of Smekday" for possible inclusion in a time capsule that will be buried for 100 years. Tip's story actually starts when her mother dreams of being abducted by aliens and a huge color-changing mole appears on her neck. On Christmas her mother disappears and the alien Boov conquer the earth. After they send all humans to a reservation in Florida, Tip decides to drive herself down there along with her cat, Pig; along the way she meets a fugitive Boov named J-Lo, who modifies her car. Together they experience all kinds of adventures as they search for Tip's mom and free the Earth. (VOYA)

Subjects: Amusement Parks; Florida; Humor

Wallenfels, Stephen.

Pod. 2010. 9781608980109. **J S**

Suddenly, strange craft appear in the skies everywhere. Everyone who is outdoors disappears immediately. Those indoors are pinned down with no hope of escape, because a ray shoots out of the hovering ships and makes anyone who ventures out disappear. The stories of fifteen-year-old Josh trapped with his father in their home in Washington State and twelve-year-old Megs trapped alone in a parking garage adjacent to a Los Angeles hotel run parallel, as no one knows what is going on, why the alien craft have appeared, or what is crewing them.

Utopia/Dystopia

All too often, communities that are built on the idea of a "perfect" society turn into a society with horrific policies that turn the utopia into a dystopia. Another one of science fiction's immersive subgenres

Adlington, L. J.

City Five. **J S**

When a society starts tattooing its members with their gene type, discrimination and racial laws grow, and the society implodes in war.

Subjects: Discrimination; Genetics; Racism; Tattoos

The Diary of Pelly D. 2005. 9780060766177.

When Toni V is conscripted to work cleaning up after a horrific war, he finds the diary of Pelly D, which tells of her life transformed from spoiled rich girl into one of the persecuted class after a hierarchy based on genetic type is adopted. (BBYA)

Subjects: Diaries; Genocide; Holocaust; Parallel Narratives; Swimming; War

Cherry Heaven. 2008. 9780061431807

Seventeen-year-old Luka, a slave in a water bottling plant, escapes and heads for the home in Cherry Heaven where she witnessed her family gunned down ten years earlier during the war. In a parallel story, two sisters, recently adopted, move with their new family to the utopian Cherry Heaven, where genetic discrimination is outlawed.

Subjects: Discrimination; Parallel Narratives; Slavery

Carman, Patrick.

Atherton. M

In Atherton, a three-tiered world, the rich and educated people live in the Highlands; serfs who labor all day live in Tabletop; and below Tabletop is the Flatlands, a desolate and danger-filled plain.

Subjects: Artificial Worlds; Mad Scientists; Slavery

The House of Power. 2007. 9780316166706.

Eleven-year-old Edgar works in the fig groves of Tabletop, and at night he climbs, looking for a treasure in the cliffs that separate those who do the work from the Highlands, from whence flows life-giving water. When he finds a book hidden in a niche in the cliffs, he is determined to climb to the Highlands and find someone who can read it for him, as books and reading are forbidden in Tabletop. (VOYA)

Rivers of Fire. 2008. 9780316166720.

As the terrain of the artificially constructed planet Atherton continues to experience cataclysmic change after collapsing down to one level, and with horrible creatures on the move, Edgar tries to warn the citizens of Tabletop that monsters are on the way.

Dark Planet. 2009. 9780316166744.

Edgar finds a way to leave Atherton and travels to the Dark Planet, where children under age twelve are kept as slaves in a place called the Silo to manufacture food for the sickly inhabitants of the polluted world. Escaping with four kids from the Silo, Edgar returns to Atherton and his friends Isabel and Samuel, who have ventured to the interior of the manufactured planet.

Collins, Suzanne.

Hunger Games. J S

Sometime in the not-too-distant future, North America has been divided into twelve districts, plus the Capitol. Each year a boy and a girl are chosen from each of the districts to compete in a *Survivor*-like reality TV show. The winner is the one who survives when all the others are dead.

Subjects: Dystopia; Reality TV Shows

The Hunger Games. 2008. 9780439023528.

> Sixteen-year-old Katniss lives in District 12, the poorest district in Panem. When her younger sister is chosen in a lottery to be the girl contestant from their district, Katniss volunteers to go in her place, certain that it is a death sentence. Peeta, the boy who is chosen, has always been in love with Katniss, but now in order to win one of them will have to kill the other along with the other twenty-two contestants. (BBYA, TTT, Quick Picks)

Catching Fire. 2009. 9780439023498.

> The Capitol was not thrilled with what Katniss and Peeta did in the previous year's game. Now that it is time for the Quarter Quell, the seventy-fifth playing of the Hunger Games, previous winners are required to compete again. With rumors of rebellion brewing, the Capitol sets out to squash it. (BBYA)

Mockingjay. 2010. 9780439023511.

> The mockingjay, the bird that is on a pin worn by Katniss, becomes the symbol of a rebellion that takes Panem over the edge into war.

Davidson, Ellen Dee.

Stolen Voices. 2005. 9781897073162. **M** **J**

> Fifteen-year-old Miri has searched and searched for her Talent, so she can be masked and bonded with the rest of her age-mates, but so far she has been unsuccessful. Her parents, two of the most important officials in the tranquil, harmonious, and very quiet walled city of Noveskina, will be devastated if she has no talent and ends up being masked as a lowly house-servant. Miri is appalled when she is given a one-year reprieve, which even though it gives her more time to find her Talent, will also put a rift between her and her beloved age-mates. So she sneaks into the Masking ceremony, only to discover that the Masker steals energy and talent from the group being masked, his hair going from gray to black and his wrinkles disappearing. Found out, and captured by the Masker, she escapes, to find her age-mates much changed. When she goes outside the walls, after a terrifying journey, she meets some people who use banned musical instruments. Miri finds life is very different than she had been taught.

Subjects: Activism; Masks; Music; Rebellion

Devita, James.

The Silenced. 2007. 9780060784621. **J** **S**

> In a world where all individual freedoms have been eliminated and the Zero Tolerance Party has crushed all dissent, fourteen-year-old Marena, the daughter of an executed dissident, joins the resistance. This story is inspired by the true life story of Sophie Scholl, a dissident who was part of the White Rose group that defied Hitler.

Dunkle, Clare B.

Martin Glass Series. Ⓜ

In a world where the government controls all information and requires residents to watch television and vote on issues such as the best color for the president's draperies, the citizens mostly spend their idle lives in domed towns.

Subjects: Activism; Dogs; Domed Cities; Robots; Siblings

The Sky Inside. 2008. 978141692422.

Thirteen-year-old Martin lives in a domed suburb, where his father is one of the few people who works, coordinating the trains that are the only portal to the supposedly desolate outside and other domed suburbs. Martin begins to snoop when his commotion-causing little sister, Cassie, one of the "Wonder Children" many families purchased, is recalled for a glitch. With his renegade robot dog, Martin finds out that his perfect world, where citizens incessantly watch television and vote daily, may not be all it is cracked up to be.

The Walls Have Eyes. 2009. 9781416953791.

Martin, along with his cyber dog, escapes from his town in an effort to find his sister and discovers that the world and society are not at all what he thought.

Fukui, Isamu.

Truancy. Ⓙ Ⓢ

In a dystopic world, the schools are used to eliminate independent thought and create a docile workforce. Students have no time for play or friendship. The teenage author was fifteen when he wrote *Truancy*, and both books in the series were nominated for the 2009 Teens Top Ten List.

Subjects: Activism; Schools; Siblings; Teenage Author

Truancy. 2008. 9780765317674. Ⓙ Ⓢ

Fifteen-year-old Tack lives in a dystopic world where the schools are used to eliminate independent thought and create a docile workforce. A group of kids called the Truancy works underground to overthrow the system, but when Tack's sister is killed in the crossfire, he decides to infiltrate them to make them pay for her death.

Truancy Origins. 2009. 9780765322623.

In this prequel to *Truancy*, Zen and Umasi, fifteen-year-old twins adopted by the mayor of Education City, take opposite sides and tactics as they rebel against the draconian system that subjugates the populace.

Halam, Ann.

Siberia. 2005. 9780553494143. **M**

> Thirteen-year-old Sloe escapes from a Siberian labor camp, intent on finding a safe place for the rescued DNA of lost species she is smuggling, in this story of a dismal future where the climate has changed and many animals have died out. (BBYA)
>
> **Subjects:** Animals; Prisons

Hautman, Pete.

Rash. 2006. 9780689869044. **S**

> The United Safer States of America is a desolate place, with fears of terrorism and lawsuits running rampant. Bo Marsten, age sixteen, is sentenced to prison for striking a classmate, after already being in trouble for having brought a rash to school. In the prison camp, where rules of normal society fly out the window, the overseer plucks Bo from the McDonald's pizza kitchen and sends him off to play illegal football. (PP)
>
> **Subjects:** Football; Prisons

Lowenstein, Sallie C.

In the Company of Whispers. 2008. 9780965848671. **S**

> In a bleak future, teenage Zeyya flees her parents' home, where they have been trying to guide her into a life that fits in with governmental expectations, to her eccentric grandmother's home, where she learns what life in mid-twentieth-century Burma was like through her grandmother's journals, photos, and memories.
>
> **Subjects:** Alternate Formats; Burma; Memories

Martinez, A. Lee.

The Automatic Detective. 2008. 9780765318343. **S**

> In mutant-filled, pollution-choked Empire City, Max Megaton, a sentient robot cab driver, turns hard-boiled detective. Like many other hard-boiled characters in noir fiction, he has a soft heart; in this case it is for the neighbor children, who have disappeared along with their parents. As he investigates and fights his own programming, Max uncovers a massive plot by infiltrating an alien group and goes up against other robots built like him, but that haven't developed the sentience that makes him so unique.
>
> **Subjects:** Adult Books for Teens; Detectives; Discrimination; Robots

Ness, Patrick.

Chaos Walking. **J** **S**

> In a world where an infection called the Noise has made the thoughts of men and animals audible and pervasive, women have disappeared and boys become men at age thirteen.
>
> **Subjects:** Dictators; Dogs; Single Sex Societies

The Knife of Never Letting Go. 2009. 9780763639310.

Todd Hewitt is almost thirteen, the age a boy becomes a man, on a planet devastated by a war with aliens that infected all the survivors with something called Noise, causing their thoughts to be broadcast. Other effects included animals being infected, causing them to talk and broadcast noise, and the end of women on the planet. In the swamp looking for apples for one of his guardians with his talking dog Manchee, Todd finds an area free of Noise and discovers a girl, Viola, who is the sole survivor of a small scouting ship crash. Things seem to be going from bad to worse in Prentisstown, precipitating Todd's guardians sending him away, out on his own with a precious knife. As Todd, Viola, and Manchee flee toward Haven, danger dogs every running step they take. (BBYA)

The Ask and the Answer. 2009. 9780763644901.

Todd and Viola finally reach Haven, only to find Mayor Prentiss has arrived before them and set himself up as president. Separated, they find themselves on opposing sides of an epic conflict.

Monsters of Men. 2010. 9780763647513.

As three armies converge on Prentisstown, Viola and Todd find themselves facing enormous moral decisions.

Prose, Francine.

After. 2003. 9780060080839. **J** **S**

After neighboring Pleasant Valley High School is shot up by a disgruntled youth, a grief and crisis counselor comes to Central High School and gradually takes over, imposing a zero-tolerance policy that expels kids for wearing red AIDS ribbons, and destroys cell phones, which are now not allowed in school. As things get creepier and creepier, good kid Tom begins to realize that kids aren't just disappearing from school—they go away and never come back. The action heats up when Tom realizes what is going on and makes an escape with his father, a friend, and her mother. (IRA YAC)

Subjects: Disappearances; School shootings; Surveillance

Shusterman, Neal.

Unwind. 2007. 9781416912040. **S**

America's second civil war, The Heartland War, ended with the "The Bill of Life," which states "that human life may not be touched from the moment of conception until a child reaches thirteen." However, between the ages of thirteen and eighteen a parent may choose to retroactively "abort" a child. Unwinds have all their parts harvested to live on in others. Connor is in enough fights that his parents decide to have him unwound. Orphaned Risa doesn't have any exceptional talent that will keep the state home where she was raised from having her unwound to make room for more abandoned babies. Lev, the tenth child in a religious family was raised as a tithe, to be sacrificed when he hit thirteen. The adventures of these three teens, as they attempt to change their fates, make for a riveting, thought-provoking page-turner. (BBYA, Quick Picks)

Subjects: Organ Harvesting; Orphans; Religion; Runaways; Sacrifice

Sleator, William.

Test. 2008. 9780810993563. **J**

Seventeen-year-old Ann is close to taking the XCAS, the standardized test that will determine whether she goes to college or faces a life of desperation and poverty, when she stumbles onto evidence of corruption related to the test.

Subjects: Cheating; Corporations; Testing

Westerfeld, Scott.

Uglies Series. **M** **J** **S**

In a future where beauty rules, beautiful young adults live in a party-filled paradise, while old people are hidden away, and younger kids, Uglies, wait for the time they will receive the plastic surgery and body sculpting that will transform them into Pretties.

Subjects: Beauty; Rebellion

Uglies. 2005. 9780689865381.

> Fifteen-year-old Tally Youngblood is looking forward to her sixteenth birthday, when she will be remade, becoming beautiful, and move to the New Pretty Town, where the Pretties party, but just before her birthday she is forced to spy on a friend who has run away rather than having the invasive extreme makeover, by infiltrating a renegade group hidden in "The Smoke." (BBYA, PP)

Pretties. 2005. 9780689865398.

> Sixteen-year-old Tally, now an empty-headed Pretty, discovers a note and a stash of pills that she had left for herself before her surgery, which will cure the hidden effects of the Pretty treatment. (IRA YAC)

Specials. 2006. 9781416947950.

> Turned into a Special, a Pretty with enhanced physical abilities, Tally is part of a team that is out to eliminate the renegades plotting revolution in New Smoke. (IRA YAC)

Extras. 2007. 9781416951179.

> Even though *Extras* is billed as the fourth in the Uglies series, it stands alone. It is the story of Aya, a kicker who films stories with Moggle, her highly modified AI self-propelled camera, in an effort to improve her face rank in a country far from Pretty Town and New Smoke. When she finds the Shy Girls, a group of thrill seekers who surf the tops of the maglev trains, she joins them, hoping to find a story to kick that will ignite movement in her face rank, but instead she finds a story that is much, much more than she ever imagined. The fame-based economy is fascinating, as is the Japanese-like future culture. (TTT)

Post-Apocalyptic SF

The end of the world as we know it is the theme of post-apocalyptic science fiction. What will happen if global warming causes sea levels to rise so high that many of the places where people now live disappear? What if the Earth wobbles, causing tides and seasons to go out of whack? What if the atmosphere becomes so poisoned that humanity has to take refuge underground? These are just a few of the questions asked by post-apocalyptic fiction. The subgenre has much in common with survival adventure, as the characters often are fighting to stay alive in a hostile world.

Bacigalupi, Paolo.

Ship Breaker. 2010. 9780316056212. **J** **S**

Nailer, a teen living with his abusive father in a shack on the Gulf Coast, is part of a crew that lives off salvage redeemed from wrecked tankers. Climate change has increased the frequency of hurricanes and tornadoes. Nailer's job is to crawl through the ductwork of wrecks, salvaging cooper wire and anything else that can be sold for food. He stakes each claim with a crew mark that matches the tattoo on his face. People who betray their crews are stripped of their crew tattoos, leaving them scarred and outcast. After a hurricane he finds a wrecked clipper, a pleasure craft belonging to people of inconceivable wealth, but aboard is one survivor still clinging to life. If she were dead, salvaging the ship would make his fortune.

Bertagna, Julie.

Exodus. **J** **S**

Global warming has raised the levels of the oceans enough that communities have flooded and food is scarce.

Subjects: Ecology; Flooding; Global Warming; Prophecies; Refugees; Underground Civilizations

Exodus. 2008. 9780802797452.

Growing up on the Wing, fifteen-year-old Mara knows that it will not be long before the island is completely inundated by the rising waters of the North Atlantic. Using ancient technology, she discovers the locations of the Sky Cities; and she convinces the rest of the people on the island to set off on a flotilla to save themselves. But when they arrive, they are not allowed in. (PP)

Zenith. 2009. 9780802798039.

Now sixteen, Mara and a group of refugees head toward Greenland but encounter a hostile welcome when their ship is sunk and they are enslaved.

Cave, Patrick.

Sharp North. 2006. 9781416912224. **S**

Miri lives in a small power generation town in Great Britain that has seen enormous changes due to the coming of a new ice age. When a familiar-looking woman is killed by the police, Miri retrieves a scrap of paper the woman was carrying, only to discover her name on it, along with the names of other women who have turned up dead. Going to the city, Miri meets Kay, a scion of one of the Great Families, who has his own reasons for befriending her in this politically turbulent, post-apocalyptic world.

Subjects: Climate Change; Great Britain

DuPrau, Jeanne.

Books of Ember. **M**

This series deals with descendants of the inhabitants of a city that went underground and forgot about the directions to emerge once it was safe again.

Subjects: Refugees; Underground Cities

The Prophet of Yonwood. 2006. 9780375875267.

Two hundred years before the time depicted in *The City of Ember*, eleven-year-old Nickie goes to the homestead of her late great-grandfather in Yonwood, North Carolina. With the world on the brink of war, there are conflicting prophecies of fiery doom.

The City of Ember. 2003. 9780385736282.

As twelve-year-olds, Doon and Lina experience Assignment Day, on which they are told what will be their jobs in the failing City of Ember. When they discover a fragment of instructions left by the founders, they come to the realization they must help the residents evacuate to the surface before it is too late. (PP)

The People of Sparks. 2004. 9780375828249.

The 400 residents of Ember are led out by Lina and Doon, finding refuge in the town of Sparks at the edge of the wasteland that had been left by the Disaster that destroyed so much of the world.

The Diamond of Darkhold. 2008. 9780375855719.

With resources scarce in Sparks, Lina and Doon return to Ember, looking for something they believe will help the blended community after finding mention of it in the few remaining pages of a book.

Grant, Michael.

Gone. **J** **S**

Suddenly, in one instant, all adults and teens over fourteen disappear and a barrier manifests, keeping the kids from leaving an approximately twenty-square-mile radius surrounding Perdido Beach, California. Soon some of the kids begin experiencing mutations and gaining unusual powers, but they are not all that is mutating. Deep under the ground a dark presence has started changing.

Subjects: Bullies; Mutations; Nuclear Power; Paranormal Abilities

Gone. 2008. 9780061448768.

Sam, who is weeks away from his fourteenth birthday, assumes a leadership role as the kids left behind in Perdido Beach try to figure out what has happened and how to survive. He leaps into a heroic role when he tries to rescue a little girl from a house fire. When all the adults and older teens disappeared, driverless cars continue moving until they crashed, stoves continue burning until turned off, and all matter of disasters happen. Along with Sam, Astrid, a brainy girl and his secret crush; Edilio, a Mexican immigrant with practical skills; and Mary, a girl who puts her own issues on a back burner, try to create order and safety in town as bullies try to take control. A little girl who can start fires, Lana, who almost dies in a car accident, finds healing powers; and a gang of troubled, rich kids from a private academy led by Caine, who has strong destructive powers, create and sometimes solve more problems. (IRA YAC)

Hunger. 2009. 9780061449079.

The kids have been living in the FAYZ for long enough to have eaten all the snack foods while the fresh foods rotted. Now hunger is rampant. More kids are developing paranormal powers, and a rift is growing between some of the kids with them and some of those without. Petey continues with his cryptic remarks, and Sam is going crazy trying to keep the community of Perdido Beach functioning. Along with some revelations about the nature of the changes in the world, new questions pop up. Action readers will love the shoot-outs at the nuclear power plant and the harrowing chase across the desert with the fuel rod.

Lies. 2010. 9780061449109.

Life in the FAYZ goes from bad to worse as those with the new paranormal powers and those without face off, and the dead begin to return.

Mahy, Margaret.

Maddigan's Fantasia. **2007. 9781416918127.** Ⓜ

In a post-apocalyptic world, Garland Maddigan lives with a traveling circus originated by her great-grandmother. When the fantasia is attacked and her father is killed, they decide to continue with their tour as they need to bring back a power generator to the city. Two strange boys with their baby sister suddenly appear, but along with them come two very strange beings, who begin following the fantasia on its lengthy and danger-filled journey.

Subjects: Circus; Performers; Science Fantasy

Patneaude, David.

Epitaph Road. **2010. 9781606840559.** Ⓙ Ⓢ

The Elijah plague that killed 80 percent of all male humans brought the new government to the conclusion that the world was better off with fewer men, so the number of men allowed in the population has been strictly regulated. Those who achieve on their tests are allowed interesting careers and the opportunity to reproduce. Kellen is preparing for his tests in a large Seattle house where he lives with his mother, aunt, and several housemates. Charlie, Kellen's father, one of the few survivors of the plague, lives on his boat in a remote area. When Sunday and Tia come to visit from Nebraska, the three teens uncover a danger that they decide warrants warning Charlie about and are thrust into a high-speed conspiracy thriller that will keep readers turning pages.

Subjects: Gender; Plagues

Pfeffer, Susan Beth.

Last Survivors. M J

This post-apocalyptic story starts when an asteroid hits the moon, shoving it out of its orbit. This causes tsunamis, volcanoes, and widespread death.

Subjects: Asteroids; Climate Change; Famine; Moon; New York; Pennsylvania; Survival

Life As We Knew It. 2006. 9780152058265.

Typical sixteen-year-old Miranda chronicles her life in a diary that changes drastically after a meteor knocks the moon into a different orbit and plunges the earth into catastrophic disasters. (BBYA, TTT)

The Dead and the Gone. 2008. 9780152063115.

In New York City, Alex Morales, a Puerto Rican American high school junior, ends up in charge of his family after they lose contact with his father, who is in Puerto Rico for a funeral, and with his mother, who works in a hospital in Queens. It is up to Alex to protect and care for his two younger sisters, Briana, fourteen, who is deeply religious, and Julie, twelve, who has always been kind of a brat. This novel is horrifyingly real, and though Alex and his sisters are heroic, they are heroic in ordinary ways, as they slowly waste away due to starvation and cold.

This World We Live In. 2010. 9780547248042.

Miranda and Alex meet a year after the apocalyptic collision of a meteor into the moon caused catastrophic changes to the world. The world is a cold, gray, dismal place with volcanic ash obscuring the sun, crops unable to grow, and food supplies growing always sparser. Miranda's family does find cause to celebrate when Matt returns from a fishing trip with a wife, and Miranda's dad, stepmother, and baby sibling show up with Alex and Julie.

Reeve, Philip.

Hungry City Chronicles. S J

In the far future, when most of the natural resources of the world have been consumed, traction cities rumble along on huge tracks, looking for other communities to consume for the resources their residents need. *Fever Crumb* (9780545207195, 2010) is the first in a prequel series set hundreds of years prior to the events in the Hungry City Chronicles.

Mortal Engines. 2003. 9780060082093.

London, after long sulking in what was once the island of Britain, has headed for the former continent of Europe, its engineers planning a daring venture. Third Class Apprentice Tom Natsworthy meets his guild's chief, saves him from an assassin, and gives chase, only to be flung down a waste chute by the Head Historian. Tom and the failed assassin Hester Shaw then set out to follow the tracks of London and fall into many adventures, including uncovering a device that was used in the six-hour war, which brought down civilization as we know it. (BBYA)

Predator's Gold. 2004. 9780060721961.

Tom and Hester, along with Pennyroyal, a famous explorer, are in an airship when they are forced to take refuge on the traction city Anchorage. They meet sixteen-year-old ruler Freya, who after hearing Pennyroyal's stories decides to move her city to America, where she thinks she will find verdant fields instead of a dead continent. (BBYA)

Infernal Engines. 2005. 9780060826376.

Tom and Hester live in Anchorage with their fifteen-year-old daughter Wren, who yearns for adventure. Unfortunately it comes to her when she is kidnapped and her parents come to the rescue. (BBYA)

A Darkling Plain. 2007. 9780060890551.

Tom and Wren find a new London rising from the ashes as united Traction Cities fight the Green Storm's efforts to establish settlements that can start farming and won't roam looking for smaller communities to devour.

Wooding, Chris.

Storm Thief. 2006. 9780439865142. **J** **S**

In a horrifying world racked by probability storms that change the nature of reality, Rail and Moa, two young thieves, try to survive after filching a strange artifact from bygone days. (BBYA)

Di's Picks

Collins, Suzanne. *Hunger Games.*

Doctorow, Cory. *Little Brother.*

Kostick, Conor. *Epic.*

Sawyer, Robert J. *WWW: Wake.*

Shusterman, Neal. *Unwind.*

Westerfeld, Scott. *Leviathan.*

Chapter 7

Fantasy

Reading fantasy can make a person hate reality since it so pales in comparison to the worlds in their heads; but for most people I think it helps them better appreciate reality. You can look at ordinary things like telephone booths, or buttons and you can see the possibilities behind them.
—Andrea, age 16

Since the advent of the <u>Harry Potter</u> series, fantasy has been riding a huge wave of popularity with teen readers. The genre, like its' sister genre science fiction, is diverse, with multiple subgenres that often have very little in common beyond a sense of wonder.

Fantasy readers are least likely to care about what age level books are written for. Adults read fantasy written for teens and children. Teens read fantasy written for adults and children.

The Harry Potter craze enticed many adults into reading young adult fantasy, and perhaps as a result, fantasy written for teens has become more sophisticated. Because of the popularity of the genre, it seems that publishers are more willing to branch out, so fantasy has become more diverse and less formulaic.

Because readers of fantasy hone their willing suspension of disbelief, they often also enjoy the other genres—science fiction, paranormal, and horror—that fall under the general rubric of speculative fiction.

Epic Fantasy

Worlds of magic where heroic teens fight evil, whether from sources mundane or magical, provide settings for the following books. Quests often play a major role: groups of friends or companions find friendship, take journeys, and face dangers together.

Abalos, Rafael.

Grimpow: The Invisible Road. 2007. 9780440239666. **M**

Grimpow and Durlib, two boys living in fourteenth-century Europe, find the fabled philosopher's stone in the hand of a dead man. The stone gives Grimpow the ability to read and to change lead into gold, and he decides he must fulfill the quest the dead man had been pursuing.

Subjects: Knights Templar; Philosopher's Stone; Quests

Benz, Derek, and J. S. Lewis.

Grey Griffins. ▣

Four card playing friends known as the Grey Griffins, all sixth graders from Avalon, Minnesota, unwittingly open a portal to the world of Faerie, allowing spriggans, witches, and goblins into their Minnesota town.

Subjects: Arthurian Legends; Gaming; Knights Templar; Secret Societies

The Revenge of the Shadow King. 2006. 9780439795746.

When the Grey Griffins—sixth graders Max, Harley, Natalia, and Ernie—play a fantasy card game, they put their hometown, Avalon, Minnesota, and its residents in danger.

The Rise of the Black Wolf. 2007. 9780439837743.

Max's billionaire father takes the Grey Griffins to Scotland for Christmas, where they find werewolves and kobolds on the loose. Morgan LeFey, seeking revenge against Max for his actions in *The Revenge of the Shadow King*, kidnaps Max's billionaire father and requires that Max assemble the legendary Spear of Ragnarok.

Fall of the Templar. 2008. 9780439837767.

Max, Harley, and Natalia travel to the Underworld to stop the evil Lord Sumner and Morgn LeFey from taking over the world now that they have the Spear of Ragnarok. The Grey Griffins must venture into the Underworld to secure the Eye of Odin, the only weapon that has a chance against the Spear of Ragnarok.

Grey Griffins: The Clockwork Chronicles. ▣

A year after the events in <u>Grey Griffins</u>, Max, Harley, Natalia, and Ernie enroll in Iron Bridge Academy, a school that trains heroes to fight against evil.

Subjects: Faerie; Knights Templar; Schools; Steam Punk

The Brimstone Key. 2010. 9780316045223.

Changelings, humans with faerie blood and paranormal powers, are targeted by the Clockwork King, who wants to steal their souls to power his clockwork war machines.

Cashore, Kristin.

Graceling. ▣ ▣

Cashore's startlingly good debut novel *Graceling*, a finalist for the first Morris Award, is only slightly connected to her second book, *Fire*; however, a third book is scheduled that is rumored to tie the two together to make up a very connected trilogy. The books are set in a world where some individuals have unusual powers and abilities, indicated by anomalies of color: either two different-colored eyes or amazingly beautiful and unusual hair or skin color.

Graceling. 2008. 9780152063962.

Gracelings are identified by their two different-colored eyes. Once they are discovered, the king takes them into his service so he can use whatever unusual talent they manifest. Katsa, niece of the king, has what appears to be the grace of killing, so she is forced to serve as her uncle's assassin. Hating what she has to do, Katsa starts up an underground movement to save any people she can, which is how she meets Prince Po, who has one eye of silver and one of gold. (BBYA, Mythopoeic, Morris Honor, TTT)

Fire. 2009. 9780575085114.

In Dells, monsters are supernaturally gorgeous animals who have intensely colored hair, feathers, fur, or scales as well as the ability to control the thoughts and actions of humans. Years before the events in Graceling and far away in the Dells, Fire, beautiful beyond belief with her fiery hair, is the only living human monster. As war approaches, strangers with minds unreadably fogged put Fire in peril. (BBYA)

Cornish, D. M.

Monster Blood Tattoo. **J** **S**

In an exquisitely crafted world with the feel of eighteenth-century England, vinagaroons sail the acidic seas, and orphans dream of being picked for a seagoing career.

Subjects: Half-Continent; Orphans; Pirates; Magic; Monsters

Foundling. 2006. 9780399246388.

Rossamund Bookchild arrived at Madam Opera's Estimable Marine Society for Foundling Boys and Girls as an infant with only one possession: a girl's name. He is hired as a lamplighter, a position for which he would have to travel far. Deceived by pirates, he ends up on the wrong boat, and starts his adventurous quest. (BBYA)

Lamplighter. 2008. 9780399246395.

Not fitting in well with the other lamplighters because of his small size and timid appearance, Rossamund befriends Threnody, a girl who wants to become a lamplighter. The lamplighters light the lamps along the Emperor's highway and keep travelers safe from monsters.

Factotum. 2010. 9780399246401.

Forthcoming.

Flanagan, John.

Ranger's Apprentice. **M** **J** **S**

This sprawling story of a battle between good and evil features courageous and loyal teens and plenty of action-filled combat. It focuses on the life of Will Treaty, who in the first book is apprenticed to the Ranger Corps.

Subjects: Action-Adventure; Orphans

The Ruins of Gorlan. 2005. 9780399244544.

> Fifteen-year-old Will, a ward of the castle, hopes to be chosen for Battleschool; but instead, because of his small stature, he is apprenticed to Ranger. (Quick Picks)

The Burning Bridge. 2006. 9780399244551.

> Will, a fifteen-year-old ranger's apprentice, and Horace, a Battleschool apprentice, are traveling along the frontier when they find a partially built bridge and uncover Morgarath's covert plans for an invasion of Araluen.

The Icebound Land. 2007. 9780399244568.

> When Will and Evanlyn, the incognito identity of Princess Cassandra, are captured by Skandians to be sold as slaves, Ranger, Halt, and Horace head to the frozen north in an attempt to rescue them.

The Battle for Skandia. 2008. 9780399244575.

> Will and Evanlyn escape from slavery, but before he and his friends can make it home, Halt discovers that the Temujai, who are attacking Skandia, also have designs on Aruluen. So they join forces to stop them.

Sorcerer in the North. 2008. 9780399250323.

> Will, no longer an apprentice, now an adult responsible for a fief on his own, is called away on a secret mission by his mentor, Halt.

Siege of Macindaw. 2009. 9780399250330.

> Arulen is in danger from a rogue knight who makes an alliance with the Scotti and holds Alyss, Will's love interest, captive in a tower. Will and Horace, along with a force of Skandians, moves in to retake Macindaw Castle and restore it to its rightful owner.

Erak's Ransom. 2010. 9780399252051.

> Will and company face desert storms and warring tribesmen when they go to rescue Erak, a high-ranking Skandian. This story takes place chronologically between *The Battle for Skandia* and *Sorcerer in the North.*

Kings of Clonmel. 2010. 9780399252068.

> A religious cult, fomenting dissent, has thrown Hibernia into turmoil, so Halt, Will, and Horace set out for Clonmel to try to restore order.

Halt's Peril. 2010. 9780399252075.

> Forthcoming.

Haydon, Elizabeth.

The Lost Journals of Ven Polypheme. M J S

Ven Polypheme, the thirteenth child born in his family, has grown up in his family's shipbuilding business and has tried his hand in every department. He is a Nain, a race much like Tolkien's Hobbits, who like to stay close to home and far from adventure, but Ven finds adventure won't leave him alone.

The Floating Island. 2006. 9780765308672.

On Ven's fiftieth birthday (the equivalent of a human turning twelve), he draws the short straw and is sent out on an inspection cruise of a new ship. Attacked by Fire Pirates known for leaving no survivors, the resourceful young Nain, ordered to scuttle the ship, figures out a way to take out all the pirates, too. After surviving the explosion of both ships, he is saved by a mermaid and rescued by a kindly captain. On their way to the captain's land they stop at the fabled Floating Island, where Ven can shout a message into the wind that will go to his parents. Ven and his friend Char, a cabin boy on the ship that rescued him, go to the Crossroads Inn, run by the captain's wife, who has very peculiar rules and interesting residents, including a talking cat.

Subjects: Ghosts; Pirates

The Thief Queen's Daughter. 2007. 9780765308689.

Hired as the King's Reporter, Ven is sent to the fabulous Gated City to seek the origin of a mysterious light stone that had been given to the King's father. Accompanied by four good friends, Ven becomes involved in a new adventure after one of them is kidnapped by the Thief Queen.

Subjects: Kidnappings

The Dragon's Lair. 2008. 9780765308696.

Ven and friends, including the mermaid-like merrow, Amariel, flee the Thief Queen's wrath and set off on a mission for the king that takes them to a kingdom where a dragon is targeting the Nain, Ven's own people and trying to start a war.

Subjects: Dragons; Mermaids

Hill, Stuart.

Icemark Chronicles. M J S

Icemark, a Nordic-like country, faces decades of battle after the Polypontian Empire plans to invade. Thirrin, princess then queen, fights to save her country.

Subjects: Snow Leopards; Vampires; Werewolves; Witches

The Cry of the Icemark. 2005. 9780439686266.

When her beloved dad is killed, Thirrin becomes queen and allies with vampires, werewolves, and talking snow leopards to defend her country, Icemark, from an invasion.

Blade of Fire. 2007. 9780439841221.

Prince Charlemagne, the son of Thirrin and Oskan, is small and lame, but he wants to be a warrior like his siblings and parents. Instead, he is sent to the Desert Lands to serve as regent for a party of exiles, where he comes into his own—just in time to return to Icemark when he is truly needed.

Last Battle of the Icemark. 2009. 9780545093293.

> Thirrin and Oskan's evil daughter Medea, taking after her grandfather Chronos, Master of the dark side, assembles a demon army that threatens the safety and security of Icemark, even as the country faces other foes.

Johansen, K. V.

The Warlocks of Talverdin. M J

The island of Eswyland is divided into three small kingdoms: Talverdin, Dunmorra, and Eswy. Maurey, a boy at a prestigious school who is tortured by the other scholars, who call him a Nightwalker, discovers he truly is half Nightwalker, but he is also the half-brother of a king.

Nightwalker. 2007. 9781551434810.

> Maurey, an orphan demoted from student to scullion when his guardian dies, discovers that there is something to the taunts of Nightwalker that the other scholars at his university grammar school call him. Imprisoned by the Chancellor, who has discovered something of his ancestry, Maurey is aided in his escape and arduous trek to Talverdin by Annot, a wilderness savvy girl who is also the Baroness of Oakhold.

Treason in Eswy. 2008. 9781551438887.

> Princess Eleanor is a pawn in political games, and Maurey tries to come to her aid when her mother and Baron Sawfield try to maneuver her into a marriage that will give control of Eswy to her mother.

Warden of Greyrock. 2009. 9781554690053.

> Maurey and Annot try to keep their borders safe, but when Annot is taken by a Nightwalker hunter, Maurey must decide whether to follow his heart and try to rescue her, or keep protecting the border.

Shadow Road. 2010. 9781554691654.

> Nethin, son of a Nightwalker and a human witch, is abducted, drugged, and secretly transported cross country in this stand-alone story. Taken across the country, he is forced to work a spell for his evil great-grandfather that will open up the shadow road and new dangers.

Kaaberbol, Lene.

Shamer Chronicles. M

Shamers can make people tell the truth, so they are often called in to solve crimes. Dina has inherited her mother's Shamer abilities.

Subjects: Deception; Dragons; Dungeons; Murder; Politics; Truth

Shamer's Daughter. 2004. 9780805081114.

> Late one night Dina's mother leaves for Dunark Castle to help solve a crime. The next day, when her mother has not returned, a stranger on a tall horse tells her that her mother needs her in Dunark. Entering the castle complex through a hidden gate, she is taken through an odiferous pit filled with dragons. Drakan has brought her to the castle because her mother is adamant that Nico, the ruler's son, who was found covered in blood next to the bodies of

his father, pregnant stepmother, and toddler brother, is innocent of their murders. Drakan, usurper to the throne, in an attempt to make Dina's mother accuse Nico, locks Dina in Nico's cell for the night.

Shamer's Signet. 2005. 9780805082173.

Told in alternating voices by Dina, now age eleven, and her brother, Davin. They are now living in the Highlands with their mother, a shamer, because the evil Drakon destroyed their former home. Drakon's cousin, Valdracu, assumes the identity of a clan ally and attempts to kidnap the Shamer and her daughter, Dina, but they escape, even though the Shamer is wounded. Dina and the grandson of the head of Clan Laclan are kidnapped and taken to Valdracu's newly built city Dracana, where she is forced to use her shamer's gift for evil to keep Valdracu from slaying his hostage.

The Serpent Gift. 2006. 9780805077704.

Dina's father is a Blackmaster, a master of illusion and lies, but Dina joins up with him in an attempt to rescue Nico and Davin, who have been captured and taken to a neighboring country as slaves.

The Shamer's War. 2006. 9780805086560.

Dina, now thirteen years old, has discovered she has multiple gifts and puts them to use helping Nico in his fight to bring down his cousin Drakon, who is relentlessly cruel in his plot to take control of Dunark.

Pierce, Tamora.

The Will of the Empress. **2005. 9780545074551.** **J** **S**

When Sandry is summoned to visit her cousin the Empress, her longtime (but now estranged) friends, Daja, Tris, and Briar, accompany her. This group of beloved characters was previously featured in Pierce's The Circle of Magic and The Circle Opens quartets.

Beka Cooper. **J** **S**

Hundreds of years before Alanna (from Song of the Lioness Quartet) was born, Beka Cooper, an orphaned sixteen-year-old, becomes a trainee in the Provost's Guard.

Subjects: Counterfeiting; Journals; Kidnappings; Missing Persons; Mysteries

Terrier. 2006. 9780375838163.

Beka Cooper's strong personality and psionic powers strengthen her, despite her painful shyness. In this police procedural-like story, Beka tries to solve the kidnappings and murders of children in Tortall and works on missing persons cases involving people who were digging for fire opals. (BBYA)

Bloodhound. 2009. 9780375914690.

Promoted to Dog at the next level, a police officer, Beka, now seventeen, and her new temporary partner investigate a counterfeiting operation. Along the way she finds romance.

Rodda, Emily.

Rondo series. **M**

From a nonagenarian great-aunt, who has always told lots of family stories, Leo Langlanderm inherits an elaborately painted music box that has very rigid rules for its use taped to its bottom.

The Key to Rondo. 2008. 9780545035354.

Leo's ornery cousin Mimi comes to stay. After she turns the key on the music box he inherited from his great-aunt, butterflies painted on it come to life and fly around his room. With a few more extra turns of the key, things go from bad to worse, and the Blue Queen leaves the box to enter this world and kidnaps Mimi's dog. Now, to save the dog, the cousins must enter the world depicted on the box.

Wizard of Rondo. 2009. 9780545115162.

When Leo notices changes to the music box that indicate the Blue Queen is up to no good, he and his cousin Mimi travel back into Rondo, the world of the music box, to once again battle the Blue Queen as they try to find a missing wizard and exonerate his apprentice.

Heroic

Heroic fantasy is full of adventure as usually reluctant teen protagonists are thrust into courageous roles. They often start out as seemingly ordinary individuals who, through sacrifice, hard work, and courage, accomplish heroic deeds. Heroic fantasy is very closely related to epic fantasy, with lots of crossover, but the main emphasis is on the heroic escapades of the protagonist rather than the journeys and quests of a larger group.

Lisle, Holly.

Moon & Sun. **M** **J** **S**

Humans rule the daylight world, but after dark the Nightlings rule. In this series fourteen-year-old Genna, a human, learns how to navigate the magical moon roads.

Subjects: Plague; World of Faerie

The Ruby Key. 2008. 9780545000123.

After losing their father and seeing their mother fall ill with the same affliction, fourteen-year-old Genna and her brother go into the woods at night to harvest a sap that may cure her. Instead of finding a cure, they are taken by the Nightlings. Aided by a Nightling slave, Genna makes a deal with Letrin, the Nightling ruler, that will save the lives of her family and village—but only if she can fulfill an almost impossible quest.

The Silver Door. 2009. 9780545000147.

> A prophecy has foretold that a Sunrider will unite the magics of sun and moon. Young Genna, under the protection of the Nightlings, is being trained to be the Sunrider, to end the war between slaves and masters, but when she is targeted by evil Kai lords, she ends up in Spire, a mysterious human city. Meanwhile, war crosses the moonroads.

Moore, John.

A Fate Worse Than Dragons. **2007. 9780441014958.** **S**

> Sir Terry has ridden across the kingdom to slay a dragon so he can win the hand of Princess Gloria. Unfortunately, just after slaying the beast he discovers that he has crossed into another kingdom—and the princess here is no one he would want to marry. Slinking home after pinning the kill on his squire, he discovers that his true love has now been pledged in an arranged marriage to Roland Westfield, the scion of a family made rich in the sliced bread business. Because Gloria wants to marry Terry, she stages a kidnapping, so he can rescue her, but Roland, feeling responsible for his unmet fiancée, takes off to find her. Sir Terry must go along too because, after all, they are headed in the same direction.

Subjects: Adult Books for Teens; Humorous; Parody; Romance

Pierce, Tamora.

Daughter of the Lioness series. **M** **J** **S**

> Sixteen-year-old Aly, the daughter of Tortall's famous woman knight Alanna (called "the Lioness") , is at odds with her parents. They think she should be doing something with her life, but don't want her to be a spy like her father.

Subjects: Gods; Nannies; Pirates; Politics; Slavery; Spies; Tricksters

Trickster's Choice. 2003. 9780375828799.

> While her mother is home from war for a visit Aly, upset over not being allowed to follow her dreams, takes off for a few days. It seems like a good idea until she is captured by pirates and sold into slavery. Purposely getting beat up to save herself from being sold as a bed slave, she luckily ends up in the household of a Duke and his two daughters by his late wife, who was royalty of the Raka. These are the people who were conquered centuries earlier when the current ruling family overran their land. A bet with the trickster god leaves Aly trying to keep the Duke's children safe, especially his oldest daughters, who have the blood of both the current royal family and of the deposed Raka royal family in their veins. (BBYA)

Trickster's Queen. 2004. 9780375828782.

> Aly, no longer a slave, is now spymaster for the Rakas, who are trying to take back the Copper Isles. Aly uses darkling, tiny shape-shifters as some of her spies while accompanying the half-Raka future queen and her family back to the capital. (BBYA)

Verrillo, Erica.

Phoenix Rising Trilogy. 🅜

Thirteen-year-old Elissa knows her mother is dead, but she wants to know who her father is. She also knows she must keep secret her ability of talking with animals.

Subjects: Animal Speakers; Prophecies; Psionic Powers; Sailing

Elissa's Quest. 2007. 9780375839467.

Elissa can talk to animals. Will that help her when her previously unknown father turns up, takes her away, and uses her as a pawn in his political plans?

Elissa's Odyssey. 2008. 9780375839481.

After escaping from the Khan, Elissa takes a job as a shipboard cook while trying to reunite with her friend, Maya, and her donkey, Gertrude, as she tries to make it home.

World's End. 2009. 9780375839504.

Fourteen-year-old Elissa flees her life as a princess when her father arranges a politically advantageous marriage for her and sends her friends away. Adventures ensue as she treks up the world's highest mountain and is captured by pirates, before fulfilling the prophecy and being reunited with her friends.

Magic and Wizards

Much of fantasy features magic. Often it is magic that sets the worlds of fantasy apart from our mundane world. Stories of magic workers are now almost always linked with Harry Potter, even though they may be very different.

Black, Holly.

Curse Workers. 🅙 🅢

In a world that seems much like ours except for the fact that gloves are always worn, some people are curse workers, whose barehanded touch can bring luck, forgetfulness, or even death.

White Cat. 2010. 9781416963967.

Cassell, the only member of his family who does not have magic, attends a boarding school. One night in his dreams he follows a white cat and ends up on the roof of the school. Suspected of attempting suicide, Cassell is suspended and returns to the filthy family home. One of his older brothers is away at college, one is married, and his mother is in prison for touching someone with her curse worker hands. Cassell discovers his family is hiding many secrets.

Dickinson, Peter.

Angel Isle. 2007. 9780385746908. 🅙 🅢

Two hundred years have passed since the Tija and Tahl, along with their respective grandparents, left the valley to find the magician called the Ropemaker, who could renew and refresh the spell that kept their valley safe in *The Ropemaker*. Now a new group must set out on a quest through time and place to find the Ropemaker and restore the protective magic.

The Tears of the Salamander. 2003. 9780385730983. **M** **J**

A talented singer, thirteen-year-old Alfredo's life changes when his family is killed in a fire, and he is whisked away to live under a volcano by an uncle who wields fire magic.

Subjects: Castratos; Orphans; Singers

Duey, Kathleen.

A Resurrection of Magic. **S**

In a world where magicians abused their powers, magic has mostly disappeared—until two young men, Franklin and Somiss, decide to bring it back by establishing a college of magic. They are the common link between two stories that take place hundreds of years apart.

Subjects: Dark Fantasy; Parallel Narratives

Skin Hunger. 2007. 9780689840937.

At Sadima's birth, her family was destroyed by a magician. Now out on her own, she comes to the city, where she keeps house for two young men who are trying to rediscover the long lost secrets of actually using real magic. In a parallel narrative, Hahp, a young man, is sent to a darkly disturbing labyrinthine school for wizardry, where failure means death. (NBA Finalist)

Sacred Scars. 2009. 9780689840951.

Taking up where *Skin Hunger* left off, Sadima, Franklin, and Somiss begin living in a cave system outside Limòri, where they continue studying magic, but Somiss has also brought in a cage-full of young street boys, whom he claims he is planning to teach magic. Actually, he has darker purposes for them. In the future timeline, Hahp learns far more true magic at the school started by Franklin and Somiss.

Gallego Garcia, Laura.

The Valley of the Wolves. 2006. 9780439585538. **M** **J**

When Dana, a poor farm girl who has always had an invisible companion, is sent far from home to the Tower to learn magic, her best friend Kai, whom only she can see, goes with her.

Kerr, P. B.

Children of the Lamp. **M**

John and Philippa Gaunt, twelve-year-old twins, find themselves experiencing strange changes and discover that they are actually djinn with magical powers.

Subjects: Djinn; Twins

The Akhenaten Adventure. 2004. 9780439670197.

Twelve-year-old twins John and Philippa Gaunt begin experiencing strange changes after their wisdom teeth are pulled. With the help of their Uncle Nimrod, they find that they are descended from djinn and have special powers.

The Blue Djinn of Babylon. 2006. 9780439670210.

When Philippa is locked away in the underground palace of the Blue Djinn to learn how to adjudicate for the djinn tribes, her twin John puts together a rescue attempt.

The Cobra King of Kathmandu. 2007. 9780439670234.

After a break-in at their house starts them on a quest that takes them to Kathmandu, twins Philippa and John Gaunt are on the trail of a murderer whose weapon is the king cobra's venomous bite.

The Day of the Djinn Warriors. 2008. 9780439932141.

With their father rapidly aging due to a Methuselah spell cast by their mother to keep them at home, twins John and Philippa hurry to figure out a way to leave. They must find someone else to take over as the Blue Djinn before their mother is lost to them forever.

The Eye of the Forest. 2009. 9780439932158.

Twins Philippa and John, along with Uncle Nimrod and others, are off to the Amazon, where an ancient Incan artifact is about to be used to unleash massively destructive power.

Larbalestier, Justine.

Magic or Madness. J S

In this version of our world, almost everyone is imbued with some degree of magic, although most don't know it, and those with a strong magical talent get closer to death every time they use it. However, if they don't use it, they descend into madness. Set in New York and Sydney, Australia, this story features American characters who speak American English and Australian characters who speak Australian English.

Subjects: Australia; New York

Magic or Madness. 2005. 9781595140708.

After her mother is institutionalized, fifteen-year old Reason goes to live with her grandmother, who is a witch in Sydney, Australia; but when she walks through a door in the kitchen she finds herself in New York. (BBYA, Norton Nebula, PP)

Magic Lessons. 2006. 9781595141248.

Reason is in Sydney to learn magic with Jay-Tee, Tom, and her grandmother, Esmerelda. Her mother, Sarafina, is in a mental institution. Meanwhile, the door that leads to New York begins to pulsate and writhe, and a reddish brown blob comes through that bites Tom and then burrows into Reason, making her feel very strange. With the door behaving so strangely, the three teens take turns watching it; but it sucks Reason through in her lightweight summer pajamas, so she ends up in New York city in a dead of winter snowstorm. She cannot go back through the door to Sydney because an awful-smelling man, who has the same smell as the blob they had decided was a golem, is now guarding it.

Magic's Child. 2007. 9781595141811.

Fifteen and pregnant, Reason now has the means to cure her mother, but when she goes to the asylum where her mad mother is living, she discovers her mother has been kidnapped by Reason's evil grandfather.

Neff, Henry H.

The Tapestry. 🅜 🅙

This winning mashup of Harry Potter, Ender, and Percy Jackson appeals to readers of all those series with its boarding school, ties to mythology, and intense training program. It is the story of Max McDaniels, who discovers he has magic potential while on a visit to a museum.

Subjects: Animals; Boarding Schools; Demons

The Hound of Rowan. 2007. 9780375838941.

Max McDaniels finds a hidden alcove in a museum with a tapestry that depicts the Cattle Raid of Cooley; then it begins to glow. Soon he finds an enigmatic letter in his pocket saying he will be contacted, discovers he is being followed by a strange man, is visited by a terrifying woman, and receives an invitation he can't refuse to attend a private boarding school in New England. When he arrives at Rowan Academy, where young people with "Potential" are trained to fight the "Enemy," he and the other apprentices are housed in rooms that magically reconfigure to suit them and assigned an animal charge they are to feed and care for. Max is paired with the last lymrill in the world, a nocturnal creature with metallic quills. They train on the Course, where they experience different scenarios as they try to achieve a goal and can move up levels as they progress.

Second Siege. 2008. 9780375838965.

Now in their second year at Rowan Academy, Max and his roommate David leave to travel across Europe in an attempt to stop the demon Astaroth from getting the Book of Thoth, which would give him mastery over everyone and everything in the world.

Fiend and the Forge. 2010. 9780375938986.

Forthcoming.

Nimmo, Jenny.

Charlie Bone series. 🅜

Charlie Bone discovers he is one of the many descendants of the Red King and has magical powers, meaning he must be sent off to boarding school. This series is often recommended as a read-alike for the Harry Potter books, particularly for readers at the younger end of the YA spectrum.

Subjects: Boarding Schools; Time Travel

Midnight for Charlie Bone. 2003. 9780439474290.

> Ten-year-old Charlie Bone lives with his mother and two grandmothers, until the day he discovers he can hear the people in photographs. That's when his great-aunts bundle him off to gloomy Bloor's Academy, where his adventures start.

Charlie Bone and the Time Twister. 2003. 9780439496872.

> Charlie must help his great uncle, Henry Yewbeam, who has dropped in from 1918, make his way back to his proper time while avoiding trouble from his evil cousin Ezekial Bloor.

Charlie Bone and the Invisible Boy. 2004. 9780439545266.

> Charlie and his friends at Bloor's Academy try to help a schoolmate who has become invisible after an encounter with a blue boa constrictor in the school's attic.

Charlie Bone and the Castle of Mirrors. 2005. 9780439545280.

> Charlie and friends set out to rescue a classmate who has been adopted by a couple who seem quite sinister.

Charlie Bone and the Hidden King. 2006. 9780439545303.

> Charlie turns twelve, but his father is still missing, his mother seems to have become enamored by an enchanter, the shadow in the portrait of the Red King has disappeared, and pets are going missing.

Charlie Bone and the Beast. 2007. 9780439846653.

> Billy's ability to talk to animals, Olivia's to create illusions, and Emma's to turn into a bird all come into play when they and Charlie go to rescue a wereboy being held in a dungeon.

Charlie Bone and the Shadow. 2008. 9780439846691.

> When Charlie travels through a painting in an attempt to rescue his ancestor from Badlock, he is accompanied by the dog Runner Bean, who becomes trapped. Charlie's friends must come to the rescue.

Pratchett, Terry.

Tiffany Aching series. **M** **J** **S**

Magically gifted Tiffany Aching is growing up in England's chalk country when her brother is taken away, and the wee free men name her their leader.

Subjects: England; Humorous; Witches

The Wee Free Men: A Story of Discworld. 2003. 9780060012366.

> Armed with an iron frying pan, a nine-year-old witch named Tiffany teams up with the Nac Mac Feegle, wee blue-tattooed, hard-headed pictsies in kilts, to rescue her kidnapped brother from the Queen of Fairyland. (BBYA, Locus)

A Hat Full of Sky: The Continuing Adventures of Tiffany Aching and the Wee Free Men. 2004. 9780060586607.

> Leaving the chalk to be tutored in witchcraft, Tiffany finds herself in some major trouble and the Wee Free Men and Granny Weatherwax step in to save her. (BBYA, Mythopoeic Award)

Wintersmith. 2006. 9780060890315.

> Winter falls in love with thirteen-year-old Tiffany at a dance, leaving the world in danger of an endless winter. (BBYA, Locus)

I Shall Wear Midnight. 2010. 9780061433047.

> Tiffany's day-to-day life as a witch on the Chalk is not as romantic and exciting as one would think; then a new danger turns up. A trip to Ankh Morpork, an encounter with Boffo, and a very interesting young man all come together to make this a satisfying conclusion to the Tiffany Aching saga.

Reisman, Michael.

Simon Bloom. M

Twelve-year-old Simon Bloom accidentally becomes the Keeper of the Order of Physics when going through the woods near his New Jersey home. Teaming up with Owen and Alysha, the three sixth graders try to save the world from villains bent on world domination.

Subjects: Physics; Science; Secret Societies

The Gravity Keeper. 2008. 9780525479222.

> When the teacher's edition of a physics text smacks Simon Bloom in the head, he discovers he can control physics, including gravity and friction, by reciting the formulas in the book. He uses his newfound power to help stop a woman with scientific formulas written all over her skin from taking over the world.

The Octopus Effect. 2009. 9780525420828.

> An infusion of octopus DNA gives Simon some unusual abilities, which he uses in battle in an undersea biology dome when he goes up against archenemy Sirabetta, who has regained her memory.

Rowling, J. K.

Harry Potter. M J S

The Harry Potter series inaugurated the current popularity of fantasy, and it has become such a part of culture in English-speaking countries that a description is hardly needed, but neither can it be overlooked. Orphaned Harry Potter lives under the stairs in the home of his aunt, uncle, and cousin, who do not like him at all. They are Muggles, people without magic who do not believe in magic, but Harry is magical. Unknown to Harry, his late parents were powerful magicians who died while fighting an evil sorcerer, but baby Harry's survival made him a legend in the wizarding world. Films have been released for the first six titles in the series, and surely the movie version of *Harry Potter and the Deadly Hallows* will soon be coming out. The order of the books is listed here for the convenience of readers. It all starts just before Harry's eleventh birthday, when he is summoned to the secret Hogwarts School of Witchcraft and Wizardry. Each book covers a subsequent school year in Harry's life as he grows from child to man. (Mythopoeic Award)

Subjects: Boarding Schools; Friends; Orphans

Harry Potter and the Sorcerer's Stone. 1998. 9780590353403.

Orphaned Harry, who has lived a miserable life under the stairs in his aunt's home, is summoned to Hogwarts School, where he develops a coterie of friends, makes a few enemies, and embarks on his magical adventures. (BBYA, IRA YAC)

Subjects: Philosopher's Stone

Harry Potter and the Chamber of Secrets. 1999. 9780439064866.

Harry is having a perfectly terrible summer vacation away from Hogwarts when his friends rescue him in a flying car. In his second year at Hogwarts, surrounded by a close-knit group of friends, he attempts to find the mysterious chamber of secrets and faces a terrifying, time-traveling foe. (BBYA, IRA YAC)

Harry Potter and the Prisoner of Azkaban. 1999. 9780439136358.

When Sirius Black breaks out of the wizarding world's high security prison, Askaban, it is rumored that he is coming after Harry. (BBYA, IRA YAC, Mythopoeic Award)

Harry Potter and the Goblet of Fire. 2000. 9780439139595.

Wizard-in-training Harry Potter is entered in the Triwizard Tournament, which thrusts him into deep danger as Voldemort takes action against him. Because of the tournament, there is no Quidditch at Hogwarts this year, but Harry does get to attend the Qidditch World Cup with his friends the Weasleys. (IRA YAC, Hugo Award, PP)

Harry Potter and the Order of the Phoenix. 2003. 9780439358064.

Now fifteen, Harry has not seen or heard from any of his Hogwarts friends over the summer vacation, but they haven't forgotten about him because The Daily Prophet has engaged on a massive smear campaign against him. Things go from bad to worse when he is banned from playing Quidditch. (BBYA, TTT)

Harry Potter and the Half Blood Prince. 2005. 9780439784542.

Voldemort and the Death Eaters are terrorizing not only the wizarding world, but also the mundane muggle world, as Harry and Dumbledore try to find a way to stop them. (BBYA, TTT)

Harry Potter and the Deathly Hallows. 2007. 9780545010221.

With Voldemort and the Death Easters in control of Hogwarts and the Ministry of Magic, seventeen-year-old Harry, Hermoine, and Ron do not return to school but quest for the Horcruxes they need to find to finally defeat the evil forces. (TTT, BBYA, Norton Nebula)

Stroud, Jonathan.

Bartimaeus Trilogy. Ⓜ Ⓙ Ⓢ

In an alternate London, the government is run by magicians. (Mythopoeic Award)

The Amulet of Samarkand. 2003. 9780786818594.

Nathaniel, a brilliant young magician's apprentice, summons Bartimaeus, a djinn, to exact revenge on a powerful magician who once humiliated him by stealing the Amulet of Samarkand. (BBYA, Mythopoeic Fantasy Award)

The Golem's Eye. 2004. 9780786818600.

Nathaniel, now fourteen, is working his way up in the government when he is assigned to track down a terrorist who is using a golem. Nathaniel enlists Bartimaeus and Kitty, a Resistance fighter, to go to Prague with him to find the golem's power source. (BBYA)

Ptolemy's Gate. 2006. 9780786818617.

Nathaniel, Kitty, and Bartimaeus join forces to fight the demons who have taken the bodies and identities of government officials. (BBYA)

World of Faerie

Don't make the mistake of equating "faerie" with Tinkerbell type fairies. The world of faerie is dark and scary. The creatures that inhabit it, fey, are stunningly beautiful, often cruel, and usually hold humans in disdain, but nevertheless become involved with them. In the world of Faerie times moves at a different speed than in the human world, so like the legendary Tam Lin, humans drawn into Faerie for a few hours often find, upon their return to the human world, they have been gone for years. The denizens of Faerie are called, fairies, fey, the fair ones, and sometimes the good neighbors. Goblins are a type of fey. These are dark, suspenseful stories.

Dunkle, Clare B.

Hollow Kingdom. Ⓜ Ⓙ Ⓢ

The Goblins who live in a gorgeous subterranean world under Hollow Hill have fertility problems, so they often look for brides with faerie or human blood.

The Hollow Kingdom. 2003. 9780805073904.

A pair of orphaned Victorian era sisters go to live at Hollow Hill, not knowing that many girls have disappeared from that spot over the years. Once they arrive, Kate has the eerie feeling she is being watched. Indeed, Marak the Goblin King is planning to make her his bride. (BBYA, Mythopoeic)

Close Kin. 2004. 9780805074970.

Em, Kate's younger sister, has always loved Seylin, a goblin who looks more like the elves in his family tree, but when he proposes and Em doesn't immediately accept, he sets out on a quest. Em goes after him, starting on her own great and dangerous adventure.

In the Coils of the Snake. 2005. 9780805081107.

Miranda always thought she would marry Marak Catspaw, but everything goes wrong when an elven girl arrives and he plans to marry her instead.

Gardner, Sally.

I, Coriander. 2005. 9780803730991. **M J**

After Coriander's Royalist father flees seventeenth-century London, she is at the mercy of her Puritan stepmother and a cruel minister. Following a beating, Coriander wakes up in another world and discovers that her beloved, gentle mother had come from Faerie, and that many of her problems in London have their roots in Faerie conflicts.

Subjects: Historical Fiction; Puritans

Kincy, Karen.

Other. 2010. 9780738719191. **J S**

There are two kinds of Others, those who inherit their otherness and those who are infected by a bite or sexual transmission. The infected are usually vampires and werewolves. Gwen is half pooka. Her birth father was one of the faerie kind who could shape-shift, and Gwen fights her own urges to transform into a horse, an owl, or a cat. She feels like an outsider in her small Washington town and wishes she knew more Others. When she and her boyfriend find a couple dead in a pond, she suspects they are water sprites, and as other deaths are in the news she begins to believe perhaps a serial killer is targeting Others.

Subjects: Mystery; Pookas; Shape-shifters

Marillier, Juliet.

Transylvanian Sisters series. **J S**

These stand-alone novels feature five talented sisters living in medieval Transylvania.

Subjects: Fairy Tales; Romance; Transylvania

Wildwood Dancing. 2007. 9780375833649.

Jenica, the sensible second daughter of the family, is running things at home while their widowed father is away trying to be cured of an illness, when her cousin tries to take charge of their household and sets out to destroy anyone from faerie that can be found. Themes in the story echo the fairy tales "The Frog Prince" and "The Twelve Dancing Princesses." (BBYA)

Subjects: Frogs; Vampires

Cybele's Secret. 2008. 9780375833656.

> Scholarly Paula travels to Istanbul with her now recovered father, who is there to purchase a rare pagan artifact. Irene of Volos maintains a library in her home that Paula visits, accompanied by Stoyan, a bodyguard hired by her father. She sees veiled women with eyes that look like those of her sister Tati, who stayed in the Other Kingdom with her love, one of the Shadow People. Now she wonders if Tati is trying to get a message to her. (BBYA)
>
> **Subjects:** Bulgarians; Istanbul

Marr, Melissa.

Faerie series. **S**

Contemporary teens get caught up in the affairs of the Faerie courts, the Summer Queen, Winter Queen, and Dark Court.

Wicked Lovely. 2007. 9780061214653.

> Aislinn can see faeries, but wishes she couldn't—especially when Keenan, the Summer King, decides to make her his queen.

Ink Exchange. 2008. 9780061214684.

> Leslie, looking for change in her life, picks a tattoo to which she is drawn, which unfortunately creates a conduit to the Faery—and to Irial, the ruler of the Dark Court.

Fragile Eternity. 2009. 9780061214714.

> In a direct sequel to *Wicked Lovely*, Aislinn, now the immortal Summer Queen, feels the pull of the Summer King; but she loves mortal Seth.

Radiant Shadows. 2010. 9780061659225.

> Ani, born half faerie and half human, is tormented by a skin hunger, a need for physical touch, as well as the ability to drain the emotions of mortal and fey alike. Meanwhile Devlin, the High Queen's assassin, has been keeping a secret from his Queen that will force the world of Faerie to the edge of war.

Stiefvater, Maggie.

Books of Faerie. **J** **S**

This contemporary series of stand-alone romantic fantasy tales, rich with music, is set in the here and now but firmly grounded in the legends of faerie.

Subjects: Assassins; Celtic Myth; Folklore; Music; Romance

Lament: The Faerie Queen's Deception. 2008. 9780738713700.

> Deirdre Monaghan, a talented, sixteen-year-old harpist, has debilitating stage fright, so her first meeting with flautist Luke Dillon is not auspicious, but surprisingly enough, with him by her side, her worries dissipate. Luke has been sent to Deirdre's typical suburban neighborhood by the faerie queen to assassinate her, but instead has

fallen in love, which puts everyone whom Deirdre cares about in peril. (BBYA, PP)

Ballad: A Gathering of Faerie. 2009. 9780738714844.

James, Deirdre's bagpipe playing best friend, has won a scholarship to Thornking-Ash, a music-focused boarding school. Nuala, a faerie, offers him unprecedented musical prowess, but savvy James knows that it will exact a price too high if he accepts. Meanwhile, solitary fey near the school are being assassinated.

Taylor, Laini.

Lips Touch: Three Times. **2009. 9780545055857.**

Kizzy, who has grown up in an odd family, knows that goblins exist, but despite a family legend and her grandmother's post-death warnings, gambles on what may be a fatal attraction. In another unforgettable tale, set in colonial India, an enticing blend of fairy tale and myth, good and evil fight for the souls of the innocent. The final tale in this collection conjures up a fantastical landscape with fanged immortals. (NBA Finalist)

Faeries of Dreamdark. M

Tough but tiny faeries try to save the world from being swallowed by the Dark.

Blackbringer. 2007. 9780399246302.

Thumb-sized fairy Magpie Windwitch is on a mission to capture all the devils that humans have released into the world, but when she comes up against Blackbringer, she realizes she may need more help than her accompanying gang of crows can provide.

Silksinger. 2009. 9780399246319.

Tiny fairy Magpie Windwitch tries to rescue Azazel, one of the five Djinn who dreamed the world into being, and his secret guardian Whisper Silksinger, who belongs to a clan long thought extinct.

Thompson, Kate.

J. J. Liddy series. M J S

The Liddy family of a small town in Ireland has always been known for their fine music and story telling.

Subjects: Ireland; Music

The New Policeman. 2007. 9780061174278.

J. J. Liddy, a fifteen-year-old whose family has always played Irish music and put on Irish dances, notices that everyone is talking about how fast time is flying. There just is not time enough for almost anything anymore. When his mother says she would like more time for her birthday, he decides that would be just the thing. Upon the advice of a neighbor, he goes through the barrier between our world and Tir na n'Og, or the land of faerie, where he discovers they have their own problems because the time from our world has been leaking into their world. Meanwhile a new fiddle-playing policeman in

Kinvara, the village where the Liddys have always lived, has a very difficult time adjusting. (BBYA)

The Last of the High Kings. 2008. 9780061175954.

This stand-alone sequel to *The New Policeman*, set a quarter of a century later, is an outstanding fantasy revolving around J. J. Liddy's family. It involves a changeling, a ghost, a pookah, Tir na n'Og, music, a monster, and yes, the last of the high kings of Ireland.

Wooding, Chris.

Poison. 2005. 9780439755702. **J** **S** **M**

When Poison's baby sister is switched during the night and nobody notices, the sixteen-year-old leaves the deadly Black Marshes and sets out on a quest to rescue her sister from the Lord of Phaerie. (BBYA, TTT)

Subjects: Changelings

Urban Fantasy

Urban fantasy has become a popular designation for almost all fantasy set in the contemporary world, but fantasy purists argue that urban fantasy must take place in a city that is prominently featured and involve the clash between humans and fey, making it a subcategory of the World of Faerie. Classics in the genre include *War for the Oaks* and *Finder* by Emma Bull and *ElseWhere* and *NeverNever* by Will Shetterly. *The Essential Bordertown*, edited by Terri Windling and Delia Sherman, is an anthology of stories that epitomize urban fantasy. Urban fantasy is often dark, and over time themes involving drugs, runaways, music, and organized crime have been popular.

Black, Holly.

Modern Faerie. **S**

Black's tales of modern faerie stand as excellent examples of urban fantasy. The stories in this series feature contemporary young women in urban settings who become involved in the affairs of the fey.

Tithe, a Modern Faerie Tale. 2002. 9780689849244.

Kaye has spent her life taking care of her mom, a talented but unsuccessful rock musician who drinks too much and hooks up with unsuitable men. After the latest boyfriend attempts to murder her mother, the two return to New Jersey to stay at Kaye's crusty grandmother's house, where as a child Kaye had faerie playmates. Hanging out with her old friend Janet, Kaye keeps hoping that her faerie friends were not just the product of an overactive imagination. One night, walking home after being attacked by Janet's boyfriend, she hears a noise in the woods and meets Roiben, a silver-haired elven knight who has been wounded. After a trip to the Seelie court under a hill, Kaye finds herself designated as a sacrifice to keep the unaffiliated fey free for seven years. This is a gruesome take on the world of faerie, along with a little romance and a generous helping of teen angst. (BBYA)

Subjects: New Jersey

Ironside: A Modern Faery's Tale. 2007. 9780689868207.

When Kaye declares her love for Roiben, he sets a seemingly impossible task for her.

Subjects: Changelings

Valiant: A Modern Tale of Faerie. 2005. 9780786282265.

Val runs away after finding her mother and boyfriend are having an affair. Living in an abandoned subway stop under the city with other teen runaways, she begins using a highly addictive drug that the fey use to stave off iron sickness. (BBYA, Quick Picks, Norton Nebula, PP)

Subjects: Drugs; Runaways

Clare, Cassandra.

Mortal Instruments. 🄢

There is much to see of the supernatural that mundanes do not see, including the Night Children, who move among them, and the Shadowhunters, who hunt them down.

Subjects: Angels; Demons; Family Secrets; Romance; Vampires; Werewolves

City of Bones. 2007. 9781416914280.

When fifteen-year-old Clary Fray witnesses a killing in a club, she confronts the killers and finds out that they are Shadowhunters, who hunt down evil and dangerous Night Children. The problem is, she shouldn't be able to see them if she is truly a mundane. And now she can't even get answers from her mother, who has been kidnapped by monsters.

City of Ashes. 2008. 9781416914297.

Now that Clary knows the identity of her father, she is set on defeating his nefarious plans, as her relationship with Simon changes and evolves. (TTT, IRA YAC)

City of Glass. 2009. 9781416914303.

When searching for a potion to cure her mother, Clary and her brother Jace face down their father in an epic battle involving werewolves, vampires, faeries, and an angel that makes allies out of enemies.

City of Fallen Angels. 2011.
Projected.

de Lint, Charles.

The Blue Girl. 2004. 9780142405451. 🄢

Imogene sees the move she makes to de Lint's legendary city of Newford as the perfect chance to shed her bad girl persona. The first day she selects conservative looking, hard-studying Maxine as her new best friend. She also starts having troubling dreams featuring her childhood imaginary friend and meets Adrian, the ghost of a boy who is said to have committed suicide by leaping off the high school roof. As in most of de Lint's oeuvre, the line between reality and faerie softens and fades, this time forcing Imogene, Adrian, and Maxine into fighting the dark side of faerie. (PP)

Vande Velde, Vivian.

Now You See It . . . 2005. 9780152053116.

When Wendy's glasses break, she finds a pair of sunglasses that just happen to have her prescription. However, with these sunglasses she suddenly starts seeing things differently because they filter magic rather than rays. The most popular and fashionable girl in school is actually an ancient crone, the geeky classmate is actually a gorgeous elf, and there are portals through space and time where she and the eighteen-year-old version of her grandmother go to fight evil. (PP)

Subjects: Alzheimer's; Humorous; Vision

Mythic Reality

This type of story is set in the concrete, nonmagical world in which the protagonist lives, but elements of myth seep into this world, or the character is drawn into the mythological world while retaining fully human qualities. Magical things may happen, but they have more to do with resolving mundane problems than with creating awe with sparkle and glamour. Readers who like this type may enjoy Jamie Martinez Wood's *Rogelia's House of Magic* in the "Psionic Powers & Unexplained Phenomena" section of chapter 5, because it also deals with little magics. Often many of the titles in this section have been referred to as urban fantasy even when they do not occur in an urban setting, which is quite perplexing and indicative of how important precision is when discussing genres and how very true it is that every book is a different experience for every reader.

de Lint, Charles.

Little (Grrl) Lost. 2007. 9780670061440. **J S**

When her family moves from the farm into the suburbs and her beloved horse is sold, T. J. is devastated. Hearing strange sounds in her bedroom wall at night, she decides to sleep on the floor and catches sight of a teenage goth-looking girl who is only six inches tall. Elizabeth is a "Little" one of a race of hidden "little people," who live under the floors and in the walls of human houses. Elizabeth is running away from home. A few days later T. J. discovers Elizabeth has only gone as far as the shed, but because her parents know that she was seen by a human, they have moved away. T. J. wants to help Elizabeth find her parents, so they decide to go to a bookstore signing by an author who has written children's books about Littles. On the way, T. J. is attacked and Elizabeth disappears. What ensues are their parallel adventures in this enticing mythic reality.

Dunmore, Helen.

Ingo. **M**

Brother and sister, Conor and Sapphire, are drawn to the sea near their Cornwall home as they look for their missing father and discover that they are part Mer themselves.

Subjects: Cornwall; Mermaids; Siblings

Ingo. 2006. 9780060818524.

> When Sapphire's father disappears, she and her brother Conor remember the song he used to sing about Ingo, a magical sea world, and his stories of the Mer folk, so when they meet some Mer people they are ready to take to the sea.

The Tide Knot. 2006. 9780060818562.

> A danger from the sea threatens the Cornwall coast with a tsunamilike disaster if the tide knot in Ingo is undone, and Sapphy and Conor must try to save their community.

The Deep. 2007. 9780060818586.

> Sapphy's mixed blood allows her to go places other Mers and humans can't, so she may be the only one who can stop the Kraken from destroying Ingo and the Cornwall coast.

Subjects: Whales

Ephron, Delia.

Frannie in Pieces. 2007. 9780060747169. **J** **S**

Fifteen-year-old Frannie is devastated when she finds her father dead, but her grief becomes more bearable when she puts together an exquisite 1,000-piece handmade jigsaw puzzle he seemingly left for her. The vivid hand-painted scene of an Italian setting whisks her into another time and place.

Subjects: Puzzles

Funke, Cornelia.

The Thief Lord. 2002. 9780545227704. **M**

Two orphaned brothers flee the aunt who wants to separate them to go to the Venice their mother always told them about. They team up with other homeless waifs, who are under the protection of another kid, the Thief Lord. The Thief Lord is commissioned to steal a wing that will restore the magic to a carousel that affects one's age.

Gaiman, Neil.

Anansi Boys. 2005. 9780060515188. **O**

Fat Charlie Nancy (who isn't fat) was often tricked by his estranged father, who lived in America. When his dad dies, he travels to Florida and ends up at the wrong funeral. An old neighbor talks to him about the brother he never knew he had; and when he returns to London the brother, Spider, turns up on his doorstep.

Charlie's fiancée, Rosey, can't tell the brothers apart, and because she never sees them together, begins to feel a building passion for Spider, whom she thinks is Charlie. Meanwhile, Charlie's shady boss has nefarious plans for him, and everything that can go wrong seems to. It seems the trickster god Anansi is involved in Charlie's life. (BBYA, Alex Award, Locus Award, August Derleth Award, Mythopoeic Award)

Subjects: Adult Books for Teens; London; Tricksters

Lester, Julius.

Time's Memory. 2006. 9780374371784. **S**

On the eve of the Civil War, Ekundayo, an African spirit that has been carried in many different people as it tries to bring peace to those in slavery, enters Nat, a slave on a Virginia plantation who loves his master's daughter, Ellen.

Subjects: Historical Fiction; Possession; Slavery

McKinley, Robin.

Dragonhaven. 2007. 9780399246753. **J S**

Fourteen-year-old Jake has grown up in a national park that is the last refuge of the few remaining dragons. It's a world divided between those who want to protect the eighty-foot-long, endangered fire breathers, and those who don't. When Jake finds a newborn dragonlet next to her dying mother, he saves her and begins raising her in secret, a decision that could close the park and end the protections for dragons.

Subjects: Dragons; National Parks

McNeal, Laura, and Tom McNeal.

The Decoding of Lana Morris. 2007. 9780375831065. **J S**

Lana is placed in a foster home for kids with special needs, just because nobody else will take a sixteen-year-old. When she buys a pad of thirteen pages of drawing paper from an antique store, she finds that the pages may have magical properties. Whatever she draws, or erases, happens.

Subjects: Autism; Disabilities; Foster Care; Romance; Special Needs

Pinkwater, Daniel.

Neddiad & Yggyssey. **M**

Elements of the *Iliad* and *Odyssey* figure into these madcap tales set in the postwar years in the mid-twentieth century.

Subjects: 1940s; 1950s; Aliens; Ghosts; Historical Fiction; Humorous; Parallel Worlds

The Neddiad: How Neddie Took the Train, Went to Hollywood, and Saved Civilization. 2007. 9780618594443.

> A 1940s postwar road trip combines comedy, fantasy, a ghost, and even space aliens. (VOYA)

The Yggyssey: How Iggy Wondered What Happened to All the Ghosts. 2009. 9780618594450.

> Iggy becomes concerned when several of the ghosts who inhabit the Hollywood hotel where she lives seems to have gone missing. She sets out on a quest to Old New Hackensack, New Jersey, a parallel world, with her friends Neddie and Seamus Finn.

Werlin, Nancy.

Impossible. 2008. 9780803730021. ⑤

> Seventeen-year-old Lucinda is the victim of an ancient curse based on the ballad "Scarborough Fair." Raised by loving foster parents after being abandoned as an infant by Miranda, her mentally ill teenage mother, Lucy has grown up to be a sensible person, the last one anyone would figure would turn up pregnant. Along with her foster parents and poodle Pierre, the household also includes Zach, a college student who had been their neighbor and moved in when his family moved away in his senior year of high school. Miranda's legacy to Lucy was a unique version of the song made famous by Simon and Garfunkel and some pages torn from her journal and hidden in a secret compartment of a bookcase. When Zack finds Miranda's journal, they discover that generations of Scarborough girls have been cursed, but that the song holds the clues to end the curse. (BBYA, NBA Finalist, PP)

> **Subjects:** Folk Songs; Literary; Pregnancy; Rape

Myth and Legend

Myths and legends often draw teen readers to the fantasy genre. Traditional myths and legends are a part of our collective history and culture, but not all myth and legend go back to ancient times. Readers who like this type may also enjoy the "Ancient History" section of chapter 3. The stories below are often based on myth and legend, but don't always qualify as myths and legends.

Farmer, Nancy.

Troll Trilogy. Ⓜ Ⓙ

> Apprentice bard Jack's adventures start when he and his sister Lucy are kidnapped by Northmen during a Viking raid.

> **Subjects:** Bards; Britain; Eighth Century; Historical Fiction; Norse Myth; Slavery; Vikings

The Sea of Trolls. 2004. 9780689867446.

> Eleven-year-old apprentice bard Jack and his younger sister Lucy are kidnapped by the Northmen and turned into slaves. When Jack offends the half-troll queen with a spell gone awry, he must set out on a quest to the icy

home of the trolls to drink from a well that will allow him to reverse the spell and save his sister from becoming a sacrifice. (BBYA)

Subjects: Berserkers; Jotunheim; Trolls

The Land of the Silver Apples. 2007. 9781416907350.

Now thirteen, Jack discovers Lucy has been taken by the Lady of the Lake, and he must travel to Elfland to save her.

Subjects: Arthurian Legend; Druids; Goblins

The Islands of the Blessed. 2009. 9781416907374.

After the village where they are living is destroyed and a vengeful spirit shows up, Jack, Thorgil, and the Bard head out on a quest to restore order.

Friesner, Esther.

Helen of Troy Duet. J S

Helen, a Spartan princess destined for fame, is feisty and independent, wanting adventure and chafing under the restrictions placed upon her as a princess.

Subjects: Girls Dressed as Boys; Greek Mythology

Nobody's Princess. 2007. 9780375875298.

Helen of Sparta is feisty and independent as she grows up and tries to participate in the same activities as her brothers. Disguising herself as a boy, she learns how to hunt, fight, and ride horses.

Nobody's Prize. 2008. 9780375875311.

Disguised as a boy, Helen stows away on Jason's ship, the *Argo*, and sets out on her own adventure during his quest for the Golden Fleece.

Friesner, Esther.

Temping Fate. 2006. 9780525477303. J S

After Ilana gets a job with Divine Relief Temps, she finds herself working for the Fates, who are only some of the mythological deities needing temporary workers.

Subjects: Humor

Geras, Adele.

Ithaka. 2006. 9780152056032. S

Klymene, a servant girl, tends Penelope in her island castle, as Penelope tries to fend off suitors while waiting for her husband Odysseus to return home to her, their son, and his dog.

Golding, Julia.

Companions Quartet. **M**

When eleven-year-old Connie is sent to live with an aunt on the rugged English sea coast, she discovers talents she didn't know she had, as well as a secret society devoted to saving mythological beings. Connie turns out to be the only Universal in the world, the only person who can communicate with all types of creatures, not just one.

Subjects: Animals; Ecology; England; Environment; Secret Societies

Secret of the Sirens. 2007. 9780761453710.

Connie, curious about what her aunt does when she goes out, stows away on a small boat. She discovers that Aunt Evelyn is a member of Society for the Protection of Mythical Creatures and is trying to save creatures who are being threatened by pollution from a local oil company.

The Gorgon's Gaze. 2007. 9780761453772.

When her parents abruptly remove her from Aunt Evelyn's home and send her to live with Great-Aunt Godiva, Connie's training ends. Now she is placed in danger from a shape-shifting monster.

Mines of the Minotaur. 2008 . 9780761453024.

When Connie begins to manifest a dangerous new power, she is expelled from the Society.

The Chimera's Curse. 2008. 9780761454403.

Kullervo, who wants to eradicate humanity for its polluting ways, sends a chimera after Connie.

Graham, Jo.

Black Ships. **2008. 9780316067997.** **S**

Annotated in the "Ancient History" section of chapter 3.

Halam, Ann.

Snakehead. **2008. 9780375841088.** **J** **S**

Perseus falls in love with Andromeda and is sent off to slay Medusa by King Polydectes, who wants Perseus out of the way. On his quest Perseus manages to save Andromeda and slay Medusa.

Humphreys, Chris.

The Runestone Saga. **S**

Sky has both Norwegian and Corsican roots; and both cultures know of people who can leave their bodies while dreaming.

The Fetch. 2006. 9780553494754.

> Fifteen-year-old Sky March and his cousin Kristin find runestones in an old trunk, which lead Sky to the discovery that he has a "fetch"—that is, a version of himself that can travel through time.

Vendetta. 2007. 9780375832932.

> Sky discovers similarities between the legends of his Corsican and Norse ancestors when he tries to evict Sigurd, his evil grandfather, who has possessed Kristin.

Possession. 2008. 9780375932946.

> In their attempt to find a way to stop Sigurd, Sky and Kristin travel back to the mid-seventeenth century for help from an ancestor who is a witch.

Lester, Julius.

Cupid: A Tale of Love and Desire. **2007. 9780152020569.** **S**

> Psyche loves Cupid even though she has never seen his face, but her sisters try to get her to break her promise to him as his mother, Venus, tries to break them up.

Levine, Gail Carson.

Ever. **2008. 9780061229626.** **M** **J** **S**

> Olus, the Akkan god of winds, has fallen in love with Kezi, who is to be sacrificed to another god in only thirty days, but if she succeeds on a quest, Kezi may achieve immortality and be able to marry Olus.

McKenzie, Nancy.

Chrysalis Queen Quartet. **M**

> Orphaned Guinevere is a ward of her aunt Queen Alyse and uncle King Pellinore in medieval Wales. Her cousin, Elaine, is obsessed with King Arthur.

Guinevere's Gift. 2008. 9780375843457.

> At age twelve Guinevere loves to ride, and one day when out on her horse she meets Llyr, a member of the Old Ones, an almost forgotten Welsh tribe that believes in a prophecy made at Guinevere's birth and has been secretly guarding her.

Guinevere's Gamble. 2009. 9780375943461.

> When all the kings of Wales are invited to a meeting, Gwen goes along and discovers a dangerous enemy in King Arthur's sister, Morgan Le Fay.

Morris, Gerald.

The Squire's Tale. **M** **J**

Various characters from Arthurian legend are thrown together with young protagonists and a touch of humor to make the tales come alive for readers at the younger end of the teen spectrum.

Subjects: Arthurian Legend

The Squire's Tale. 1997. 9780395869598.

> Fourteen-year-old Terence becomes squire to Sir Gawain and discovers the secret of his parentage.

The Squire, His Knight, and His Lady. 1999. 9780395912119.

> When Gawain is imprisoned, young Terence must rescue him. (BBYA)

The Savage Damsel and the Dwarf. 2000. 9780395971260.

> Sixteen-year-old Lady Lynet escapes her besieged castle to request help from King Arthur. (BBYA, VOYA)

Parsifal's Page. 2001. 9780618055098.

> Eleven-year-old Piers goes to Arthur's court, where he discovers that Parsifal is in dire need of a page who knows the rules of chivalry. (IRA YAC)

Ballad of Sir Dinaden. 2003. 9780618190997.

> Raised to be a knight, young Dinaden would prefer to be a minstrel. (VOYA)

The Princess, the Crone, and the Dung-Cart Knight. 2004. 9780547014807.

> Thirteen-year-old Sarah deviates from her quest to find the one who killed her mother when she sees Queen Guinevere and Sir Kay being kidnapped and goes to inform King Arthur.
>
> **Subjects:** Hate Crimes; Jews

The Lioness and Her Knight. 2005. 9780618507726.

> Sixteen-year-old Luneta finds romance when she is escorted to the home of her mother's friend, where she will live for a year near her cousin Ywain and Rhience, who has taken a vow to live as a fool for one year.

The Quest of the Fair Unknown. 2006. 9780618631520.

> Fulfilling a promise to his dead mother, seventeen-year-old Beaufils goes to Camelot to find the father he has never known.

Riordan, Rick.

Percy Jackson and the Olympians. **M** **J** **S**

Percy Jackson, a kid with a bent for trouble, discovers that he is a half-blood: his unknown father was a god.

Subjects: ADHD; Camps; Greek Myth

The Lightning Thief. 2005. 9780786856299.

Kicked out of another school, Percy is sent to a camp for kids who are half-bloods, half-human and half-god, where he finds out more about his own history and takes on a quest to restore Zeus's lightning bolt to save humanity. (BBYA, PP, Film)

The Sea of Monsters. 2006. 9780786856862.

Percy Jackson, the son of Poseidon and a mortal woman, is off on a far-ranging adventure with his friends Annabeth, another half-blood, and Tyson, a Cyclops, as they try to save Camp Half-Blood, as well as Grover, a satyr who has been captured by a cyclops. (VOYA)

The Titan's Curse. 2007. 9781423101451.

A quest to rescue Artemis and Annabeth takes Percy, Grover, Thalia, Zoë Nightshade, and newly found half-blood Bianca on a journey across an America filled with monsters to find them and save Olympus. (VOYA, IRA YAC)

The Battle of the Labyrinth. 2008. 9781423101468.

In his fourth summer at Camp Half-Blood, Percy, along with his demigod friends, ventures into the Labyrinth after discovering that it could be providing an opening for danger to penetrate the camp. (VOYA)

The Last Olympian. 2009. 9780739380338.

Nearly sixteen, Percy and friends face down the Titans in an epic battle centered in New York City, as a giant heads for the city and Olympus fights its own battles.

Sandell, Lisa Ann.

Song of the Sparrow. **2007 9780439918480.** **J** **S**

Elaine lives with her father in one of King Arthur's military camps in fifth-century Britain, where she falls in love with Lancelot; but then Gwynivere arrives.

Subjects: Arthurian Legend; Britain; Fifth Century; Lady of Shallot; Verse Novels

Scott, Michael.

Secrets of the Immortal Nicholas Flamel Series. **J** **S**

Contemporary California twins are swept into a world of magic and mythology after they meet an immortal alchemist and his wife, who have been living since the fourteenth century.

Subjects: Alchemy; Dee, John; Flamel, Nicholas; Golems; Immortality; Joan of Arc; London; Machiavelli; Paris; San Francisco; Twins; Valkyries; Vampires; Werewolves

The Alchemyst. 2007. 9780385903721.

Fifteen-year-old twins Sophie and Josh find summer jobs in San Francisco and are sucked into a world of mayhem after golems steal an important book called the Codex from Josh's bookstore-owning boss, who turns out to be Nicholas Flamel, an alchemist born in the fourteenth century who developed a formula for immortality. (IRA YAC)

The Magician. 2008. 9780385733588.

Sophie, Josh, and Nicholas continue to look for the Codex, as Nicholas and his wife Pernelle, imprisoned in Alcatraz, continue to age one year for every day that it is missing.

The Sorceress. 2009. 9780385735292.

Sophie and Josh end up in England after Paris is left in ruins and meet Gilgamesh, Billy the Kid, and William Shakespeare.

Necromancer. 2010. 9780385735315.

Josh and Sophie are back in San Francisco, but Dr. John Dee is still after them, and Machiavelli is at Alcatraz to release the monsters locked up there for the final battle.

Spinner, Stephanie.

Quicksilver. 2005, 9780440238454. **J S**

Hermes tells of his myriad experiences with Persephone, Perseus, Medusa, Odysseus, and the Trojan war.

Subjects: Greek Myth

Vande Velde, Vivian.

The Book of Mordred. 2005. 9780618507542. **J S**

Three women—Alayna, whose daughter has been kidnapped and needs help; magical Nimue, who is close to Merlin; and Kiera, the fifteen-year-old who had been kidnapped at age five—and their relationships with Mordred, the son of Arthur.

Subjects: Arthurian Legend

Fairy Tales

Retelling and reworking traditional fairy tales and folktales, sometimes in fractured humorous remakes, is a growing trend in publishing and in novels for teens and adults. In these stories familiar characters and storylines are presented with new twists and different perspectives. Many readers will be well acquainted with some of the stories told in the following novels, and other stories are seemingly brand new, but with a tone that elicits the underlying feeling that the story has been told before.

Bunce, Elizabeth.

A Curse Dark as Gold. 2008. 9780439895767. **J S**

This retelling of Rumpelstiltskin is set during the Industrial Revolution in England. It is the story of Charlotte and Rosie Miller, who take over operation of the family's struggling, and perhaps cursed, mill upon their father's death and try to make a go of it. When Jack Spinner, a strange little man, shows up, claiming to be able to spin a room full of straw into gold, it looks like their problems may be solved. (BBYA, Morris)

Subjects: Historical fiction; Rumpelstiltskin

Calhoun, Dia.

White Midnight. 2003. 9780374383893. **M** **J**

Fifteen-year-old asthmatic Rose, knowing she is thought ugly, is happy trying to breed new varieties of apples in her spare time, but she is terrified when her parents sell her to Master Brae, who owns Greengarden. She is fearful when told she will be living and working in the Bighouse, where "the Thing," a terrifying creature, lives in the attic. Then she is told she must marry "the Thing." (BBYA)

Subjects: Beauty and the Beast

Farley, Terri.

Seven Tears into the Sea. 2005. 9780689864421. **J** **S**

When she was ten, seventeen-year-old Gwen was recued from drowning by a strange man and her family moved away from the beach. Now that she has returned to California to help her grandmother, she falls in love with Jesse, who has a strange proclivity for eating raw fish.

Subjects: Romance; Selkies

Ferris, Jean.

Twice Upon a Marigold. 2008. 9780152063825. **M** **J** **S**

Part comedy, part tragedy, part two. A year after they started living happily ever after, Queen Marigold and King Chris are at odds with each other for no reason—and so are the five dogs, who all want the same blue dog toy. Queen Olympia, who suffered amnesia and turned into a decent person called Angela after falling in the river and being swept away at their wedding, regains her memory and her streak of cruelty, and returns to the palace with Lazy Susan, Sleeping Beauty's sister. Sending the King, Ed, and Magnus to the dungeon to await execution for treason, Olympia rewrites the constitution. Meanwhile, Marigold and Christian find a secret way into the dungeon. They seek a way to fix things and save the lives of their adopted dads and their friend. This sequel to *Once Upon a Marigold* is full of malapropisms and kindness.

Subjects: Humor; Malapropisms; Trolls

Flinn, Alex.

Beastly. 2007. 9780060874162. **J** **S**

Conceited Kyle Kingsbury turns into a hideous beast after playing a cruel prank on a new, goth-looking, girl at his school. One unthinking act of kindness allows him an opportunity for redemption and to turn back into himself; but he will have to be kissed by his own true love within two years for that to happen. In his beastly form, the chances don't look too likely. (Quick Picks, IRA YAC, PP, Film)

Subjects: Beauty and the Beast

A Kiss in Time. **2010. 9780060874193.**

Talia, the over-protected sixteen-year-old Princess of Euphrasia, falls into a 300-year sleep after pricking her finger on a spindle. In the present day, Jack, age seventeen, is a total slacker whose well-to-do parents have sent him on a tour of Europe. He escapes his tour group and with his buddy Travis tries to find a beach, but due to their boorish behavior they are given bad directions that take them into Euphrasia, where Jack kisses Talia awake. When her dad the king blows up about her irresponsibility in destroying the kingdom by putting it to sleep since she was foolish enough to touch a spindle, she runs away back to Miami with Jack. Jack knows he is not her true love, his distant parents agree to allow her to sleep on an air mattress on the floor of the den for a week, and Jack's outsider little sister sort of befriends Talia.

Subjects: Sleeping Beauty

George, Jessica Day.

Sun and Moon, Ice and Snow. **2008. 9781599901091. J S**

A tenderhearted unnamed heroine is gifted with the ability to speak with animals after she rescues a trapped white reindeer, who is unable to grant her wish that her oldest brother be healed from debilitating depression. In a land that winter will not release, her family has become more impoverished each year, with no money to dower the girls. When a huge white bear shows up and offers wealth in exchange for the nameless girl, called pika or lass, to spend a year and a day with him in a palace, she agrees to go with him, not knowing she is embarking on a major adventure. (BBYA)

Subjects: East of the Sun, West of the Moon

Hale, Shannon.

Book of a Thousand Days. **2007. 9781599900513. J S**

Dashti, a resourceful maid, keeps a diary while imprisoned in a tower with her mistress, Lady Saren, who has refused to marry Lord Khasar. (BBYA)

Princess Academy. **2005. 9781582349930. M J**

The residents of Mount Eskel eke out a subsistence living by quarrying linder, a rare and beautiful stone that is found nowhere else in the kingdom, and trading it for foodstuffs when the rare traders come through. When the priests forecast the crown prince will marry a girl from Mount Eskel, all the girls from Miri's village are sent to a Princess Academy to be trained for a year before meeting the prince. By reading some of Tutor Olana's books, Miri discovers the rarity of the linder and its true worth. She also discovers that she can use Quarry-speech, a kind of telepathy that is linked to the linder. When Prince Steffan of Danland leaves the day after he arrives, bandits show up to kidnap his fiancée, not knowing that the prince had not yet chosen a princess. This gives Miri and the others opportunities to show leadership, cleverness, and heroism. (Newbery Honor)

Books of Bayern. Ⓜ Ⓙ Ⓢ

The books in this grouping of stand-alone stories share characters, but were not originally published as a series. However, all have a fairy tale theme, some familiar, some seemingly totally original.

Goose Girl. 2003. 9781582348438.

On her way to a neighboring kingdom to marry, Princess Ani is attacked by her lady-in-waiting, who takes her possessions and place. Surviving as a goose girl called Isi, Ani tries to save her horse and reclaim her life. (PP)

Enna Burning. 2004. 9781582348896.

After goose girl Isi marries the prince, Enna returns to the forest, where she uses her talent for fire to help fight Bayern's enemies; when she is captured by the enemy, Isi, Finn, and Razo attempt to rescue her.

River Secrets. 2006. 9781582349015.

Razso's prodigious memory for details gets him sent on a diplomatic mission to Tira after the war is over. (TTT, PP)

Forest Born. 2009. 9781599901671.

Rin, Razo's sister, returns to the city with her brother, where she finds war is looming. She joins Queen Isi, Enna, and Dasha as they try to retrieve Isi's kidnapped son.

Leavitt, Martine.

Keturah and Lord Death. 2006. 9781932425291. Ⓙ Ⓢ

When sixteen-year-old orphan Keturah becomes lost in the woods following a legendary hart, she encounters Lord Death. Her storytelling skills lead him to spare her life for a day, as long as in that time she can find her true love. (PP, NBA Finalist)

Subjects: Scheherazade; Storytelling

Levine, Gail Carson.

Fairest. 2006. 9780060734084. Ⓜ Ⓙ

Aza isn't beautiful, but she can sing, and in the world of Ayortha, that is of major importance. When the queen discovers that Aza can not only sing beautifully, but also throw her voice, she is enlisted to make the queen sound good.

Subjects: Cyrano; Singing; Snow White

Martin, Rafe.

Birdwing. 2005. 9780439211673. Ⓜ Ⓙ

In a Grimms' retelling of "Six Swans," one of the brothers is left with one swan wing. This is his story. Prince Ardwin is quite accomplished at princely pursuits despite his physical difference, but he also has the ability to understand animal speech. He sets out on a journey to escape an arranged marriage that would require him to cut off his wing.

Subjects: Six Swans

Moore, John.

The Unhandsome Prince. 2005. 9780441012879. **S**

Caroline is practically perfect—not only extremely attractive, she is also well organized, which helps her find the frog prince in the swamp after endless weeks of catching and kissing frogs in a very systematic way. But something is wrong—the prince is not handsome! Well, some may say he is kind of cute, but definitely not handsome. Caroline has been banking on this opportunity, so even though she is unwilling to marry Prince Hal, who is actually more dorky looking than anything, she seizes on the loophole that she may be able to marry one of his brothers. Of course there are time constraints, because Hal could turn back into a frog. Emily goes to the palace with Caroline because she needs to find a mentor since her mother, the witch who turned Hal into a frog, is now dead. With Rapunzel and Rumpelstiltskin joining in, Hal tries to find a way to keep the kingdom from bankruptcy, marry Caroline off to one of his handsome brothers, and get the girl of his dreams.

Subjects: Adult Books for Teens; Frog Prince; Humorous; Parody; Rapunzel; Rumpelstiltskin

Murdock, Catherine Gilbert.

Princess Ben. 2008. 9780618959716. **J** **S**

After her parents are assassinated, Princess Benevolence is sent to live with her hateful aunt Queen Sophia. After she is locked away in a tower, she finds a secret room and a book from which she begins to learn magic.

Napoli, Donna Jo.

Bound. 2004. 9780689861758. **M** **J** **S**

Xing Xing, lives with her stepmother and stepsister in a cave in fourteenth-century China. (BBYA, PP)

Subjects: China; Cinderella; Historical Fiction

Breath. 2003. 9780689861741. **J** **S**

Inspired by the tale of the Pied Piper, this grim historical novel set in late thirteenth-century Hameln, Germany, details the horrors of life and disease during a rat and fungal infestation, as related by Salz, a twelve-year-old with cystic fibrosis. (BBYA, PP)

Subjects: Cystic Fibrosis; Germany; Historical fiction; Pied Piper

Pattou, Edith.

East. 2005. 9780152052218. **M** **J** **S**

In this retelling of the fairy tale "East of the Sun and West of the Moon," Rose is the ninth daughter of a mapmaker and his wife. When a mysterious white bear offers her family prosperity if Rose goes with him, she does, and learns that the bear is a prince under a spell cast by the jealous Troll Queen. Eventually she must embark on a journey that spans the icy North to reclaim her love. (BBYA, PP)

Subjects: East of the Sun West of the Moon; Fairy Tales; Norse Mythology; Weaving

Vande Velde, Vivian.

Stolen. 2008. 9780761455158. **M** **J** **S**

After a witch's cottage is burned down, a twelve-year-old girl with absolutely no memories is found running through the woods. The couple who find her believe she is Isabelle, who was stolen away by a witch six years earlier. (VOYA)

Subjects: Amnesia

Yolen, Jane, and Adam Stemple.

Pay the Piper: A Rock 'n' Roll Fairy Tale. 2005. 9780765311580. **J**

Teen journalist Callie McCallan escapes being spirited away by a piper on Halloween because she was working with headphones on when all the other teens and children in town were taken away. Setting out to search for her brother, she is picked up by the guitar player of her favorite band and discovers she must break a faerie curse placed on the band's flute player to release him and all the teens and children, who were taken as his tithe to faerie. (Locus Award)

Subjects: Faerie; Pied Piper; Rock Music

Troll Bridge: A Rock 'n' Roll Fairy Tale. 2006. 9780765314260. **J**

Sixteen-year-old Moira is a harp-playing musical prodigy who is one of twelve Dairy Princesses for the State Fair. She rushes from rehearsal with the Minnesota Orchestra to a photo shoot on the Trollholm bridge just in time to see the other eleven princesses and the photographer snatched up by a giant troll and swept away into the river. Grabbing his shirttail, Moira follows along and ends up in Trollholm. A popular pop group made up of the three Griffson brothers is on a road trip when they approach the bridge, and a fox telepathically orders youngest brother Jakob to follow him. When the brothers' car gets to the center of the bridge, a wall of water sweeps them off and directly into Trollholm. The three brothers are captured by the troll and hung, one each, in the pantries of his three wives. Jakob escapes by tricking one of the troll's sons. When Moira and Jakob meet up, they join forces, and with the advice of Fossegrin, the fox, they attempt to rescue Jakob's brothers and the other Dairy Princesses.

Subjects: Foxes; Jack in the Beanstock; Minnesota; Music; Trolls

Animal Fantasy

Animal fantasy has long been popular with teen readers, particularly those at the youngest end of the spectrum. Stories in this section may deal with real animals fighting for survival, mythological creatures, or even shape-shifters, people who spend some of their time in animal form.

Atwater-Rhodes, Amelia.

The Kiesha'ra Series. J S

Two races of shape-shifters, birds and snakes, have been so long at war that their populations have been decimated.

Hawksong. 2003. 9780385734929.

> The young rulers of each kingdom, Danica Shardae and Zane Cobriana, are weary of losing everyone they love, and decide to end the war by marrying.

Snakecharm. 2004. 9780385734936.

> As Zane and Danica await the birth of their first child, the peace between the Avian and Serpiente peoples is imperiled after fears arise about how a mixed-race royal heir will be accepted.

Falcondance. 2005. 9780385731942.

> Nineteen-year-old Nicias, whose falcon parents were exiled and stripped of their powers, is trying to learn how to control his own falcon magic, while serving as a guard to Oliza, the heir to both the avian and serpiente thrones.

Wolfcry. 2006. 9780440238867.

> The Wyvern court is being torn apart as both avian and serpiente suitors want to win Oliza. But all changes when she is kidnapped by mercenaries and taken deep into wolf territory. (IRA YAC)

Wyvernhail. 2007. 9780385734363.

> Hai, who is half serpiente and half avian, sees visions of a grim future if Oliza comes back to take the throne; so Hai must give up all she loves to ensure the peace and safety of both races.

Browne, N. M.

Silverboy. 2007. 9781582347806. M

> Fifteen-year-old Tommo, a spellgrinder's apprentice, escapes from his cruel taskmaster, but finds it difficult to hide, as he has turned silver after years spent grinding the magical stones. He teams up with Akenna, a fisherman's daughter, and is aided by a flock of birds with human faces.

Subjects: Birds; Magic

Carey, Janet Lee.

Dragon's Keep. 2007. 9780152064013. M J S

> Merlin prophesied that Rosalind would become the queen to restore her family to greatness, but since she was born with a finger that looks like a dragon's claw, it is doubtful that she will ever live to become queen—especially after she is carried away by a dragon to mind his children. (BBYA)

Subjects: Curses; Dragons; Princesses

D'Lacey, Chris.

Last Dragon Chronicles. M

College student David Rain rents a room in a house where a woman who makes dragons of clay lives with her young daughter, Lucy, who worries about an injured squirrel.

Subjects: Aliens; Boarding Houses; Ceramics; Dragons; Ecology; Polar Bears; Squirrels

The Fire Within. 2005. 9780439672436.

After being given his own tiny clay dragon named Gadzooks, David writes a story for Lucy and discovers that there may be more to Liz's ceramic dragons than first appears.

Icefire. 2006. 9780439672467.

David writes an essay about dragon history, and one of his classmates accidentally "quickens" a dragon egg.

Fire Star. 2007. 9780439901857.

David and his girlfriend Zanna investigate changes in the arctic as aliens turn out to have a connection to the dragons.

Fire Eternal. 2008. 9780545051637.

Even though David has been missing in the arctic for five years, Zanna, the mother of his daughter, Lucy, and Liz have not given up on him.

Dark Fire. 2010. 9780545102728.

David Rain returns after five years with dragons who have dark fire.

de Lint, Charles.

Dingo. 2008. 9780142408162. J S

It is love at first sight for seventeen-year-old Miguel when he sees recent Australian import Lainey and her dog outside his father's comic and music store. Lainey and her twin Em are actually shape-shifters who only sometimes take their dingo form. Miguel's enemy Johnny falls for Em, and all four of them end up visiting the dream lands to try to free the girls from a power that is threatening them.

Subjects: Australians; Canada; Dingoes; Dogs; Shapeshifters

George, Jessica Day.

Creel series. M J S

Orphaned Creel becomes a friend to dragons, finds a new life in the capital, and hones her needlework skills.

Subjects: Dragons; Embroidery; Seamstresses; War

Dragon Slippers. 2007. 9781599902753.

Orphaned Creel and her family have fallen on hard times, so her aunt comes up with an idea to save them all by sacrificing Creel to a dragon.

After all, everyone knows a gallant knight will save her. However, Creel befriends the dragon, who it turns out does have a treasure horde, but it isn't made up of gold or gems. She ends up with a comfortable pair of slippers that she wears to the king's city, where she plans to make her fortune with her embroidering skills. Unfortunately the odious princess from the neighboring antagonistic kingdom, who is in town to marry the crown prince, becomes fixated on Creel's shoes, shoes which are more than they seem. In fact, the shoes may be important when humans and dragons are sucked into a horrible war. (VOYA)

Dragon Flight. 2008. 9781599901107.

Even though she is inundated with orders, dressmaker Creel, a friend to dragons, accepts a mission of traveling to a distant desert land to gather intelligence on a king who has a force of hundreds of dragons and is planning to conquer Faravel.

Dragon Spear. 2009. 9781599903699.

While Creel and Luka plan their wedding, dragon Queen Velika is kidnapped, so they must rush to her aid.

Goodman, Alison.

Eon: Dragoneye Reborn. **2008. 9780670062270.**

In this world inspired by Chinese mythology, twelve dragons look over the people and protect them. Each dragon lends its power to one Dragoneye, who will work to harness their inner strength and their dragon's magic. Sixteen-year-old Eona has no hope of becoming a Dragoneye, both because she is crippled and because she is female. Nevertheless, she disguises herself as eleven-year-old Eon and, when the mysterious rule of the Dragons chooses her, Eona is forced into a game of political intrigue where the penalty is worse than death. (BBYA, IRA YAC)

Subjects: Chinese Mythology; Dragons; Girls Dressed as Boys

Harrison, Mettie Ivie.

The Princess and the Hound. **2008. 9780061131899.** M J

Prince George posses the forbidden ability of talking to animals. When he sees the close relationship between Princess Beatrice, to whom he is engaged for political purposes, and her dog, he hopes they will find a link.

Martini, Clem.

Feather and Bone: The Crow Chronicles. M

A gathering of crows, the Mob, meets every year at the Gathering Tree to share stories, find mates, discuss issues, and dispense justice.

The Mob. 2004. 9781553375746.

The Kinaars, a crow family, are called together by Kalum, their Chooser, who tells their stories; but this year the teasing of a cat by a group of young crows results in a death, so justice must be dispensed.

The Plague. 2005. 9781553376675.

> Murder, disease, and abduction beset the Kinaar crows. Kyp sets out to rescue Kym, who has been captured by humans looking into the plague that has been decimating the crows.

Judgment. 2006. 9781553377566.

> Kyp, now leader of a flock of rescued crows, leads them south as they look for a new place to live because they are threatened by the fanatical Collection.

Oppel, Kenneth.

Darkwing. **2007. 9780060850548.** **M** **J**

> A prehistoric precursor to modern bats, Dusk, a chiropter, who is not like the others, discovers that some of his differences may actually be advantages as the colony faces deadly danger. (VOYA)

Subjects: Bats; Dinosaurs; Prehistoric Animals

Paolini, Christopher.

Inheritance. **J** **S**

Eragon and his dragon partner Saphira end up on a quest to right the wrongs in the empire perpetrated by the evil King Galbatorix. Paolini was only fifteen when he wrote *Eragon*, and his family self-published it. It was subsequently picked up by Knopf and became a major best seller. Many of the fantasy tropes surrounding dragons are found here.

Subjects: Dragons; Teenage Author

Eragon. 2002. 9780440240730.

> When a beautiful blue dragon named Saphira hatches from what looks like a blue stone, Eragon bonds with her, becoming the first independent dragon rider in more than a century. (Film)

Eldest. 2005. 9780440238492.

> After being successful in battle, Eragon travels to the land of the elves to further his education. (TTT)

Brisingr. 2008. 9780375826726.

> Eragon continues his quest to find a weapon that will let him slay Galbatorix, in this long, battle-filled installment. (IRA YAC)

Alternate and Parallel Worlds

Some stories postulate that parallel worlds exist alongside ours. Differences between real and parallel worlds may be subtle, with parallel worlds that look, smell, and feel almost exactly like ours. At the other end of the spectrum, the differences may be so vast that the parallel world is almost completely alien. Many of these stories operate on the premise that there is a continuum of worlds, with those closest the most similar and those farther away the most different, but all are reached through a rent in the fabric of reality. Many of the tales dealing with parallel worlds involve travel between worlds. Usually alternate worlds are fully realized in a different reality, where our world does not even exist. Obviously setting is an important element of these stories, and whether the parallel world is similar or vastly different, these books provide escapist appeal.

Readers may also enjoy stories in chapter 6 that are set in alternate and parallel worlds.

Anderson, M. T.

Game of Sunken Places. 2004. 9780545200080. **M**

Gregory and Brian, both age thirteen, are spending two weeks with Gregory's Uncle Max in Vermont, where they enter an adventure through a board game and encounter elves and trolls as well as many dangers.

Subjects: Dark Fantasy; Elves; Games; Ogres; Trolls; Uncles; Vermont

Banner, Catherine.

The Last Descendants. **J** **S**

Members of a family in Malonia, a medieval-like country in a parallel world, are linked by a prince exiled to contemporary England. Like Christopher Paolini, Isamu Fukui, and Amelia Atwater-Rhodes did with their stories, the author wrote this as a teen.

The Eyes of a King. 2008. 9780375838750.

Leo attends military school in Malonia and cares for his younger brother, but his life becomes exciting when he finds a blank book and upon its pages the story of two teens from a parallel world begin to appear, along with family secrets and tales of the history of his troubled country.

Voices in the Dark. 2009. 9780375838774.

Several years after the events in *The Eyes of a King*, fifteen-year-old Anselm Andros lives in a Malonia terrorized by thugs, and the threat of magic and homosexuality both becoming criminal offenses.

Bray, Libba.

Gemma Doyle series. **J** **S**

In Victorian England, Gemma Doyle discovers a portal to other worlds at her finishing school.

Subjects: Boarding Schools; England; Historical Fiction; India; Literary; Nineteenth Century

A Great and Terrible Beauty. 2003. 9780385730280.

After sixteen-year-old Gemma has a vision of her mother dying, it actually happens. Gemma is sent back to England to attend Spence Academy, where she discovers strange and creepy things happening that take her into the Realms. (BBYA, TTT)

Rebel Angels. 2005. 9780385730297.

Gemma and her friends travel into the Realms again as she attempts to bind the magic she loosed. (BBYA, TTT)

The Sweet Far Thing. 2007. 9780385730303.

As Gemma prepares for her London debut, she tries to restore magic in the Realms and keep friends and family safe. (TTT)

Brennan, Herbie.

The Faerie Wars Chronicles. M J

Two boys, one from our world, one from the Purple Kingdom, become friends as they experience adventures between the different worlds.

Faerie Wars. 2003. 9780765356741.

Pyrgus Malvae, a crown prince in his world, is sent to our world for safety. There he meets Henry Atherton, who takes care of elderly Mr. Fogarty's yard. Mr. Fogarty, a retired bank robber and physicist, creates a new portal to return Pyrgus to his world. When Henry and Mr. Fogarty go through to the Purple Kingdom, they find more adventure than they bargained for. (BBYA, TTT, VOYA)

The Purple Emperor. 2004. 9781582348803.

Henry returns to the Purple Kingdom when Pyrgus and his sister are exiled after the evil Lord Hairstreak has resurrected their dead father.

Ruler of the Realm. 2006. 9781582348810.

Holly Blue, now Queen of the Faeries of the Light, is trying to negotiate for peace with the Faeries of the Night, when Henry shows up in a flying saucer and kidnaps her.

Faerie Lord. 2007. 9781599901206.

Two years after he last visited the Purple Kingdom, Henry is visited by Pyrgus, who is now middle aged and asking for help because a plague has hit faerie, causing extremely fast aging.

Colfer, Eoin.

Airman. **2008. 9781423107507.** J S

Conor Broekhart has always been obsessed with flight. After all, he was born in a hot air balloon over the 1878 World's Fair. When he is imprisoned on an island after stumbling across a treasonous plot, he builds a flying machine to escape. (BBYA)

Subjects: Flight; Historical Fiction

Collins, Suzanne.

Underland Chronicles. M

Eleven-year-old Gregor discovers a secret subterranean world where he may be the prophesied liberator.

Gregor the Overlander. 2003. 9780439678131.

Three years after their father disappeared, eleven-year-old Gregor is in the laundry room of his New York apartment watching his toddler sister, Boots, while doing chores, when she finds an open heating vent and goes through. As a responsible brother, he dives after her into a rabbit-hole of a descent into the Underland, where they are met by giant cockroaches, who take them to a bizarre town where purple-eyed people ride the backs of bats. Gregor fits the prophecy of an overlander who will come to help them in their war against the evil rats. Anxious to get home, he reluctantly accepts that he must work with the underworlders when he finds out that his father may be held hostage by the rats. (VOYA)

Gregor and the Prophecy of Bane. 2004. 9780439650755.

With the rats intent on killing Boots, Gregor, along with his bat and cockroach allies, sails across the Underland sea to find and kill the leader of the rats.

Gregor and the Curse of the Warmbloods. 2004. 9780439656238.

When a devastating plague that threatens to wipe out all mammal life hits the Underworld, Gregor and Boots are summoned for help, but their mother insists on going with them.

Gregor and the Marks of Secret. 2006. 9780439791458.

Gregor must return to fulfill his destiny as a warrior to help the Underlanders, when Queen Luxa discovers all the mice have been spirited way by Bane, who is now eight feet tall and quite mad.

Gregor and the Code of Claw. 2007. 9780439791434.

Full-scale war erupts, and it may take Gregor's death to end it.

Dekker, Ted.

The Lost Books series. M J S

The Lost Books series follows the adventures of four Forest Guard teen recruits—Johnis, Silvie, Billos, and Darsal—who are to find the seven Lost Books of History that have power over the past, present, and future. This series is a follow-up to Dekker's Circle series, which was written for adults, and it is also published in graphic novel format.

Subjects: Christian; Time Travel

Chosen. 2008. 9781595543592 (novel); 9781595546036 (graphic novel).

A football game, in which tightly rolled human hair is used as the ball, is played to choose new leaders from among the sixteen- and seventeen-year-olds who have just been allowed to join the Forest Guard in their fight against the Horde. Rejected for service, Johnis, small and bookish, stands on the sidelines. He does the unthinkable when he becomes the one to take the ball over the finish line, which makes him one of the four chosen leaders. The four are then sent on a quest, where they are ambushed by the Horde. Johnis is able to see two kinds of mythical creatures, the evil, batlike Shataiki and the cute, furry Roush.

Infidel. 2008. 9781595543639 (novel); 9781595546043 (graphic novel).

Will Johnis betray his companions to rescue his mother, who has been enslaved by the Horde?

Renegade. 2008. 9781595543714 (novel); 9781595546050 (graphic novel).

Billos goes renegade and ends up in Paradise, Colorado, after accepting powers from Marsuvees Black.

Chaos. 2008. 9781595543721 (novel); 9781595546067 (graphic novel).

Some thought dead are found, and an evil Shataiki seems on the verge of seeing the fruition of his plan, as the Forest Guard teens try to fight him in our world.

Lunatic. 2009. 9781595543738.

When Johnis, Silvie, and Darsal finally return home, they find they have been gone for five years and that everything they had left was gone, including Thomas Hunter and the Forest Guard. The lakes of Elyon are red, the healing waters gone.

Elyon. 2008. 9781595543745.

Finally, it is time for the ultimate clash of good and evil that will resolve the future of the chosen.

Fletcher, Charlie.

Stoneheart Trilogy. M

Twelve-year-old George Chapman discovers a parallel London, where statues walk and talk, carvings fly, and a girl named Edie follows objects through time.

Stoneheart. 2007. 97814231017582007.

Twelve-year-old George Chapman accidentally breaks off a bit of a carving on the museum building and suddenly finds himself being chased by a pterodactyl, which only moments before had been a decoration on a building; Teaming up with Edie, who can travel back in time by touching an object that had been there, they meet the Gunner, a statue, and learn that they are in the middle of a war between the spits and the taints, who live in a parallel world so close that in our world they are statues and carvings.

Ironhand. 2008. 9784423101772.

George and Edie find themselves in more danger, as George must face three extreme challenges and Edie sees her own death. Meanwhile, the Gunner is imprisoned in an underground lake and faces final annihilation.

Silvertongue. 2009. 9781423101796.

When time stops, the war between the spits and taints escalates, and George and Edie are the only humans not frozen. Now George must combat the Dark Knight if he is to keep from being turned to stone.

Funke, Cornelia.

Inkworld Trilogy. M J S

Meggie's life with her father Mo has been quiet and book-filled until a stranger appears at the door and sends them fleeing. The Inkworld Trilogy is a booklover's series, a landscape filled with books from the very first page.

Subjects: Books; Reading

Inkheart. 2003. 9780545046268.

Meggie's mother went missing several years ago, and now her father refuses to read aloud. He was such a fine reader that he had once read a band of villains out of a book, and now they want him to read some of their cohorts out. (VOYA, PP, Film)

Inkspell. 2005. 9780439554015.

Meggie goes into Inkworld, a world inside a book, where she tries to change the future of her family. (IRA YAC)

Inkdeath. 2008. 9780439866286.

Dozens of characters and subplots come together in the concluding volume of this booklover's feast.

Hoffman, Mary.

Stravaganza. J S

Stravagante are people using some kind of talisman who can travel between the worlds, our world and the world of Talia, which is home to cities very similar to those in our world's sixteenth-century Italy.

Subjects: Italy; Talismans; Time Travel

Stravaganza: City of Masks. 2002. 9781582349176.

In a parallel world, a city analogous to our Venice is ruled by a mysterious masked woman. Arianna, a girl from that world, has hatched a dangerous plan to stay in Bellezza to attempt to become a mandolier, but the plan is ruined when she finds Lucien, a strangely attired boy and cancer victim from our world. Lucien is chosen as a mandolier, which brings him to the attention of Senator Rodolofo, a philosopher scientist and a favorite of the ruling Duchessa. Rodolfo knows exactly why Lucien, now called Luciano, was transported to Bellezza because he too is a Stravagante.

Stravaganza: City of Stars. 2003. 9781582349824.

Fifteen-year-old Londoner Georgia has no friends and an abusive stepbrother, who torments her relentlessly. When she finds a figurine of a winged horse in an antique shop, she knows she has to have it even though she normally hoards her money for horseback riding. One night she falls asleep in her twenty-first-century bedroom with the figurine clutched in her hand and wakes up in Remora, an alternate fifteenth-century Sienna, where she is mistaken for a boy. Political intrigue, romance, family relationships, and a thrilling horse race, as well as a real winged horse, contribute to this fully realized tale.

Stravaganza: City of Flowers. 2005. 9781582347493.

> Sky, a mixed-race, seventeen-year-old boy from twenty-first-century London, finds himself in Florence-like Giglia, where he poses as a novice monk as the political machinations of the ruling family reach a crescendo.

City of Secrets. 2008. 9781599902029.

> Seventeen-year-old dyslexic Matt is not fond of books, but it is a book that serves as the talisman that transports him to Padavia, the Talian equivalent of Padua. There he meets Luciano, another Stravagante from his own time.

City of Ships. 2010. 9781599904917.

> Isabel is transported to the city Classe, where her new friend Flavia, a merchant, becomes an outcast and pirate.

Jones, Diana Wynne.

The Game. 2007. 9780142407189. **M**

> Raised by her grandparents after her parents disappeared, Hayley is suddenly sent off to her aunts in Ireland, where for the first time she can interact with other young people and gets involved in what they call "The Game," an activity that takes them into the mythosphere.

The Merlin Conspiracy. 2003. 9780060523206. **S** **J** **M**

> Arianrhod Hyde, known most commonly as Roddy, and her best friend Grundo have spent their lives traveling with the King's progress as the children of court magicians. The islands of Blest maintain their magic and safety because the king constantly travels from town to town, accompanied by his court and the Merlin. Nick, from our world, has always wanted to travel between worlds and has suddenly and inexplicably ended up in another world, where he is mistaken for a novice magician. In Blest, Roddy and Grundo uncover a conspiracy. As Nick tries to make his way through a labyrinth between worlds that will take him to a powerful magician who can help him find his way home, he finds Roddy, who has cast a spell requesting help. He promises to help her; and eventually all three teens come together.

> **Subjects:** Time Warp

Chrestomanci. **M** **J** **S**

> The Chrestomanci is a person who has nine lives and can be called upon for help when things go bad between the multiple parallel worlds. Jones has returned to this world time and time again, with the first book in the series published in 1977 and the most recent one published in 2006. The books have also been reissued in omnibus editions, most recently in 2008, bringing them to a whole new audience.

> **Subjects:** England; Magic; Witches

Lives of Christopher Chant. 1988. 9780060298777.

Christopher Chant seems strangely devoid of magic despite coming from a magical family, but his nine lives mean he will soon be in charge of maintaining the magical balance between worlds, and his strange dreams take him to other worlds.

The Magicians of Caprona. 1980; reissued 2001. 9780060298784.

Brothers Tonino and Paolo Montana belong to one of two powerful spell-casting families in Caprona, a city-state in a parallel world.

Charmed Life. 1977; reissued 2001. 9780060298760.

Orphaned siblings Gwendolyn and Erick "Cat" Chant are summoned to Chrestomanci Castle, where the extent of their powers and personalities is exposed.

Witch Week. 1982; reissued 2001. 9780060298791.

Four students, in an alternate contemporary London where witchcraft is a capital offense, discover they have powers. The Chrestomanci steps in to help save them from the Inquisition.

Conrad's Fate. 2005. 9780060747459.

High in the English Alps at Stallery Mansion, twelve-year-old Conrad is hired as a page so he can find out whom he is supposed to kill to fix his bad Karma. At the mansion he meets Christopher Chant, another new page, who has come from a different world, looking for a missing friend.

The Pinhoe Egg. 2006. 9780061131240.

Marianne Pinhoe's grandmother is losing her mind, so Marianne has to train as the next Gammer to handle the magic in her family, who distrust the people at Chrestomanci Castle. Finding a mysterious egg in the attic, Marianne gives it to Cat Chant. Soon it hatches a whole new flock of problems.

Knox, Elizabeth.

Dreamhunter Duet. ⓜ ⓙ ⓢ

In Southland, a place much like Edwardian era New Zealand, Dreamers go to The Place, where they retrieve dreams that can be shared in Dream Palaces.

Dreamhunter. 2006. 9780312535711.

Laura and Rose, fifteen-year-old cousins, live in a world very much like our early twentieth century, where a strange land has been discovered that only allows a few in to experience strange dreams, that can then be carried outside and shared with theater audiences. (BBYA)

Dreamquake. 2007. 9780312581473.

Laura, now a dreamhunter, has definite opinions about how the government is exploiting the dreams. (BBYA, Printz Honor)

Lynch, Scott.

Gentlemen Bandits series. [o]

Orphaned Locke Lamora becomes an accomplished con man as he comes of age in Camorr.

Subjects: Adult Books for Teens; Gambling; Orphans; Thieves

The Lies of Locke Lamora. 2006. 9780553588941.

This genreblend of fantasy and crime caper features orphaned Locke Lamora, who was sold into a life of thievery as a child and became the leader of the Gentleman Bandits, who steal with élan. (BBYA)

Red Seas under Red Skies. 2007. 9780553804683.

After traveling to Tal Verrar, Locke and Jean devise a perfect caper, since Tal Verrar is home to Sinspire, the most exclusive gambling house in the world.

Moesta, Rebecca, and Kevin J. Anderson.

Crystal Doors series. [M] [J]

Fourteen-year-old Gwen and Vic consider themselves twin cousins, as their fathers were identical twins and their mothers, sisters. They've lived together with Vic's dad Cap ever since Gwen's parents were killed and Vic's mother went missing.

Island Realm. 2006. 9780316112956.

Twin cousins, Gwen and Vic, are swept into another world when they walk through some sort of experiment Uncle Cap has set up with crystals. In the world Elantya, which is a hub for doors between many worlds, they discover that their mothers were from a different world, and that Elantya is under attack.

Ocean Realm. 2007. 9780316112963.

Vic and Gwen are kidnapped by Azric, who was responsible for the deaths of Gwen's parents, and now wants them to open the portal that will allow his army to overtake Elantya.

Sky Realm. 2008. 9780316010542.

After facing Azric on land and sea, Vic, Gwen, and friends must face him in the sky when they accompany Sharif to the flying city of Irrakesh, where his father, the Sultan, is dying.

Nix, Garth.

The Keys to the Kingdom. [M] [J]

Arthur Penhaligon must go up against seven other worldly people as he tries to acquire the seven keys to the kingdom.

Subjects: Asthmatics; Keys; Seven Deadly Sins

Mister Monday. 2003. 9780439703697.

On the first day of school, when Arthur Penhaligon tries to explain to his gym teacher that he has asthma and cannot run the cross country, he is brushed off, but he decides to try it anyway and ends up nearly dying of an asthma attack. Just as he is about to lose consciousness, a strange man shows up and gives him a strange piece of metal that looks like a key and a clock hand. Strangely, his attack clears up and he gets healthier, but some terrifying dog-faced Fetchers show up to take it away from him. As an illness that makes people sleep sweeps through the city, Arthur finds that he can see a strange house that no one else seems to see. Mr. Monday, who gave him the key, is the person he must battle to get back out of the house, where he encounters strange beings, and strange and terrifying things keep happening.

Grim Tuesday. 2004. 9780439703703.

No sooner has Arthur defeated Mister Monday than greedy Grim Tuesday forecloses on the earth. Now Arthur must find more of the Will and acquire the second Key.

Drowned Wednesday. 2005. 9780439700863.

Lady Wednesday, who was cursed with gluttony, lives as a gigantic white whale in the Border Seas. She summons Arthur, but he ends up running across the pirate Feverfew, who enslaves all in his path.

Subjects: Pirates

Sir Thursday. 2006. 9780439700870.

Unable to return to his own world because a double is there holding his family hostage, Arthur is drafted into the Glorious Army of the Architect by Sir Thursday.

Lady Friday. 2007. 9780439700887.

While Leaf is held hostage by Lady Friday, Arthur continues to seek more portions of the Will.

Superior Saturday. 2008. 9780439700894.

Arthur, now immortal, tries to hide his identity and powers as he searches the House for the sixth key.

Lord Sunday. 2010. 9780439700900.

Arthur's final confrontation and the culmination of the series comes when he faces Lord Sunday, who is different than all his other challenges, as the house is falling apart, something that could herald the end of the human world.

Sanderson, Brandon.

Alcatraz series. M J

Alcatraz Smedry discovers, at age thirteen, that he is part of a talented family that has been targeted by the evil librarians who control and sometimes distort all information. One of the things the evil librarians have done is to make sure all prisons are named after members of the Smedry family. Alcatraz's talent is destruction.

Subjects: Action Adventure; Humorous; Librarians

Alcatraz Versus the Evil Librarians. 2007. 9780439925525.

> Alcatraz Smedry has grown up in foster care, but suddenly on his thirteenth birthday, he receives a bag of sand, which is almost immediately stolen by a cult of evil librarians bent on world domination.

Alcatraz Versus the Scrivener's Bones. 2008. 9780439925532.

> As Alcatraz Smedry continues the quest started in *Alcatraz Versus the Evil Librarians,* he is picked up in a flying glass dragon and ends up dealing with specters in the vast underground warren of the Library of Alexandria.

Alcatraz Versus The Knights of Crystallia. 2009. 9780439925556.

> Alcatraz visits the city of Crystallia with his grandfather Leavenworth, his father, and Bastille, and he finds the city under siege by the Evil Librarians.

Shinn, Sharon.

General Winston's Daughter. **2007. 9780670062485.** **J** **S**

When eighteen-year-old Averie Winston goes to Chiarrin to meet her father, the commanding officer, and her fiancé, she falls in love with the brilliant colors and fascinating people of the recently conquered land. After dissidents bomb the marketplace, she takes Jalessa, an injured fabric seller, home and hires her as her personal maid. This thoughtful look at colonialism, national identity, and war is memorable and very well done.

Subjects: Colonialism; Terrorism; War

Safe-Keepers Trilogy. **M** **J** **S**

Safe-Keepers are entrusted with secrets that they cannot reveal, Truth-Tellers tell truths, and Dream-Makers grant wishes.

The Safe-Keeper's Secret. 2004. 9780142403570.

> Two bastard children are raised by the village Safe-Keeper, where the parentage of one of them is kept ever secret. (BBYA)

The Truth-Teller's Tale. 2005. 9780142407844.

> Mirror twins Eleda and Adele, one a Safe-Keeper and the other a Truth-Teller, find truths and secrets, not to mention romance and dreams, when a dancing master and his apprentice visit the village.

The Dream-Maker's Magic. 2006. 9780142410967.

> Kellen, a girl raised as a boy, and Gryffin, an abused, crippled orphan, are both outcasts at school, and thus begins a friendship that may turn into more with the revelation of a Dream-Maker.

Shusterman, Neal.

Skinjacker series. **J** **S**

Everlost is a world where the spirits of teens and children who are caught halfway between life and death must keep moving and follow myriad rules while staying away from a resident monster.

Everlost. 2006. 9780689872372.

Nick and Allie are killed in a car wreck, but become trapped in a limbo-like world. (IRA YAC, VOYA, PP)

Everwild. 2009. 9781416958635.

Is the fate of Everlost to be determined in battle?

Thal, Lilli.

Mimus. 2005. 9781550379242. **J** **S**

In a world that never existed, but is curiously like the Germanic kingdoms of the middle ages, Prince Florin is summoned to a neighboring kingdom to celebrate the end of a war, whereupon he is taken prisoner and turned into a "soulless" jester who lives in the stables. (BBYA)

Subjects: Fools; Jesters; Princes; Prisoners

Time Travel

Time travel appears in both science fiction and fantasy. In fantasy, the time travel is not accomplished by using a technological or scientific medium but rather by magic or some unexplained phenomenon. Often slippage through time occurs. Readers who like the historical settings in the time travel novels may also enjoy historical fiction.

Alexie, Sherman.

Flight. 2007. 9780802170378. **S**

Zits, a fifteen-year-old mixed-race teen, travels through 150 years of history, bouncing into one life after another as he experiences other people's lives. (BBYA)

Subjects: Acne; Adult Books for Teens; AIM; Foster Children; Historical Fiction; Little Big Horn; Mixed-Race; Native Americans; Orphans

Bloor, Edward.

London Calling. 2006. 9780375843631. **M**

Annotated in chapter 3.

Curry, Jane Louise.

The Black Canary. 2005. 9780689864780.

While his musical family is visiting London, James, who is biracial, goes through a shimmering portal in the basement of their flat and ends up in the seventeenth century, where he discovers the musical abilities he never wanted to use may be his route to survival.

Subjects: Historical Fiction; Mixed Race; Time Slip

Moonshower, Candie.

The Legend of Zoey. **2006. 9780440239246.** **M**
  Annotated in chapter 3.

Peck, Dale.

The Drift House. **J**
  Following 9/11, Mr. and Mrs. Oakenfeld send their three children, Murray, Charles, and Susan, to stay with their Uncle Farley in a boat-like mansion in Canada.

  Subjects: Mermaids; Parrots; Pirates; Stepfamilies

  The First Voyage. 2005. 9781582349695.
    Arriving from New York, the three Okenfeld children and Uncle Farley are swept away out of the Bay of Eternity onto the Sea of Time, where they encounter all kinds of adventures.

  The Lost Cities. 2007. 9781582348599.
    While visiting for the summer, a tidal wave throws Charles and the parrot into a tree and sends Susan and Uncle Farley in his floating house on a journey through time and space, leaving it up to Murray to make sure they can finally make it home.

Weyn, Suzanne.

Reincarnation. **2008 . 9780545013239.** **J** **S**
  A green stone plays a part in the lives of a boy and a girl, who fall in love through several time periods in which they are reincarnated.

  Subjects: Reincarnation

Short Stories

Short stories often receive short shrift when talking about fantasy for young adults, but the following anthologies make a good starting place for readers tying to find authors they like. Readers who like fantasy short stories should also check the short story section of chapter 10, as there are several collections and anthologies that cover not only fantasy but also science fiction and horror or paranormal.

Berman, Steve, ed.

Magic in the Mirrorstone. **2008. 9780786947324.** **J** **S**
  This anthology of fifteen enchanting stories, from big name authors and others who should eventually be big names, offers a range of stories that will have something to captivate every fantasy reader. Holly Black's urban fantasy features homeless teens and a unicorn. Cassandra Clare's Lovecraftian story will appeal to those who love creepy stories, especially

all the Cthulu fans. Cecil Castellucci's Hollywood tale features alternate realities and the power of one young actress. Tiffany Trent's story features a character from her Hallowmere series. Beth Bernobich is a new talent, and her fairy tale with an Asian setting, "Pig, Crane, Fox: Three Hearts Unfolding," is a winner, as is "Out of Her Element" by E. Sedia, a story about a Victorian girl with consumption and a salamander. It has the atmosphere and feel of Libba Bray's Gemma Doyle series and Jenny Davidson's novel *The Explosionist*. Berman's comments about each author following their brief bios at the end of the book are hysterical.

Pierce, Tamora, and Josepha Sherman, eds.

Young Warriors: Stories of Strength. 2006. 9780375829628. **J** **S**

Fifteen stories of warriors by Bruce Holland Rogers, S. M. Stirling and Jan Stirling, Janis Ian, Holly Black, Pamela F. Service, Esther Friesner, India Edghill, Mike Resnick, Tamora Pierce, Laura Anne Gilman, Margaret Mahy, Doranna Durgin, Rosemary Edghill, Lesley McBain, and Brent Hartinger.

Weiss, M. Jerry, and Helen S. Weiss.

Dreams and Visions : Fourteen Flights of Fantasy. 2006. 9780765351074. **J** **S**

An anthology of fourteen fantasy stories by Joan Bauer, Suzanne Fisher Staples, Charles de Lint, Michael O. Tunnell, Rich Wallace, Patrice Kindl, S. L. Rottman, David Lubar, Mel Glenn, Nancy Springer, John H. Ritter, Sharon Dennis Wyeth, Neal Shusterman, and Tamora Pierce, some well known for fantasy and some known for other genres.

Di's Picks

Cashore, Kristin. *Graceling*.

Duey, Kathleen. A Resurrection of Magic.

Flinn, Alex. *Beastly*.

Marillier, Juliet *Wildwood Dancing*.

Taylor, Laini. *Lips Touch: Three Times*.

Werlin, Nancy. *Impossible*.

Chapter 8

Mystery and Suspense

> *I adore mystery. There's something simply thrilling about curling up in the evening with an exciting mystery and an inquiring mind as to what will happen next. Mystery novels let my imagination take off and dream of situations full of adventure and excitement that I could never comprehend on my own.*—Elle, age 14

Mysteries for teens, like horror, experienced a period of stagnation from which the genre is just now emerging. In 1989 Audrey B. Eaglen wrote in *School Library Journal*, "Young adult readers who like science fiction, fantasy, or romances have a plethora of titles available to them at every reading level and every level of sophistication. . . . It's another story for the YA mystery fan." In 2000 Shelle Rosenfeld discussed the lack of mystery novels for teens in *Booklist*. In recent years YA mysteries have become more plentiful. In 2000 only two of the fifty-nine fiction titles that made the Best Books for Young Adult list were mystery or suspense. In 2009 the tally was seven out of seventy-three fiction titles. The Morris Award for Young Adult debut novels was first awarded in 2009, and three of the four honor books, *Madapple* by Christina Meldrum, *Me, the Missing, and the Dead* by Jenny Valentine, and *Absolute Brightness* by James Lecesne are suspense titles.

Part of the reason for this reversal of trends may be that the young adult literary market is booming, or perhaps that some of the new talents have taken on the genre, including 2010 debut novelists like Anna Jarzab, Karen Kincy, Y.S. Lee, Josh Berk, and James Leck, whose first novels, which are mysteries, may account for the increase in popularity. In any case, this is a boon for those teen readers who like mystery and suspense.

Mysteries are defined as stories that hinge on detection. A crime has been committed or is suspected and a character investigates. They often involve realistic settings and characters either in the present or the past as well as some kind of puzzle. Suspense keeps the reader guessing what happens next while often building a feeling of imminent danger or impending doom.

This chapter is organized with historical mysteries first, followed by contemporary mysteries, then suspense novels.

Historical Mysteries

Mysteries with historical settings have dual appeal. They engage readers looking for the thrills and chills inherent in a mystery, as well as the readers who like to learn about bygone times and cultures. Keep in mind that for teens, "historical" means anything that occurred before they were born, which differs from the definition of historical fiction for adults. To a thirteen-year-old, the 1970s seem almost as remote and exotic as the seventeenth century.

Arnold, Tedd.

Rat Life. 2007. 9780142414316. **J S**

Fourteen-year-old Todd, an aspiring writer of gross tales who lives in Elmore, New York, and works in his parents' motel, befriends a young Vietnam veteran, who may hold clues to the mystery of a body that turned up in the river. (Edgar Award)

Subjects: 1970s; Elmore, New York; Vietnam Veteran

Cadnum, Michael.

The King's Arrow. 2008. 9780670063314. **M J S**

Eighteen-year-old Simon, the son of a dead Norman officer and an English noblewoman, finds himself in danger after he is invited on a hunt with the king. Unfortunately, he is present when the king is killed by an arrow shot by Walter Tirel.

Subjects: Tirel, Walter; Twelfth Century; William II, King

Hoffman, Mary.

The Falconer's Knot: A Story of Friars, Flirtation and Foul Play. 2007. 978-1599902296. **J S**

When sixteen-year-old nobleman Silvano becomes the prime suspect in a murder committed with his dagger, he flees to a Franciscan friary, where he mixes pigments for decorating a basilica. As more murders occur, Silvano and Chiara, who dreams of love and family despite living in a neighboring abbey, set out to solve the crimes.

Subjects: Fourteenth Century; Italy; Renaissance; Romance; Samurai

Hoobler, Dorothy, and Thomas Hoobler.

Seikei Samurai series. **M J**

Seikei, a fourteen-year-old in eighteenth-century Japan, becomes a crime solver after being adopted by Samurai Judge Ooka.

Subjects: Eighteenth Century; Japan

The Ghost in the Tokaido Inn. 1999. 9780142405413.

In eighteenth-century Japan, Seikei, a fourteen-year-old boy, witnesses a crime. His bravery in stepping forth to clear the one who was falsely accused brings him the respect of Judge Ooka, who then hires Seikei to investigate the crime and solve the mystery. (BBYA, IRA YAC)

The Demon in the Teahouse. 2001. 9780142405406.

Seikei, the adopted son of a samurai judge, goes undercover in a tea house to try to find a serial killer who is targeting geishas in eighteenth-century Japan.

In Darkness, Death. 2004. 9780142403662.

When a well-guarded lord is murdered, and the only clues include an origami butterfly and the rope used by the killer to escape, ninjas are suspected; so Judge Ooka and Seikei step in to investigate. (VOYA, Edgar Award)

Subjects: Ninjas

The Sword That Cut the Burning Grass. 2005. 9780399242724.

An official of the Shogun sends Seikei on a mission to retrieve the fourteen-year-old Emperor, who has run away, but after finding him, he is kidnapped, making things more difficult—especially since it seems there is a move afoot to overthrow the Shogun.

A Samurai Never Fears Death. 2007. 9780399246098.

Seikei and his adopted father, Judge Ooka, visit Osaka, where Seikei's birth family lives, to investigate a smuggling case. They find Seikei's siblings implicated in murder and smuggling.

Seven Paths to Death. 2008. 9780399246104.

Different portions of a map appear as tattoos on the backs of several men who have turned up dead. As Seikei and Judge Ooka investigate, they find a connection to a cache of arms and a possible threat to the emperor.

Subjects: Tattoos

LaFevers, R. L.

Theodosia and the Serpents of Chaos. 2007. 9780618999767. **M**

In 1906, Theodosia Throckmorton spends lots of time at her parents' Museum of Legends and Antiquities, where she has the paranormal ability to see the curses that are attached to various artifacts that show up there. When an Egyptian scarab amulet goes missing, Theodosia takes the case to find it. (VOYA)

Subjects: 1900s; Curses; Egyptology; Museums; Twentieth Century

Lee, Y. S.

The Agency. **J S**

In the 1850s Mary, a condemned twelve-year-old orphan, was saved from the gallows when she was whisked away to be educated at an unusual school. Five years later she is sent out as a spy.

Subjects: Convicts; London; Mixed-Race; Nineteenth Century; Orphans; Spies; Victorian Era

A Spy in the House. 2010. 9780763640675.

> Seventeen-year-old Mary is sent to an upper-class household as companion to a young lady to covertly search for clues about smuggling and fraud. She keeps running up against a young engineer.

The Body at the Tower. 2010. 9780763649685.

> Mary, in disguise as an errand boy, investigates a murder at the construction site where a clock tower is being built at the Houses of Parliament.

Lisle, Janet Taylor.

Black Duck. 2006. 9780142409022. **J** **S**

> A contemporary teen elicits the tale of adventure his elderly neighbor Ruben Hart experienced after finding a body on the beach when he was young and being drawn into a deadly world of gangs, rum-running, and murder. (BBYA)

Subjects: 1920s; Prohibition

Springer, Nancy.

Enola Holmes Mysteries. **M** **J**

> Enola, age fourteen, is the much younger sister of Sherlock and Mycroft Holmes, but the mystery-solving gene runs strong throughout the family.

Subjects: 1880s; London

The Case of the Missing Marquess. 2006. 9780399243042.

> When her mother goes missing, Enola heads off to London searching for her. Along the way she uncovers the case of a kidnapped marquess, a case she solves using her deductive skills.

The Case of the Left-Handed Lady. 2007. 9780142411902.

> On the run from her older brothers, who want to send her to a boarding school, Enola, utilizing disguises, sets up shop in London as a perditorian, a finder of the lost.

The Case of the Bizarre Bouquets. 2008. 9780399245183.

> When Dr. Watson goes missing, Enola finds clues in the flowers sent to his wife.

Updale, Eleanor.

Montmorency. **M** **J**

> When a thief survives a fall through a skylight by becoming a specimen and case study for an ambitious surgeon in late nineteenth-century London, he learns about the new sewer system and devises new double identities for himself.

Subjects: Burglars; London; Nineteenth Century; Spies; Surgeons; Victorian

Montmorency: Thief, Liar, Gentleman? 2004. 9780439580366.

> Montmorency sets himself up as a gentleman using the proceeds from his burglaries, as his scruffy hired man Scarfer navigates the sewer system to commit his thefts. (BBYA)

Montmorency on the Rocks: Doctor, Aristocrat, Murderer? 2005. 978-0439606776.

> Montmorency and friends have two mysteries to solve, one involving a London bombing and the other infant deaths in Scotland.

Montmorency and the Assassins: Master Criminal, Spy? 2006. 978-0439683432.

> Twenty years after his last adventure, Montmorency looks into anarchist plots, taking him from London to Italy, Scotland, and New Jersey. (PP)

Montmorency's Revenge. 2007. 9780439813747.

> Scotland Yard calls on Montmorency for help in identifying the Italian anarchist who was responsible for his friend's death, because there is fear he will target the British royal family as Queen Victoria nears death.

Contemporary Mysteries

Mystery readers who seek characters, settings, and stories they can more closely identify with will find them in contemporary mysteries. The realism of a story set in the present intensifies the mystery and the suspense, intellectually and emotionally drawing in readers. It's as if these stories present the tacit premise, "imagine something like this happening to you."

Abrahams, Peter.

Reality Check. 2009. 9780061227660. **J S**

> Sixteen-year-old injured football star Cody drops out of high school in rural eastern Colorado when he is benched for injuries and his wealthy girlfriend is sent to an exclusive boarding school in Vermont. Wanting what is best for Clea, Cody breaks up with her so she can have a fresh start at her new school. When she goes missing, Cody hops in his car and heads east to join the search. (Edgar Award)
>
> **Subjects:** Boarding Schools; Horses; Missing Persons

Echo Falls. **M J**

> Thirteen-year-old Ingrid Levin-Hill, the daughter of the chief of police of small town Echo Falls, Connecticut, finds herself involved in various mysteries.

Down the Rabbit Hole. 2005. 9780060737016.

> Busy with her role as Alice in a local performance of *Alice in Wonderland*, and short on time, thirteen-year-old Ingrid Levin-Hill becomes lost while running to soccer practice. A woman helps her on her way, but when Ingrid finds out the woman was murdered that same day, she begins investigating on her own.

Behind the Curtain. 2006. 9780060737061.

While investigating her football-playing brother's sudden increase in muscle, which she suspects is due to steroids, eighth-grade sleuth Ingrid is kidnapped, escapes from the trunk where she was stashed, and starts looking for her kidnapper.

Into the Dark. 2008. 9780060737085.

Ninth grader Ingrid finds a dead body on her Grandfather's land. When he becomes the prime suspect, she must use her sleuthing prowess to clear his name.

Alexander, E. M.

Death at Deacon Pond. **2006. 9781897073421.**

One night at a party in the woods with her friend Seth Roberts, Kerri Langston goes off to pee and hears a voice crying "help me." Then she falls onto a body, which Seth identifies as Mark Travers, a reclusive man whom he had met when delivering groceries from the market where Kerri works. There is no way Kerri could have heard him call out, because he had been dead for hours. A year ago, when her father died, Kerri had visions that have marked her as a freak. Now she knows that Mark's death is somehow related to her father's murder, even though her father's death was determined to be a suicide. When it turns out that Mark was involved in the marijuana trade and that there are no records from the grocery store that Seth had ever delivered to him, Seth comes under suspicion. Meanwhile Kerri's visions lead her to believe that a young woman is in deadly peril.

Subjects: Marijuana; Psionic Powers

Bauer, Joan.

Peeled. **2008. 9780399234750.** 🅜 🅙

High school journalist Hildy Biddle tries to uncover the truth behind the haunted happenings being reported in the local newspaper that are having an effect in her small New York apple-growing community. (VOYA)

Subjects: Journalists; New York

Berk, Josh.

The Dark Days of Hamburger Halpin. **2010. 9780375856990.** 🅙 🅢

Sixteen-year-old Will Halpin, deaf and overweight, transfers from a school for the deaf to a public high school, where he ends up becoming friends with Devon Smiley, another bright social outcast. When the obnoxious but popular football star is killed on a field trip to a coal mine, Will and Smiley start sleuthing.

Subjects: Deaf; Humor; Murder

Brooks, Kevin.

Black Rabbit Summer. **2008. 9780545057523.** 🅢

Just before leaving for college, a group of five teens who had been friends when they were children decide to get together one last time at a carnival. The reunion is

not fun—one of them goes missing and becomes the suspect in the disappearance of a celebrity.

Subjects: Carnivals; Drugs; Missing Persons

Dowd, Siobhan.

The London Eye Mystery. 2008. 9780375849763. **M**

Ted and Kat saw their cousin Salin get on the London Eye, an enclosed Fer-
ris wheel-like sightseeing attraction on the banks of the Thames, but when
the ride was over, Salin was gone. Twelve-year-old Ted, who thinks differently and may have some form of autism, uses his skills to solve the mystery
ahead of the police. (BBYA)

Subjects: Baseball; Cousins; London; Missing Persons; Siblings

Feinstein, John.

Sports Series. **M** **J**

Stevie Thomas and Susan Carol Anderson are two eighth graders from very
different places and backgrounds who become friends and eventually
costars of their own TV show after winning a basketball journalism contest.

Subjects: Basketball; Football; Journalists; Sports; Tennis

Last Shot: A Final Four Mystery. 2005. 9780375931680.

> Stevie and Susan Carol win a journalism contest with a prize that sends
> them to New Orleans to cover the Final Four tournament. Then they
> find out one of the players is being blackmailed to throw the game.
> (Edgar Award, PP)

Vanishing Act: Mystery at the U.S. Open. 2006. 9780375835926.

> Susan Carol and Stevie scores press box tickets for the U.S. Open in
> New York. When a Russian tennis superstar is kidnapped between the
> locker room and tennis court, they jump in to investigate.

Cover Up: Mystery at the Superbowl. 2007. 9780375942471.

> Even though Stevie is fired from their TV show, he still ends up with a
> Superbowl press pass, and he and Susan Carol uncover a doping scandal.

Change Up: Mystery at the World Series. 2009. 9780375856365.

> Stevie and Susan Carol, while interviewing the Washington National's
> rookie pitcher, sense something strange in his demeanor. Their subse-
> quent investigation uncovers a shadowy past.

Ferguson, Alane.

Forensic Mystery series. **S** **J**

Cameryn Mahoney, the seventeen-year-old daughter of the county coroner
in Silverton, Colorado, has always been fascinated by forensics and plans
on becoming a forensic pathologist. She gets a chance to put her interest to
use in working as her father's assistant.

Subjects: Bipolar Disorder; Coroners; Forensics; Mental Illness; Silverton, Colorado

The Christopher Killer. 2006. 9780670060085.

> A serial killer who strangles his victims and places a St. Christopher medal around the neck of each of his victims has killed Rachel Geller, who was a friend of Cameryn's. Now as Cameryn investigates, she may become the next victim.

Angel of Death. 2006. 9780670060559.

> Cameryn's teacher is found dead and burned in his own bed, with no other signs of fire in evidence. Meanwhile, Cameryn's personal life is also getting complicated, with her estranged mother coming back and a romance with an Eagle Scout.

Circle of Blood. 2008. 9780670060566.

> When Cameryn's mother Hannah picks up a young female hitchhiker, the girl steals Hannah's wallet. Later, the girl turns up dead. While trying to keep her bipolar mother out of the investigation, Cameryn discovers the girl was trying to escape from a polygamous cult.
>
> **Subjects:** Polygamists

Dying Breath. 2009. 9780670063147.

> Seventeen-year-old Cameryn is falling in love with Justin, the young deputy sheriff, when they investigate a case of two celebrities who drowned without water while sitting in a Durango eatery. They are also investigating the mysterious death of a reclusive eccentric, a case that Cameryn is kicked off of because the perpetrator, her former boyfriend, now a murderous psychopath, left a note to her at the scene.

Gratz, Alan M.

Horatio Wilkes Mysteries. **J** **S**

Boarding school student Horatio Wilkes finds himself solving contemporary mysteries with strong parallels to Shakespeare's plays.

Subjects: Shakespeare; Tennessee

Something Rotten. 2007. 9780803732162.

> Horatio Wilkes goes to Denmark, Tennessee, the home of his boarding school roommate Hamilton Prince, for a vacation shortly after Hamilton's mother marries his uncle following his father's death. After Horatio and Hamilton find a video recording of Rex, Hamilton's father, they begin a murder investigation into his poisoning. Readers who know Hamlet will enjoy this ironic takeoff. (Quick Picks, PP)
>
> **Subjects:** Denmark, Tennessee; Ecology; Environment; Hamlet; Poison

Something Wicked. 2008. 9780803736665.

> Visiting the Scottish Highland Games with his friend Mac and Mac's dislikable girlfriend Beth, Horatio is drawn into a mystery when Mac's grandfather, the owner of the mountain that is the site of the Games, is found murdered.
>
> **Subjects:** Highland Games; Macbeth; Scotland

Green, John.

Paper Towns. 2008. 9780525478188. **S**

When they were kids, Margo Roth Spiegelman was Q's best friend. Now a month before high school graduation, Margo has disappeared after taking Q on a night of pranks involving dead fish and a depilatory. Worried that Margo may have committed suicide, Q and his friends start tracking her down, using clues she has left behind. (BBYA, TTT, IRA YAC, Edgar Award)

Subjects: Maps; Missing Persons; Pranks

Hautman, Pete, and Mary Logue.

Bloodwater Mysteries. **M** **J**

Fourteen-year-old science geek Brian and seventeen-year-old high school newspaper reporter Roni don't have much in common, except that they both are drawn to mysteries to solve in the town of Bloodwater, Minnesota.

Subjects: Asian Americans; Bloodwater, Minnesota; Humorous; Korean Americans; Reporters

Snatched. 2006. 9780142407950.

After meeting in the principal's office, Roni and Brian team up to find out what happened to popular Alicia, star of the school play, who has been kidnapped after getting out of the hospital following a beating.

Skullduggery. 2007. 9780399243783.

On a field trip, Roni and Brian find a badly injured professor on a pile of bones. The professor gives Brian an artifact and tells him to save the bluff. Along the way of solving the mystery, Roni and Brian encounter real estate developers and run across environmental concerns.

Subjects: Anthropology

Doppelganger. 2008. 9780399243790.

When browsing a missing children Web site, Roni finds a photo of a boy who disappeared at age three and who, in the photo of what he would look like now, is the spitting image of Brian. As Roni and Brian delve into Brian's mysterious past, his adoptive parents seem reluctant to tell him everything.

Subjects: Missing Children

Henderson, Lauren.

Scarlett Wakefield series.

Scarlett, a sixteen-year-old student at an exclusive London private school, has a huge crush on Dan McAndrew, so when she is invited to an elite party that he will attend, she goes. Her dreams turn into a nightmare after he kisses her and then dies in her arms.

Subjects: Boarding school; Orphans

Kiss Me Kill Me. 2008. 9780385734875.

Sixteen-year-old Scarlett Wakefield transfers from an exclusive school in the city to Wakefield Collegiate, a boarding school run by her grandmother. She has a past she wants to hide, but now someone is threatening to expose her. Is it possible that she really killed her big crush with a kiss? A threatening note impels her to investigate what could be a murder.

Kisses and Lies. 2009. 9780385734899.

Now that Scarlett knows Dan really was murdered, she tries to find out why and by whom. After clearing one suspect, she is off to Scotland with her American friend Taylor, to investigate another suspect at Dan's family home.

Subjects: Scotland

Kiss in the Dark. 2010. 9780385737777.

Scarlett becomes a pariah at Wakefield Hall Collegiate when Plum, her enemy, transfers in and turns everyone against her, but it doesn't stop her from becoming involved in a new mysterious death that may be connected to her parents' fatal accident.

Jarzab, Anna.

All Unquiet Things. 2010. 9780385738354. **S**

A year after the murder of his ex-girlfriend, Neily begins to believe that perhaps the wrong person has been sent to prison. After the murder, Carly's uncle, the father of her best friend/cousin Audrey, was convicted. Neily and Audrey are both outcasts now at Brighton Day School, Neily because some think he killed Carly and Audrey because her dad was convicted of the crime. They join forces to find out who shot Carly and why.

Leck, James.

The Adventures of Jack Lime. 2010. 9781554533640. **M** **J**

In this episodic novel, Jack Lime, seventeen-year-old narcoleptic private investigator, takes on a variety of cases that come up at his high school, ranging from stolen bikes to murder.

Subjects: Humor; Narcolepsy; Private Investigators

Pagliarulo, Antonio.

Celebutantes. **O**

Madison, Park, and Lexington, the Hamilton triplets, may be heiresses to billions, but that doesn't stop the sixteen-year-olds from solving mysteries—*Gossip Girl* style.

Subjects: Chick Lit; Manhattan; Triplets; Wealth

On the Avenue. 2007. 9780385734042.

When one of the Hamilton triplets is suspected of killing a fashion editor, the girls combine forces to find the real perpetrator.

In the Club. 2008. 9780385734738.

The Hamilton family's new Manhattan nightclub is the scene of a murder, and the triplets look for clues.

To the Penthouse. 2008. 9780385734745.

When a promising young sculptor is found dead, the triplets set out to clear their friend.

Peet, Mal.

The Penalty. 2007. 9780763633998. **S**

In a fictionalized South American country, sports reporter Paul Faustino is drawn into a mystery involving the occult religion, Veneration, after El Brujito, the soccer phenomenon of the San Juan team, falls apart on the field and disappears during a soccer match.

Subjects: Journalists; Soccer

Olsen, Sylvia.

Middle Row. 2008. 9781551438993. **J S**

When seventeen-year-old Vince, the son of white bigots, falls in love with Raedawn, a girl from the Rez, he is drawn into a mystery. Raedawn is determined to find out what happened to Dune, who has been missing since the first day of school. Dune was a quiet artist without any friends, who always sat in the middle of the bus, not with either the First Nations kids at the front or the white kids at the back. (Quick Picks)

Subjects: High-Low; Missing Persons; Native Americans

Reiss, Kathryn.

Blackthorn Winter. 2006. 9780152054793. **J S**

Juliana, age fifteen, is forced to accompany her siblings and their mother to an English artists' colony when her parents agree to a trial separation and her mother decides to restart her art career. When Julia starts investigating the murder of her mother's old friend from art school, she ends up putting them all in danger.

Subjects: Artist Colony; England; Murder

Sorrells, Walter.

First Shot. 2007. 9780525478010. **J S**

David Crandall's mother was murdered two years ago, but the case was never solved. Now David is beginning to think his abusive headmaster father may have been responsible.

Subjects: Abuse; Boarding School; Marksmen

Westerfeld, Scott.

So Yesterday. 2004. 9781595140005. **J** **S**

Hunter is a "cool hunter." He looks for new trends and fads, but ends up embroiled in a missing persons mystery after his boss disappears. (BBYA)

Subjects: Activism; Fads; Trends

Zusak, Markus.

I Am the Messenger. 2005. 9780375830990. **S**

After Ed Kennedy, a nineteen-year-old cabbie, foils a robbery, he starts receiving playing cards in the mail that direct him to his next good deed. Who is sending the cards, and why? (BBYA, Printz Honor)

Subjects: Australia; Cards

Suspense

Suspense stories in YA fiction include some type of crime or suspected crime and an element of not knowing what will or did happen. Sleuthing is not necessarily an aspect. These stories feature tension and uncertainty that is often psychological. They are usually dark.

Readers who like suspense, and particularly the heart-pounding sense of impending doom, may also find books they enjoy in chapter 2, particularly in the "Abuse" section, with books like *Living Dead Girl* by Elizabeth Scott, about a teen who was kidnapped by a predator when she was in elementary school and is now being forced to find his next victim.

Alphin, Elaine Marie.

The Perfect Shot. 2005. 9781575058627. **S**

Brian, captain of his school's basketball team, still mourns the death of his best friend/girlfriend, Amanda, who was murdered, and whose father, a former cop, is being tried for the murder. Now a school assignment about Leo Frank, who was wrongly convicted of a murder and lynched in 1915, makes him wonder if Amanda's father is also going to be convicted of a crime he didn't commit.

Subjects: Murder

Bodeen, S. A.

The Compound. 2008. 9780312578602. **J** **S**

A wealthy father builds an underground compound where his family could survive a nuclear war, but when they all lock themselves in, one of his twin sons is left outside. Six years after they move into the compound, after all kinds of things have gone wrong, fifteen-year-old Eli discovers that all is not as it appears to be. (Quick Picks)

Bradbury, Jennifer.

Shift. 2008. 9781416947325. **J** **S**

Two friends, Chris and Win, head cross-country on bicycles the summer after graduating from high school, but only Chris makes it back for college. What happened on the trip? Where is Win? The FBI wants to know. (BBYA)

Subjects: Bicycling; Missing Persons

Brooks, Kevin.

Kissing the Rain. 2004. 9780439577427. **S**

Moo Nelson, an outcast, butt of many jokes, and unhappy teen, witnesses a murder. Whether he tells what he saw or not, there doesn't seem to be any possible good outcome for him, in this story told in stream-of-consciousness fashion.

Subjects: Murder; Outcasts

The Road of the Dead. 2006. 9780439786232. **S**

Fourteen-year-old Ruben Ford knows his sister is dead before word reaches the family in London. Violence stalks him and his brother Cole as they go to Dartmoor to find Rachel's killer and retrieve her body. (BBYA, TTT, PP)

Subjects: England; Murder; Siblings

Cooney, Caroline B.

Code Orange. 2005. 9780385732604. **M** **J**

When Mitty Blake finds an envelope full of hundred-year-old smallpox scabs, he fears he may be infected and infectious. A group of bioterrorists kidnap him, believing they may be able to use him as a weapon. (IRA YAC)

Subjects: Bioterrorism; Smallpox

Diamonds in the Shadow. 2007. 9780385732611. **J** **S**

The Finch family takes in a family of refugees from Africa, and Jared begins to believe something is not quite right about them. They don't look or act like a family. Meanwhile a fifth person who arrived from Africa poses a huge danger, not only to the refugees, but to the Finches as well. (Quick Picks)

Subjects: Africa; Blood Diamonds; Refugees

Fields, Terri.

My Father's Son. 2008. 9781596433496. **J** **S**

Kevin spends weekends with his dad, who is well off and works for a computer company. But he mostly lives with his mom, who has little money and does data entry for a living. A good student with aspirations of going to Yale, Kevin has just started his first romance when his father is arrested as a notorious serial killer, DB25. As Kevin's life veers abruptly off course, his girlfriend Emily claims he is stalking her, his best friend starts going out with her, his father refuses his visits, he gets in fights, and he is suspended from school. (Quick Picks)

Subjects: Serial Killers

Galloway, Gregory.

As Simple as Snow. 2005. 9780399152313. **O**

When a new goth-style girl named Anna, who writes obituaries for fun, starts at his school, the unnamed narrator is surprised that she notices and likes him. He is left to puzzle out what happened to her after she disappears just before Valentine's day, leaving behind a dress next to a hole in the ice. (BBYA, Alex Award)

Subjects: Adult for Teens; Disappearances; Goth

Hall, Barbara.

The Noah Confessions. 2007. 9780385733298. **S**

Instead of receiving a car for her sixteenth birthday, Lynnie is given a manuscript box hiding the details of her late mother's involvement in a murder.

Subjects: Murder

Lecesne, James.

Absolute Brightness. 2008. 9780061256271. **J** **S**

Fifteen-year-old Phoebe is not thrilled when her fourteen-year-old flamboyantly gay cousin, Leonard Pelkey, appears at their house. Leonard soon starts doing makeovers in Phoebe's mother's salon, then he disappears. (Morris Honor)

Subjects: Gay Boys; Homophobia; Missing Persons; Murder

Marks, Graham.

Zoo. 2005. 9781582349916. **S**

This page-turner starts with the kidnapping of seventeen-year-old Cameron Stewart off a San Diego street in broad daylight. It follows his escape with the use of a lethal can of air freshener from the kidnappers in Seattle and his journey home again. Along the way Cameron finds a gorgeous girl, a kindly vet student who takes care of his gunshot wound, and a reporter who uncovers the true business his parents are in and its link to eugenics.

Subjects: Eugenics; Kidnapping

Meldrum, Christina

Madapple. 2008. 9780375851766. **S**

Aslaug was raised in almost total isolation by her mother, who taught her all about plants and world religions. After her mother's sudden death, she discovers she has an aunt and cousins in a nearby town. Through trial transcripts and flashbacks, the reader discovers Aslaug is on trial for murdering her mother, and later, for two other deaths. (BBYA, Morris Honor)

Subjects: Arson; Herbalists; Murder; Religion

Michaels, Rune.

Genesis Alpha. 2007. 9781416918868. **J** **S**

Josh plays an online interactive game with his older brother Max, who is off at college, until suddenly Max is arrested for the murder of a girl. The media go wild, in part because Josh was conceived to save Max's life by providing stem cells. Left at home alone while his parents try to contend with Max being held in jail, Josh discovers the murdered girl's sister lurking in a shed. He must keep Rachel's presence secret, because she has cut herself, leaving blood evidence, and threatens to say Josh kidnapped her and tortured her. As Rachel and Josh delve into Max's online persona, Josh worries if he is too much like his brother.

Subjects: Gaming; Murder

Mitchard, Jacquelyn.

Now You See Her. 2007. 9780061116841. **J** **S**

Why would a girl who has it all—beauty, talent, and brains—stage her own abduction? Unreliable narrator Hope Shay, aka Bernadette Romano, plots her own kidnapping with the older boyfriend she has met while attending a performing arts school.

Subjects: Acting; Kidnapping; Mental Illness

Oates, Joyce Carol.

Freaky Green Eyes. 2003. 9780064473484 . **J** **S**

When Franky Pierson's mother disappears, Franky wants to believe she just went away; but her family's secrets get in the way. She knows her father, a former football hero and sports celebrity broadcaster, has another side.

Subjects: Abusive Relationships; Domestic Violence; Missing Persons

Plummer, Louise.

Finding Daddy. 2007. 9780385901130. **J** **S**

Mira's mother and grandmother won't tell her much about her father. One evening when she is home alone, she does some snooping and finds a photo album of pictures of her with her dad. She also discovers that his name is different than the one she thought it was. Enlisting the help of a hacker friend, Mira finds an e-mail address and contacts her dad. But then awful things start happening, starting with the disappearance of her dog. (Quick Picks)

Subjects: Abuse; Hackers; Psychopaths

Scott, Elizabeth.

Stealing Heaven. 2008. 9780061122804. **J** **S**

Eighteen-year-old Dani and her mother make their living moving from town to town, changing their names as they rob and move on, but when they move to Heaven, Dani is befriended by her next target and falls for a cop. Now she begins to examine her life. (BBYA)

Subjects: Grifters; Thieves

Sorrells, Walter.

Hunted. **J** **S**

Chass, short for Chastity, and her mother are always ready to move, their suitcases packed and by the front door.

Fake ID. 2005. 9780525475149.

> On Chass's sixteenth birthday, her mother disappears, leaving behind a car filled with fake IDs. If Chass can't find her in six days, she will end up in foster care.
>
> **Subjects:** Missing Persons

Club Dread. 2006. 9780525476184.

> When Chass witnesses the murder of a pop star, she infiltrates a secret society to which he belonged.
>
> **Subjects:** Celebrities; Murder; Secret Societies

Whiteout. 2009. 9780525421412.

> In the middle of a Minnesota blizzard, Chastity trips over a dead body.
>
> **Subjects:** Arson; Minnesota; Murder

Springer, Nancy.

Blood Trail. 2003. 9780823417230. **J**

As Booger heads home after a visit to the local swimming hole, his best friend, Aaron, tells the seventeen-year-old football player that he is scared and asks him to telephone him in ten minutes. When Booger telephones, the answering machine picks up after several rings, even though Aaron should be home. Booger calls back and gets Aaron's much smaller twin brother Nathan on the line, who tells him that Aaron is not at home. When he sees police cars go past, Booger knows that something has happened at Aaron's house. Arriving on the scene, Booger discovers that Aaron has been brutally slain with more than seventy stab wounds. He talks to the police, but withholds the name of who Aaron was afraid of, until he is called back in for a lie detector test. When he admits that Aaron was afraid of Nathan, it ends up on the news. Booger becomes a pariah, with people in the community decrying him for further hurting Aaron's family, when surely it had to have been some deranged sociopath who murdered Aaron. With the help of his sister, Booger comes to realize the truth. (IRA YAC, Quick Picks)

Subjects: Murder; Twins

Valentine, Jenny.

Me, the Missing, and the Dead. 2008. 9780060850692. **S**

Lucas Swain is inexplicably drawn to an urn of ashes he finds at a taxi company. The urn seems to give him the impetus to look into the disappearance of his father, which happened five years earlier. (BBYA, Morris Honor)

Subjects: Cremains; London; Missing Persons

Weatherly, Lee.

Kat Got Your Tongue. 2007. 9780385751179. **J S**

The people at the hospital tell her that she was hit by a car, and that her name is Kathy. They send her home with Beth, who they say is her mother; but she can't remember anything. She doesn't feel like a Kathy. She prefers being called Kat. She doesn't like the clothes in Kathy's closet or the music that belonged to Kathy. The girls Beth said were her friends seem to hate her. So who is she? Why can't she remember?

Subjects: Amnesia

Werlin, Nancy.

Double Helix. 2004. 9780803726062. **J S**

When Eli takes a job working for Wyatt, a man his father loathes, he at first admires him. Then he begins to notice Wyatt's manipulations and machinations. When Eli discovers a secret elevator, he uncovers new secrets. (BBYA, PP)

Subjects: Genetic Engineering

Wynne-Jones, Tim.

A Thief in the House of Memory. 2004. 9780374400194. **J S**

When Dec was ten years-old, his mother disappeared. Along with his father, his little sister, and his father's girlfriend, the family has moved out of the ancestral mansion into a more ordinary house that isn't filled with the memories of Lindy. Now at age sixteen, Dec spends more and more time up at Steeple Hall, and his sister Sunny likes to go there too, but one day they find a massive bookcase tipped over on top of the body of a man who had picked up Dec hitchhiking. As family secrets slowly unfold, Dec's life and family are illuminated. (BBYA)

Subjects: Hitchhikers; Mansions

1

2

3

4

5

6

7

8

Di's Picks

Alexander, E. M. *Death at Deacon Pond.*

Alphin, Elaine Marie. *The Perfect Shot.*

Ferguson, Alane. <u>Forensic Mystery series.</u>

Fields, Terri. *My Father's Son.*

Green, John. *Paper Towns.*

Meldrum, Christina. *Madapple.*

Plummer, Louise. *Finding Daddy.*

References

Eaglen, Audrey B. 1989. "Murder, They Write." *School Library Journal* (January): 39.

Rosenfeld, Shelle. 2000. "The Case of the Missing Mystery Series." *Booklist,* May 1.

Chapter 9

Romance

Romance adds the personal touch. I can find myself "similarizing" between my life and the story. I also love the different emotions inspired by romance and liking someone. Romance novels touch the heart and open up the mind for me.—Lizzie, age 14

Teens are romantic creatures by nature. Many teens are involved in romantic relationships, and many who are not think about them, dream about them, and hope for them. Although almost every novel written for teens has some element of romance, the novels in this chapter revolve around the romantic elements. This type of novel focuses on emotions, but unlike adult romances, it does not have to end with a happily ever after. In fact, in these books the ever after is often ignored. Instead, the focus is on starting a dating relationship.

Contemporary romance, Chick Lit, and historical romance are covered in this chapter, but romance occurs in all types of teen fiction.

There are also some romance series. They fall into two major types. One follows the romantic quest of a character through a few books, and the other follows individual girls from a group of friends.

Readers looking for more teen romance should consult Carolyn Carpan's *Rocked by Romance.*

Contemporary Romance

Some teens enjoy romance tales set in the here and now, perhaps because they like characters they can easily envision or identify with.

Barkley, Brad, and Heather Helper.

Dream Factory. 2007. 9780525478027. **S**

When the costumed characters at Disney World go on strike, several teens are hired to fill in, including Ella to perform as Cinderella because the costume fits, and Luke, who has a sweltering time in the furry Dale (of Chip and Dale fame) costume. Romance ensues.

Subjects: Amusement Parks; Disney World; Jobs; Strikes

Bauer, Joan.

Best Foot Forward. 2005.9780142406908. **M** **J**

In this stand-alone sequel to *Rules of the Road*, Jenna Boller, high school junior, discovers an embezzlement plot at Gladstone Shoes, trains a new employee who is dangerously attractive, and tries for romance with a boy who really understands retail.

Benway, Robin.

Audrey, Wait! 2008. 9781595141910. **S**

Audrey breaks up with Evan because he really only cares about his band, but they vow they will remain friends. When she hears the song he wrote about their breakup, she is not happy, but she figures it will blow over. Unfortunately for her, it takes off—Evan gets a record contract, and pretty soon even her Dad, who has no idea it is about her, is humming it. The catchy tune has taken the world by storm, rocketing up the charts and making Audrey famous—or is it infamous?—as the girl who broke the heart of The Do-Gooders lead singer. Her fame leads to serious difficulties at the ice cream shop in the mall, where she works and is finding romance. (BBYA)

Subjects: Humor; Rock Bands

Brian, Kate.

Fake Boyfriend. 2007. 9781416913672. **J** **S**

High school seniors Vivi and Lane dream up a plan to keep their friend Izzy from going back to the boyfriend who dumped her just before prom. They create the perfect boyfriend online, but then Izzy wants to meet him in real life.

Megan Meade's Guide to the McGowan Boys. 2005. 9781416900313. **J** **S**

When her military parents go overseas, sixteen-year-old Megan, who does not want to give up soccer or a "normal" high school experience, moves in with family friends, the McGowans, who happen to have seven sons. As if suddenly going from only child to one of eight and to being the only girl in a family with seven "brothers" weren't enough, it turns out a couple of the McGowan boys are HOT.

Subjects: Asperger's Syndrome; Brothers; Siblings; Soccer

Burnham, Niki.

Royally Jacked. 2004. 9780689866685. **J** **S**

When fifteen-year-old Valerie's mom announces she is a lesbian and is moving in with her girlfriend, everything starts falling to pieces. Valerie's dad, former protocol chief for the White House, is out of a job, at least until the next election. So when the choice comes between staying in Washington with her mom and the vegan girlfriend or going to a tiny Alpine country where her dad has been hired as protocol chief for the royal family, Val opts for Europe and finds a prince.

Subjects: Americans Abroad; Royalty

Cabot, Meg.

Pants on Fire. 2007. 9780060880170. **J** **S**

Katie's life looks perfect the summer before her senior year of high school, but she knows it's all built on lies. When her former friend, Tommy, now gorgeous, returns to town, she finally has to face up to what she has done.

Subjects: Lies; Reputation

Teen Idol. 2004. 9780060096182. **J** **S**

When Luke Striker, a teen movie star, comes to town to research a role, advice columnist and high school junior Jenny Greenley is the only one entrusted with his true identity. (TTT, PP)

Subjects: Journalism; Movie Stars

All American Girl. **M** **J** **S**

Samantha, a suburban Washington, D.C., teen artist, becomes the American equivalent of a princess when she averts an assassination attempt on the president of the United States, is appointed teen ambassador to the United Nations, and falls in love with David, the president's son.

Subjects: Artists; Humor; Politicians

All American Girl. 2002. 9780060294694.

Fifteen-year-old Samantha has lots going on in her life: having a crush on her sister's boyfriend, dying all her clothes black, and saving the president's life. Art is the bright spot in her life until her parents send her to an art class with David, the president's son. (IRA YAC, Quick Picks, PP)

Ready or Not. 2005. 9780060724504.

Samantha Madison, now sixteen, is invited to Camp David for Thanksgiving with her boyfriend, the president's son, and his family. When he says they will play Parcheesi, she thinks it is a code word for have sex, so she tries to get out of going. Meanwhile the president stages a town meeting at her high school and comes out with a policy that she doesn't agree with, causing her to blurt out something cringe-worthy. (IRA YAC, PP)

Cohn, Rachel.

Cyd Charisse series. **S**

California girl Cyd Charisse, a barista, loves her surfer boyfriend, from whom she was separated by her mom and stepdad.

Subjects: Baristas; Surfers

Shrimp. 2005. 9780689866135.

In this sequel to *Gingerbread* (see chapter 1, "Coming-of-Age" section), Cyd Charisse is back in San Francisco starting senior year and trying to get back together with her surfing boyfriend Shrimp.

9

10

11

12

Cupcake. 2007. 9781416912170.

> After graduating from high school, Cyd moves to New York, becoming roommates with her brother and helping him with his cupcake business. She is looking for new love, but then Shrimp, who had been surfing in New Zealand, turns up again.

Elkeles, Simone.

Fuentes Brothers. S

> The sexy, gorgeous Fuentes brothers have issues. Their gang member dad was killed several years ago, and Alex, the oldest brother, had to join the gang to keep the family safe. When he goes off to college, his brother Carlos goes to live in Mexico, where he becomes involved in gang activity.

Subjects: Brothers; Gangs; Latinos

Perfect Chemistry. 2009. 9780802798237.

> When a tough gang member, Alex Fuentes, and a perky cheerleader, Brittany Ellis, are assigned to work together as lab partners, neither one is happy. However, Alex and Brittany have much more complex lives than the facades they show at school and so, even though they seem to have nothing in common, they find themselves in love with each other. (Quick Picks)

Rules of Attraction. 2010. 9780802720863.

> Carlos Fuentes is not happy to be sent to Colorado to live with his college student brother, Alex, after a year in Mexico and gang involvement. Framed for drugs, the high school senior is forced to move into the home of one of Alex's professors, who happens to have a daughter, Kiara, who is studious, outdoorsy, and enamored of classic cars. Sometimes opposites do attract.

Ferraro, Tina.

How to Hook a Hottie. 2008. 9780385734387 J S

> Seventeen-year-old Kate is dedicated to the goal of becoming a millionaire by age twenty, so when people ask her advice on snaring a boyfriend, she starts a matchmaking business venture with her friend Jason.

Subjects: Advice Columns

Friedman, Aimee.

A Novel Idea. 2005. 9781416907855. J S

> In this romantic comedy, friendship and love are found at a teen book club when Norah, needing an extracurricular activity for her college applications, starts a book group at a local store and discovers some very attractive readers.

Subjects: Book Clubs; Books; Humor; Reading

Goldblatt, Stacey.

Stray. 2007. 9780802720856. **J** **S**

The summer after her sophomore year, Natalie Kaplan finds herself straying from her veterinarian mother's strict rules when she falls for Carver Reed, a just graduated family friend who has moved into her house to work in the veterinary practice for the summer.

Subjects: Dogs; Veterinarians

Jones, Carrie.

Belle series. **O**

Belle, a high school senior, has been known as half of Belle and Dylan throughout high school, but when Dylan confesses that he is gay, her whole life changes. In the small town in Maine where she lives, no news stays secret for long.

Subjects: Gay Boys; Maine; Small Towns

Tips on Having a Gay (ex) Boyfriend. 2007. 9780738710504.

High school senior Belle has her life planned out. After graduation and college she will marry Dylan and live happily ever after, but that all changes when he announces that he is gay. Will she ever find love again?

Love and Other Uses for Duct Tape. 2008. 9780738712574.

Belle is getting through her senior year with the help of her new boyfriend, Tom, but her seizures are occurring more frequently, and her best friend Em has a new problem.

Kantor, Melissa.

Confessions of a Not It Girl. 2004. 9780786818082. **J** **S**

High school senior Jan Miller is convinced that she will always be a failure at romance, because her crush keeps trying to set her up with someone else. Meanwhile, her best friend is out to snare an older man.

Subjects: Humor; Private Schools

If I Have a Wicked Stepmother, Where's My Prince? 2005. 9780786809615. **J**

High school sophomore Lucy Norton finds her life turned upside down when she is forced to move to Long Island because her father remarries. She is subjected to life with a stepmother and two stepsisters who remind her of the Cinderella story. Now she needs her own Prince Charming, but is he Sam from the art room, or Connor, the gorgeous basketball player? (TTT, PP)

Subjects: Step-families

Kephart, Beth.

Undercover. 2007. 9780061238949. **J** **S**

Elisa, a high school sophomore, ghostwrites love notes for boys to give to the girls they like, à la Cyrano de Bergerac, but she faces conflict when her crush wants to hire her to write letters for his crush.

Subjects: Cyrano de Bergerac; Love Letters; Writing

Mackall, Dandi Daley.

Crazy in Love. 2007. 9780142411575. **J** **S**

When high school senior Mary Jane is accused of taking another girl's boyfriend, a boy she really likes, her two inner voices argue with each other, especially after the boy becomes available.

Madigan, L. K.

Flash Burnout. 2009. 9780547194899. **S**

Fifteen-year-old Blake, a talented photographer, has two supportive parents and two girls in his life. Marissa is his photography class partner, and Shannon is his perfect girlfriend, who is pretty, smart, and popular. Blake's relationships come into conflict when he takes a photo of a homeless woman in a dangerous part of Portland and she turns out to be Marissa's missing meth-head mom. (Morris Award, BBYA)

Subjects: Photography; Cheating; Portland, Oregon

Miller, Sarah.

Inside the Mind of Gideon Rayburn. 2007. 9780312333768. **S**

Attending an exclusive boarding school on a fluke, Gideon is dared by his roommates to seduce sexy Molly McGarry, whom he does like; but he also adores Pilar Benitez-Jones.

Subjects: Boarding Schools; Humor; Private Schools

Nelson, Jandy.

The Sky Is Everywhere. 2010. 9780803734951.

Seventeen-year-old Lennie is heartbroken when her nineteen-year-old sister, a talented actress, suddenly dies. As Lennie, who lives with her grandmother and uncle, tries to survive her grief, she turns to Toby, her sister's boyfriend, and falls in love with Joe, a new boy in town.

Peters, Julie Anne.

Far from Xanadu. 2005. 9780316159715. **S**

Mike Szabo thinks she has found true love when a new girl, named Xanadu, starts attending her small town Kansas school. To say that Mike's family is dysfunctional is a very kind understatement. Her beloved alcoholic father, whom she looks exactly like and is named for, took an intentional header off the town's water tower. Her mother, who has not spoken to Mike in two years, is committing suicide by eating. Her older brother shut down the family's plumbing business, a business that Mike loved, without ever even paying the bills. Xanadu is gorgeous but straight, and Mike hopes that by becoming her best friend she may be able to win her heart. Mike's other best friend is Jaimie, a male cheerleader, who is flamboyantly gay and also unable to find love in their small town, instead looking for it on the Internet.

Subjects: Gay Boys; Kansas; Lesbians; Unrequited Love

Shaw, Tucker.

The Hookup Artist. 2006. 9780060756222. **J** **S**

Lucas has a reputation for matchmaking at Thomas Jefferson High School in Denver. He is hopeless at love himself, and can't find a boyfriend, but he is great at finding boyfriends for his two best friends, Cate and Sonja, whom he works with in a Mexican restaurant. When Derek, "the hottest guy ever," starts attending TJ High, Lucas tries to hook him up with Cate, but mysteriously it seems that Derek keeps flirting with him.

Subjects: Gay Boys; Matchmakers

Shulman, Polly.

Enthusiasm. 2006. 9780399243899. **S**

When Julie's best friend, Ashleigh, develops an enthusiasm for Jane Austen, the two sophomores crash a dance at an exclusive boy's school in search of a twenty-first-century Mr. Darcy, and both end up falling for the same boy.

Subjects: Austen, Jane

Snadowsky, Daria.

Anatomy of a Boyfriend. 2007. 9780385733205. **O**

The year Dominique turns seventeen, she falls in love for the first time, is kissed for the first time, has sex for the first time, goes off to college, loses her grandmother, breaks up with her boyfriend, and begins to discover herself.

Subjects: First Love; Loss of Virginity

Soto, Gary.

Accidental Love. 2006. 9780152054977. **J** **S**

High school freshman Marisa is a tough girl in a tough neighborhood. After a fight she accidentally winds up with someone else's cell phone, which turns out to belong to a nerdy boy who goes to a magnet school. Suddenly fascinated by him, she switches schools, joins the chess club, and finds first love.

Subjects: Latino

Wood, Maryrose.

Sex Kittens and Horn Dawgs Fall in Love. 2006. 9780385732772. **M** **J**

Fourteen-year-old Felicia is a poet, the daughter of divorced parents, a student at the Manhattan Free Children's School, and madly in love with gorgeous science prodigy Matthew. She and her two best friends call themselves the sex kittens, their school The Pound, and their male schoolmates horn dawgs. One way for Felicia to get close to Matthew is to propose a science project for the annual school science fair that will draw his attention. Together they decide to explore "X," that undefined thing that makes people fall in love. Through interviews and observations they explore the love lives of friends and family.

Subjects: Private Schools; Research Projects

Zarr, Sara.

Sweethearts. 2008. 9780316014557. **S**

In elementary school Jennifer Harris was the fat-girl outcast who shoplifted treats and ate in secret. Her only friend was Cameron Quick, who had his own load of problems. He moved away in fifth grade and then died. Fast forward to senior year of high school, and Jennifer has morphed into self-confident popular Jenna Vaughn, complete with a popular boyfriend and crowd. Suddenly, on her birthday, a card arrives from Cameron. Tales of his death, it seems, were greatly exaggerated, but how could he have gone eight years without ever contacting her? In any case, now he is back, and a horrible event from their childhood haunts Jenna. (BBYA, IRA YAC)

Zusak, Markus.

Getting the Girl. 2003. 9780439389501. **S**

Cameron Wolfe falls for Octavia, one of the girls his older brother will discard after a relationship lasting a few weeks. Cam is the quiet brother in his family, not like his soccer star brother Steve or his charming fighter brother Rube, who have no trouble getting girlfriends. This sequel to *Fighting Reuben Wolfe* stands alone as a romance.

Chick Lit

Teen Chick Lit usually follows the stories of groups of friends, with emphasis on romance, and even though they often touch on tougher issues, the tone is light. The support of friends is of major importance. Brand names, designer clothes, and hip references play a major role, and often the characters attend posh prep schools.

In recent years, teen Chick Lit has exploded into a huge subgenre, with numerous series and numerous titles in most of the series. This section looks at a few of the titles available.

Readers who enjoy this subgenre have a new resource, *Teen Chick Lit* by Christine Meloni (Libraries Unlimited, 2010) to find even more titles to pursue.

Brashares, Ann.

The Sisterhood. **J** **S**

It all starts the summer four lifelong best friends are to spend their first pro-
longed time apart and follows the ups and downs and loves and losses they
experience through the next four summers.

The Sisterhood of the Traveling Pants. 2001. 9780553494792.

> Before Lena goes to Greece for a summer with her grandparents,
> Bridget goes to soccer camp in Mexico, Carmen goes to spend the sum-
> mer with her father, and Tibby stays home to work in a discount store;
> the four fifteen-year-olds discover that a pair of jeans bought at a sec-
> ondhand store seems to have the magical ability to look perfect on each
> and every one of them. Going their separate ways, they keep in touch
> by sending each other the pants and letters about their adventures.
> This best seller launched a popular series, as well as a movie. (BBYA,
> PP, Film)

The Second Summer of the Sisterhood. 2003. 9780385731058.

> One year after the events in *The Sisterhood of the Traveling Pants*, Tibby is
> off to Virginia to participate in a film program , Bridgit travels to Ala-
> bama to see her grandmother, Lena copes with a long-distance ro-
> mance, Carmen is faced with her mother entering the dating world,
> and the magical pants don't seem to be working.

Girls in Pants: The Third Summer of the Sisterhood. 2005. 9780553375930.

> The famous pants are ready for the their third summer of adventures
> and the last summer before Carmen, Lena, Tibby, and Bridget all go off
> to college in different places. (TTT)

Forever in Blue: The Fourth Summer of the Sisterhood (alternate title: *The
Sisterhood of the Traveling Pants 2*). 2007. 9780385734011.

> As Carmen, Lena, Tibby, and Bridget have gotten older and finished
> their first year at university, they try to find a way to reconnect. As the
> four are now adults, the issues are also more adult, making this install-
> ment more suitable for older teens. (Film)

Burnham, Niki.

Goddess Games. 2007. 9781416927006. **J** **S**

> Three teen girls take summer jobs at an elite spa in the ski town of Juniper,
> Colorado. Claire, a local, has found God and is trying to change the life of
> drinking and partying she had entered with her rich boy boyfriend, Drew; a
> competitive runner is trying to race away from tragedy and train to make a
> permanent mark in the world; and Seneca, the daughter of a once major
> Hollywood star, wants to make contacts that will put her mother's career
> back on track. The three are brought together as roommates in employee
> housing and find friendship and romance.

> **Subjects:** Colorado; Resorts; Roommates

Cabot, Meg.

The Princess Diaries. 🇯 🇭

Greenwich Village high school student, Mia Thermopolis finds her life changed when it is revealed that she is actually heir to a small kingdom and must learn to behave like a princess, with humorous results. The series starts when Mia is in ninth grade and follows her exploits through high school in diary format. The ten novels in the series are interspersed with several novellas dealing with specific events in Mia's life.

Subjects: Diaries; Genovia; Grandmothers; Humor; New York; Royalty

The Princess Diaries. 2000. 9780380978489.

When her European father, who she never knew was a prince, is diagnosed with testicular cancer, fourteen-year-old Mia is named heir to the Kingdom of Genovia and must suffer her terrifying Grandmere's tutelage on being a princess. (BBYA, IRA YAC, Quick Picks, Film)

Princess in the Spotlight. 2001. 9780060294656.

After a few embarrassing events, Mia finally has become comfortable with her self and her situation, but as she is crushing on her best friend's brother, the media want to know what is on her mind as the latest royal celebrity. (Quick Picks)

Princess in Love. 2002. 9780060294670.

Despite episodes of embarrassment, Mia is beginning to accept her role as a princess while celebrating two Thanksgiving dinners and preparing to fly to Genovia for Christmas. (IRA YAC, Quick Picks)

Princess in Waiting. 2003. 9780061543647.

Mia discovers new aspects of her princess role when she spends Christmas in Genovia and meets the people of Genovia for the first time. Meanwhile, she misses her boyfriend Michael and yearns to be back with him.

Subjects: Christmas

Project Princess 4½. 2003. 9780060571313.

Mia and friends undertake a charitable project of building a house for the less fortunate.

Princess in Pink. 2004. 9780060096106.

Mia really wants to go to the prom, but her plans are in peril because Michael doesn't want to go, and a strike threatens to stop the prom altogether. (IRA YAC)

Subjects: Prom

Princess in Training. 2005. 9780060096137.

Lilly nominates Mia as a candidate for president of the student body, but Mia's heart is uptown, where Michael has started college.

Subjects: Student Council

The Princess Present 6½. 2005. 9780060754334.

> Lilly and Michael accompany Mia to Genovia for Christmas.

> **Subjects:** Christmas

Party Princess. 2006. 9780060724535.

> When the student government goes broke, Grandmere comes up with a diabolical plan to raise money and make Mia even more famous.

Sweet Sixteen Princess 7½. 2006. 9780060847166.

> Grandmere has gone too far when she determines Mia's sixteenth birthday celebration should be the topic of a reality TV series.

Valentine Princess 7¾. 2006. 9780060847180.

> Mia recounts her first Valentine's day with Michael, who was decidedly unromantic.

> **Subjects:** Valentine's Day

Princess on the Brink. 2007 9780060724566.

> Junior year should bring Mia some respite, but Lilly again nominates her for student body president, and Michael is off to Japan for a year abroad.

> **Subjects:** Student Council

Princess Mia. 2008. 9780060724634.

> Depressed over her breakup with Michael, Mia is has a hard time writing a speech, until she finds the diary of an ancestor.

Forever Princess. 2009. 9780061232923.

> In the finale to the series, Mia writes a romance novel rather than her final class project, claims she wasn't accepted to college, and tries to figure out what she feels for current boyfriend, J. P., and ex-boyfriend Michael, who has turned up again. The story is told in Mia's diary entries along with text messages with friends. The novel Mia "writes," *Ransom My Heart* (9780061700071), was also published in 2009.

> **Subjects:** Romance Novels

Calonita, Jen.

Secrets of My Hollywood Life. M

Sixteen-year-old Kaitlin Burke, a TV star, assumes a new persona so she can spend a hiatus living as a typical teen, but she still has to fulfill publicity tasks for her show.

Subjects: TV Stars

Secrets of My Hollywood Life. 2006. 9780316154437.

> Wearing a wig, putting on a British accent, and dressed in dowdy clothes, Kaitlin attends her best friend's school, where she discovers people are much the same, whether in Hollywood or high school. (PP)

Secrets of My Hollywood Life : On Location. 2007. 9780316154390.

Kaitlin's life just gets more hectic when she goes on location for a feature film and people from her past keep showing up, including an ex-boyfriend, her current boyfriend, and a longtime rival.

Secrets of My Hollywood Life : Family Affairs. 2008. 9780316117999.

A new actress who has been added to the cast of the TV show starts spreading rumors that threaten Kaitlin, so Kaitlin teams up with her archrival Sky to salvage both of their careers.

Paparazzi Princess. 2009. 9780316030649.

Now seventeen, Kaitlin is facing the end of the show she has been on since she was four. She is pulled in different directions by her mom, her agent, and her friends as she tries to cope with losing something that was a huge part of her existence for most of her life.

Broadway Lights. 2011. 9780316030656.

Landing a part in a Broadway play, starlet Kaitlin and entourage are spending the summer in New York.

Freeman, Martha.

1000 Reasons Never to Kiss a Boy. 2007. 9780823420445. **J** **S**

When sixteen-year-old Jane goes into the walk-in fridge at work, she surprises her boyfriend Eliot, who is making out with another girl. As part of her recovery from the breakup, she starts penning a list of 1000 Reasons Never to Kiss a Boy, but along the way falls in love.

Friedman, Aimee.

South Beach. **S**

Holly and Alexa, both sixteen, sometimes friends and sometimes enemies, find themselves vacationing together.

South Beach. 2005. 9780439706780.

Alexa and Holly go to South Beach for spring break, where Holly tries to get back together with Diego, who was her first kiss at age thirteen, but now seems to be more interested in Alexa. (PP)

French Kiss. 2006. 9780439792813.

Alexa heads to Paris and Holly to England for spring break their senior year. When Alexa's boyfriend, Diego, leaves, she invites Holly to come to Paris.

Hollywood Hills. 2007. 9780439792820.

Holly and Alexa are off to LA and a fabulous celebrity wedding, but will they make it back to New Jersey in time to graduate?

Gabel, Claudia.

In or Out. **J**

At the beginning of ninth grade, lifelong friends Marnie and Nola swear to be best friends forever, but when one wants to be part of the IN crowd and the other doesn't, the relationship suffers.

In or Out. 2007. 9780439918534.

When Marnie starts hanging out with Lizette, fashion and social arbiter of the high school, she abandons Nola, her lifelong best friend who finds friendship with a cute boy.

Loves Me, Loves Me Not. 2007. 9780439918541.

Now enemies, Marnie runs for student council, while Nola loves having Matt as a best friend, but is crushed every time he talks to or about his long-distance girlfriend.

Sweet and Vicious. 2008. 9780439918565.

With Homecoming approaching, former friends Marnie and Nola, now enemies, contrive to show each other up and find the perfect date.

Friends Close, Enemies Closer. 2008. 9780439918572.

After Marnie and Lizette get into a fight, Marnie is suddenly OUT, but Nola, with her string of male admirers, is looking like she may be IN.

Kantor, Melissa.

The Breakup Bible. 2007. 9780786809622. **J** **S**

Jen Lewis is happy with the way her junior year in high school is shaping up. She is features editor of the school newspaper and is in love with her boyfriend, Max, the paper's general editor. But on the day that Max breaks up with her for another girl, everything changes.

Limb, Sue.

Girl, 15. **J** **S**

Jess Jordan, an aspiring comedian with a wicked sense of humor, lives in England with her mum. She has two very good friends: Flora, who is beautiful and popular, and Fred, who is as socially awkward as Jess. Jess's father in Cornwall sends her a horoscope every morning.

Subjects: British; Comedy; Gay Dads; Humor

Girl, 15, Charming But Insane. 2004. 9780440238966.

While trying to get her crush, Ben, to notice her, fifteen-year-old Jess has a mishap involving minestrone soup in her bra and a video camera at a party. (PP)

Girl, Nearly 16: Absolute Torture. 2005. 9780385732161.

Jess heads out on a road trip with her mum and gran to see her father. She has hopes of her parents reuniting, but those hopes are dashed when she finds out her dad is gay. Meanwhile she worries about how Fred and Flora are doing back at home.

Girl, Going on 17: Pants on Fire. 2006. 9780385732185.

Jess has had a wonderful summer with Fred as her boyfriend, but now, as school starts again, he seems to not want anyone to know they are a couple.

Girl, Barely 15: Flirting for England. 2008. 9780385735384.

In this prequel, Jess enlists Fred's help to pretend to be her boyfriend to discourage the attentions of the French exchange student who is living in her house.

Ny, Jeanine Le.

Once Upon a Prom. J

A month before the prom, three high school seniors who are friends dream about it and plan for the perfect evening.

Dream. 2008. 9780545028158.

Tara may be head of the prom committee, but it isn't going to do her much good if she can't find a date for the prom. Meanwhile her friend Jordan, who should take Prom Queen with no problem is rebelling, and Nisha's parents may not even let her go to the prom.

Dress. 2008. 9780545031813.

With the prom two weeks away, the three friends still face conflicts. Tara is trying to retain control of the prom committee, Jordan is thinking too much about a boy who is not her boyfriend, and Nisha's parents have picked out a prom date for her even though she is planning to go with her boyfriend.

Date. 2008. 9780545031820.

With the three friends at odds, will they be able to make the prom the dream they have always had? Nisha will have to sneak out if she is to go, Jordan will have to decide what she really thinks about being prom queen, and Tara will have to decide between two boys.

Parker, Jade.

Making a Splash. J

Robyn, Caitlin, and Whitney land summer jobs at Paradise Falls water park.

Robyn. 2008. 9780545045407.

Instead of being assigned to one of the fun parts of the water park, Robyn is relegated to Splash, the little kids' section, where her boss is her best friend Caitlin's irritating older brother, Sean. The longer Robyn works at Splash, the more she begins to think Caitlin's opinions about Sean are wrong, because he really is attractive and interesting.

Caitlin. 2008. 9780545045414.

Caitlin's job is lifeguarding at one of the pools at Paradise Park, where the cute boys hang out. She falls for Tanner, who works in the next lifeguard station, and when she sees him kissing another girl, she is devastated. It doesn't help that her best friend and her brother are now a couple.

Whitney. 2008. 9780545045414.

Even though Whitney's family has lots of money, her dad has decided she has to work for the summer. When she discovers that her wealthy ex-best friend Marci is renting the entire park for a party, she turns to her new friends Caitlin and Robyn for support.

Preble, Laura.

Queen Geeks. **J**

Fifteen-year-old Shelby Chapelle has always been an outsider, living with her widowed inventor dad and the robot that takes care of them

Subjects: Activism; Friendship; Humor

The Queen Geek Social Club. 2006. 9780425211649.

When a freakishly tall girl moves into the neighborhood, she becomes Shelby's best friend. Becca Gallagher is also fifteen, but she has plans for social domination of the school. Together the two girls start the Queen Geek Social Club, finding new friends and romance.

Queen Geeks in Love. 2007. 9780425217177.

Shelby and Fletcher are a couple, but love shakes up the Geek Queens when Becca and Amber fall for the same guy.

Prom Queen Geeks. 2008. 9780425223383.

The Geek Queens plan an alternative prom that will cost a lot less money, be a lot more work, and provide far more fun than the traditional prom

Schneider, Robyn.

Better Than Yesterday. 2007. 9780385733465. **O**

Skylar, Marissa, Charley, and Blake are staying at Hillyard Prep for the summer session before their senior year. When Blake goes missing Skylar and Charley, reluctant allies, go to New York looking for him on the party circuit of wealthy, badly behaved teens.

Triana, Gaby.

The Temptress Four. 2008. 9780060885670. **J** **S**

Following graduation from their Florida high school, four best friends, Fiona, Killian, Yoli and Alma, go on a long-planned Caribbean cruise even though a fortune teller has warned them that one of them will not return.

Wilcox, Mary.

Hollywood Sisters. [J] [M]

After Jessica's sister Eva becomes a TV star, shy thirteen-year-old Jess accompanies her to the set every morning.

Subjects: Alternate Formats; Celebrities; Hollywood; Latinas; Mysteries; Scripts; Sisters; TV

Backstage Pass. 2006. 9780385733540.

When TV actress Eva is targeted by the tabloids and someone is giving them insider information, Jess, her younger sister, investigates.

On Location. 2007. 9780385733557.

A prankster is delaying the shooting schedule for Eva's sitcom, so thirteen-year-old Eva investigates so the show can go on.

Caught on Tape. 2007. 9780385733564.

The Ortiz family moves to Beverly Hills for Eva's career, which means Jessica must change schools and leave her friends behind. Meanwhile she develops a crush on Eva's costar.

Star Quality. 2008. 9780385735278.

When lockers are broken into at her new school, Jessica, as the new girl, comes under suspicion. Meanwhile, Eva's fame gives her more commitments, which means shy Jessica may have to take her place at a talent show at their grandmother's community center.

Truth or Dare. 2009. 9780385735285.

When Eva lands a part in a movie being filmed in a house reputed to be haunted, Jessica is on the set, this time hired on as an extra.

Soap Opera

Soap opera novels often feature characters who are celebrities, or at least wealthy. They feature steamy plots with lots of drama, including betrayals, new relationships, and alliances. Often shopping, drugs, alcohol, and sex feature prominently. The best known of this type is still *Gossip Girl*. Its impact has been so great that Christine Meloni, in *Teen Chick Lit*, calls this subgenre "Gossip Chick Lit."

Soap opera is closely related to Chick Lit but has heavier themes, more sex, more drug use, and far less true friendship.

Dean, Zoey.

The A-List series. [O]

Anna Percy, a smart New Yorker, is offered an internship in LA for her last semester of high school ,where she meets the glitterati of the West Coast teen world. This series has been called "witty and risqué."

Subjects: Film

The A-List. 2003. 9780316734356.

When Anna Percy is offered an internship for a literary agent in LA in lieu of a final semester at her posh Manhattan prep school, she jumps at the chance to go stay there with her divorced father. Things really start happening in the first class cabin of the plane when the gorgeous Ben Birnbaum, a freshman at Princeton, saves her from her horrible bore of a seatmate and invites her to attend an Oscar winner's wedding with him. That starts what looks to be possibly the best twenty-four hours in her life, which turns into a very crazy time when she meets his jealous (female) friends. (Quick Picks)

Girls on Film. 2004. 9780316734752.

When Anna dumps Ben for someone who is a good guy but doesn't quite light her fire, Ben refuses to go back to Princeton until they can resolve their relationship. Meanwhile her life is complicated by a visit from her sister, who has just checked out of rehab.

Blonde Ambition. 2004. 9780316734745

While working as an intern on a teen soap opera, Anna ponders the differences between true love and true lust. (Quick Picks)

Tall Cool One. 2005. 9780316735087.

Anna and Sam head to Mexico to check out a resort Anna's father is thinking about purchasing and end up lost in the desert, while Dee imagines funeral ensembles.

Back in Black. 2005. 9780316010924.

Anna, Sam, Cammie, and Dee take a girls' trip to Las Vegas, where they encounter Anna's best friend from New York, who is with Anna's old crush.

Some Like It Hot. 2006. 9780316010931.

As Anna, Sam, Cammie, and Dee prepare for the prom, they find even more life drama.

American Beauty. 2006. 9780316010948.

As graduation nears, Anna thinks about her relationship with Ben, Cammie continues her investigation into her mother's death, and Sam tries to reestablish her relationship with Eduardo.

Heart of Glass. 2007. 9780316010962.

Anna and Cammie, caught trespassing on a private beach, end up doing their community service by working on a fashion show for poor teens.

Beautiful Stranger. 2007. 9780316113526.

Anna and Sam head to New York for the rest of the summer following high school graduation.

California Dreaming. 2008. 9780316113533.

In this conclusion of the series, Anna wonders if she really wants to spend the next four years at Yale, while Sam questions whether she is really ready to get married.

Mayer, Melody.

The Nannies. **s**

Kiley's life in La Crosse, Wisconsin, with her loving parents is fine, but she will not be able to achieve her dream of attending Scripps Institution in California to become an oceanographer unless she can get in-state tuition by being picked for the *Platinum Nanny* reality TV show. She is picked as a finalist, but because she is underage, her overprotective but underwhelming mother goes to California with her.

Lydia had been the pampered daughter of two high-powered Texas doctors until they decided their mission in life was to work in a remote Brazilian village. She's spent all her teen years in the jungle, getting all her information about contemporary American life from the occasional magazine that comes her way, until her aunt, who is an ESPN tennis commentator and life partner of a famous tennis player, asks her to come to Bel Air and play nanny to their young children.

Esme, in the United States illegally, is trying to avoid the gangs that have destroyed her life. Going to pick up her parents from the Beverly Hills mansion where they work as domestics, she comes to the attention of their TV producer employer and his trophy wife, who move her into their guesthouse so she can be the nanny to their children.

Kiley, Lydia, and Esme may come from vastly different backgrounds, but now they are in the same boat. Fortunately being a nanny isn't a 24/7 job, and the three experience all that southern California has to offer, including romance.

The Nannies. 2005. 9780385732833.

Kiley, Lydia, and Esme, three seventeen-year-old girls in LA, start their friendship despite their disparate backgrounds as they take up their duties as nannies. (Quick Picks)

Friends with Benefits. 2006. 9780385732840.

The three teens from *The Nannies* are back and about two weeks into their stints caring for the kids of the rich and famous. Lydia is scheming a way to make some big money; Esme is torn between her long-term boyfriend, who escaped a gang to become an EMT, and Jonathan, the hunky son of her boss; and Kiley, while trying to keep her young charges safe, suspects that the gorgeous male supermodel she is dating only likes her as a friend.

Have to Have It. 2006. 9780385733519.

When her boss is busted for drugs, Kiley has to find another job quickly or go back home. Meanwhile Esme has to go to Jamaica with the family she works for, but she has a problem with that because she is an undocumented immigrant.

Noël, Alyson.

Art Geeks and Prom Queens. 2005. 9780312336363. **s**

When sixteen-year-old Rio moves with her family from New York to posh Newport Beach, California, she becomes friends with a couple of the art geeks, until a popular cheerleader notices her expensive clothes and invites her into the popular clique. In the clique Rio ends up having far too much to do with sex and drugs, but when it all goes wrong, Rio turns things around. (TTT)

Von Ziegesar, Cecily.

It Had to Be You: A Gossip Girl Prequel. [S]

Three fifteen-year-olds, Serena van der Woodsen, Blair Waldorf, and Nate Archibald, live a life of privilege and designer labels in Manhattan while attending an exclusive prep school.

Gossip Girl series. [S]

A Web site, written anonymously, spreads all the gossip and tawdry escapades of Manhattan's elite teens. The stories are rife with drug and alcohol use, sex, and nefarious goings on. The popular book series became a television series, and one of the younger characters, Jenny Humphrey, is featured in a sequel series, It Girl.

Subjects: Television

Gossip Girl. 2002. 9780316910330.

Rumors fly when Serena van der Woodsen returns to a posh, Upper East Side private school after supposedly being expelled from boarding school. Meanwhile, her bulimic best friend Blair is having trouble sharing the spotlight. (Quick Picks, PP)

You Know You Love Me. 2002. 9780316911481.

Blair deals with stress related to her upcoming seventeeth birthday, college interviews, her cheating boyfriend Nate, and her mother's impending wedding. Serena, meanwhile, deals with the affection of Dan, an unpopular poet, and wins a film festival. (Quick Picks)

All I Want Is Everything. 2003. 9780316912129.

Blair has officially ditched Nate, who is now dating fourteen-year-old Jenny. Serena and Blair, now best friends again, vacation in St. Bart's, where Serena catches the eye of a rock star and Blair catches the eye of Aaron—her new stepbrother!

Because I'm Worth It. 2003. 9780316909686.

Serena is rocketed to supermodel fame, while Blair attempts to patch up her botched Yale interview and skirts an affair with a married man. Poet Dan gets published in the *New Yorker*, while Nate lands himself in rehab.

I Like It Like That. 2004. 9780316735186.

Nate and his new girlfriend Georgie team up with Serena and Blair for spring break in Sun Valley, Idaho. Jenny, back in New York, has a new boyfriend; Dan deals with the pressure of being a published writer.

You're the One That I Want. 2004. 9780316735162.

Serena and Blair open their college acceptance letters together. Serena visits Yale, Harvard, and Brown, meeting a new beau at each; she is wait-listed for Yale. Nate and Blair are on-again and off-again, while Serena and Jenny do a photo shoot together.

Nobody Does It Better. 2005. 9780316735124.

> Jenny and Serena continue their modeling careers while Blair contemplates her future. Hunky poet Dan resorts to alcohol to deal with his problems.

Nothing Can Keep Us Together. 2005. 9780316735094.

> With graduation near, Serena lands a part in a remake of *Breakfast at Tiffany's,* which makes Blair jealous. Nate is back with Serena, while Blair has a new boyfriend—Lord Marcus Beaton-Rhodes. Jenny, being younger than the other characters, looks for a boarding school.

Only in Your Dreams. 2006. 9780316011822.

> After spending some time in London with Marcus, Blair breaks up with him and returns to New York for a final summer before college. Unfortunately, her parents insist that Blair get a job, so she lands an internship with a fashion designer and moves in with Serena. *Breakfast at Fred's* is moving along, but Serena's acting isn't up to par. Dan gets a job at The Strand and Nate works in the Hamptons fixing up his lacrosse coach's house, hooking up with several girls in the process.

Would I Lie to You? 2006. 9780316011839.

> After growing tired of modeling for a fashion designer, Blair and Serena head off with Nate to a party in Connecticut being thrown by Serena's brother.

Don't You Forget About Me. 2007. 9780316011846.

> Serena, Blair, and Nate continue on in their messy love triangle. There are rumors of a sequel to *Breakfast at Fred's,* Nate decides to sail around the world with his father's mentor, and Serena and Blair make up for good before heading to college.

Historical Romance

A historical setting can be very romantic, with long, sweeping dresses and a large number of royals running around. The formality of bygone days adds a special allure to historical romances. Also, some teens like to learn something when they read, and they absorb historical facts as well as ambiance. Though teens often define historical fiction as anything set in a time before they were born, most historical romances take place in a more distant past, before the twentieth century.

Many of the teens who enjoy historical romance will find historical fiction, which often has a generous portion of romance, satisfying.

Doyle, Marissa.

Leland Sisters. ◨ ⬛

Twins Persephone and Penelope Leland are born the same day as Princess Victoria. Now nearing their eighteenth birthdays, they will be leaving the schoolroom and their study of magic with their governess, Melusine Allardyce, called Ally, to make good matches, as proper Victorian young ladies should.

Subjects: Alternate Worlds; Fantasy; Magic; Mystery; Twins; ; Victorian Era

Bewitching Season. 2008. 9780805082517.

> When twin sisters Persephone and Penelope arrive in London for the season, they discover that Ally, who had been sent ahead to put the business of creating their debut season's wardrobes in process, has disappeared. Ally's father, a bookseller, has divined that she is being held somewhere in the dilapidated Kensington Palace.

Betraying Season. 2009.9780805082524.

> With both her sister and her governess happily married, Pen goes to Ireland to further her magic studies, where she is courted by Niall, the son of Lady Keating. Unfortunately, Lady Keating has diabolical plans involving Pen.

Godbersen, Anna.

Luxe. **S**

> Called a combination of *The Age of Innocence* and *Gossip Girls*, the Luxe series features high society teens, their dramas, and romances in New York during the Gilded Age.

Subjects: 1890s; 1900s; Gilded Age

The Luxe. 2008. 9780061345661.

> The series starts with the funeral of society beauty Elizabeth Holland in the last year of the nineteenth century and introduces her circle of socialites. (PP)

Rumors. 2008. 9780061345692.

> Scandal threatens Elizabeth Holland's sister and friends as the truth behind her death remains murky.

Envy. 2009. 9780061345722.

> As one of the characters refuses to take her place in society, the sparkling newlyweds hide their loathing of each other.

Splendor. 2009. 9780061626319.

> New York's young socialites continue in their wild ways while Henry experiences war, Penelope meets a prince, and the new century rolls in.

Parker, Jade.

To Catch a Pirate. 2007. 9780439026949. **J S**

> Sixteen-year-old Annalisa is en route to the Caribbean island Mourning, where her father is to be governor, when the ship is attacked by pirates and a treasure is stolen. Annalisa's father, suspected of complicity in the theft, is sent to prison, so she sets out to find the pirates, retrieve the treasure, and free her father. One of the pirates had stolen a kiss from her, and she finds herself strangely attracted to him.

Subjects: Caribbean; Georgian Era; Pirates

Short Stories

Abbott, Hailey, Melissa de la Cruz, Aimee Friedman, and Nina Malkin.

Mistletoe. 2006. 9780439863681. **S**

Four romantic stories take place in December, around Christmas and Hanukkah.

Busby, Cylin, ed.

First Kiss (Then Tell). 2008. 9781599902418. **J** **S**

Short stories, poems, essays, and comics about first kisses by popular authors Deb Caletti, Micol Ostow, Cecil Castellucci, Jon Scieszka, Amy Kim Ganter, Shannon Hale and Dean Hale,Nikki Grimes, Lisa Papademitriou, Paul Ruditis, Leslie Margolis and Sarah Mlynowski, Robin Wasserman, Roz Chast, Naomi Shihab Nye, Justine Larbalestier, Alyson Noël, David Levithan and Nick Eliopulos, Scott Westerfeld, Donna Jo Napoli, and Lauren Myracle.

Subjects: Comics; Essays; Poems; Short Stories

Di's Picks

Benway, Robin. *Audrey, Wait!*

Cabot, Meg. *All American Girl.*

Doyle, Marissa. *Bewitching Season.*

Elkeles, Simone. *Perfect Chemistry.*

Wood, Maryrose. *Sex Kittens and Horn Dawgs Fall in Love.*

Zarr, Sara. *Sweethearts.*

Chapter 10

Alternate Formats

Some readers love stories told in different ways, alternatives to straightforward, narrative text. So even though the books in this section are linked by format rather than genre, like genre, categorizing these different but related types of reading experiences together helps put readers and books together.

This chapter has two major divisions. The first section features stories that are told in unconventional narrative formats. These may be verse, instant messages, diary entries, or myriad other unusual forms for a novel. Anthologies and collections that do not fit into any of the specific genre sections are also included here. The first part of this section features a variety of text-based stories, is followed by a subsection of verse novels, and concludes with short stories.

The second section, "A Visual Feast," features stories in which visuals play a major role, including illustrated novels, a format growing in popularity after decades of readers believing that illustrations were just for kids; graphic novels, a huge and growing category; and picture books for teens, a short section, but one of interest to some teen readers. Manga is hugely popular with teens and a huge publishing area. For lack of space, only a few are included here as examples.

Verse, Epistolary, Text-Message Novels, and More

The books in this section are primarily text based. Though some have illustrations, the stories are conveyed mostly through words, whether they are in verse, in letters, on sticky notes, in diaries, or written as school assignments. The diversity of formats presented here is amazing, and the creativity alone shown in these presentations appeals to teen readers..

Stories told through notes and letters are almost as intimate as those told through journals or diaries. Along with the sometime sense of voyeurism, this type of book creates a relationship between the reader and the characters who are writing. Fans of this type of writing enjoy novels written as text messages, instant messages, or e-mails, as well as novels told entirely in dialogue. Often more than one format type appears in a book, interspersing different modes such as notes with text messages and diary entries or poems.

Jonsberg, Barry.

Am I Right or Am I Right? 2007. 9780375843518. **J** **S**

Sixteen-year-old Calma works at a neighborhood grocery to be close to her crush; avoids her dad, who has just come back into her life; tries to discover whom her mother is seeing; and also tries to find out why her best friend is covered in scratches and bruises. Calma's story is told through narrative text, movie scripts, and notes posted on the refrigerator.

Subjects: Abuse; Australians; Crushes; Humorous; Issues; Notes; Romance; Scripts; Work

Kluger, Steve.

My Most Excellent Year: A Novel of Love, Mary Poppins, and Fenway Park. 2008. 9780803732278. **S** **J**

Multiple voices, school assignments, instant messages, diary entries, and letters to dead heroes tell the story of high school juniors Alejandra Perez, T. C. Keller, and Augie Hwong in ninth grade, their most excellent year. That was the year that Ale, a Mexican diplomat's daughter, started attending a school in suburban Boston, where she became friends with motherless T. C. and Augie, friends so close they consider themselves brothers.

Subjects: Asian Americans; Baseball; Contemporary; Deaf Children; Diaries; Gay Boys; Instant Messages; Letters

Lowry, Brigid.

Follow the Blue. 2004. 9780823418275. **J** **S**

Using postcards, lists, poems, how-to instructions, and more, fifteen-year-old Bec tells the story of what happened when her parents went away for a month, leaving her and her younger siblings in Perth with a grumpy housekeeper.

Subjects: Australia; Contemporary; Family; Humor; Poems; Postcard

Things You Either Hate or Love. 2007. 9780312363086. **J** **S**

Through lists and diary entries, fifteen-year-old New Zealander Georgia tells her story of how she tries to make enough money to attend a concert of her favorite band.

Subjects: Contemporary; Diaries; Humor; Lists; New Zealand

Moriarty, Jaclyn.

The Murder of Bindy Mackenzie. 2006. 9780439740517. **J** **S**

Eleventh grader Bindy Mackenzie knows she's smart, talented, and attractive; it's just other people who sometimes don't get it. In this novel created with notes, diary entries, and school assignments, a new American teacher has brought in the concept of building community in Bindy's Australian high school by assigning each student to a small group for a program called Friendship and Development, or FAD. Unfortunately, Bindy's group is made up of six people she really doesn't like. Quirky characters (mostly Bindy), misunderstandings, a mystery, and some interesting plot twists all work well together to make this quite different in the end than Moriarty's previous books.

Subjects: Australia; Crime; Diaries; Mystery; Notes; School Assignments

The Year of Secret Assignments. 2004. 9780439498814. **J** **S**

Assigned to write to pen pals at a rival school, tenth-grade best friends Lydia, Emily, and Cassie end up writing to Charlie, Seb, and Matthew, three boys from Brookfield High, with resultant pranks, friendships, and romances. The story is told in letters, notes, transcripts, quizzes, and fake subpoenas. (BBYA, IRA YAC)

Subjects: Australia; Contemporary; Epistolary Novels; Letters; Romance

Myracle, Lauren.

Internet Girls. **J** **S**

Three tenth graders, Zoe, Maddie, and Angela, lifelong friends, instant message their stories using the abbreviations and conventions prevalent in the medium.

Subjects: Atlanta; Contemporary; E-mail; Epistolary Novels; Friends; Instant Messaging

TTYL. 2004. 9780810948211.

The avowed friendship between Zoe, Maddie, and Angela starts to fray when devout Zoe starts a relationship with a teacher, Maddie makes a spectacle of herself after getting drunk at a frat party, and Angela experiences a series of crushes on bad boys. (Quick Picks)

TTFN. 2006. 9780810959712.

Now sixteen, the three friends are still IMing, even though Angela has moved to California, Maddie has started hanging out with stoners, and Zoe has worries about her sexuality.

L8R, G8R. 2007. 9780810912663.

As seniors Angela, Zoe, and Maddie are agonizing over boyfriends and college when one of their old enemies comes into the picture.

Nelson, Marilyn, and Tonya C. Hegamin.

Pemba's Song: A Ghost Story. 2008. 9780545020763. **J** **S**

Pemba is unhappy that her mother has moved her from Brooklyn, New York, to Colchester, Connecticut, which is full of rich white people. In their new home, a colonial house, Pemba sees a strange girl in a mirror. Phyllis, a slave who lived in the house centuries ago, makes her presence known as Pemba starts to do research with eccentric old Abraham on the African American history of her new town. Told through poetry, song, and prose.

Subjects: Connecticut; Family; Ghosts; Paranormal; Poems; Slavery; Songs

Perkins, Lynne Rae.

Criss Cross. 2005. 9780060092740. **J**

Debbie and Hector, along with various friends, sit in Hector's dad's truck one night a week during the summer and listen to a radio show called *Criss Cross.* Meanwhile, Debbie's necklace makes a journey of its own, passing through the hands of several people. The narrative is interspersed with illustrations, haiku, and interesting formatting and styles. (BBYA, Newbery Award)

Subjects: Friends; Haiku; Illustrated Novels; Poetry

Walsh, Marissa.

A Field Guide to High School. 2007. 9780385734103. **J**

In this book within a book, when Andie's sister heads off for Yale, she leaves the eighth grader a clever field guide to help her through high school.

Subjects: Contemporary; Family; Field Guides

Wittlinger, Ellen.

Heart on my Sleeve. 2004. 9780689849978. **S**

Two high school seniors, Chloe and Julian, meet when checking out a college, and fall in love through e-mails, instant messaging, and letters.

Subjects: College Admissions; E-mail; Epistolary Novels; Instant Messaging; Romance

Verse Novels

Novels in verse usually utilize free verse, but some, most particularly those by Helen Frost, tell a story using poetic forms such as sestinas and sonnets. Many teens are poets, which brings in some of the audience for this type. Reluctant readers often select verse novels, which often have lots of white space on a page, because they can be read quickly.

Some are of high literary interest, such as those by Printz Honor awardee Hemphill, whereas others appeal more to those who want a good sensational story told quickly, like those by Ellen Hopkins.

Bingham, Kelly.

Shark Girl. 2007. 9780763632076. **J**

Fifteen-year-old Jane Arrowood survives a shark attack, but loses her arm.

Subjects: Amputations; Issues; Sharks

Corrigan, Eireann.

Splintering. 2004. 9780439535977. **S**

The members of a dysfunctional family are changed by the attack of a stranger who is high on PCP. (BBYA)

Subjects: Assault; Drugs; Dysfunctional Family; Issues

Fields, Terri.

After the Death of Anna Gonzales. 2003. 9780805071276. **J** **S**

> Verse novel told in various voices of students and staff of a high school, after a freshman girl commits suicide.

Subjects: Issues; Latinas; Suicide

Frost, Helen.

The Braid. 2006. 9780374309626. **J** **S**

> In this story told in braided verse, the Scottish highland clearances in the 1850s separate two sisters. (BBYA)

Subjects: Braided Verse; Historical Fiction; Nineteenth Century

Diamond Willow. 2008. 9780374317768. **M** **J**

> When returning home on her dogsled, Native Alaskan teen Willow runs into a log, blinding her dog. Unwilling to put the dog down as her parents want, she runs away to her grandparents', and on the way becomes lost in a blizzard. Each poem is shaped like a diamond.

Subjects: Adventure; Alaska; Blizzard; Concrete Poetry; Contemporary; Dogs; Mixed Race; Survival

Keesha's House. 2003. 9780374340643. **M** **J** **S**

> This powerful and authentic verse novel tells the tales of several different kids whose messed up lives take a turn for the better when they find respite at Keesha's house, which is really owned by Joe, who was taken in by an aunt when he needed help as a teen. Stephie, a tenth grader, is pregnant; Harris has been kicked out of his home by parents who can't accept that he is gay; and Dontay has run away from his foster family after messing up on some of their rules. (BBYA, Printz Honor, PP)

Subjects: Foster Care; Gay Boys; Homelessness; Issues; Pregnancy; Sestinas; Sonnets

Fullerton, Alma.

Walking on Glass. 2007. 9780060778514. **S**

> A free verse novel about a boy whose mother attempted suicide and lies in a coma. (Quick Picks)

Subjects: Coma; Issues; Mental Illness; Suicide

Hemphill, Stephanie.

Things Left Unsaid: A Novel in Poems. 2005. 9780786818501. **J** **S**

> When seventeen-year-old Sarah befriends Robin, she leaves her good girl image behind, but when mentally ill Robin attempts suicide, Sarah must discover who she really is.

Subjects: Issues; Mental Illness; Suicide

Your Own, Sylvia: A Verse Portrait of Sylvia Plath. 2007. 9780375937996. **s**

This fictionalized biography of Sylvia Plath is told through the voices of friends, family, and others. (BBYA, Printz Honor)

Subjects: Biography; Poets

High, Linda Oatman.

Sister Slam and the Poetic Motormouth Road Trip. 2004. 9781582348964.J. **s**

Laura Crapper and her best friend, Twig, go on a hip-hop road trip to celebrate graduation by attending a poetry slam in New Jersey.

Subjects: Contemporary; New Jersey; New York; Poetry Slam; Road Trip

Hopkins, Ellen.

Burned. 2006. 9781416903543. **s**

Seventeen-year-old Pattyn leaves her abusive Mormon family to visit an aunt on a remote Nevada ranch, where she falls in love and becomes pregnant.

Subjects: Abuse; Issues; Pregnancy

Impulse. 2007. 9781416903567. **s**

Three teens in a mental hospital, all of whom attempted suicide, become friends. (Quick Picks)

Subjects: Abortion; Cutting; Gay Boys; Issues; Sexual Abuse

Tricks. 2009. 9781416950073. **s**

Heart-wrenching tales in verse of five teens from different parts of the country who end up selling themselves in Las Vegas.

Subjects: Issues; Las Vegas; Prostitution

Crank series. **s**

Based on the author's experiences dealing with her daughter, who was a methamphetamine addict, these free verse novels are gritty and heart-wrenching.

Subjects: Drug Abuse; Foster Care; Issues; OCD; Pregnancy; Rape; Runaways; Teen Mother

Crank. 2004. 9780689865190.

High school junior Kristina Georgia Snow is practically perfect until she goes to visit her estranged father, reinvents herself as bad girl Bree, and starts using crank, crystal meth. (IRA YAC, Quick Picks)

Glass. 2007. 9781416940906.

In this stand-alone sequel to *Crank*, new mother Kristina just can't stay away from the highs she enjoys on meth, and starts a downward spiral. (Quick Picks)

Fallout. 2010. 9781416950097.

Hunter, Autumn, and Summer must deal with the fallout of being the children of a meth addict as they face all kinds of issues as teens.

Koertge, Ron.

Shakespeare. **J**

9

Fourteen-year-old Kevin discovers poetry after losing his mother and suffering a baseball setback.

Shakespeare Bats Cleanup. 2003. 9780763629397.

Kevin's life revolves around baseball until he comes down with mononucleosis. He picks up a notebook and a book about poetry in an attempt to fend off boredom. He is still crazy about baseball, but when he returns to play, his position has moved to riding the pine (sitting the bench) with kids he once thought of as losers.

10

Subjects: Baseball; Issues; Poets; Writing

Shakespeare Makes the Playoffs. 2010. 9780763644352.

Kevin is back in the game, but he hasn't given up his newly found passion for poetry. He has a girlfriend but finds himself thinking more often of a girl who is a friend, and he continues to grieve for his mother and resent that his father has started dating.

11

Subjects: Baseball; Issues; Poets; Romance

Myers, Walter Dean.

12

Street Love. 2006. 9780060280802 **J** **S**

The story of Damien and Junice, star-crossed teen lovers from very different backgrounds, is told in hip-hop verse. (BBYA, PP)

Subjects: Hip-hop; Romance

Sandell, Lisa Ann.

Song of the Sparrow. 2007. 9780439918480. **J** **S**

Annotated in the "Myth and Legend" section of chapter 7.

Sones, Sonya.

One of Those Hideous Books Where the Mother Dies. 2004. 9780689858208. **J** **S**

When fifteen-year-old Ruby's mother dies of cancer, she must move to California to live with her movie star father. (BBYA, IRA YAC, PP)

Subjects: Death; Hollywood; Issues; Movie Stars

Stone, Tanya Lee.

A Bad Boy Can be Good for a Girl. 2006. 9780553495096. **S**

Told in verse, three very different girls relate their experiences with a player who dumps each when he either gets what he wants or discovers he never will get it. The girls form an understanding after they write warnings about him in the back of Judy Blume's *Forever* in the library. (Quick Picks, IRA YAC)

Subjects: Contemporary; Friends; Libraries

Wolf, Allan.

New Found Land. 2004. 9780763621131. **J** **S**
Annotated in chapter 3.

Short Stories

Sometimes readers want to sample many authors, try several different takes on one theme, or just don't have time for an entire novel. The following books bring together collections of stories that suit such situations. Short story collections that fit into one specific genre are included in the appropriate genre chapters.

Almond, David, ed.

Click. 2007. 9780439411387. **J** **S**
This unique novel, a collaborative venture by ten award-winning and highly regarded writers, covers more than a century and several characters, but starts and ends with Maggie, or Margaret as she is called later in life. Part historical fiction and part speculative fiction, telling stories set in post–World War II Japan and futuristic New York, this amazing novel told in short stories revolves around people touched by Gee, George Keane, a famous photographer. Maggie and Jason, his grandchildren, inherit items from him that have a profound impact on their lives. Authors are David Almond, Eoin Colfer, Roddy Doyle, Deborah Ellis, Nick Hornby, Margo Lanagan, Gregory Maguire, Ruth Ozeki, Linda Sue Park, and Tim Wynne-Jones.

Subjects: Historical Fiction; Photography; Speculative Fiction

Gaiman, Neil.

M Is for Magic. 2007. 9780061186455. **J** **S**
This collection features nine of Gaiman's eerie short stories, along with a poem.

Subjects: Fantasy; Magic

Jones, Diana Wynne.

Unexpected Magic. 2004. 9780060555351. **M** **J** **S**
Fifteen short stories and one novella showcase Jones's diverse talents in science fiction and fantasy.

Subjects: Fantasy; Magic; Science Fiction

Lanagan, Margo.

Black Juice. 2005. 9780060743901. **S**
Ten strange, inventive, literary stories from an award-winning Australian author. This collection includes the heart-wrenching, Nebula award-winning "Singing My Sister Down." (BBYA, Printz Honor)

Subjects: Fantasy; Horror; Literary; Science Fiction; Speculative Fiction

Red Spikes. 2007. 9780375843044. **S**

Lanagan's stories are always startling and unexpected. (BBYA)

Subjects: Fantasy; Horror; Literary; Science Fiction; Speculative Fiction

White Time. 2006. 9780060743932. **J S**

More unexpected and unusual stories for teens. (BBYA)

Subjects: Fantasy; Horror; Literary; Science Fiction; Speculative Fiction

Levithan, David, and Daniel Ehrenhaft, eds.

21 Proms. 2007. 9780439890298. **S**

Prom stories by Elizabeth Craft, Cecily von Ziegesar, Holly Black, Sarah Mlynowski, Billy Merrell, Adrienne Maria Vrettos, Daniel Ehrenhaft, Aimee Friedman, Brent Hartinger, Will Leitch, Jacqueline Woodson, E. Lockhart, Melissa de la Cruz, Libba Bray, Ned Vizzini, Lisa Ann Sandell, Rachel Cohn, Jodi Lynn Anderson, Leslie Margolis, David Levithan, and John Green.

Subjects: Contemporary; Prom; Romance

Myers, Walter Dean.

What They Found: Love on 145th Street. 2007. 9780385321389. **J S**

Connected stories revolve around the people who live in the 145th Street neighborhood in Harlem. (BBYA, Quick Picks)

Subjects: Family; Friends; Harlem; Romance

November, Sharyn, ed.

Firebirds: An Anthology of Original Fantasy and Science Fiction. 2003. 9780142501429. **S J**

Sixteen of the best science fiction and fantasy authors writing today contributed stories featuring teens dealing with issues in a science fiction or fantasy setting. The included authors are Delia Sherman, Megan Whalen Turner, Sherwood Smith, Nancy Springer, Lloyd Alexander, Meredith Ann Pierce, Michael Cadnum, Emma Bull, Patricia A. McKillip, Kara Dalkey, Garth Nix, Elizabeth E. Wein, Diana Wynne Jones, Nancy Farmer, Nina Kiriki Hoffman, and Laurel Winter. (BBYA, VOYA)

Subjects: Fantasy; Science Fiction

Firebirds Rising. 2006. 9780142409367. **J S**

Outstanding science fiction and fantasy stories for teens were contributed by some of the top current fantasy and science fiction writers, including Pierce, Nina Kiriki Hoffman, Alison Goodman, Charles de Lint, Diana Wynne Jones, Ellen Klages, Sharon Shinn, Kelly Link, Patricia A. McKillip, Carol Emshwiller, Francesca Lia Block, Kara Dalkey, Alan Dean Foster, Tanith Lee, Pamela Dean, and Emma Bull. (BBYA)

Subjects: Fantasy; Science Fiction

Paulsen, Gary.

How Angel Peterson Got His Name and Other Outrageous Tales About Extreme Sports. 2003. 9780440229353. **M J**

Autobiographical stories showcase some of the extreme things young teen boys do, such as establishing a speed record by being towed on skis behind a car, going over a waterfall in a barrel, and wrestling a bear.

Subjects: Humor; Sports

Peck, Richard.

Past Perfect, Present Tense: New and Collected Stories. 2004. 9780142405376. **M J**

A collection of Richard Peck's previously published short stories, along with two stories written for this collection.

Subjects: Contemporary; Historical

Up All Night. 2008. 9780061370762. **J S**

Short stories by six outstanding young adult authors, including Peter Abrahams, Libba Bray, David Levithan, Patricia McCormick, Sarah Weeks, and Gene Luen Yang, about what keeps their protagonists up all night. The reasons range from the loss of a parent in war to a monkey's quest.

Subjects: Contemporary; Issues; Suspense

Graphic and Illustrated Novels

Visuals have become more and more important in teen books in the last few years. Graphic novels have exploded in popularity, but novels with illustrations are now being published for teens, and there are also picture books for teens.

New formats are continually evolving. An example of this is Chris Wooding's *Malice* (2009, 9781407103945), a perfect blend of traditional text and graphic novel formats that complement each other that has action taking place in both the real world and the graphic novel world

The technology of e-books readers will no doubt have an effect in the future, with video perhaps being incorporated.

Illustrated Novels

Novels combining text, illustrations, comics, and sometimes even realia may appeal to kinetic learners or teens who just like a mixed media combination of ways of getting a story across. Illustrated novels are becoming more popular with teens. *Leviathan* by Scott Westerfeld (annotated in chapter 6) is a good example.

Ehrenhaft, Daniel. Illustrated by Trevor Ristow.

Drawing a Blank: Or How I Tried to Solve a Mystery, End a Feud, and Land the Girl of My Dreams. 2006. 9780060752521. **S**

> Wealthy, seventeen-year-old, aspiring graphic novelist Carlton Dunn IV treks to Scotland to rescue his father, who has been kidnapped because of an age-old feud, and finds himself teamed up with Aileen, a girl who is remarkably like the heroine in his comics.
>
> **Subjects:** Contemporary; Graphic Novels; Romance; Scotland

Kinney, Jeff.

Diary of a Wimpy Kid. **M** **J**

> Greg Heffley chronicles his hilarious middle school experiences in his journal, which uses pictures and text.
>
> **Subjects:** Comics; Diaries; Humor

> *Diary of a Wimpy Kid.* 2007. 9780810993136.
>
>> When Greg, who is small for his age, starts middle school, he discovers that his best friend Rowley is on his way up the popularity scale. (TTT, IRA YAC)

> *Diary of a Wimpy Kid: Rodrick Rules.* 2008. 9780810994737.
>
>> The middle son in the family, Greg, must deal with Roderick, a mean older brother, who presents no end of trouble, as well as with a little brother who gets away with everything. (VOYA, TTT)

> *Diary of a Wimpy Kid: The Last Straw.* 2009. 9780810970687.
>
>> When Greg's dad tries to get him to toughen up, Greg thinks he can sidestep the issue, but then his dad threatens to send him to military school.

> *Diary of a Wimpy Kid: Dog Days.* 2009. 9780810983915.
>
>> Greg's account of how he spent his summer vacation, which was not the best time of his life, between horrifying sights in the shower room at the pool and his mother's attempts to get him involved in a book club.

Lane, Dakota.

The Secret Life of It Girls. 2007. 9781416914921. **S**

> Photo-essay-like style tells stories of several girls, using their social networking pages, instant messaging, photos, doodles, diary pages, and more. (Quick Picks)
>
> **Subjects:** Contemporary; Diaries; Friends; Instant Messaging; Issues; MySpace; Photographs

Myers, Walter Dean.

Autobiography of My Dead Brother. 2005. 9780060582913. **J S**

Jesse, age fifteen, has always admired Rise, his "blood brother," but when Rise starts dealing drugs, Jesse puzzles out his own thoughts through his drawings of Rise and the creation of a comic. (BBYA, IRA YAC, NBA Finalist, PP)

Subjects: Artists; Drugs; Friends; Issues

Stewart, Sean, Jordan Weisman, and Cathy Brigg.

Cathy series. **S**

This interactive trilogy combines journal entries, illustrations, Web sites, phone numbers, notes, and various objects, which seventeen-year-old Cathy uses in her quest to find out what has happened to her missing boyfriend, Victor.

Subjects: Asian Mythology; Diaries; Illustrated Novels; Immortality; Notes; Paranormal; Phone Numbers; Photographs; Realia; Romance; Suspense; Web Sites

Cathy's Book : If Found Call (650) 266-8233. 2008. 9780762433469.

When looking for her much older boyfriend, who has disappeared after breaking up with her, seventeen-year-old Cathy finds out he wasn't exactly who she thought he was, and now she is thrust into danger.

Cathy's Key: If Found Please Call 650-266-8233. 2008. 9780762430857.

On a bus trip back from going to visit a psychic, Cathy, grieving for her dead father, meets Jewell, a very shady girl, who turns out to be an immortal like her missing ex-boyfriend.

Cathy's Ring: If Found, Please Call 650-266-8263. 2009. 9780762435302.

Realizing everyone she cares about is endangered by her presence, Cathy decides to leave town to draw Ancestor Lu's hired assassins away, but her friends have different ideas.

Wooding, Chris.

Malice. 2009. 9780545160438. **M J S**

A secret, difficult-to-obtain comic book depicts horrifying adventures, with characters who look exactly like missing children and teens. When his friend disappears, teenager Seth hunts down a copy of *Malice* and then performs a ritual that takes him into the comic, where clockwork monsters terrorize and kill the readers who have been physically sucked into the comic. The parts of the story happening in our world are in text; the parts that take place in Malice are depicted in graphic novel format.

Subjects: Clockwork; Graphic Novels; Horror; Legends; Monsters

Zimmer, Tracie Vaughn.

42 Miles. 2008. 9780618618675. **M**

In this illustrated verse novel, thirteen-year-old JoEllen divides her life between weeks in the city with her mother and weekends on the farm with her father.

Subjects: Family; Illustrated Novels; Issues; Ohio

Graphic Novels

Graphic novel fans are quick to let you know that graphic novels are a format, not a genre. In fact, graphic novels can appear in any genre, including nonfiction, but there are also many readers who enjoy the graphic novel format as a genre. Reading graphic novels requires a whole different skill set than reading text novels. The illustrations often indicate mood and elucidate character and help propel the story through action.

The following graphic novels include nonfiction, fantasy, science fiction, adventure/thriller, romance, contemporary, historical, and paranormal.

Manga, an important type of graphic novel, is huge with teen audiences. The publishing of manga is more like the publishing of magazines, with new series entries constantly being published.

Readers who enjoy graphic novels and manga may wish to consult Michael Pawuk's *Graphic Novels: A Genre Guide to Comic Books, Manga, and More* for more in-depth coverage.

Abadzis, Nick.

Laika. 2007. 9781596431010. **J S**

> A novel based on the true story of Laika, the dog the Soviets shot into space.
>
> **Subjects:** Dogs; Historical ; Soviet Union; Space Travel

Abel, Jessica, and Gabriel Soria.

Life Sucks. 2008. 9781596431072. **S**

> Dave, who looks like an ordinary convenience store clerk, is actually a vegetarian vampire who was turned by the store owner, who wanted someone who would rotate the hot dogs when ordered. When a beautiful goth girl comes into the store, Dave is smitten, but will he be able to protect her from vampire surfer Wes? (Quick Picks)
>
> **Subjects:** Convenience Stores; Goth; Paranormal; Surfers; Vampires; Vegetarians

Black, Holly.

The Good Neighbors. **J S**

> It's not wise to talk about the fey or faerie folk, so those who are wise refer to them by other names—such as "the good neighbors."
>
> **Subjects:** Fantasy; World of Faerie

> *The Good Neighbors: Kin.* 2008. 9780439855624.
>
> > After sixteen-year-old Rue Silver's mother disappears, Rue starts seeing beings nobody else seems to see. Her life takes another turn for the worse when her father is arrested for murdering a student, and she begins to realize that perhaps her mother wasn't even human, but one of the fey. (Great Graphic Novels for Teens, Quick Picks)

The Good Neighbors: Kith. 2009. 9780439855631.

> Rue travels into the world of faerie, attempting to save humans from her faerie relatives.

Cabot, Meg.

Avalon High: Coronation. **M**

Contemporary teens who are reincarnations of figures from Arthurian legend find conflict at Avalon High, where Mr. Morton the World Civilizations teacher (the reincarnation of Merlin) gives them some guidance. This manga series is based on Cabot's *Avalon High* novel.

Subjects: Arthurian Legend; Fantasy; Manga; Reincarnation; Romance

The Merlin Prophecy. 2007. 978061177071.

> After Ellie, a teen, starts attending Avalon High, she also starts dating Will, who is the reincarnation of King Arthur. Soon she experiences flashes of memory that tie her to her previous life. (PP)

Homecoming. 2008. 9780061177095.

> Ellie, the reincarnation of the Lady of the Lake, has to convince Will that he is Arthur before Friday, or all will be lost. Her plans are thrown into disarray when Marco, Will's brother and possibly the reincarnation of Mordred, is released from a mental hospital.

Hunter's Moon. 2009. 9780061177095.

> With Homecoming in less than twenty-four hours, Morgan, who is running for Homecoming Queen against Ellie, is willing to sabotage her to win, but Ellie doesn't have time to deal with such machinations, because the world as we know it will end if she can't convince Will of his true identity.

Castellucci, Cecil.

The Plain Janes. 2007. 9781401211158. **J** **S**

> After a terrorist attack in Metro City, Jane's protective parents move her to a small town. On the first day at her new school she meets a table full of girls, all with Jane in their names. Together they form P.L.A.I.N.—People Loving Art In Neighborhoods. Unfortunately, the community confuses their art attacks with terrorism. (PP)

Subjects: Activism; Art; Contemporary

Eldred, Tim.

Grease Monkey: A Tale of Growing up in Orbit. 2006. 9780765313263. **J** **S**

> When the population of Earth became too small to be sustainable, a galactic alliance helped the remaining inhabitants rebuild so they could fight off future attacks. In order to have a large enough population, gorillas were rapidly evolved, but even though they are now intelligent and competent, many humans still think of them disdainfully as mere animals. Cadet Robin Plotnik, a teenage human, sees this firsthand when he takes up his duties on the space station *Fist of Earth*, where

he is assigned to work under Chief Mechanic Gimbensky, a gorilla who keeps the all-woman Barbarian Squad's space craft flight and fight ready. (BBYA)

Subjects: Primates; Racism; Science Fiction

Gaiman, Neil. Illustrated by P. Craig Russell.

Coraline. 2008. 978006082544. **M**

After stumbling into a strange passage out of her family's new home, Coraline finds people who look like her own parents but aren't, and upon returning home discovers her parents are missing. To save her parents she must strike a deal with the other mother. This scary tale, originally published as a novella, was on the Best Books for Young Adults list and won the Hugo Award. It was also made into a movie.

Subjects: Horror; Paranormal

Gipi.

Notes for a War Story. 2007. 9781596432611. **O**

In this dark graphic novel, Giuliano, Christian, and Little Killer, three teen boys in an unnamed war in an unnamed country, start working for Felix, a war profiteer. (BBYA, Great Graphic Novels for Teens)

Subjects: Adventure; War

Horowitz, Anthony, and Antony Johnston.

Alex Rider: The Graphic Novel. **M** **J**

This graphic novel series retells the stories from Horowitz's <u>Alex Rider</u> series. Fourteen-year-old Alex works for MI6, Britain's top intelligence agency.

Subjects: Adventure; Espionage; Manga; Spies

Stormbreaker: The Graphic Novel. 2006. 9780399246333.

When his secret agent uncle is killed, orphaned Alex Rider is recruited to work for the British intelligence agency. This particular graphic novel owes more to the movie adapted from Horowitz's book than to the novel itself.

Point Blank: The Graphic Novel. 2008. 9781844281121

Alex continues his work with MI6 and investigates a school in the French Alps. (Quick Picks)

Skeleton Key: The Graphic Novel. 2009. 9780399254185.

Alex is off to Skeleton Key, an island near Cuba, where he must fight against a man who is willing to use a nuclear bomb to make Russia the dominant world power.

Lat.

Kampung Boy. 2006. 9781596431218. **M** **J**

Life in a small Malaysian village in the 1950s is illuminated in this graphic novel memoir of a Muslim boy growing up surrounded by rubber tree plantations. (BBYA)

Subjects: Asian; Historical Nonfiction; Malaysia; Multicultural; Muslims

Murphy, Sean.

Off Road. 2005. 9781932664300. **J** **S**

Home from college on a visit, three manly young men go four-wheeling in a bright yellow jeep and end up stuck in a swamp. (BBYA)

Subjects: Contemporary; Friendship; Humorous

Petrucha, Stefan.

Beowulf. 2007. 9780061343902. **M**

Beowulf comes from across the sea to slay the monster Grendel, who has been terrorizing and eating humans at Heorot for a dozen years.

Subjects: Heroes; Monsters; Myth and Legend

Stassen, Jean-Philippe.

Deogratias: A Tale of Rwanda. 2006. 9781596431034. **O**

Deogratias, a Hutu man, loses his mind in the genocide that shook Rwanda in the 1990s, after he witnesses the horrific death and destruction. (BBYA)

Subjects: Genocide; Issues; War

Tamaki, Mariko. Illustrated by Jilliam Tamaki.

Skim. 2008. 9780888997531. **O**

Skim, a Canadian of Japanese ancestry, tells her story in dialogue and diary form. Attending a Catholic girl's school while exploring Wicca is only one of the things that makes her an outsider, but she does have a best friend. Suicide, depression, love, sexuality questions, crushes, and cliques fill out this graphic novel of tortured teen life. (BBYA, Great Graphic Novels for Teens)

Subjects: Asian American; Coming-of-Age; Issues; Lesbians; Multicultural; Wicca

Wood, Don.

Into the Volcano. 2008. 9780439726719. **M**

A couple of brothers, a mysterious trip to an island, an auntie living on the beach in a Winnebago, a gorgeous surfer, fabled pearls, murderous plots, volcanic eruptions, earthquakes, and family ties all combine in a quick to read adventure. (BBYA)

Yang, Gene Luen. Illustrated by Lark Pien.

American Born Chinese. 2006. 9781596433731. **J** **S**

Three stories in one include the tale of the Monkey King, who wants to prove he is deity; a Chinese American boy who has a crush on a blond girl; and a boy whose life is disrupted when his stereotypical cousin visits. The three stories entwine with synergy in the end, making this a powerful tale of identity and self-acceptance. (BBYA, Printz Award, NBA Finalist)

Subjects: Asian American; Chinese American; Fables; Multicultural; Racism

Picture Books for Teens

These picture books are not written for the preschool crowd. Their shape and format may resemble books for the very young, but the stories are for teens, and the complex artwork is, too. In some of the following books, the illustrations enhance the text. *The Arrival* by Shaun Tan is entirely illustrations, with no text at all, but a sensitive story is conveyed without words.

Myers, Walter Dean. Illustrated by Javaka Steptoe.

Amiri & Odette. 2009. 9780590680417. **J** **S**

This modern retelling of *Swan Lake* is set in the gritty, urban Swan Lake Projects and perfectly captures the emotions of Amiri, a contemporary warrior.

Subjects: Issues; Multicultural; Romance

Myers, Walter Dean. Illustrated by Christopher Myers.

Blues Journey. 2003. 9780823416134. **M**

Poetry inspired by blues music is illustrated with blue ink, white paint, and brown paper.

Subjects: Blues; Music; Poetry

Selznick, Brian.

The Invention of Hugo Cabret. 2007. 9780439813785. **M**

Orphaned Hugo lives in the walls of a train station in 1930s Paris, where he tries to fix a mysterious automaton, hoping it will write him a message from his father. This illustrated novel won a Caldecott Award. (BBYA, NBA Finalist)

Subjects: 1930s; Automatons; Clockwork; Historical Fiction; Paris; Robots

Tan, Shaun.

The Arrival. 2007. 9780439895293. **M** **J** **S**

This wordless book can be interpreted in many different ways: as a story of immigration, as a fantasy story, or as science fiction. (BBYA)

Subjects: Fantasy; Immigration; Issues; Science Fiction

Di's Picks

Castellucci, Cecil. *The Plain Janes.*

Frost, Helen. *Keesha's House.*

Myers, Walter Dean. *What They Found: Love on 145th Street.*

Stone, Tanya Lee. *A Bad Boy Can Be Good for a Girl.*

Tan, Shaun. *The Arrival.*

Wooding, Chris. *Malice.*

Chapter 11

Multicultural

I just like reading about other places, it's like a way to go there without leaving here.—anonymous middle schooler

The world today is growing increasingly smaller, and many American teens have traveled abroad or met teens from other countries who now live in the United States. Today's teens are intensely curious about other countries and cultures and other ways of life. Multicultural characters and themes can be found in almost any genre. However, this chapter deals with people living on the Earth in or near to our own time, so most of the books described here would also fall into the contemporary or issues genres (Chapters 1 and 2). Reading books about diverse cultures introduces readers to what may seem an exotic way of life, but usually ends up showing how much as humans we are alike. On the other hand, readers from the culture portrayed generally identify with the feelings and challenges portrayed in these stories.

> The publication of books related to people from under-re presented communities continues to lag. Despite a handful of big hits, the numbers haven't changed much in the past twenty years.—Cynthia Leitich Smith, Segregation and Shelf Space (www.cynthialeitichsmith.com/lit_resources/ diversity/multicultural/segregation.html)

Multicultural is often used only to describe minorities in the United States; but this chapter includes books that depict a broad range of cultures, including Hmong, Swedish, Latino, African American, and others. Some of these stories deal with cultures around the world; others deal with minority populations in the United States as well as American teens going to other countries.

This chapter is organized in three sections. "Teens Around the World" stories feature protagonists from non-American countries. A bridging section, "Americans Abroad," features teens experiencing other countries. Titles described in "Closer to Home" feature teens from the Americas, including Native Americans and Latinos.

Readers who like novels dealing with protagonists who have multicultural identities may also enjoy books from the "Ethnic and Racial Identity" subsection in chapter 1. They may also want to check out some of the resources on Cynthia Leithich Smith's Web page Exploring Diversity: Themes & Communities (www.cynthialeitichsmith.com/lit_resources/diversity/multicultural/ communities.html).

Teens Around the World

Books can provide windows into the way people live in other lands. Currently Africa and Asia are the settings that predominate in teen fiction. Fascinating settings can be a strong appeal in these stories, as can the characters who populate them.

Africa

Novels set in Africa differ from African American novels, in that they portray other cultures and are often even somewhat historical. Even if the time is not specified, many of these stories reflect life as it was two to three decades ago. Some depict everyday life in different cultures, while others address tough issues that are unique to the countries and cultures in which they are set.

Jansen, Hanna.

Over a Thousand Hills I Walk with You. 2006. 9781575059273. **J** **S**

In a novel based on true events, Jeanne, a Rwandan girl, witnesses horrible events when the political upheaval in her country forces her family, who are subsequently massacred, to flee their home in the middle of the night. (BBYA)

Subjects: Genocide; Rwanda

Kessler, Cristina.

Our Secret, Siri Aang. 2004. 9780399239854, **M** **J**

Namelok, called "our sweetest one," is a twelve-year-old Maasai girl who lives in Kenya. She befriends a black rhino and her baby, naming the little rhino Siri Aang, In a time when her band is undergoing drastic changes. Namelok, doesn't want to go through the ceremony that will make her a woman.

Subjects: Genital Mutilation; Kenya; Maasai

Asia

Many of the stories set in Asia deal with tough issues faced by teens there, such as sexual slavery, poverty, and culturally imposed isolation. While the conventional wisdom is that teens like to read books with protagonists a couple of years older than themselves, many of the issue-driven novels set in other cultures appeal to older teens despite their younger protagonists. Perhaps it is because the younger protagonists are facing very adult situations in their own lives.

The settings within Asia are diverse, with novels set in Afghanistan, India, and Sri Lanka.

Hosseini, Khaled.

The Kite Runner. 2003. 9781573222457. **O**

Amir, the son of a wealthy Afghan merchant in Kabul, betrays his best friend, Hassan, the son of his father's servant. (Alex Award)

Subjects: Adult Books for Teens; Afghanistan

A Thousand Splendid Suns. 2007. 9781594489501. **O**

> Set in Afghanistan during the period of anti-Soviet fighting by the mujahideen, civil conflict, and the rule of the Taliban, Hosseini's novel explores the lives and friendship of two women who are married to the same brutal husband. The elder, Mariam, was forced into the marriage at age fifteen due to her illegitimate status, while the younger, Laila, entered her marriage after losing her parents as casualties of war. (BBYA)
>
> **Subjects:** Adult Books for Teens; Afghanistan

Irani, Anosh.

The Song of Kahunsha. 2007. 9781571310620. **S**

> Ten-year-old Chamdi leaves the Bombay orphanage, the only home he has ever known, to look for his father. He finds the streets far worse than he ever imagined.
>
> **Subjects:** Adult Books for Teens; India; Orphanage

McCormick, Patricia.

Sold. 2006. 9780786851713 **S**

> Thirteen-year-old Nepalese Lakshmi is told by her stepfather that she is being sent to work in India as a maid; but instead she is sold into sexual slavery to work in a Calcutta brothel. (BBYA, NBA Finalist, PP)
>
> **Subjects:** India; Prostitution; Sri Lanka

Perkins, Mitali.

Secret Keeper. 2009. 9780385733403. **J** **S**

> Asha and her sister Reet, along with their mother, move in with their uncle's family and their grandmother in Calcutta after their father moves to America to look for work. When Asha hit adolescence, she had to give up playing tennis and cricket, and now because of her father having lost his engineering job, she has to give up school as well, even though she is a brilliant student. Dreaming of going to the United States and earning a doctorate in psychology, Asha sits on the roof of the house in Calcutta, writing in her journal. That is where she meets Jay, the boy next door, an eccentric painter. This tale of forbidden but chaste love, loss, and family solidarity really pulls at the emotions. The place and time come to life as well as the characters.
>
> **Subjects:** 1970s; India

Selvadurai, Shyam.

Swimming in the Monsoon Sea. 2005. 9780887768347. **J** **S**

> Orphaned thirteen-year-old Amrith confronts his feelings about his birth family and discovers his sexuality when his Canadian cousin Niresh comes to Sri Lanka. (BBYA, PP)
>
> **Subjects:** Canadians; Sri Lanka

Sheth, Kashmira.

Keeping Corner. 2008. 9780786838592. **M** **J**

Twelve-year-old Leela becomes a widow before she is ever a wife, when her husband dies before they ever live together. Following custom, her head is shaved and she must not leave the house for a year. As India's fight for independence grows, she questions her caste's customs. (BBYA)

Subjects: 1940s; Historical Fiction; India

Venkatraman, Padma.

Climbing the Stairs. 2008. 9780399247460. **M** **J**

Fifteen-year-old Vidaya, the daughter of a progressive Bombay family in the 1940s, plans to go to college, but when her father is beaten and left brain injured in a riot, the family must move in with Vidaya's grandfather, where women live a very traditional and restricted life. (BBYA)

Subjects: 1940s; India

Down Under

Recent years have seen a globalization of teen novels, particularly among authors who write in English. There are many authors from Australia and New Zealand who are read in the United States. Their novels can be found in various chapters throughout this guide. Readers who like novels set in Australia and New Zealand may want to check the index for books by Markus Zusak, Melina Marchetta, Justine Larbalestier, Garth Nix, Judith Clarke, Tim Winton, Sonya Harnett, Alyssa Brugman, Jaclyn Moriarty, and John Marsden.

Abdel-Fattah, Randa.

Ten Things I Hate About Me. 2009. 9780545050555. **M** **J** **S**

Sixteen-year-old Jamie is blond and blue-eyed at school, but at home the Lebanese Australian is Jamilah, a devout Muslim with a widowed dad. Only one person knows about her dual identities—John, a boy she met online.

Subjects: Australia; Lebanese Australians; Muslims

Marchetta, Melina.

Jellicoe Road. 2008. 9780061431838. **S**

Seventeen-year-old Taylor Markham was abandoned by her drug addict mother at age eleven. Now she is a leader at the boarding school she attends in rural Australia. (BBYA, Printz Award)

Subjects: Abandonment; Boarding Schools; Family Secrets

Americans Abroad

There are several books about life abroad seen through the lens of American teens traveling to various countries. Outsiders looking in on cultures and people quite different from what they have grown up with is one of the appeal factors of this type.

Hogan, Mary.

Pretty Face. 2008. 9780060841119 **S**

Hayley is sent to Italy for the summer, leaving LA and her weight-obsessed mother behind as well as her best friend and her crush, who has a crush on her BFF. Staying outside Assisi, Italy, with her mother's old friend's family, she finds she does not have access to an Internet connection, much less a computer. So she starts walking into Assisi each day, seeing the sights and climbing ever higher on the hills. This story includes great travel details, a cute Italian boy, first love, and coming-of-age as Hayley discovers herself and deals with her body image. (PP)

Subjects: Body Image; Italy; Plus Size; Romance

Mackall, Dandi Daley.

Eva Underground. 2006. 9780152054625. **J** **S**

High school senior Eva is fine with her life in Chicago and resentful when her father drags her to Communist Poland, where he is teaching in an underground school.

Subjects: Poland

Perkins, Mitali.

Monsoon Summer. 2004. 9780385731232. **J** **S**

Jazz, a successful fifteen-year-old-businesswoman in partnership with her male best friend, is dismayed that her mother, who was adopted from an orphanage in India as an infant, is taking the family to India, where she will be starting up a clinic next to the orphanage where she was found. Jazz feels she has no talent as a do-gooder, so she attends a private school, where she meets some of the community's wealthier teens, instead of volunteering at the orphanage. Eventually she tours the orphanage and decides to volunteer there, while she helps the girl sent to help her family around the house start up a business of her own.

Subjects: Entrepreneurs; Indian Americans; Orphans

S.A.S.S.—Students Across the Seven Seas. **J** **S**

Students Across the Seven Seas is a program that takes American students to other countries to study. Individual books by different authors feature different protagonists visiting various countries and finding romance. They all visit some of the tourist sites in the countries.

Subjects: Romance; Travel

Ostow, Micol.

Westminster Abby. 2005. 9780142404133.

After being caught by her parents lying about time spent with her boyfriend James, Abby is sent to London for the summer to study. She meets, and likes, Ian from Manchester, but then James turns up.

Subjects: England

Strauss, Peggy Guthart.

Getting the Boot. 2005. 9780142404140.

Seventeen-year-old Kelly loves boys and fashion, so an opportunity to study in Italy seems too good to be true, but after getting together with Joe, a boy in the program who likes to party, she is at risk of being booted out.

Subjects: Fashion; Italy; Partying

Jellen, Michelle.

Spain or Shine. 2005. 9780142403686

Elena, an aspiring playwright, gets into the S.A.S.S. program by claiming she wants to research her Spanish roots, but in truth she wants to experience Spanish nightlife and beaches.

Subjects: Latinas; Spain

Hapka, Cathy.

Pardon My French. 2005. 9780142404591.

Nicole's parents really want her to go to Paris, but she doesn't want to leave her boyfriend, Nate, and her other friends, even for one semester.

Subjects: France

Nelson, Suzanne.

Heart and Salsa. 2006. 9780142406472.

Cat is not happy living in Boston, where her family moved when her mother remarried, so she is excited to be spending the summer in Oaxaca, Mexico, with her best friend from Arizona. But when Sabrina shows up with her boyfriend, Cat finds her experience much different than she had planned.

Subjects: Mexico

The Sound of Munich. 2006. 9780142405765.

While Siena is in Germany, she tries to find the man who helped her father's family escape from behind the Iron Curtain, along the way finding friendship and romance.

Subjects: Germany

Gerber, Linda.

Now and Zen. 2006. 9780142406571.

> Nori wants to get away from the drama surrounding her parents' divorce, so she takes the chance to go to Japan, the country of her ancestors, where she pretends to be Japanese and shows a gorgeous German student around.

Subjects: Germans; Japan; Japanese Americans

9

Apelqvist, Eva.

Swede Dreams. 2007. 9780142407462.

> Sixteen-year-old Calista fell in love with Swedish exchange student Jonas when he attended her school in Wisconsin. Now she is in the S.A.S.S. program so she can visit him in his homeland.

Subjects: Sweden

10

Ferris, Aimee.

*Girl Overboard.*2007. 9780142407998.

> Marina's S.A.S.S. experience takes place on a yacht in the Caribbean, where she and a cute shipmate from Australia get to visit the Bahamas and the Dominican Republic.

Subjects: Australians; Bahamas; Caribbean; Cruises; Dominican Republic

11

12

Gerber, Linda.

The Finnish Line. 2007. 9780142409169.

> Mo, a ski jumper, is off to Finland to train with other ski jumpers as well as discover all things Finnish.

Subjects: Finland; Skiers

Supplee, Suzanne.

When Irish Guys Are Smiling. 2008. 9780142410165.

> Still grieving for her dead mother and wanting to get away from her pregnant stepmother, seventeen-year-old Delk is off to Connmerra in Ireland for a semester.

Subjects: Ireland

Liu, Cynthia.

Great Call of China. 2009. 9780142411346.

> Cece, a Texan born in China, uses her S.A.S.S. semester to try to find her birth family.

Subjects: Adoption; China; Chinese American

Ostow, Micol.

Up Over Down Under. 2010. 9780142410561.

> Two girls are signed up for environmental programs as part of S.A.S.S. American Eliza goes to Melbourne, while Aussie Billie goes to Washington, D.C.

Subjects: Australia; Environment

Closer to Home

Novels in this section feature North American protagonists with multicultural backgrounds and show the diversity of cultures on this continent as well as the diversity of issues faced by various groups.

Native American

Novels featuring authentically portrayed Native Americans are unfortunately few and far between. In the past Native Americans, the first people to inhabit the Americas, were both demonized and romanticized in our literature. Even today, books about Native Americans often focus on the way Indians looked, dressed, and lived in the past. Very few books for teens dealing with Native American life have been published in the last few years. Many readers would like to see more new titles and authors emerging in this area in the coming years.

That said, Joseph Bruchac, an Abenaki, is quite prolific. His middle school novels usually have paranormal elements, but feature contemporary Native American characters. His BBYA novel *Dawn Land* will be published in graphic novel format in October 2010. Award-winning author Sherman Alexie, a Spokane, has now also written a teen novel and hopefully will write more.

Alexie, Sherman.

Absolutely True Diary of a Part-Time Indian. 2007. 9780316013697 . **J** **S**

> Accidentally breaking his geometry teacher's nose takes fourteen-year-old Arnold off the rez and makes him the only Indian in his new school. Now he isn't the funny-looking smart kid anymore, but a basketball star with a hot girlfriend. (BBYA, NBA, PP)

Subjects: Basketball; Spokane

Bruchac, Joseph.

Nightwings. 2009. 9780061123184. **M**

> Thirteen-year-old Paul lives with his Abenaki grandfather while both his parents are deployed to the Middle East. A TV producer wants Paul's grandfather to lead a crew up a mountain in search of a legendary treasure, and when he refuses, the producer has him and Paul kidnapped.

Subjects: Abenaki; Kidnapping; Treasure

Whisper in the Dark. 2005. 9780060580896. **M**

Thirteen-year-old orphaned Maddie, a descendant of a Narragansett sachem, lives with her aunt in Rhode Island, where she encounters a legendary clawed monster.

Subjects: Narragansett

Skeleton Man. **M**

Scary stories based on folklore and set in New York feature Molly, a contemporary Mohawk sixth grader who uses Mohawk legends to save her family.

Skeleton Man. 2001. 9780060290757.

After her parents fail to come home one night, sixth grader Molly is sent to live with an uncle she has never even heard of before, who locks her up at night. Molly's dreams lead her to find her parents, who have also been kidnapped by the "uncle." A spooky tale, based on Mohawk folklore.

The Return of Skeleton Man. 2006. 9780060580926.

Molly, age twelve, is at a retreat center in Northern New York with her parents when she begins to suspect that the legendary Mohawk monster, Skeleton Man, is back.

Taylor, Drew Haydon.

Night Wanderer: A Native Gothic Novel. 2007. 9781554510993. **S**

Sixteen-year-old Anishinabe Tiffany Hunter lives in the Native community of Otter Lake in northern Ontario. Her father is upset with her dating a white boy, and the household has recently taken in a boarder, Pierre L'Enfant. Pierre lives in their dark basement and only goes out at night. In fact, Pierre is a vampire with a long and interesting history.

Subjects: Vampires

African American

Novels featuring African American protagonists run the gamut from upper-middle-class contemporary romance-like stories to gritty urban tales of the disenfranchised. This is one of the most active and growing areas of publishing in teen fiction. Harlequin entered the field with the Kimani Tru line and Kensington with the Dafina line, both publishing urban fiction featuring African American teens.

Currently the trend in African American fiction tends more to the gritty urban type of tale or soap opera Chick Lit; however, more literary and thought-provoking works by authors such as Angela Johnson, Sharon Draper, Jacqueline Woodson, and Walter Dean Myers are still being published. Readers who enjoy reading African American novels will also find several titles of interest in chapter 1 in the "Ethnic and Racial Identity" subsection and numerous titles in the subject index under African Americans.

Bluford High Series. ⬛ ⬛

This highly popular and successful series, written by several authors, centers on the students at Bluford High School, who experience life in an urban setting and face many different challenges. Originally published by Townsend Press, a small publisher, the reprints are published by Scholastic. The unattractive covers on the originals have been no deterrent to readers; even reluctant readers are willing to overlook them for the easy-to-read stories that relate to their real lives and issues.

Schraff, Anne.

Lost and Found. 2001, reissued 2007. 9780439898393.

High school sophomore Darcy Wills becomes friends with her new lab partner Tarah and Tarah's boyfriend Cooper, who stand by her when her younger sister disappears. (PP)

A Matter of Trust. 2003, reissued 2007. 9780439865470.

Darcy tries to ignore the taunts of her former grade school best friend; but when Brisana tries to take Darcy's boyfriend away, she has to take action.

Secrets in the Shadows. 2003, reissued 2007. 9780439904858.

Roylin Bailey regrets stealing from Mr. Miller to buy a gift that he wants to use to win over new girl Korie Archer.

Someone to Love Me. 2003, reissued 2007. 9780439904865.

Cindy's new boyfriend. Bobby, seems wonderful, but then he starts ordering her around and then abusing her.

Subjects: Abuse

Langan, Paul.

The Bully. 2003, reissued 2007. 9780439865463.

Moving from Philadelphia to California has not saved Darrell Mercer from bullying.

Subjects: Bullies

Payback. Original title: *The Gun.* 2003, reissued 2007. 9780439904872.

Tyray Hobbs, Bluford freshman, has always been a bully, but now that Darrell Mercer has stood up to him, everybody isn't as afraid of him, and he is going to need to do something drastic to keep people in fear.

Subjects: Bullies

Schraff, Anne.

Until We Meet Again. 2003, reissued 2007. 9780439904889.

Darcy Wills finds that the summer she was so looking forward to is filled with disappointment when Hakeem moves, and she worries about her ailing grandmother.

Langan, Paul.

Blood Is Thicker. 2003, reissued 20079780439904896.

When his father gets sick and the family loses their home, Hakeem Randall has to leave Bluford and go live in Detroit with relatives.

Subjects: Detroit

Brothers in Arms. 2003, reissued 2008. 9780439904902.

Martin Luna wants revenge for the death of his little brother.

Summer of Secrets. 2004, reissued 2008. 9780439904919.

Darcy is hiding a secret, which when revealed will change her life.

The Fallen. 2006. 9781591940661.

Martin is in trouble at school, and back in his neighborhood he is being hunted by gun-toting Frankie.

Shattered. 2006. 9781591940692.

Darcy starts her junior year, trying to keep things together with Hakeem, and is devastated when she learns her closest friends have been lying to her.

Search for Safety. 2006. 9781591940708.

Ben McKee, a new sophomore at Bluford, faces abuse from a drunken stepfather at home.

Subjects: Abuse; Alcoholism

Kern, Peggy.

No Way Out. 2008. 9781591941767.

Orphaned Bluford freshman Harold Davis gets involved in a drug-dealing ring after his grandmother suffers injuries in a fall, with complications related to her diabetes. Discovering that the part-time job at the corner grocery won't begin to make a dent in the medical bills, he takes up the offer of a neighborhood thug, but finds he can't destroy lives in good conscience. (Quick Picks)

Subjects: Diabetes; Drugs

Langan, Paul.

Schooled. 2008. 9781591941774.

Lionel Shepherd's dream is to play in the NBA but with the difficulties he is having in school no scout will ever even see him. (Quick Picks)

Subjects: Basketball

Divine, L.

Drama High series. S

Sixteen-year-old Jayd Jackson lives in Compton, California, but is bussed to a predominantly white high school in the South Bay area of Los Angeles.

This urban fiction series has lots of soap opera qualities, as well as a touch of the paranormal in Jayd's interest in her family's conjure woman history.

Subjects: California; Urban Fiction

The Fight. 2006. 9780758216335.

> At the beginning of her junior year, as one of thirty students from Compton bussed into South Bay High School, sixteen-year-old Jayd has dumped her playa boyfriend, but his new girlfriend won't leave her alone. (Quick Picks)

Second Chance. 2006. 9780758216359.

> Sixteen-year-old Jayd, who is one of the African American teens being bussed from Compton to South Bay High School, starts dating a half-Jewish white boy.

Jayd's Legacy. 2007. 9780758216373.

> Jayd, age sixteen, still with her Jewish boyfriend Jeremy Weiner, is falling seriously in love, but with Homecoming approaching she also has to worry about Nellie, who may end up being the first African American elected to the Homecoming court.

Frenemies. 2008. 9780758225320.

> Ever since she was elected Homecoming princess, Nellie seems to have changed. But she isn't the only one. Jayd is beginning to have serious doubts about Jeremy's commitment to her. (Quick Picks)

Lady J. 2008. 9780758225344.

> Sixteen-year-old Jayd, who is attending a predominantly white high school after being bussed in from Compton, has broken up with her Jewish boyfriend Jeremy. She decides it is time to pay some attention to her heritage. After all, she comes from a long line of conjure women.(Quick Picks)

Courtin' Jayd. 2008. 9780758225368.

> Jayd is finding drama both at home and in her relationships. She doesn't want to be Rah's rebound girlfriend, and he doesn't want her ex, Jeremy, on the basketball team. (Quick Picks)

Hustlin'. 2009. 9780758231055.

> Jayd tries to stay out of the drama, but Mickey is going to have her baby soon, and Rah, Jayd's boyfriend, is having wishes with his baby mama. (Quick Picks)

Keep It Movin'. 2009. 9780758231079.

> Jayd did get a car for Christmas, but it isn't the greatest, and Mickey, Jayd's friend who is pregnant, is being sent off to a continuation school. (Quick Picks)

Holidaze. 2009. 9780758231093.

> Valentine's Day is fast approaching, but Jayd is still mourning her friend Tre, and she is tired of all the drama with her boyfriend, Rah.

Culture Clash. 2010. 9780758231116.

> After not being impressed with the way Cultural Awareness Day is being celebrated at South Bay High, Jayd is involved in starting an African Student Union. Emilio, a new Latino sophomore student, seems to be crushing on her as much as she is crushing on him.

Cold as Ice. 2010. 9780758231130.

Millner, Denene, and Mitzi Miller.

Hotlanta Series. **S**

A pair of Atlanta twins with all the accoutrements of the upper middle class find ties to the grittier side of town when they uncover secrets about their prominent businessman stepfather, and their own bio dad is released from prison. Lauren is a wild child, and Sydney is prim and proper.

Subjects: Atlanta; Crime; Twins; Wealth

Hotlanta. 2008. 9780545003087.

> Sydney and Lauren Duke live a brand-name-filled life in a Buckhead mansion in Atlanta. For twins, they have little in common except for their looks. When their real father is released from prison, one wants to see him and the other doesn't. (Quick Picks, PP)

If Only You Knew. 2008. 9780545003094.

> The twins spend more time with family in the bad part of town as they discover more about their materialistic mom, ex-con dad, and wealthy stepfather. (Quick Picks)

What Goes Around. 2009. 9780545003100.

> Lauren and Sydney discover they have more in common than they thought as they have to work together to bring the truth to light and expose what is going on with their wealthy but dishonest stepfather.

Woodson, Jacqueline.

After Tupac & D Foster. **2008** . **9780399246548.** **M** **J**

> Three friends in an African American neighborhood in New York enter adolescence against a background of Tupac's music. The narrator and Neeka have been friends forever, but suddenly a new girl, a foster child they call D Foster, appears on their block. All three are passionate about their love for Tupac and his music, setting this story firmly in its time. (BBYA, Newbery Honor)

Subjects: 1990s; Foster Care; Friendship; New York; Rap Music

Asian American

These novels feature Asian American teens who live in the mainstream of American life, yet who do not look like most of their peers. They sometimes face discrimination and often have to deal with different family expectations.

Headley, Justina Chen.

Girl Overboard. 2009. 9780316011297. **M** **S**

All fifteen-year-old Syrah Chen ever wanted to do was be a professional snowboarder, but her plans are crushed when her mother and Chinese American billionaire father ban her from the sport after she gets caught in (and survives) an avalanche. Syrah finds refuge in drawing manga and eventually organizes a fund-raiser for a girl fighting leukemia.

Subjects: Chinese Americans; Fund-raising; Snowboarders; Wealthy

Hirahara, Naomi.

1001 Cranes. 2008. 9780385905411. **M** **J**

Sent off to stay with her grandparents while her parents try to iron out their marital difficulties, twelve-year-old Angela Kato spends the summer folding origami cranes for the family business and comes to know and appreciate her stern grandmother and her Japanese heritage.

Subjects: Japanese Americans; Origami

Lamba, Marie.

What I Meant . . . . 2007. 9780375840913. **J** **S**

Fifteen-year-old Sang, with a Sikh father and white American mother, finds her life thrown into upheaval when her demanding aunt comes from India to stay with the family. Sang's plans to get rid of her are turned around.

Subjects: Aunts; Indian Americans; Mixed Race; Sikhs

Na, An.

The Fold. 2008. 9780399242762. **M** **J** H.

Korean American Joyce Kim is not sure what to do when her aunt offers to pay for surgery to make Joyce's eyes look more Western the summer before her senior year of high school.

Subjects: Body Image; Korean Americans; Plastic Surgery

Shea, Pegi Deitz.

Tangled Threads: A Hmong Girl's Story. 2003. 9780618247486. **M**

After spending ten years in a Thai refugee camp, thirteen-year-old Mai Yang and her grandmother are finally moving to Providence, Rhode Island. Once there, Mai's American cousins try to make her over, while she still tries to honor her grandmother's Hmong ways.

Subjects: Hmong Americans; Laotian Americans

Sonnenblick, Jordan.

Zen and the Art of Faking It. 2007. 9780439837095. **M**
  Annotated in chapter 1.

9

Wong, Joyce Lee.

Seeing Emily. 2005. 9780810957572. **J**
  In this novel told in free verse, sixteen-year-old Emily, the daughter of Chi-
  nese immigrants, is a talented artist who finds too many people trying to
  mold her into who they think she should be. Sent off to stay with an aunt in
  Taipei, she comes into her own.
  Subjects: Chinese Americans; Taiwan; Verse Novels

10

Yoo, Paula.

Good Enough. 2008. 9780060790851. **J S**
  Patti Yoon's Korean American parents have extremely high expectations
  for the musically accomplished high school senior, who is on track to be val-
  edictorian. She must score 2300 on her SATs and get into Harvard, Yale, and
  Princeton.
  Subjects: Humor; Korean Americans

11

Latino

   Books with Hispanic protagonists run the gamut of characters and plots,
from stories of teens whose families may have been in what is now the United
States for 400 years to those of teens living in Latin American countries or trying
to make it into the United States. Under the broad umbrella of "Latino," many
cultures are represented, from Mexican to Mexican American to Cuban to Guatemalan.

12

Alegria, Malin.

Estrella's Quinceañera. 2006. 9780689878091. **J S**
  Estrella would prefer to not have a Quinceañera now that she is going to a
  ritzy private school on a scholarship.
  Subjects: California; Mexican American; Quinceañera; Romance

Sofi Mendoza's Guide to Getting Lost in Mexico. 2007. 9780689878114. **S**
  In hopes of snaring her crush, Sofi decides to defy her overly protective parents and go to Mexico for a house party just before prom and graduation. .
  When she and her two friends head home, she is turned back at the border
  for having a fake green card. Sofi has lived in California since she was four.
  Now her parents are going to find out that she didn't go where she was supposed to go. Fortunately she has an aunt she has never met who lives in
  Tijuana with her family, which consists of a disabled husband, two young
  sons, and a daughter Sofi's age. As Sofi waits for resolution of her green

card problem and a way home, she learns how to live with no Internet access, no telephone, and an outdoor bathroom. As Sofi tries to figure out if she is Mexican, American, or just what, she discovers her own ties to her family roots and finds love.

Subjects: California; Identity; Immigration; Mexican Americans; Mexicans; Mexico

Hobbs, Will.

Crossing the Wire. 2006. 9780060741389. **J** **S**

Victor Flores, at age fifteen, is the sole support of his mother, brother, and two sisters, feeding the family by raising corn. When the bottom falls out of the corn market, he knows that for them to survive he must go to El Norte, becoming an illegal immigrant. Victor's journey is fraught with peril. On the way to Nogales on a bus he is almost deported to Guatemala because he can't prove his Mexican citizenship and he looks Guatemalan, being originally from Chiapas, Mexico. He meets many people with many stories on his dangerous journey. Hobbs excels at depicting the wilderness as Victor travels through the frigid Chiricahua mountains and across the border with a man almost crippled by a beating from vigilantes, until they are both captured and deported by the Border Patrol. The rugged landscape of the rocky desert is illuminated when Rico supposedly finds them a coyote who will accept payment from the brother in Tucson, but in reality has signed himself and Victor to carry water and food for heavily loaded human mules who are smuggling drugs.

Subjects: Adventure; Immigration; Mexicans; Poverty; Smuggling; Survival

Johnson, LouAnne.

Muchacho. 2009. 9780375861178. **S**

Eddie Corazon had promised his mom he would graduate from high school, which is why he is attending an alternative high school rather than dropping out, but in a neighborhood full of drug dealers and gangs, he's not sure he can make it. When he meets Lupe, a smart girl who has transferred in to get away from bullies, he falls in love and starts seeing a future. The culture of New Mexico Hispanics is well portrayed. (BBYA, Quick Picks)

Subjects: Alternative Education; New Mexico; Poets; Romance

Osa, Nancy.

Cuba 15. 2003. 9780385732338. **J**

Violet Paz has never been very interested in her cultural heritage—neither her Polish ancestry from her mother nor her Cuban ancestry from her father—but now the Chicago teen's Cuban grandmother wants to throw her a big Quinceañera, even though Violet has already had her fifteenth birthday and does not want to wear ruffles and a tiara. Required to perform a comedic speech, Violet decides to use incidents from her family's life and comes up with "the Loco Family." (BBYA)

Subjects: Cuban Americans; Polish American; Quinceañera

Resau, Laura.

The Indigo Notebook. 2009. 9780385736527. **J** **S**

Zeeta's fifteen years have been spent traveling the globe with her mother, Layla, an itinerant English teacher and free spirit. On a flight to Ecuador, they interact with Wendell, a teen boy who looks like an Otavaleno but talks and walks like an American, and also with Jeff, who personifies everything Zeeta has always wished for in a "normal father." After settling in Otavalo, Zeeta makes friends in the marketplace and runs into Wendell again, who needs an interpreter. Adopted as an infant, he has traveled to Ecuador seeking his birth parents. Zeeta teams up with him to translate the letters he has written to his birth parents over the years and to help him in his quest to find them. A crystal that had been wrapped in his blankets when he was delivered to his real parents, the parents who raised him, is his only clue. Meanwhile Zeeta discovers why it is essential to be sure what one wishes for is what one truly wants.

Subjects: Adoption; Ecuador; Mystery; Native Americans; Romance

Red Glass. 2007. 9780385734660. **J** **S**

Sophie lives in Tucson with her English mother, Mexican stepfather, Bosnian refugee great-aunt Dika, and Pedro, a six-year old foster brother who came into their lives when his parents and the party they crossed the border with all died in the desert. After eight months of living with the family, Pedro has finally begun talking, and they find his relatives in a small Oaxaca town. With her parents unable to make a trip to Mexico, Sophie is to take Pedro to visit his grandparents and extended family, accompanied by Dika, Dika's boyfriend Mr. Lorenzo, and his teen son Angel. During the week-long drive to Pedro's village and the week they spend visiting, the entire party bonds with each other and with Pedro's family, but then Mr. Lorenzo and Angel head off to Guatemala to retrieve Angel's mother's jewels. When they don't return, Sophie starts on a perilous journey that will prove who she really is to herself. The details of life in a Mexican village and Sophie's journey from Tucson to Guatemala are vividly and memorably drawn. (BBYA, VOYA, IRA)

Subjects: Bosnians; Guatemala; Guatemalans; Mexicans; Mexico

What the Moon Saw. 2006. 9780385733434. **M** **J**

Fourteen-year-old Clara Luna has never met her grandparents because her father was an illegal immigrant to the United States. Now she has received a letter from them in Spanish inviting her to spend the summer with them in Oaxaca, Mexico. (BBYA)

Subjects: Mexican Americans; Mexicans

Ryan, Pam Muñoz.

Becoming Naomi Leon. 2004. 9780439269971. **M**

Naomi Leon Outlaw lives in a trailer park with her great-grandmother and little brother, who is a funny-looking kid but very smart. When their mother turns up with a new boyfriend years after abandoning them and has a plan to gain custody of Naomi to get some welfare money, the two kids and their grandma travel to Oaxaca with neighbors to look for their father. There she finds family she never knew. Great depiction of contemporary Mexican culture. (Pura Belpré Honor Book, Schneider Family Middle-School Book Award)

Subjects: Art; Disabilities; Latinos; Mexico

Sitomer, Alan Lawrence.

The Secret Story of Sonia Rodriguez. 2008. 9781423110729. **J S**

Sonia, the oldest daughter and first U.S.-born kid in her family, is determined to succeed in school and life, despite the fact that her pregnant mother relies on her to take care of her younger siblings, cook the meals, and keep the house spotless. Her beloved father, who works three jobs, is almost never home. Her older brother is always stoned, and her "drunkle," her mother's criminal brother, is always lusting after her. She does have an African American best friend whom she doesn't get to spend enough time with, and she meets a gorgeous Salvadoran boy working in a pet shop. But then her mother and aunt decide that Sonia needs to experience Mexico, so they send her to visit her cigar-smoking Abuelita on a rancho in Mexico. There she learns a lot about her roots and the plight of the residents, including her young widowed cousin. (Quick Picks, IRA YAC)

Subjects: Family; Mexican Americans; Mexico; Salvadorans; Substance Abuse; Widows

Soto, Gary.

The Afterlife.

Annotated in chapter 5.

Subjects: Mexican Americans

Facts of Life: Stories. 2008. 9780152061814. **M**

Ten short stories about growing up Latino in California.

Subjects: Latino; Mexican Americans

Help Wanted. 2005. 9780152052010. **J S**

Ten stories of California Latino teens dealing with jobs, relationships, family, friends, and romantic entanglements.

Subjects: Latino; Mexican Americans

Di's Picks

Alegria, Malin. *Sofi Mendoza's Guide to Getting Lost in Mexico.*

Alexie, Sherman. *Absolutely True Diary of a Part-Time Indian.*

Hogan, Mary. *Pretty Face.*

Kessler, Cristina. *Our Secret, Siri Aang.*

Perkins, Mitali. *Secret Keeper.*

Resau, Laura. *The Indigo Notebook.*

Woodson, Jacqueline. *After Tupac & D Foster.*

Chapter 12

Resources

Many things have changed since the 1997 publication of the first edition of *Teen Genreflecting*. Library services to teens have exploded, with more libraries offering more services to teens all the time. The literature has experienced an amazing boom cycle, with many young adult titles becoming best sellers. With all this attention to young adult/teen services, it is no wonder that resources for working with teen readers have also grown in scope and availability.

Working with Teens

Alessio, Amy, ed. *Excellence in Library Services to Young Adults*. 5th ed. ALA/YALSA, 2008. 97808389-8457-4.

Anderson, Sheila B. *Extreme Teens: Library Services to Nontraditional Young Adults*. Libraries Unlimited, 2005.

Booth, Heather. *Serving Teens Through Readers' Advisory*. ALA, 2007. 978-0838909300

Gorman, Michele, and Tricia Suellentrop. *Connecting Young Adults and Libraries: A How-to-Do-It Manual*. 4th ed. Neal-Schuman, 2009.

Jones, Patrick, Maureen L. Hartman, and Patricia Taylor. *Connecting with Reluctant Teen Readers: Tips, Titles, and Tools*. Neal-Schuman, 2006. 9781555705718.

Kan, Katharine L. *Sizzling Summer Reading Programs for Young Adults*. ALA, 2006. 9780838935637.

Bibliographies of Books for Teens

Barr, Catherine. *Best Books for High School Readers, Grades 9–12*. Libraries Unlimited, 2009. 9781591585763.

Barr, Catherine. *Best Books for Middle School and Junior High Readers, Grades 6–8*. Libraries Unlimited, 2009. 9781591585732.

Bodart, Joni Richards. *Radical Reads 2: Working with the Newest Edgy Titles for Teens*. Scarecrow Press, 2010. 9780810869080

Holley, Pam Spencer. *Quick and Popular Reads for Teens*. ALA, 2009. 978-0838935774. From Popular Paperbacks and Quick Picks for Reluctant Young Adult Readers.

Honnold, Rosemary. *Teen Reader's Advisor*. Neal-Schuman, 2006. 9781555705510.

Keane, Nancy J. *Big Book of Teen Reading Lists: 100 Great, Ready-to-Use Book Lists for Educators, Librarians, Parents, and Teens*. Libraries Unlimited, 2006. 9781591583332.

McDaniel, Deanna J. *Gentle Reads: Great Books to Warm Hearts and Lift Spirits, Grades 5–9*. Libraries Unlimited, 2008. 9781591584919.

Schall, Lucy. *Genre Talks for Teens: Booktalks and More for Every Teen Reading Interest*. Libraries Unlimited, 2009. 9781591587439.

Online Resources

Adbooks—http://groups.yahoo.com/group/adbooks/

Bistro Book Club (Formerly Center for Adolescent Reading)—http://www.teensread.org

Genrefluent Teen Page—http://www.genrefluent.com/teentalk.htm

Reading Rants—http://www.readingrants.org/

Richie's Picks—http://richiespicks.pbworks.com/

Teen Librarian—http://teenlibrarian.co.uk/ A British site for teen librarians.

Teen Reads.Com—http://teenreads.com/

YALSA—http://www.ala.org/ala/mgrps/divs/yalsa/yalsa.cfm

YALSA-BK—http://lists.ala.org/wws/info/yalsa-bk

Other Professional Development Resources

ALAN: The Assembly on Literature for Adolescents—http://www.alan-ya.org/

YALSA—http://www.ala.org/ala/mgrps/divs/yalsa/yalsa.cfm

Genre-Specific Resources

Multicultural

Dawson, Alma, and Connie Van Fleet, eds. *African American Literature: A Guide to Reading Interests*. Libraries Unlimited, 2004. 9781563089312.

Martínez, Sara E. *Latino Literature*. Libraries Unlimited, 2009. 978-1591582922.

York, Sherry. *Booktalking Authentic Multicultural Literature: Fiction, History, and Memoirs for Teens*. Linworth Publishing, 2008. 9781586832995.

Nonfiction

Fraser, Elizabeth. *Reality Rules!: A Guide to Teen Nonfiction Reading Interests*. Libraries Unlimited, 2008. 9781591585633.

Fantasy

Fichtelberg, Susan. *Encountering Enchantment: A Guide to Speculative Fiction for Teens*. Libraries Unlimited, 2007. 9781591583165.

Herald, Diana, and Bonnie Kunzel. *Fluent in Fantasy: The Next Generation*. Libraries Unlimited, 2008. 9781591581987.

Hollands, Neil. *Read On . . . Fantasy Fiction: Reading Lists for Every Taste*. Libraries Unlimited, 2007. 9781591583301

Lynn, Ruth Nadelman. *Fantasy Literature for Children and Young Adults: A Comprehensive Guide*. Libraries Unlimited, 2005. 9781591580508

Graphic Novels

Brenner, Robin. *Understanding Manga and Anime*. Libraries Unlimited, 2007. 9781591583325.

Goldsmith, Francisca. *Reader's Advisory Guide to Graphic Novels*. American Library Association, 2010. 9780838910085.

Gorman, Michele. *Getting Graphic: Comics for Kids*. Linworth, 2008. 9781586833275.

Pawuk, Michael. *Graphic Novels: A Genre Guide to Comic Books, Manga, and More*. Libraries Unlimited, 2007. 9781591581321.

Romance

Carpan, Carolyn. *Rocked by Romance: A Guide to Teen Romance Fiction*. Libraries Unlimited, 2004. 9781591580225.

Meloni, Christine. *Teen Chick Lit: A Guide to Reading Interests*. Libraries Unlimited, 2010. 9781591587569.

High-Low Books for Middle School

This list features a recent selection of high interest, low reading level books for middle school age readers. A variety of genres and formats are included. Each entry lists the publication date that corresponds to the ISBN (not necessarily the first publication of the book), the number of pages, and the reading level.

Acampora, Paul. *Defining Dulcie.* ISBN 9780142411834. 2008. 168pp. RL 4

Avi. *Crispin: At the Edge of the World.* ISBN 9781423103059. 2008. 234pp. RL 4.8

Bluford High series:

    Schraff, Anne. *Lost and Found.* ISBN 9780439898393. 2007. 133pp. RL 4.7

    Schraff, Anne. *A Matter of Trust.* ISBN 9780439865470. 2007. 125pp. RL 4.6

    Schraff, Anne. *Secrets in the Shadows.* ISBN 9780439904858. 2007. 126pp. RL 4.7

    Schraff, Anne. *Someone to Love Me.* ISBN 9780439904865. 2007. 162pp. RL 4.5

    Langan, Paul. *Bully.* ISBN 9780439865463. 2007. 190pp. RL 4.7

    Langan, Paul. *Payback.* ISBN 9780439904872. 2007. 123pp. RL 4.7

    Schraff, Anne. *Until We Meet Again.* ISBN 9780439904889. 2007. 144pp. RL 4.8

    Langan, Paul. *Blood Is Thicker.* ISBN 9780439904896. 2007. 156pp. RL 4.8

    Langan, Paul. *Brothers in Arms.* ISBN 9780439904902. 2008 152pp. RL RL 4.2

    Langan, Paul. *Summer of Secrets.* ISBN 9780439904919. 2008. 142pp. RL 4.6

    Langan, Paul. *The Fallen.* ISBN 9781591940661. 2007. 133pp. RL 4.2

    Langan, Paul. *Shattered.* ISBN 9781591940692. 2007. 123pp. RL 4.4

    Langan, John. *Search for Safety.* ISBN 9781591940708. 2007. 128pp. 4.1

    Kern, Peggy. *No Way Out.* ISBN 9781591941767. 2009. 140pp. RL 4.1

    Langan, Paul. *Schooled.* ISBN 9781591941774. 2009. 140pp. RL 4.9

Bossley, Michele Martin. *Bio-Pirate.* ISBN 9781551438931. 2008. 109pp. RL 4

Bowen, Carl. *20,000 Leagues Under the Sea.* ISBN 9781434204974. 2008. 63pp. RL 3 (graphic novel)

Brouwer, Sigmund. *Absolute Pressure.* ISBN 9781554691302. 2009. 159pp. RL 3.9

Brouwer, Sigmund. *Chief Honor.* ISBN 9781551439150. 2008. 166pp. RL 3.9

Brouwer, Sigmund. *Maverick Mania.* ISBN 9781554690473. 2008. 163pp. RL 4.5

Brouwer, Sigmund. *Scarlet Thunder.* ISBN 9781551439112. 2008. 172pp. RL 4.5

Brouwer, Sigmund. *Thunderbird Spirit.* ISBN 9781554690459. 2008. 185pp. RL 4.4

Cammuso, Frank. <u>Knights of the Lunch Table</u>, no. 1, *Dodgeball Chronicles.* ISBN 9780439903226. 2008. 141pp. RL 2.2 (graphic novel)

Carroll, Michael. *Quantum Prophecy: The Awakening.* ISBN 9780142411797. 2008. 264pp. RL 4.1

Choyce, Lesley. *Skate Freak.* ISBN 9781554690428. 2008. 108pp. RL 3.6

Crew, Gary. *End of the Line.* ISBN 9781598899153. 2008. 73pp. RL 3.6

Denman, K. L. *Perfect Revenge.* ISBN 9781554691029. 2009. 102pp. RL 3.3

Denman, K. L. *Shade.* ISBN 9781551439310. 2008. 106pp. RL 3.1

Grant, Vicki. *Nine Doors.* ISBN 9781554690732. 2009. 102pp. RL 3.4

Jaimet, Kate. *Slam Dunk.* ISBN 9781554691326. 2009. 166pp. RL 4.7

Jaramillo, Ann. *La Linea.* ISBN 9780312373542. 2008. 135pp. RL 4.3

Kibuishi, Kazu. *Amulet 1: The Stonekeeper.* ISBN 9780439846813. 2008. 185pp. RL 2

Landy, Derek. *Skulduggery Pleasant.* ISBN 9780061231179. 2008. 392pp. RL 4.9

Levine, Gail Carson. *Fairest.* ISBN 9780060734107. 2008. 326pp. RL 4.0

Lowry, Lois. *Gossamer.* ISBN 9780385734165. 2008. 154pp. RL 4.4

McClintock, Norah. *Marked.* ISBN 9781551439921. 2008. 103pp. RL 4

McClintock, Norah. *Watch Me.* ISBN 9781554690398. 2008. 94pp. RL 3.7

Nelson, Blake. *Paranoid Park.* ISBN 9780142411568. 2008. 180pp. RL 3.7

Pfeffer, Susan Beth. *Life As We Knew It.* ISBN 9780152061548. 2008. 347pp. RL 4.7

Polak, Monique. *121 Express.* ISBN 9781551439761. 2008. 104pp. RL 4.2

Riordan, Rick. <u>Percy Jackson & the Olympians</u>:

    Lightning Thief. ISBN 9780786838653. 2006. 377pp. RL 4.7

    Sea of Monsters. ISBN 9781423103349. 2007. 279pp. RL 4.5

    Titan's Curse. ISBN 9781423101482. 2008. 312pp. RL 4.2

    Battle of the Labyrinth. ISBN 9781423101499. 2009. 361pp. RL 4

Rud, Jeff. *Crossover.* ISBN 9781551439815. 2008. 170pp. RL 4.7

Rud, Jeff. *Paralyzed.* ISBN 9781554690596. 2008. 169pp. RL 4.6

Slade, Arthur. *Megiddo's Shadow.* ISBN 9780553495072. 2008. 290pp. RL 4.4

Smith, Jeff. <u>Bone series</u>:

    Out from Boneville. ISBN 9780439706407. 2005. 138pp. RL 2.4

    The Great Cow Race. ISBN 9780439706391. 2005. 132pp. RL 2.4

    Eyes of the Storm. ISBN 9780439706384. 2006. 174pp. RL 2.6

    The Dragonslayer. ISBN 9780439706377. 2006. 168pp. RL 2.6

    Rock Jaw: Master of the Eastern Border. ISBN 9780439706360. 2007. 128pp. RL 2.2

    Old Man's Cave. ISBN 9780439706353. 2007. 118pp. RL 2.7

    Ghost Circles. ISBN 9780439706346. 2008. 150pp. RL 2.5

    Treasure Hunters. ISBN 9780439706339. 2008. 136pp. RL 2.9

    Crown of Horns. ISBN 9780439706322. 2009. 212pp. RL 2.4

Stevenson, Robin. *Dead in the Water.* ISBN 9781551439624. 2008. 169pp. RL 4.3

Stone, Jeff. <u>Five Ancestors series</u>:

    Tiger. ISBN 9780375830723. 2005. 196pp. RL 5

    Monkey. ISBN 9780375830747. 2006. 189pp. RL 4.3

    Snake. ISBN 9780375830761. 2007. 193pp. RL 4.4

    Crane. ISBN 9780375830785. 2008. 248pp. RL 4.8

    Eagle. ISBN 9780375830846. 2008. 223pp. RL 4.7

Tate, Nikki. *Venom.* ISBN 9781554690718. 2009. 168pp. RL 4

Varrato, Tony. *Fakie.* ISBN 9781897073797. 2008. 142pp. RL 4.7

Walters, Eric. *Splat!* ISBN 9781551439860. 2008. 110pp. RL 4.3

Author/Title Index

Subject Index

About the Author

DIANA TIXIER HERALD is Library Media Coordinator, Mesa County Valley School District, where she is responsible for one K–12, twenty-four elementary, and thirteen secondary school libraries. She is a frequent presenter at national conferences and a consulting editor for Readers' Advisor Online. Diana is author of two previous editions of this guide, as well as *Genreflecting*, *Fluent in Fantasy*, and *Strictly Science Fiction*, and editor of the <u>Genreflecting Advisory series</u>.